Lecture Notes in Artificial Intelligence   4897

Edited by J. G. Carbonell and J. Siekmann

Subseries of Lecture Notes in Computer Science

Matteo Baldoni   Tran Cao Son
M. Birna van Riemsdijk   Michael Winikoff (Eds.)

Declarative Agent Languages and Technologies V

5th International Workshop, DALT 2007
Honolulu, HI, USA, May 14, 2007
Revised Selected and Invited Papers

 Springer

Series Editors

Jaime G. Carbonell, Carnegie Mellon University, Pittsburgh, PA, USA
Jörg Siekmann, University of Saarland, Saarbrücken, Germany

Volume Editors

Matteo Baldoni
Università di Torino, Dipartimento di Informatica
Via Pessinetto 12, 10149 Turin, Italy
E-mail: baldoni@di.unito.it

Tran Cao Son
New Mexico State University, Department of Computer Science
P.O.Box 30001, MSC CS, Las Cruces, NM 88003, USA
E-mail: tson@cs.nmsu.edu

M. Birna van Riemsdijk
Ludwig-Maximilians-Universität München, Institut für Informatik
Oettingenstr. 67, 80538 Munich, Germany
E-mail: riemsdijk@pst.ifi.lmu.de

Michael Winikoff
RMIT University, School of Computer Science and Information Technology
GPO Box 2476V Melbourne, Australia
E-mail: michael.winikoff@rmit.edu.au

Library of Congress Control Number: 2007942738

CR Subject Classification (1998): I.2.11, C.2.4, D.2.4, D.2, D.3, F.3.1

LNCS Sublibrary: SL 7 – Artificial Intelligence

ISSN   0302-9743
ISBN-10   3-540-77563-3 Springer Berlin Heidelberg New York
ISBN-13   978-3-540-77563-8 Springer Berlin Heidelberg New York

Springer is a part of Springer Science+Business Media

springer.com

© Springer-Verlag Berlin Heidelberg 2008
Printed in Germany

Typesetting: Camera-ready by author, data conversion by Scientific Publishing Services, Chennai, India
Printed on acid-free paper   SPIN: 12211814   06/3180   5 4 3 2 1 0

Preface

The workshop on Declarative Agent Languages and Technologies (DALT), in its fifth edition this year, is a well-established forum for researchers interested in sharing their experiences in combining declarative and formal approaches with engineering and technology aspects of agents and multi-agent systems.

DALT 2007 was held as a satellite workshop of AAMAS 2007, the 6th International Joint Conference on Autonomous Agents and Multiagent Systems, in May 2007 in Honolulu, Hawai'i. Following the success of DALT 2003 in Melbourne (LNAI 2990), DALT 2004 in New York (LNAI 3476), DALT 2005 in Utrecht (LNAI 3904), and DALT 2006 in Hakodate (LNAI 4327), the workshop again provided a discussion forum to both (a) support the transfer of declarative paradigms and techniques to the broader community of agent researchers and practitioners, and (b) to bring the issue of designing complex agent systems to the attention of researchers working on declarative languages and technologies.

The aim of the DALT workshop is to stimulate research on formal and declarative approaches both for developing the foundations of multi-agent systems as well as for all phases of engineering multi-agent systems, i.e., for specification and modeling, for implementation, and for verification. By providing a forum for the presentation of ideas addressing both of these aspects, DALT encourages the integration of formal and declarative techniques and methods that are based on solid theoretical foundations, in the engineering of multi-agent systems.

As agents are increasingly endowed with mechanisms for behaving flexibly and autonomously in open and dynamic environments, it becomes more and more important that they are engineered to ensure both adaptability *and* a certain level of predictability. While providing a certain level of predictability is important for any software, it is especially important for multi-agent systems in which the agents are autonomous and adaptive. Formal and declarative technologies both for specification and verification as well as for implementation can provide this required predictability. Ensuring a certain level of predictability is important for the adoption of multi-agent technology in practice, as users have to trust a multi-agent system to behave as required even though the agents are autonomous and adaptive.

An ongoing challenge for the DALT community is the investigation of formal and declarative techniques for the specification and implementation of rational agents. Moreover, techniques for structuring a multi-agent system and for facilitating cooperation among agents such as organizational views of agent systems, norms, teams, coordination mechanisms, and argumentation and negotiation techniques are becoming increasingly important and are challenging for DALT. Further, there are several areas that have commonalities with multi-agent systems and to which declarative agent languages and technologies can be applied, such as the Semantic Web, service-oriented systems, component-based systems, security, and electronic contracting.

There is thus an ongoing and even increasing demand for formal and declarative approaches for the development of multi-agent systems. In this volume, we report on the latest results in this area.

The volume contains the 11 contributed articles that were selected by the Programme Committee for presentation at the workshop, divided into four sections, as well as two invited articles, originally presented as short papers at AAMAS 2007, that have been extended by their authors. The four sections focus on *modeling* (one paper), *goals* (three papers), *foundational concepts* (four papers), and *communication* (three papers). Of the two invited articles, the first "Joint Conversation Specification and Compliance" is by S. Paurobally and M. Wooldridge, while the second "Interoperation in Protocol Enactment" is by A. K. Chopra and M. P. Singh. The volume also includes the article "Agent-Oriented Modelling: Declarative or Procedural?" by Leon Sterling. Professor Sterling, from the University of Melbourne, was the invited speaker for this edition of DALT.

We would like to thank all authors for their contributions, the members of the DALT Steering Committee for their precious suggestions and support, and the members of the Programme Committee for their excellent work during the reviewing phase.

November 2007

Matteo Baldoni
Tran Cao Son
M. Birna van Riemsdijk
Michael Winikoff

Organization

Workshop Organizers

Matteo Baldoni   University of Turin, Italy
Tran Cao Son   New Mexico State University, USA
M. Birna van Riemsdijk   Ludwig-Maximilians-Universität München,
         Germany,
Michael Winikoff   RMIT University, Melbourne, Australia

Programme Committee

Marco Alberti   University of Ferrara, Italy
Natasha Alechina   University of Nottingham, UK
Grigoris Antoniou   University of Crete, Greece
Matteo Baldoni   University of Turin, Italy
Cristina Baroglio   University of Turin, Italy
Rafael Bordini   University of Durham, UK
Keith Clark   Imperial College London, UK
Ulle Endriss   University of Amsterdam, Netherlands
Benjamin Hirsch   Technical University Berlin, Germany
Shinichi Honiden   National Institute of Informatics, Japan
John Lloyd   Australian National University, Australia
Viviana Mascardi   University of Genova, Italy
John-Jules Ch. Meyer   Utrecht University, Netherlands
Enrico Pontelli   New Mexico State University, USA
M. Birna van Riemsdijk   Ludwig-Maximilians-Universität München,
         Germany,
Munindar P. Singh   North Carolina State University, USA
Tran Cao Son   New Mexico State University, USA
Chiaki Sakama   Wakayama University, Japan
Wamberto Vasconcelos   University of Aberdeen, UK
Christopher Walton   University of Edinburgh, UK
Mirko Viroli   University of Bologna, Italy
Michael Winikoff   RMIT University, Melbourne, Australia

Additional Reviewers

Martin Caminada   Berndt Farwer   Sebastian Sardina
Nirmit Desai   Yasuyuki Tahara

Steering Committee

João Leite	New University of Lisbon, Portugal
Andrea Omicini	University of Bologna-Cesena, Italy
Leon Sterling	University of Melbourne, Australia
Paolo Torroni	University of Bologna, Italy
Pınar Yolum	Bogazici University, Turkey

Sponsoring Institutions

Matteo Baldoni has partially been funded by the European Commission and by the Swiss Federal Office for Education and Science within the 6th Framework Programme project REWERSE number 506779 (cf. http://rewerse.net), and he has also been supported by the MIUR PRIN 2005 "Specification and verification of agent interaction protocols" national project.

M. Birna van Riemsdijk has been supported by the EU project SENSORIA (IST-2005-016004), which is part of the 6th Framework Programme.

Table of Contents

Contributed Papers: Communication

Agent-Oriented Modelling: Declarative or Procedural?

Leon Sterling

Department of Computer Science and Software Engineering
University of Melbourne, Australia
leonss@unimelb.edu.au

Abstract. The use of agent-oriented models in developing complex, distributed, open, heterogeneous software is advocated. Agent-oriented models at the analysis level and design level are described, and a case study presented. We muse how modelling activity relates to the classical debate of whether knowledge is declarative or procedural.

1   Background

My introduction to Artificial Intelligence came in a subject attended in 1976, in my final year of a Science degree at the University of Melbourne. An interesting topic presented in the class was whether knowledge was declarative or procedural. Declarative knowledge was characterised as being part of the logic tradition, with its application in robot planning as per STRIPS [5]. Procedural knowledge was characterised as encoding knowledge in procedures to be executed, and was typified by the natural language understanding program, SHRDLU [16] operating in the blocks world.

Five years later, I was introduced to Prolog [3] in the context of a postdoctoral research position at the University of Edinburgh. Prolog seemed to resolve the declarative v procedural debate. Knowledge was clearly both. Good Prolog code could be read declaratively, but also had a clear, programmable, procedural interpretation. In the broader research world, the debate died down, perhaps coincidentally.

Many researchers became excited about Prolog, myself included. The declarative aspect and the ability to reason about knowledge seemed to guarantee it an important place in Artificial Intelligence and Software Engineering. Well-written Prolog code had a definite elegance. Prolog received increased prominence through the Japanese Fifth Generation Project.

Prolog was not ideal, however. Throughout the 1980's, researchers enthusiastically worked on improved logic programming languages. Two issues which were addressed were concurrency and state. A natural extension in the 1990's and 2000's has been to agents, which promote autonomy and distribution. Many agent researchers have a logic programming background and see agents as being able to address (some of) Prolog's limitations.

M. Baldoni et al. (Eds.): DALT 2007, LNAI 4897, pp. 1–17, 2008.

While many Prolog applications were built, the language failed to make much impression on mainstream software developers. One problem was that programming in Prolog was not entirely straightforward - it required a different way of thinking. My fifteen years of teaching Prolog to graduate and undergraduate students highlighted that Prolog only suited certain learning styles. Another problem was the lack of a design level [11].

In trying to promote agents, avoiding some of Prolog's mistakes, and becoming aware of software engineering, I have been led to modelling. It has been important to better separate the stages of analysis and design. When invited to give a presentation at DALT2007, I wondered how my current agent-oriented modelling research fitted with the active research of the DALT community. A light-hearted revisiting of the declarative v procedural debate came to mind and forms the context for this paper.

The paper is organised as follows. The next section presents agent-oriented modelling, including a discussions of models, agent-oriented software engineering, and the introduction of a case study, a device for mediating intimacy. Section 3 discusses the conceptual space for the modelling work. Section 4 introduces analysis level models, goal models and role models, and presents the case study models. Section 5 introduces design level models, agent models and system overview diagrams, and demonstrates them for the case study. The models combine aspects of the ROADMAP [6,7] and Prometheus [10] methodologies. While there is little discussion about implementation, anecdotal experience at the University of Melbourne suggests that a system well designed can be implemented relatively easily. Section 6 presents some brief comments on declarative v procedural, and the paper concludes.

2   Agent-Oriented Modelling

Agents do not need introduction to the DALT community. However, in the circumstances, a brief perspective from the Intelligent Agent Laboratory at the University of Melbourne is appropriate. Agents are a good metaphor for conceptualizing a socio-technical system. A *socio-technical system* has been defined as one that includes hardware and software, has defined operational processes, and offers an interface, implemented in software, to human users. Within the lab, we have been building agent-oriented models for a range of diverse socio-technical systems, including a smart home [12], a framework for evaluating educational objectives [14], and airport optimization. The last has resulted in an Australian Research Council Linkage grant on modeling air traffic control with an industry partner. Before explaining our agent-oriented modeling, we discuss agent-oriented software engineering, a topic that has emerged in the last ten years.

2.1   Agent-Oriented Software Engineering

How does one build a multi-agent system? The research community has a diversity of opinions on what to emphasise. The theoreticians claim that once the theory is established, the practice will be straightforward to implement, and so emphasis should be on theory. The architects claim that if you have the right architecture, all the rest will follow. The language developers claim that given the right programming language, it is straightforward for agent developers to be able to build multi-agent systems.

My claim is different. A multi-agent system is a system with a significant software component. We should build on what has been learned about developing software over the last forty years. The perspective I advocate for building multi-agent systems is a software engineering perspective, which can be loosely identified with a systems engineering perspective.

The following analogy may be helpful to appreciate software engineering. Consider the task of building a small shed for storage in the backyard of a house, a common hobby for Australian men in previous decades. Many men and women may be successful with this task, particularly if they had a practical bent. However, just because someone built such a storage shed, would not immediately qualify he or she to build a thirty-floor office building. There is extra knowledge needed, about building materials, structures, regulations, for example. Now consider the task of writing a computer program to process data. Many men and women may be successful with this task, particularly if they had a technical bent. However you wouldn't automatically trust that person to write an air traffic control system. The missing discipline and knowledge is loosely covered by the area of software engineering.

A definition of software engineering, developed for Engineers Australia, is *a discipline applied by teams to produce high-quality, large-scale, cost-effective software that satisfies the users' needs and can be maintained over time.*

Significant words in the definition include discipline, which implies an underlying body of knowledge; users, which implies the need for requirements; teams, which implies the need for communications and interfaces; over time, which implies that the system must be able to be changed without becoming brittle; high-quality which suggests performance criteria, not only functional capabilities; and large-scale, which means different architectural considerations about performance and other qualities. Understanding costs and trade-offs in design will be important. Also important will be recognising the needs of stakeholders, not only users.

Agent-oriented software engineering then suggests applying software engineering principles to the development of multi-agent systems. It can be presumed that the multi-agent system will follow a system development lifecycle. There will be a stage of gathering requirements. Once the requirements have been elicited, they are analysed. The analysis goes hand in hand with design, where trade-offs are expected to be needed to allow the building of a system that meets users' requirements, both functional and non-functional. The system must be implemented, tested and maintained. All these stages should be supported by methods and tools within an overall methodology. Many agent-oriented software engineering methodologies have been developed. One useful collection is in [2].

Rather than applying software engineering principles to the development of multi-agent systems, the term agent-oriented software engineering can also be interpreted as using agent concepts in the development of software. It is primarily this alternate interpretation that is adopted in this paper. Before addressing the case study, it is worth thinking a little about the nature of models and modeling.

2.2   What Is a Model?

Modelling is empowering in a practical sense. If you can model, you are a significant part of the way to building something useful. Let us consider 'what is a model?' A definition taken from Wordnet (wordnet.princeton.edu) is that a model is a *hypothetical description of a complex entity or process*. A model is constructed to aid in building the system we have in mind. To paraphrase Parnas' well-known characterisation of specifications, a model should be as complex as it needs to be to reflect the issues the system is being built to address, but no more complex.

What are some examples of models? A common school project for primary school children is to build a model of the solar system. In such a model, there is at least some depiction of individual planets, and the sun. More detailed models may include moons of planets and asteroids. Better students may try and get some idea of distance of planets from the sun, by either placing the planets in an order, or some scaled representation of distance. More ambitious students may add a dynamic element to the model by having the planets move around their orbit. Building a good model of the solar system clearly stretches the abilities of primary school children, and usually their parents.

Agent-oriented models will emphasise goals, activities, and interactions, as will be described in the next section on the conceptual space. In my experience, agent-oriented models are a natural way for understanding a system, and allow for appreciation of a system by external, non-technical stakeholders.

2.3   Secret Touch Case Study

To illustrate agent-oriented modeling, we introduce an application domain investigated in a research project conducted at the University of Melbourne. The project was conducted within the Smart Internet Technology Cooperative Research Centre. The research project, entitled 'Mediating Intimacy: Strong-Tie Relationships' used ethnographic techniques to study how people may use technology to mediate intimacy [8]. Ethnography focuses on participatory data collection to understand activity as it happens. The data may provide a rich source of ideas for technological products. The motivation of the project was to explore novel technology use for a 'smart Internet.' Technology in social settings needs to demonstrably fulfill the felt needs relating to the social environments. These needs typically include many that are high-level, cognitive, emotional, and hard to measure, such as playfulness, being engaged in an activity, expressing feelings, and privacy.

Workbooks and diaries were produced by six couples, documenting interactions the couples had throughout the day. From this data, scenarios, or sequences of activities, were created suggesting technological devices to assist in mediating intimacy. This view of a scenario is consistent with the agent-oriented models to be introduced shortly.

One scenario developed was Secret Touch. Secret Touch envisaged a software system on a small pocket device, which communicates with a partner's similar device. Partners can interact discretely and remotely through physically moving the device in their pocket, causing their partner's device to move in an identical fashion.

Inspiration: - Couples wanting to communicate in private. Being playful. Individuals like fiddling with toys.

Scenario: - They both reach in their pockets during work. She feels that he is fiddling with the device. She turns the device in the other direction, engaging in playful activity.

Several interactive sessions led to the Secret Touch multi-agent software system design, which we model in Sections 4 and 5. A range of products was designed to cater for diverse opinions about the desirability of intelligent Secret Touch devices. Table 1 contains the product range, listed from simplest to most complex.

Table 1. Secret Touch Product Range

Name	Description	Details
Flirt	Risk and openness to flirtation	Open channel, full-duplex communication, i.e. always on
Discrete Flirt	Partner chooses level of accessibility	Choice of open channel or modes: ON, OFF, PASSIVE
Fiddler's Choice	Response possibly from agent	Add learning or remembering to either of the above
Guessing Game	Who or what is that?	An open, dynamic system - partners and devices change

The simplest device, Flirt, transforms all device movement into touches, which are instantaneously sent to the partner's device, as well as immediately transforming all touches received into movement. Simultaneously incoming and outgoing movements are resolved by the device itself, which then moves in a direction reflecting the vector sum of both touches - potentially a real tug-of-war situation. The discrete version, Discrete Flirt, enables partners to engage in a turn-taking dialogue, and allows a device to be switched off or set to passively receive touches and replay them later, for example, when the important meeting at work is over. Fiddler's Choice is an intelligent, learning device. A partner may allow the device to respond if unable to personally engage. Fiddler's Choice can also be used solo, in which the partner is actually a software agent.

3   Conceptual Space

Agent-oriented models need agent-oriented concepts, such as goals and roles. These terms are not used consistently across the agent community. Rather than defining each individual concept, we introduce a conceptual space within which to view systems and classify models.

A key feature of our conceptual space is to layer concepts. The conceptual space consists of three layers: an environment layer, a system design layer, and a motivation layer. Three layer architectures have a long history in Artificial Intelligence and agents. The layers give a way to structure the set of models.

The layers represent an amalgam of the software development stage and level of abstraction. The more abstract, the earlier in the software development lifecycle, and the more accessible to external stakeholders without a technical background. Conversely, the lower the level, the more useful it is to developers, and the later in the software lifecycle.

Loosely, models within the motivation layer are developed during requirements elicitation and analysis. Models in the system design layer are developed during architectural design, and the environment layer is populated during detailed design, and fleshed out in implementation and deployment.

Two kinds of entities inhabit the models within the conceptual space: abstract entities and concrete entities. *Abstract entities* exist neither in space nor in time, that is they cannot be localized. Examples of abstract entities are mathematical objects like numbers and sets, *modelling abstractions* like goals and roles, as well as *types*. *Concrete entities* exist at least in time. They subsume physical entities that exist in both time and space, and virtual entities that exist merely in time. Examples of physical entities are humans and machines. Examples of virtual entities are actions and events.

We describe the three layers from the most abstract to the least abstract. The *motivation layer* contains abstract modelling concepts needed for defining requirements and purposes of a system. Arguably, the most foundational are the *goals* of the system, which must be modelled, as well as *roles* responsible for achieving the goals. Here goals represent functionalities expected from the system, while roles are capabilities of the system required for achieving the functionalities. Focussing on both goals and roles is important in our experience.

The organisational structure of roles, consisting of relationships and dependencies between them, are identified within the motivation layer. The motivation layer should contain *social policies* that constrain interaction and the behaviour of any agents playing the roles. They can represent anything from access rights to social norms to obligations. Social policies are identified based on the relationships and dependencies between roles.

Permeating the entire conceptual space is knowledge. I believe knowledge should be made explicit as much as possible. Knowledge at the motivation layer includes norms and obligations, and also details about the environments and contexts within which the system is situated and operates. Knowledge of being at work, location, time, are examples of knowledge relevant for the Secret Touch system.

The *system design layer* consists of design notions. The central one among them is the concept of agent. We define an *agent* as an autonomous entity situated in an environment capable of both perceiving the environment and acting on it. Each agent belongs to some *agent type* that, in turn, is related to one or more roles from the motivation layer. The decision whether to model an entity as an active and autonomous entity - agent - or rather as a passive, servant entity - *object* - is based on the criterion of helpfulness. That is, if using the abstraction of agent helps the designer, maintainer, or user to develop, maintain, or use the socio-technical system, an entity included by it should be modelled as an agent. For example, from the perspective of maintenance and usage, it can be helpful to model an e-mail system as an agent, even though the system may have been designed and implemented using concepts at the lower abstraction level. Similarly, a software agent for finding citations can be modelled and designed as an agent, but implemented as an HTML script.

Agents enact roles by performing *activities*. Each activity instantiates some *activity type* that specifies functionalities defined by goals at the motivation layer. Activities are started and sequenced by *rules*. Rules thus determine when goals are to be achieved. Rules also govern interactions between agents performed within activities. Rules thus carry out social policies defined at the motivation layer. Rules are triggered by *perceptions* of events by an agent and/or by the *knowledge* held by an agent. An activity consists of actions where each action belongs to some *action type*. Most of these words are used slightly differently by different researchers. The description here serves as an informal metamodel. For example, in the Secret Touch scenario, a rule would be triggered by the physical perception of a change in the pocket device. What an agent is designed to perceive is influenced by social policies.

The environment is populated by concrete agents and concrete objects. By concrete agents and objects, we mean entities, which have concrete manifestations - *concretisations* - in the environment. Examples of concrete agents are a human, a robot, a dog, and a software agent, and as examples of concrete objects serve a book, a car, and a Web service. A concrete agent like a human may be a concretisation of the corresponding agent represented at the system design layer. Analogously, a concrete object of the environment layer may correspond to a conceptual object represented at the system layer. Concrete agents and objects belong to the respective *concrete agent types* and *concrete object types*, such as agent and object types of a specific software platform. They are derived from the agent types and conceptual object types of the system design layer. Likewise, *behavioural construct types* of the environment layer are based on the activity types and rules of the system design layer. Behavioural construct types are instantiated by the corresponding *behavioural constructs*.

A concrete agent or object can be described by a set of attributes where an attribute is either a numeric attribute or a non-numeric attribute. A numeric attribute, like a weight, can be represented as a numerical value, while a non-numeric attribute, like the colour, is more vague and subjective. At the environment layer of the conceptual space, the counterparts of action types of the system design layer are *concrete action types*. Here an environment can be either a real physical environment or a virtual one, like a simulated environment. A concrete action performed by one agent can be perceived as an *event* by other agents. For example, a message sent by one software agent to another is perceived as a message received event by the latter. Events belong to *event types*.

An extra level of structuring can be added to the concepts, namely that of viewpoints. Three useful viewpoints are organization and interaction within the system, motivation and behaviour, and the explicit information that is needed for the system, which will of necessity vary in different environments and contexts. In [13] , a complete description of the models is given. Some of them are described in the next two sections. Nonetheless it is useful to see in Table 2, a populated table of models structured by layer and viewpoint.

Table 2. Agent-oriented Models

Abstraction layer	Viewpoint		
	Interaction	*Information*	*Behaviour*
Motivation layer	Role models and organisation models and models of social policies	Environment models	Goal models and motivational scenarios
Design layer	Models of acquaintances, interaction models	Knowledge models and service models	Behaviour models and scenarios
Environment layer	Agent interface and interaction specifications	Data models and service specifications	Agent behaviour specifications

4   Motivation Layer Models

We now give examples of models from the motivation layer. We present two goal models (from the behaviour viewpoint) and one role model (from the interaction viewpoint). The models are ROADMAP models, constructed with the REBEL tool [7]. The Secret Touch case study was developed using a combination of the ROADMAP and Prometheus methodologies. Using analysis level models from other methodologies such as Tropos or MaSE would be similar.

Goal models have three types of components: - goals represented by parallelograms, roles represented by stick figures, and quality goals represented by clouds. Figure 1 contains the overall goal model for the Secret Touch system. The overall goal, Secret Touch, has two sub-goals, Flirt and Communicate. A Partner role is responsible for the Flirt, which by nature is Risky and Playful, the associated quality goals shown in the diagram. The Flirt goal can be achieved via the sub-goal Initiate Touch. First, a Touch Initiator role initiates the flirt. This involves timely achievement of the sub-goal, Capture Touch and accurately Translating device Movement Into a software data Touch.

Returning to Figure 1, another way to achieve the Flirt goal is via the sub-goal Respond to Flirt. Responding is possible only for the intelligently learning Fiddler's Choice product. The goal is to appropriately respond to an incoming touch in a way that somehow matches. The Choreographer's role is to Recognize an Incoming Touch and Propose an appropriate counter-movement or Touch Movement. This concept builds on habits that often develop within relationships.

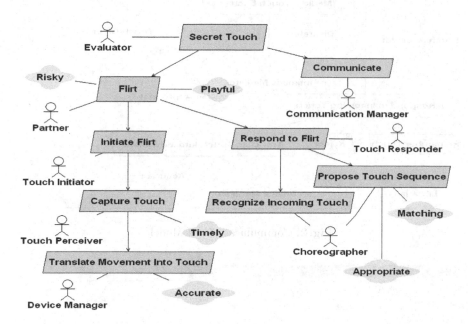

Fig. 1. Secret Touch Goal Model

Figure 2 depicts the set of sub-goals under the Communicate goal. Note that goal models are naturally presented hierarchically. Continuing the explanation, an incoming touch must be Noticed and Responded to, whereas an outgoing touch should be Given. The goal to Remember an incoming Touch, a sub-goal of Respond to Incoming Touch, is available only in the Fiddler's Choice design. The Mediate Touch Exchange goal allows a partner to choose availability in the Discrete Flirt product.

Figure 3 shows the Touch Acceptor Role Model. The list of responsibilities includes goals associated with the Touch Acceptor in the goal-model diagrams, for example Notice Incoming Touch. Constraints may document how a quality goal is to be achieved, or access to knowledge. Actions resulting from partner availability are listed. The lists of responsibilities and constraints make it easy to give feedback. They represent important detail of how system behaviour is envisaged, thus generating lively discussion during requirements elicitation sessions.

The role and goal models facilitated real communication with the researchers, who were non-technical clients. The flexibility and high-level nature of the models enabled the software engineer who developed the models to present very

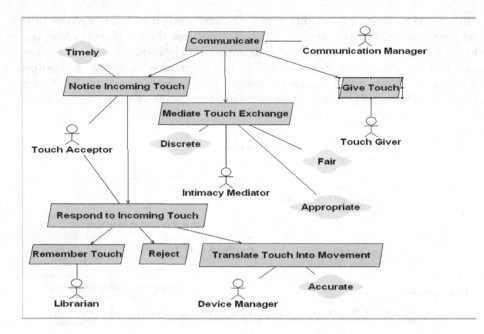

Fig. 2. Communicate Goal Model

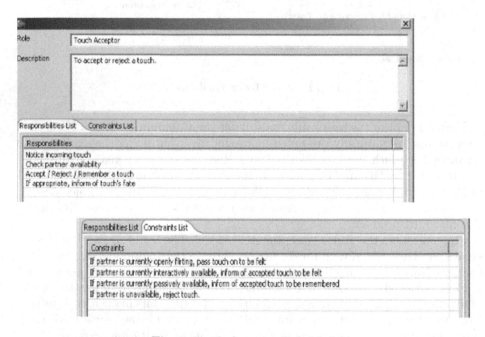

Fig. 3. Touch Acceptor Role Model

high-level abstractions to the clients. This is important for communication with non-technical people. The usefulness of agent concepts was confirmed by survey results and other feedback. Of particular interest were the quality goals, which also sparked useful discussions. For example, one major requirement was found to be missing in the original proposed system - described variously as playfulness, flirting, teasing.

Discussion of the constraints in an Intimacy Mediator role, presented for discussion in the first iteration, clarified that a major requirement was missing, as mentioned above, most precisely called enabling a tug-of-war between partners. Re-thinking these requirements based on the valuable feedback led to the two products, Flirt and Discrete Flirt, and to the Mediate Touch Exchange goal in Figure 1 above being completely absent from the basic Flirt product. During a second feedback presentation, survey responses were overwhelmingly positive. The interaction designers perceived that their initial feedback was accurately understood and also fairly well incorporated into the requirements analysis and design of the system.

The importance of the agent-human analogy was explicitly captured in the survey responses. The survey question about whether the agent paradigm was useful for understanding the proposed system received a unanimously positive response. Quality goals were confirmed to be useful for capturing intangible requirements and goals, as often encountered in social contexts. The interaction designers reacted very positively to the quality goals in ROADMAP. The value of quality goals became clearer in the second feedback session, in which documentation of the requirements was more complete.

5   Design Layer Models

In this section we give some examples of design layer models. We concentrate on the architectural design level rather than the detailed design level. In the Secret Touch case study, Prometheus was used for the design level. We give an example of an interaction diagram from the interaction viewpoint, agent coupling diagrams, and a system overview diagram which gives an overview of the sytem behaviour and interactions. Details about the diagrams can be found in [10]. The diagrams were built using PDT, the Prometheus Design Tool available at www.cs.rmit.edu.au/agents/pdt.

The process that was loosely followed was Choose agents for roles; Specify behaviour using interaction diagrams and protocols; Describe the overall system behaviour and interactions with a system overview diagram.

The goal models in Figures 1 and 2 had many roles. These were combined into four agents. The intimacy handler agent covered five roles: evaluator, touch giver, communication manager, touch acceptor and intimacy mediator. The partner handler agent covered three roles: touch initiator, partner, and touch responder. The device handler agent covered the device manager, touch feeler and touch perceiver roles, while the resource handler agent covered the librarian and choreographer roles. This is depicted in Figure 4.

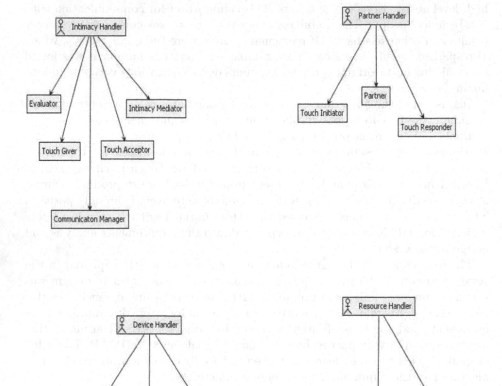

Fig. 4. Agent-Role Coupling Diagram

Figure 5 describes an interaction between the partner handler, device handler, and intimacy handler. The various messages exchanged and percepts observed proceed sequentially down the page. The interaction starts with the perception of a desire to flirt, and ends with the touch being returned to the sender.

The final diagram (Figure 6) described in this section is the system overview diagram which describes the agents in the system (denoted as rectangles), the percepts they sense (denoted as splats), the protocols they have (double-headed arrows between agents), and actions taken (arrows). Consider the top right agent, the device handler. It has three percepts: BeginEnd Touch, Movement, and Find an accepted Touch, three actions: Inform of Perceived Touch, Move Device, and Inform Touch was Felt, and is involved with two protocols with the Touch handler agent, namely Touching and Being Touched.

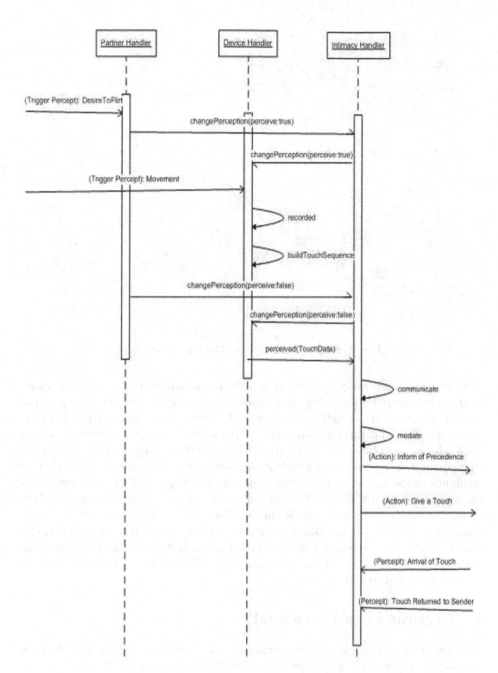

Fig. 5. Agent Interaction Diagram

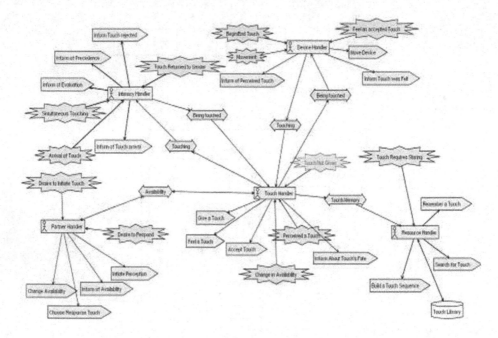

Fig. 6. Secret Touch System Overview Diagram

System overview diagrams may seem a little complicated to begin with. However, as the name implies, they do provide a good overview of the logical structure of the system, including the protocols between agents and which agent perceives what and takes which action. Prometheus contains a detailed design level where capabilities and plans are developed for each agent. The designs are implementation language independent. The designs can be turned into code in a straightforward way using the agent programming language JACK (www.agent-software.com) or JADE [1]. We have done a student project discussing how to decide which agent language is suitable for which design. Factors that were considered include compatibility of internal architecture, interoperability, dynamic behaviour, complexity of design, compatibility of physical environment with agent platform constraints, connectivity, distribution, and learning curve versus maintenance cost.

6   Declarative or Procedural?

The last two sections have given examples of agent-oriented models. Models are ideally executable, and that is essentially the case here. It is reasonably straightforward to translate the models into software. This is unsurprising as methodologies such as ROADMAP and Prometheus, which have been described, were developed for the purpose. Rapidly prototyping models has been presented by [15], among others. It would be also straightforward to translate into an object-oriented language such as Java. We have abundant experience within the Intelligent Agent lab at the University of Melbourne with over 100 student projects in the graduate Intelligent Agent subject building agent designs and many implementing them.

What is the status of the models described above? Are they declarative? Are they procedural? Are they hybrid, as is claimed for BDI agents? If they are best understood as being declarative, then one would want to prove theorems about their declarative content, such as completeness. If they are best understood as procedural, one would want to prove theorems about termination and other procedural properties.

In the presentation at DALT, I was asked about when properties needed to proved about the models. My response was that it was perhaps counter productive to prove theorems too early. During elicitation, the non-technical stakeholders need to be encouraged to engage, and proofs don't encourage engagement by non-technical stakeholders. Later during design, one may try to prove that quality attributes may be met.

Many properties need greater definition in order to progress. Security is a quality attribute that is essential. But the exact level of security needs much greater definition and understanding of how the property should be interpreted. I am sure that designs will contain proofs as aids to establish correctness of designs, but we have some way to go, before we can describe systems appropriately.

Some properties, of course, will never be proved formally. To take an example from the Secret Touch system, a desirable property is to be flirtatious. Almost certainly a user study would be needed to track user response and engagement with the system to fully ascertain whether it is flirtatious. That would be preferable to a theory of flirtatiousness.

Having raised the question of evaluation, we need to address it a little more explicitly. There are implicit questions about which are the best concepts for modelling. For example, how should roles be defined. Detailed examination is beyond the scope of this paper. Evaluation is hard to do formally. From anecdotal experience, the models scale. For one larger student project reported in [12] the analysis level models were over 90 pages, yet were easy to read and assess. The high level models are understandable by non-experts. More technical models in the dsign and environment layers are ones that would benefit from more formalization and verification, and work needs to be done on which methods might work best.

To conclude this section, I would like to consider the adjective *elegant*. From my experience with Prolog, there is no doubt that elegance is desirable. As O'Keefe stresses in the 'Craft of Prolog', Elegance is not optional. What is true for Prolog should be true for agent models. In our agent group we have had numerous discussions about the elegance of agent-oriented models, both ours and others. Reviewers should be encouraged to discuss elegance along with correctness. So, I suggest that declarativeness is analogous to elegance. Perhaps we will have a track at future DALT meetings as EALT, Elegant Agent languages and technologies.

7 Conclusions

Agent-oriented models have been presented including goal models and role models. Models are conceived as belonging to an abstraction layer, closely related to the stage in the software development lifecycle. Three layers, a motivation layer, a design layer and an environment layer were discussed. The models can be given another dimension through viewpoints. The models were demonstrated with a case study of a device for mediating intimacy. At the University of Melbourne, we have used agent-oriented modelling on a range of projects, and have anecdotal evidence that the models at the motivation level are useful for non-technical people to appreciate agent technology. Finally, in light-hearted spirit, I suggested that declarativeness might be re-cast as elegance.

Acknowledgments. It was a pleasure to have the opportunity to give an invited talk, and to share some of the thoughts in this paper. There are many people that have influenced my thinking. The Dagstuhl in June 2006 with topic 'PROMAS meets AOSE' was good for clarifying the range of ways that researchers think about developing multi-agent systems. The path from Prolog to agents was influenced by the lightweight ARPEGGIO project [4], especially in discussions with Maurizio Martelli and Viviana Mascardi. Even more influential has been the Melbourne Agents community, including Liz Sonenberg, Lin Padgham, Simon Goss, Adrian Pearce, Michael Winikoff, Shanika Karunasekera, Kendall Lister, Ayodele Oluyomi, and Kevin Chan. Four people deserve particular mention and thanks. Thomas Juan persuaded me that agent-oreinted software engineering was a good area of study and influenced ROADMAP development. Kuldar Taveter was responsible for the conceptual space, and viewpoints, and we are colloboarating on a book on agent-oriented modelling. Ann Boettcher developed the Secret Touch case study and has spent a lot of time thinking how to combine ROADMAP and Prometheus models. Finally Bin Lu helped with converting the paper to the appropriate LaTeX style. The research was supported by grant LP0348797 from the Australian Research Council and two grants from the Smart Internet Technology Cooperative Research Centre.

References

1. Bellifemine, F., Caire, G., Greenwood, D.: Developing Multi-Agent Systems with JADE. Wiley, Chichester (2007)
2. Bergenti, F., Gleizes, M., Zambonelli, F. (eds.): Methodologies and Software Engineering for Agent Systems: The Agent-Oriented Software Engineering Handbook. Kluwer, Dordrecht (2004)
3. Clocksin, Mellish: Programming in Prolog. Springer, Heidelberg (1981)
4. Dart, P., Kazmierczak, E., Martelli, M., Mascardi, V., Sterling, L., Subrahmaniam, V., Zini, F.: Combining Logical Agents with Rapid Prototyping for Engineering Distributed Applications. In: Tilley, S., Verner, J. (eds.) Proc. STEP 1999, pp. 40–49. IEEE Computer Society Press, Los Alamitos (1999)

 5. Fikes, R.E., Nilsson, N.J.: STRIPS: A new approach to the application of theorem proving to problem solving. Artificial Intelligence 2, 189–208 (1971)
 6. Juan, T., Pearce, A., Sterling, L.: ROADMAP: Extending the Gaia Methodology for Complex Open Systems. In: Johnson, W., Cristelfranchi, C. (eds.) AAMAS 2002. Proc. First International Joint Conference on Autonomous Agents and Multi-Agent Systems, pp. 3–10. ACM Press, New York (2002)
 7. Kuan, P., Karunasekera, S., Sterling, L.: Improving Goal and Role Oriented Analysis for Agent Based Systems. In: ASWEC 2005. Proc. Australian Software Engineering Conference, Brisbane, Australia, pp. 40–47 (2005)
 8. Kjeldskov, J., Gibbs, M., Vetere, F., Howard, S., Pedell, S., Mecoles, K., Bunyan, M.: Using Cultural Probes to Explore Mediated Intimacy. Australian Journal of Information Systems (Special Issue), 102–115 (2004)
 9. O'Keefe, R.: The Craft of Prolog. MIT Press, Cambridge (1990)
10. Padgham, L., Winikoff, M.: Developing Intelligent Agent Systems. John Wiley, Chichester (2004)
11. Sterling, L.: Patterns for Prolog programming. In: Kakas, A.C., Sadri, F. (eds.) Computational Logic: Logic Programming and Beyond. LNCS (LNAI), vol. 2407, pp. 374–401. Springer, Berlin (2002)
12. Sterling, L., Taveter, K., and the Daedalus Team: Building Agent-Based Appliances with Complementary Methodologies. In: JCKBSE 2006. Proc. Joint Conference on Knowledge-Based Software Engineering, Tallinn, Estonia, pp. 223–232. IOS Press, Amsterdam (2006)
13. Sterling, L., Taveter, K.: The Art of Agent-Oriented Modelling. MIT Press, Cambridge (2008)
14. Stern, L., Sterling, L.: Toward Agents for Educational Software. In: Proc. ED-MEDIA 2006, Association for the Advancement of Computing in Education, pp. 2040–2047
15. Taveter, K., Sterling, L.: An Expressway from Agent-Oriented Models to Prototype Systems. In: Proc. Workshop on Agent-Oriented Software Engineering, Hawaii, pp. 192–206 (May 2007)
16. Winograd, T.: Understanding Natural Language. Academic Press, London (1972)

Joint Conversation Specification and Compliance

Shamimabi Paurobally[1] and Michael Wooldridge[2]

[1] University of Westminster, London W1W 6UW, U.K.
S.Paurobally@westminster.ac.uk
[2] University of Liverpool, Liverpool L69 3BX, U.K.
mjw@csc.liv.ac.uk

Abstract. Formal specifications of protocol-oriented agent interactions have focused mainly on the semantics of the constituent agent communication language (ACL). In existing work, the semantics of a conversation policy is derived from the semantics of its individual communicative actions (CA) and there is no notion of persistency and compliance to the whole conversation policy. We argue that a proper theoretical treatment of conversations cannot be simply derived compositionally from the semantics of individual CAs. Accordingly, we develop a theory of joint conversations that is independent of its constituent CAs. We treat the process of a group following an interaction protocol as a persistent joint communicative action (JCA) by the group. This paper specifies the $\mathcal{L}_{JCA}$ logic based on Cohen and Levesque 1990 joint intention (JI) theory [2] and develops a framework in $\mathcal{L}_{JCA}$ logic for representing and reasoning about joint conversations. We define compliance in a joint conversation and we prove salient properties of joint conversations. Amongst others, we prove the existence of a Nash equilibrium in a bilateral interaction, and that our framework ensures an agent's compliance to the rules of the interaction in the sense that each participant jointly intends to uphold the whole conversation and to adhere to the conversation policy.

Keywords: compliance, joint conversation, communicative action, intention.

1   Introduction

Social interactions, such as cooperation, coordination and negotiation, are enacted through a variety of agent communication languages (ACLs) and interaction protocols (IPs). An ACL (for example KQML, FIPA ACL [5]) specifies the individual communicative acts (CAs), typically as classes of asynchronous messages modelled on the theory of speech acts. An interaction protocol, like the contract net protocol (CNP), or an English auction protocol, aims to specify the message sequences that lead to a end state such as a (*sold* ∧ *closed*) auction. Ideally, in an agent world, each message would be the content conveyed by an individual communicative act of the ACL. However, the published specifications of protocols suffer from ambiguities and incompleteness. This lack of precision arises from the inherent inexpressiveness of diagrammatic representations such

M. Baldoni et al. (Eds.): DALT 2007, LNAI 4897, pp. 18–35, 2008.

as Petri-nets [11] and AUML [1], and from a focus on a conceptual level of discussion using informal language rather than mathematics. Consequently, while the published protocol specifications may well be helpful for comprehension, in practice they are inadequate for formal verification of correctness.

Proposed semantics for ACLs and conversation policies can be categorised into belief-intention semantics (as in FIPA ACL [5]), commitment-based semantics [17] and joint intention (JI) [2] based semantics [7]. In all of these cases, the semantics of the interaction protocols (IPs) have been proposed as the postconditions holding after two or three CAs. Their approach is to first specify the semantics of the individual CAs in the ACL in the belief-intention, commitment-based or JI theories respectively. Then the semantics of the conversation policies are specified as what holds after sending two or three of the CAs in sequence. For example, in [7] and [14], conversation policies are given as sending a *request* CA followed by an *agree* CA, or a *offer* CA followed by an *inform* CA. The semantics of such conversation policies are defined as what commitment holds after each CA without taking into account the whole protocol. As in [12], the semantics of interaction protocols are derived from the postconditions of each CA. We argue that existing approaches such as the above-mentioned are inadequate for specifying and reasoning about the semantics of conversation policies for three main reasons.

The *first* reason is that a conversation between a group of agents, with respect to an IP, involves more than the aggregate of the individual CAs. Communication essentially requires a framework of mutual mental states (beliefs, knowledge, goals, intentions) and these mental states influence each other. As for joint actions, a conversation may require that the sending of an individual CA by one agent depends on another agent's utterances. When a conversation is underway, each participant has a part to perform when it is their turn to respond. The performance of an agent's part has to occur with respect to the other participants' intentions, leading to some notion of joint commitment and joint control over the *whole* conversation and not only for some of the CAs. Thus a conversation is more than the sequence of its CAs.

The *second* reason is that there is the need for compliance and persistency of this compliance throughout the whole conversation according to the rules of the interaction. For example, when the bidder x and the auctioneer y are involved in an English auction, each time x makes a bid, y should inform x whether its bid was successful or not. The auctioneer y should not arbitrarily choose to stop complying to the protocol and withdraw without a consensus between the participants. Although [7] specifies the semantics of several speech-acts in terms of persistent goals, there is no notion of compliance and persistency to follow the whole protocol. For example, [7] does not define the *inform* CA as a persistent goal and this is correct. However, there would be no notion of persistent goal to be achieved and thus no compliance in a conversation policy that contains one or more *inform* CAs.

The *third* limitation of existing approaches in the semantics for conversation policies lies in that we should be able to specify what it means to follow an

IP independent of its constituent CAs and ACL. What is the semantics of the conversation policy that sequences the CAs $phrase_1$, $thing_2$, $sentence_3$ and $word_4$? We should be able to specify what it means to follow such a conversation policy. A group engages in such a conversation in order to cooperate and jointly achieve some goal. This translates to a group member jointly intending the group's goal because in some way contributing to the group's goal helps that member to satisfy its own individual goal. We can refer to a group following an auctioning protocol without needing to know which specific CAs are used. Thus semantics for IPs are different from the ACL semantics.

Against the above three arguments, it can be seen that there are a number of social constraints on an agent and consequently on a group when carrying out a conversation. Our paper advances the state of the art by proposing an approach based on the joint intention theory in order to remedy the above shortcomings. We specify the $\mathcal{L}_{JCA}$ logic and propose a framework to represent joint conversations and compliance to such conversations. We ensure that we reason about the whole conversation instead of its CAs separately. We prove salient properties of joint conversations expressed in $\mathcal{L}_{JCA}$ such as Nash equilibrium exists between two agents interacting according to an IP. We also define persistency throughout a conversation by specifying what it means for an agent to comply to a conversation policy and proving such compliance holds in our framework, in the sense that the agents share a joint intention with the group to follow the actions allowed by the IP and the framework.

The remainder of this paper is structured in the following way. Section 2 gives an overview of the JI theory. In section 3, we specify the syntax, semantics and axioms in the $\mathcal{L}_{JCA}$ logic. In section 4, we develop a framework for joint conversations in $\mathcal{L}_{JCA}$ and we define two notions of compliance to an IP. Section 5 specifies and proves salient properties holding in joint conversations in our framework. Section 6 discusses related work on the semantics of conversation policies. Section 7 concludes and identifies possible avenues for future work.

2   Joint Intention Theory

Previously proposed semantics for ACLs include belief-intention semantics as in FIPA ACL [5], commitment-based semantics [17] and joint intention (JI) based semantics [3]. These semantics lead to similar styles of semantics for IPs. The 1997 semantic specification for FIPA ACL is expressed using a logic of belief and intention. While this specification is informative, it has been criticised on various grounds [16], not least that it is unverifiable. We consider that a belief logic is a useful ideal for giving epistemic status to the consistent, but not necessarily true, internal propositions that can be used by a designer to express and reason about information internal to an agent. Treating intention in a similar way is also a useful ideal for succinct reasoning about a goal state. The durability of the Belief-Desire-Intention paradigm for practical deliberative agents also provides anecdotal justification for this sort of reasoning.

In the case of the JI theory [3] based semantics for CAs [14], the mental states of the agents incorporate mutual belief between two agents about their respective

Table 1. Notation Used in the Paper

Bel-Int axiom	$I_i\alpha \leftrightarrow B_i I_i\alpha$ [9]
G	$\{s, H\}$
$OCCURRING\ \gamma$	γ occurs at the current time point [2]
$I_G p$	$\forall i \in G\ (I_i p)$
$E_G p$	$\forall i \in G\ (B_i p)$
$K_i p$	i knows p
$EK_G p$	$\forall i \in G\ (K_i p)$
$MB\ s\ r\ p$	Mutual belief between s and r that p
$MB\ G\ p$	$\forall i \in G, j \in G\ (MB\ i\ j\ p)$
$JPG\ s\ r\ p\ q$	s and r have JPG p wrt. q
$JPG\ G\ p\ q$	$\forall i \in G, j \in G\ (JPG\ i\ j\ p\ q)$
$JI\ s\ r\ \gamma\ q$	$JPG\ s\ r\ (DONE\ \{s,r\}.[UNTIL$ $(DONE\ \{s,r\}.\gamma)(MB\ s\ r\ (\{s,r\}.\gamma))]?;\gamma)\ q$
$JI\ G\ \gamma\ q$	$\forall i \in G, j \in G\ (JI\ i\ j\ \gamma\ q)$
$C_G p$	$EK_G\alpha \wedge EK_G^2\alpha \wedge \ldots \wedge EK_G^m\alpha \wedge \ldots$
Atomic process	ϖ
Complex process	γ
Atomic JCA α	$\mathcal{JCA}((s,H).\varpi)$
Complex JCA β	$\mathcal{JCA}(G.\gamma)$
q	$MB\ G\ (\neg(DONE\ G.(\beta\|abort)))$

persistent goal to have an action a done unless it is considered to be impossible or irrelevant. Given that our aim in this paper is to consider interoperation and teamwork within a group when following an IP, we find that the theory of JI best fits the types of commitments we need for specifying participation in a conversation. Thus, in this section, we provide an overview of the JI theory although we do not faithfully re-use Cohen and Levesque's [2] notation for beliefs, intentions and goals. JI theory is specified in first order modal logic with dynamic logic [6] and epistemic logic connectives [9], including the KD45 axioms for belief. The Kripke semantics of JI theory is given in [2]. ($HAPPENS\ \gamma$) and ($DONE\ \gamma$) [2] respectively denote that the process γ will happen next or has just happened. $BEFORE$ and $AFTER$ are defined using $HAPPENS$, where $BEFORE\ p\ q$ states that p comes before q.

Regarding mental states, let $B_i p$ denote agent i believes proposition p. Let $G_i p$ and $I_i p$ denote that i has respectively the goal and intention that p holds. A group G has mutual belief ($MB\ G\ p$) about p if everyone believes p, i.e. ($E_G\ p$), and if everyone believes that everyone mutually believes p. ($MG\ x\ y\ p$) denotes two agents x and y have a mutual goal p and this holds if they mutually believe that p is a goal of both agents. ($PGOAL\ x\ p\ q$) denotes that an agent x has a persistent goal to achieve p relative to q: it persists in having the goal to achieve p until it believes that p is true, or is impossible or irrelevant by q being false. An intention ($INTEND$) is a persistent goal in which the agent is committed to performing an action believing throughout that it is doing the action [2]. The expression ($PWAG\ x\ y\ p\ q$) states that an agent x has a *persistent weak achievement goal (PWAG)* with respect to agent y to achieve p relative to q. ($PWAG\ x\ y\ p\ q$) is defined as a disjunction of the following conditions 1) agent x does not believe p and has a persistent goal to achieve p, 2) if agent x believes that p holds or that p is impossible or that q is false, then x has the persistent goal to bring about the corresponding mutual belief with y [7].

($JPG\ x\ y\ p\ q$) denote that two agents x and y have a joint persistent goal (JPG) p with respect to q and the JPG holds if: 1) there is mutual belief that p is not currently true, 2) it is a mutual goal to bring about p, 3) p will remain a weak mutual goal until there is a mutual belief that p is either true, p will never be true, or q is false. Mutual belief in each other's PWAG towards the other agent establishes JPG between two agents if one PWAG is relative to the other [2]. Joint intention (JI) between two agents is defined as a joint persistent goal to perform an action believing throughout that the agents are jointly doing the action. We denote the JI between the members of a group G to achieve λ with respect to q as ($JI\ G\ \lambda\ q$) through group PWAG defined in [8]. In table 1, we summarise the abbreviations that we use in the rest of this paper.

3   Logic of $\mathcal{JCA}$

Joint actions are actions involving a number of agents performing interdependent actions to achieve some common intention or goal (for example two or more people dancing together, driving together in a convoy or as in this paper taking part in a conversation) [13]. If an agent is involved in a joint action, then it has a part of the overall action to perform, and it must know when and how to perform its part. The agents in a group are collectively committed to performing the joint action until the goal of the joint action has been achieved. This is the teamwork formalised by the joint intention theory.

Many joint actions involve communication before and during the action execution. For example, agent x may request agent y that they carry a table together or perform negotiations together in an electronic transaction. Normally, a group of agents engage in a dialogue to reach an agreement to carry out a joint action together after the dialogue. We consider the act of participating in a dialogue between two or more agents as a joint action. More specifically, we call actions that involves communication as joint communicative actions (JCAs). This paper specifies the logic and properties of JCAs and, in this section, we specify the logic for JCA, $\mathcal{L}_{JCA}$.

3.1   Syntax of $\mathcal{L}_{JCA}$

The syntax of $\mathcal{L}_{JCA}$ is based on the syntax of the JI theory (see section 2), consisting of dynamic logic connectives, and temporal and epistemic modalities. We refer to dynamic logic programs as processes in this paper. A process can be an atomic process ϖ or a complex process, γ. A complex process can itself be defined as sequential, alternative, iterative and test, as per the normal propositional dynamic logic (PDL) syntax [6]. In addition, in $\mathcal{L}_{JCA}$, a process can be a joint communicative act (JCA) denoted as $\mathcal{JCA}(G.\gamma)$

PDL Processes: $\gamma ::= \varpi \mid \gamma_1; \gamma_2 \mid \gamma_1 \cup \gamma_2 \mid \gamma^* \mid A? \mid null \mid abort$
$\mathcal{L}_{JCA}$ processes: $\gamma ::= i.\gamma \mid \mathcal{JCA}((s, H).\varpi) \mid \mathcal{JCA}(G.\gamma)$

The complex process $(\gamma_1; \gamma_2)$ denotes executing the sub-process γ_1 followed by γ_2, the process $(\gamma_1 \cup \gamma_2)$ is either γ_1 or γ_2 non-deterministically, γ^* denotes zero or more iterations of process γ. A state test operator "?" allows sequential composition to follow only if the tested state holds. A *null* process represents no execution, while an *abort* process results in a failed state.

We extend the program logic of dynamic logic to include processes of type $i.\gamma$, where agent i executes process γ. For example, i executing a *bid* CA is denoted as $i.bid$, and j performing a *negotiation* process is denoted as $j.negotiation$. We define the dynamic logic process $\mathcal{JCA}((s, H).\varpi)$ as an atomic JCA between a speaker s and one or more hearers H, by indicating the atomic action ϖ is in the context of a conversation.

$\mathcal{JCA}((s, H).\varpi)$ is the sending of the CA, ϖ, from the speaker s to hearer H, or the execution of an atomic action by s, both *within the context of a joint conversation*. A CA such as a KQML performative or a FIPA ACL CA is *not* an atomic JCA action. In the expression $(\mathcal{JCA}((s, H).\varpi))$, the CA is ϖ. Thus a CA such as *request, inform* or *offer* has their associated belief intention semantics. In addition, we formulate the beliefs and intention that hold with each utterance of a CA in the context of a conversation, independent of the semantics of the particular CA.

More specifically, a sender has a number of intentions: his intention to convey the meaning of the CA, his illocutionary intention to send the message through and his perlocutionary intention for the hearer to believe or act in some way. Mutually accepted conventions such as a shared ACL and IP make it unnecessary for the sender to explicitly convey all these intentions for each CA. Similarly our definition of JCAs include a number of intentions that are regarded as mutually accepted conventions for agent conversations. For example, in our theory for JCAs, it is no longer enough for a hearer to believe that the sender intended the hearer to believe or do something. We also require that any actions are performed within the context of a joint conversation. Thus a sender sends a CA because in addition, he believes that there is a joint intention between the sender and the hearer for the sender to make such an utterance. The hearer expects the sender to send the CA. The sender may be responding to any previous utterance from the hearer according to both agent's beliefs about the IP.

An example atomic JCA is $\mathcal{JCA}((auctioneer, bidder).accept)$, where an auctioneer sends an *accept* CA to a bidder. This is in the context of a joint conversation, where there should be a joint intention between the two agents for the auctioneer to send the CA *accept* to the bidder. This would probably be during an auction, where the auctioneer is replying to a bid from the bidder. Thus the bidder expects the auctioneer to send *accept*, and on receiving the CA, the bidder changes his beliefs accordingly.

The complex process $\mathcal{JCA}(G.\gamma)$ generalises the above atomic JCA, $\mathcal{JCA}((s, H).\varpi)$, to apply to a group G performing a joint conversation γ. Here

γ could be a single CA, such as in $\mathcal{JCA}(\{auctioneer, bidder\}.bidder.bid)$. The process γ could also represent a whole English auction protocol, for example:

$\mathcal{JCA}(\{auctioneer, bidder_1, \ldots, bidder_n\}.$
$\quad (auctioneer.post; (bidder_i.bid; auctioneer.request\_higher\_bid)^*;$
$\quad bidder_j.bid; (auctioneer.(accept|withdraw))))).$

The semantics of $\mathcal{JCA}(G.\gamma)$ ensures that there is JI between G throughout the conversation to perform the allowable sequences in the IP.

Alternatively, $\mathcal{JCA}(G.\gamma)$ could represent part of a protocol, for example:

$\mathcal{JCA}(\{auctioneer, bidder_1, bidder_2, bidder_3\}.$
$\quad ((bidder_i.bid; auctioneer.request\_higher\_bid)^*)),$

where only the bidding part of the English auction is represented. The JI between the auctioneer and the bidders still hold since they still need to commit to perform the sub-protocol as a team, and this is ensured by the semantics of a JCA.

3.2 Semantics of $\mathcal{L}_{JCA}$

The logic $\mathcal{L}_{JCA}$ can be given a formal possible worlds semantics using an extended multi-relational Kripke model. We extend Cohen and Levesque's model theory for JI [2]. Thus, we assume a set of possible worlds W each one consisting of a sequence of events, temporally extended infinitely in past and future. A model for $\mathcal{L}_{JCA}$ is a structure:

$M = (W, E, T, R_\gamma, V, R_{B_i}, R_{G_i})$. W is a non-empty set of worlds. The function V is an assignment from sets of possible worlds to propositions. E is a set of primitive event types. $T \subseteq [\mathcal{Z} \to E]$ is a set of possible courses of events (or worlds) specified as a function from the integers to elements of E. The world is populated by a non-empty set of agents and a group of agents is a non-empty subset of the world population. In the model, i denotes an agent in the relations for modalites expressing mental states. R_γ, R_{B_i} and R_{G_i} are accessibility relations on the worlds in W (in order to model processes, beliefs and goals respectively). The relation R_{B_i} is serial, transitive, and Euclidean and R_{G_i} is serial. $B_i p$ denotes agent i believes proposition p. $G_i p$ denotes that i has goal p. The semantics of intention $I_i p$ is given in [2] in terms of the persistent goal of i to intentionally perform an event that will bring about p.

$I_i p \stackrel{\text{def}}{=} (PGOAL\ i\ \exists e(DONE\ i[(B_i\ \exists e'(HAPPENS\ i\ e'; p?)) \wedge$
$\quad \neg(GOAL\ i\neg(HAPPENS\ i\ e; p?))]?; e; p?))$

Complex processes are generated from the set of atomic processes, and the semantics of the standard dynamic logic processes can be found in [6]. The formula $[\gamma]A$ has the intended meaning: A holds after executing process γ.

Let the formula $(AGENT\ i\ \gamma)$ denote that only the agent i can do action γ [2]. $i.\gamma$ denotes the action expression $i.\gamma$ is occurring now at the current time point. The following is a definition of $i.\gamma$ using the dynamic logic "[ ]" operator.

$M, w \models [i.\gamma]p$ iff $\forall w' \in W(wR_{i.\gamma}w' \wedge (AGENT\ i\ \gamma) \rightarrow M, w' \models p)$

The semantics of $\mathcal{JCA}((s, H).\varpi)$ and $\mathcal{JCA}(G.\gamma)$ are given below. We have different formulations for atomic and complex JCAs because we can declare the sender s and hearer H of an atomic JCA, as (s, H), and the associated CA as ϖ. However for a complex JCA, $\mathcal{JCA}(G.\gamma)$, we refer in terms of a group of agents G involved in carrying out the process γ, which could itself be a JCA.

The fixed point definition of the atomic JCA from sender s to hearer(s) H with the CA ϖ presupposes the following:

- There is JI between s and H to do the JCA, unless the conversation is aborted or over. $\lambda = JI\ s\ H\ \mathcal{JCA}((s, H).\varpi)\ (MB\ s\ H\ \neg abort | \neg(DONE\ s.\varpi))$
- It is mutual belief between s and H that H intends s to do ϖ. $\delta = MB\ s\ H\ (I_H\ (DONE\ s.\varpi))$. Further mutual belief between s and H that H intends s to do the JCA is captured by the JI in λ.
- s intends that having sent the CA, ϖ, H believes that s both intended the JCA and has done the atomic JCA.
  $\mu = I_s((DONE\ s.\varpi) \rightarrow B_H((DONE\ s.\mathcal{JCA}((s, H).\varpi))$
  $\wedge I_s(DONE\ \mathcal{JCA}((s, H).\varpi))))$

Given the success of these beliefs and intentions, s does send the CAs ϖ, given by $s.\varpi$ at the end of the definition of an atomic JCA.

For atomic JCA: $\mathcal{JCA}((s, H).\varpi) \stackrel{\text{def}}{=} (\lambda \wedge \delta \wedge \mu)?; s.\varpi$

The semantics of a complex JCA, $\beta = \mathcal{JCA}(G.(s.\varpi; \gamma))$, first states that there is a JI in G to carry out $(s.\varpi; \gamma)$ as a JCA with respect to q (see table 1). Here q gives the conditions for stopping a conversation by q being false. q is defined in table 1 and the conditions are that 1) it is mutual belief in the group that not all the actions in the JCA, β, have been executed, or 2) it is mutual belief that the conversation has not been aborted. We include timeouts in aborted conversations. We define a complex JCA to consist of the following processes (successful testing of the conditions), where $\beta = \mathcal{JCA}(G.(s.\varpi; \gamma))$:

- There is a JI in G to carry out $(s.\varpi; \gamma)$ as a JCA with respect to q.
  $\theta = (JI\ G\ (DONE\ G.\beta)?\ q)$.
- Executing the atomic JCA with CA ϖ. $\alpha = \mathcal{JCA}((s, G').\varpi)$,
  where $G' = G \backslash \{s\}$
- Given that the atomic JCA α has been performed, ensuring that there is a joint intention to do the rest of the complex JCA.
  $\nu = JI\ G((DONE\ \alpha)?; \mathcal{JCA}(G.\gamma))\ q$
- Doing the rest of the JCA, $\mu = \mathcal{JCA}(G.\gamma)$

Thus a complex JCA is defined as $\mathcal{JCA}(G.(s.\varpi; \gamma)) \stackrel{\text{def}}{=} (\theta?; \alpha; \nu?; \mu)$.

Our definition of a complex JCA, β, requires that the joint intention to perform β persists throughout the conversation, taking into account the point at which the conversation has reached. In this way, our definition captures the persistency required in following an interaction protocol.

3.3   Axiomatisation of $\mathcal{L}_{JCA}$

Both atomic and complex JCAs are perlocutionary acts that produce an effect on the addressee's side, where the sender intends the receiver to react, believe or do something, according to its utterance. In this section, we formulate axioms to express the effect of performing a JCA on the mental states of group participants. We use the notation summarised in table 1 in specifying the axioms in this section. Recall that an atomic JCA with CA, ϖ, is denoted by $\alpha = \mathcal{JCA}((s, H).\varpi)$, and a complex JCA is denoted by $\beta = \mathcal{JCA}(G.\gamma)$. Let $G = \{s, H\}$.

Axiom 1 states that the CA associated with a JCA is also performed when the JCA is carried out. This axiom holds because in the semantics of atomic JCA, the process $s.\varpi$ is carried out when s possesses the correct intentions.

Axiom 1. $(DONE\ \alpha) \rightarrow (DONE\ s.\varpi)$

Axiom 2 states that in an intended JCA, the sender s also intends its associated CA. Axiom 2 can be derived from axiom 1 and the side-effect of intentions.

Axiom 2. $I_s(DONE\ \alpha) \rightarrow I_s(DONE\ s.\varpi)$

Axiom 3 states that sending a CA implies that it is mutual belief between the sender and the hearer that the sender intended the associated JCA. The axiom can be proved from an atomic JCA's semantics and from *Bel-Int* Axiom.

Axiom 3. $E_G(DONE\ s.\varpi) \rightarrow (MB\ s\ H\ I_s(DONE\ s.\alpha))$

Axiom 4 states that in a conversation the group mutually believes that it intends to carry out the conversation. This axiom can be obtained from the semantics of a complex JCA (since carrying out a complex process involves joint intention in G), and from *Bel-Int* Axiom (see table 1).

Axiom 4. $(OCCURRING\ G.\beta) \rightarrow (MB\ G\ I_G\ (DONE\ G.\beta))$

Axiom 5 formulates a hearer's H beliefs on receiving a JCA. The hearer believes that the sender s intended H to believe that s intended the JCA before actually sending the CA associated with the JCA. Axiom 5 can be derived from axiom 3 where the intentions of the sender are mutually believed in a group.

Axiom 5. $B_H(DONE\ s.\alpha) \rightarrow B_H I_s B_H([(I_s(DONE\ \alpha))?; \alpha](DONE\ s.\varpi))$

Axiom 6 states that after a conversation, everyone believes that everyone intended to do the interaction before actually doing it, and everyone believes that everyone intended for everyone to believe their intentions. This axiom follows from generalising axiom 5 and from the JI in the definition of a JCA.

Axiom 6. $E_G(DONE\ G.\beta) \rightarrow$
      $(E_G(BEFORE\ (DONE\ G.\beta)\ (I_G(DONE\ \beta))) \wedge (JI\ G\ \beta\ q))$

Axiom 7 states that the receiver of a JCA believes that he has also received the associated CA. This axiom is inferred from axiom 5.

Axiom 7. $B_H(DONE\ \alpha) \rightarrow B_H(DONE\ s.\varpi)$

Axiom 8 states that it is mutual belief in G that everyone in G must perform the JCA β together as a joint intention. Thus, if everyone believes that everyone intends to perform a conversation, then the joint intention of this JCA is mutual belief within the group. This axiom is entailed from the semantics of JCA and that JI entails mutual belief about the group's intentions.

Axiom 8. $E_G I_G(DONE\ G.\beta) \rightarrow MB\ G\ (JI\ G\ G.\beta\ q)$

Axioms 1, 2 and 7 can also be modified to reflect the sender's and hearers' intentions and beliefs for complex JCAs β.

4 A Framework in $\mathcal{L}_{JCA}$ for Joint Conversations

In this section, we use the $\mathcal{L}_{JCA}$ logic to develop a framework for joint conversations between a group of agents according to an IP. We first express the assumptions for shared conventions, then we provide an example for forming a group of interacting agents, and finally we specify two notions of compliance to the rules of a joint conversation.

4.1 Assumptions

We make the following assumptions about the representation of an interaction protocol and the sharing of the interaction protocol and its semantics within the group.

Assumption 1. *A group G participating in a joint conversation has prior mutual knowledge about the shared ACL and its semantics. Let a theory for the ACL shared between G with CAs γ' be denoted by $\Delta(G, \gamma')$, then assumption 1 is given as $((OCCURRING\ JCA(G.\gamma)) \wedge (\Delta(G, \gamma') \rightarrow \Delta(G, \gamma))) \rightarrow (C_G\Delta(G, \gamma'))$.*

Assumption 1 expresses that the chosen ACL and the semantics of its CAs is mutual knowledge within the interacting group. What an agent says by its utterance (locutionary understanding) and what is meant by that utterance (illocutionary understanding) are mutual knowledge after an agent's utterance.

Assumption 2. *Possible paths of actions can be inferred from an interaction protocol. An interaction protocol can imply a JCA complex process, with the possible paths as its sub-processes. The constituent actions are labelled with the perpetrator of that action. $\mathcal{JCA}(G.\gamma)$ represents the sequences of actions in the IP using the sequential and alternation PDL program operators. Let a theory of the interaction protocol be denoted as $\Pi(G, \gamma')$ where G is the group of agents following the IP and γ' represents all the paths of actions derivable from the the the IP. Assumption 2 is formulated as $(\Pi(G, \gamma') \wedge [\gamma]p) \rightarrow (\exists i \in G, (<G.\mathcal{JCA}(i.\gamma_i)> p))$ where $\gamma = \gamma_1; \ldots \gamma_i; \ldots \gamma_n$, and $[\gamma]p \leftrightarrow \neg <\neg\gamma> p$.*

Assumption 2 states that we can represent an interaction protocol in PDL as possible sequences of actions. In addition, for each action in the IP, the IP specifies which agent does that action. For example, in an auction, one possible sequential path is ($auctioneer.post$; $bidder_1.bid$; $auctioneer.call\_bid$; $bidder_2.bid$; $auctioneer.accept$; $auctioneer.close$).

Assumption 3. *A group of agents uses an interaction protocol to carry out a conversation. The IP, $\Pi(G, \gamma')$, and its semantics are common knowledge within the group.*

$$((\Pi(G, \gamma') \rightarrow (DONE\ \mathcal{JCA}(G.\gamma))) \wedge I_G(DONE\ \mathcal{JCA}(G.\gamma))) \rightarrow C_G\Pi(G, \gamma')$$

Assumption 3 states that all interacting agents know which IP is being used during the conversation. Thus assumptions 2 and 3 results in all the agents knowing the permissible actions and their perpetrators in a conversation.

Assumption 4. *An agent knows if it is a member of G and knows its role in the conversation.*

$$\mathcal{JCA}(G.\gamma) \rightarrow (\forall i \in G(K_i((i \in G) \wedge I_i(DONE\ i.\gamma_i)))) \ where\ \gamma = \gamma_1; \ldots \gamma_i; \ldots \gamma_n$$

We assume an agent's awareness of its membership in a group and its role according to that IP. We show how this can be achieved in section 4.2.

Assumption 5. *Each agent in G has individual goals and intentions, and mutually believe so about the other agents too.*

$$\forall i \in G\ \exists \gamma, \mu((PGOAL\ i\ (DONE\ i.\gamma)\ q) \wedge I_i\ (DONE\ \mu)$$
$$\wedge\ MB\ G\ ((PGOAL\ i\ (DONE\ \gamma)\ q) \wedge I_i\ (DONE\ \mu)))$$

It is also mutual belief in G that for each agent to achieve its individual goals, it has to participate in the conversation.

$$\forall i \in G((PGOAL\ i\ (DONE\ i.\mu)\ q) \wedge I_G\ (DONE\ \mathcal{JCA}(G.\gamma)) \rightarrow$$
$$(MB\ G\ (DONE\ \mathcal{JCA}(G.\gamma)) \rightarrow (DONE\ \mu)))$$

Assumption 5 expresses that an agent is intensional – it believes it can achieve its individual goals by intending to participate and participating in the joint conversation. Thus, agents are rational and participate in a joint conversation for individual goal satisfaction.

4.2   Example Group Formation

A group of agents is formed because its members choose to collaborate in a dialogue or a joint action, leading to the satisfaction of the member's own individual goals. Here, we focus on one to many IPs because they encode the ideas of group interaction such as the contract net protocol or auctions. One to many protocols, where only one member can perform a one-to-many interaction, can be simplified to the bilateral case or extended to many-to-many protocols. We use an English auction as an example. Before the group is formed, an auctioneer has a goal $(DONE \ \lambda)$ to be achieved through group collaboration. He also has a goal $(DONE \ \gamma)$ for a conversation with other agents such that they can coordinate to achieve λ after the conversation. Thus, γ, as the JCA, is the process of conversing and λ is what is agreed to be performed after the dialogue. The auctioneer wants to first form a group to carry out γ, the joint conversation. Here, as an example of group formation, the auctioneer sends a call for participation with the goal to engage in a joint conversation followed by an acceptance or refusal from the receivers. Let $(c\_f\_participation \ a \ r \ \gamma \ q)$ denote a call for participation from auctioneer a to receivers r for achieving the goal $(DONE \ \gamma)$ relative to q. Let the group of agents that include only a and r be denoted by G_a. Let cfp denote the action of sending the cfp CA, whose formal semantics can be found in [5]. Note that γ is a JCA and is of type $\mathcal{JCA}(G.\beta)$.

The semantics of the $c\_f\_participation$ with the cfp CA is given in $\mathcal{L}_{JCA}$ as:

$$(c\_f\_participation \ a \ r \ \gamma \ q) \triangleq (B_a \neg\gamma)?; I_a((DONE \ \gamma) \wedge (JI \ G_a \ G_a.\gamma \ q) \wedge$$
$$B_{G_a} I_a((DONE \ G_a.\gamma) \wedge (JI \ G_a \ G_a.\gamma \ q)))?; cfp$$

We define the semantics of $c\_f\_participation$ as a intends to achieve the JCA γ and for G_a to adopt this as a joint intention. a also intends for G_a to believe these intentions. On receiving a $c\_f\_participation$, an agent r $(r \in G_a)$ may choose to respond with an acceptance or a refusal to be a member of the group to perform JCA γ. The semantics of $(accept \ r \ a \ \gamma \ q)$ with the $accept$ CA is:

$$I_r((DONE \ \gamma) \wedge (BMB \ r \ s \ (PWAG \ r \ a \ (DONE \ \gamma) \ q)))?; accept$$

If r refuse, then all commitments are discharged and r is not a member of the group involved in the joint conversation. If r accepts, then r is integrated in the group and participates in the joint conversation. Let G' be re-initialised to the group containing only a. Theorem 1 states that: if r accepts a call for participation from a followed by r being added to the group G (the sequence of actions in the premise of theorem 1), then there is a JPG in G to carry out the JCA γ.

Theorem 1. $\models (DONE \ [((c\_f\_participation \ a \ r \ \gamma \ q); (accept \ r \ a \ \gamma \ q))?])$
$\rightarrow (JPG \ G \ (DONE \ G.\gamma) \ q)$, where $G := (G' \cup \{r\})$.

Proof. Assume that an acceptance follows the call for participation without any inteferring intermediary action and that it is mutual belief that messages are not lost. From the semantics of $c\_f\_participation$, agent a on sending a $c\_f\_participation$ has the intention for a JI to be adopted by the group. Since, r sends an $accept$, then it must have received the $c\_f\_participation$ and thus believes $(DONE \ a.c\_f\_participation)$ and from axiom 5, $B_r I_a((DONE \ \gamma) \wedge (JI \ G \ G.\gamma \ q) \wedge B_G I_a((DONE \ G.\gamma) \wedge (JI \ G \ G.\gamma \ q)))$, more specifically $B_r I_a(JI \ G \ G.\gamma \ q)$. On receiving an $accept$, again from axiom 5:

$B_a I_r BMB \ r \ a(PWAG \ r \ a(DONE \ \gamma)q) \wedge B_a B_r I_a(JI \ G \ G.\gamma \ q)$. More specifically, $B_a I_r BMB \ r \ a \ (JPG \ r \ a \ (DONE \ \gamma) \ q)$ from the definition of JPG as mutual belief in each other's $PWAG$. From axiom Bel-Int, we have $(JPG \ \{r, a\} \ (DONE \ G.\gamma) \ q)$. Each receiver that sends an $accept$ shares the same mutual beliefs with a, and thus we have $(JPG \ G \ (DONE \ G.\gamma) \ q)$.

4.3 Compliance in a Joint Conversation

To conduct a coherent conversation, all members of a group must adhere to the requirements for a joint conversation and this is for each member's benefit in achieving their own goal. During a joint conversation, a group's compliance to the IP and the rules of interaction is dependent on the members' joint intention to uphold the joint conversation and its rules. An initial indication of this intention for compliance is the acceptance to a call for participation. In addition, throughout the joint conversation, there has to be mutual belief and intention within the group of each member's joint intention to comply to the rules of the interaction. To this end, we define below two notions of compliance – standard and strong compliance. First we define *standard compliance* in a joint conversation, which stands as the minimum requirements for conducting a joint conversation. We assume that each member in the group G believes that it is a member of G and this is mutual belief in G.

Standard Compliance

Definition 1. *Group members intentionally show standard compliance to the rules governing a joint conversation, according to protocol $\Pi(G, \gamma')$ and the $\mathcal{JCA}(G.\gamma)$ conversation, if the following conditions hold:*

(STD1) All the members in G have a joint intention to uphold the joint conversation by jointly intending $\mathcal{JCA}(G.\gamma))$ and this is mutual belief in G.

(STD2) i jointly intends with G the sequences of actions derivable from $\Pi(G, \gamma')$.

(STD3) If the IP specifies that i has to perform CA_i, then i both individually and jointly intends to perform $\mathcal{JCA}_i$, where $(\mathcal{JCA}_i \rightarrow CA_i)$.

(STD4) If $\mathcal{JCA}(G.\gamma)$ triggers the end state λ, that is $[\mathcal{JCA}(G.\gamma)]\lambda$, then it is the joint intention of the group to achieve $(\lambda?)$.

(STD5) Each member jointly intends to achieve its share of $\mathcal{JCA}(G.\gamma)$ and this is mutual belief.

(STD6) The members retain their joint and individual intentions until the whole joint conversation is terminated.

In section 5, we prove that following our assumptions in section 4.1, our framework ensures standard compliance.

Strong Compliance. We also define a stronger notion of compliance, called *strong compliance* if the participants in a joint conversation are cooperative, helpful and prevent violation of the compliance.

Definition 2. *In a joint conversation, strong compliance by G to protocol $\Pi(G, \gamma')$ and the $\mathcal{JCA}(G.\gamma)$ conversation holds, if the following conditions hold:*

(M1) G shows standard compliance to performing the $\mathcal{JCA}(G.\gamma)$ process according to the interaction protocol $\Pi(G, \gamma')$.

(M2) Members of G are cooperative in that when receiving a message, they always reply even if they reply negatively with a refusal or a rejection.

(M3) Members of G do not violate the IP and hence do not violate compliance, even though another participant's or the group's goal may be in conflict with their own goal.

(M4) Members of G are helpful, that is if possible they help other members comply to the rules in the joint conversation. Helpful may be defined in terms of repeating parts of the protocol in the pursuit of everyone's compliance.

Having developed a framework in $\mathcal{L}_{JCA}$ for representing and reasoning about joint conversations, we use this framework to define and prove properties regarding a member's and a group's mental states in a joint conversation. In so doing, we prove that, following the assumptions in section 4.1, the members in G exhibit standard compliance in our framework.

5 Properties of Joint Conversations

In this section, we formulate and prove relevant theorems that arise from the $\mathcal{L}_{JCA}$ logic after a group of interacting agents has been formed with the joint intention of participating in a conversation. Theorems 3, 4 and 5 are useful for reasoning about joint conversations because they show that each participant believes that the other members of the group will cooperate with them in the conversation and that cooperation indeed is the best action for them. Again, we use the notation summarised in table 1.

Theorem 2 states that it is mutual belief in G that the group's intention to carry out the conversation as a JCA implies a member's intention for the group's conversation to satisfy each member's own goal.

Theorem 2. *MB G $(I_G(DONE\ \mathcal{JCA}(G.\gamma))) \wedge I_i(DONE\ \gamma_i) \rightarrow$*
    MB G $(I_i(DONE\ \mathcal{JCA}(G.\gamma_i)))$ where $i \in G$

Proof. From the definition of JCA and JI *(MB G $(DONE\ \mathcal{JCA}(G.\gamma))) \rightarrow$ $(MB(JPG\ G\ (DONE\ G.\gamma)\ q))$.* From theorem 1, *(JPG G $(DONE\ G.\gamma)$)* holds during a conversation. Given this JPG between G, then by assumption 5, there is mutual belief in G that each agent's goal can be achieved in the conversation, that is, *MB G $(I_i DONE\ \mathcal{JCA}(G.\gamma_i))$.*

Theorem 3 states that an agent chooses to do its part of a JCA process rather than not performing and ignoring its part.

Theorem 3. *It is mutual belief in G, that performing $\mathcal{JCA}(G.\beta)$ together requires each member in G to do its part of $\mathcal{JCA}(G.\beta)$. More formally, Let predicate do_part(G, i, β, β_i) hold if i in group G performs the JCA process β_i in the complex process β.*

(MB G $(I_G(DONE\ \mathcal{JCA}(G.\beta)))) \rightarrow (\forall i \in G(JI\ i\ G\ do\_part(G, i, \beta, \beta_i)\ q)))$
    where $\beta = \beta_1; \ldots \beta_i; \ldots \beta_n$

Proof. Given the semantics of JCAs, the premise implies $(JI\ G\ G.\beta\ q)$. This pre-supposes $MB\ G\ (JPG\ G\ (DONE\ G.\beta)\ q)$. From theorem 2 and assumption 5, it is mutually believed that each member i intends the conversation to achieve the overall goal of the conversation and its own goal:

$$MB\ G\ I_i\ ((DONE\ \mathcal{JCA}(G.\beta)) \wedge$$
$$(BEFORE(DONE\ \mathcal{JCA}(G.\beta))\ I_i(DONE\ \beta_i)) \rightarrow I_i(DONE\ \beta_i)).$$

The intention of the group is thus to achieve each member's individual goal for the conversation. From the definition of stepwise execution using JI [3], if a team intends to do a sequence of actions, the agents of any of the steps will jointly intend to do the step relative to the group's intention. From assumption 2, the conversation can be represented as a stepwise execution where, from assumption 4, a member knows which is her part. The preconditions for stepwise execution is thus fulfilled, implying that the agents of any of the steps will jointly intend to do the step relative to the group's intention, that is $(\forall i(JI\ i\ G\ do\_part(G, i, \beta, \beta_i)\ q))$.

Theorem 4 extends theorem 3 for a JCA consisting of two CAs performed by two different agents. Theorem 4 states that a hearer responds to a sender when it is its turn because of their beliefs about each other's actions in the context of a JCA.

Theorem 4. *If a group G intends the JCA β, where β stipulates that a hearer r (in G) replies with the communicative act ϖ_r after receiving ϖ_s from agent s (in G), then agent r both performs ϖ_r and intends the JCA associated with ϖ_r.*
$$MB\ G\ (I_G\ (DONE\ \mathcal{JCA}((s,r).(\varpi_s; \varpi_r)))) \rightarrow$$
$$I_r\ \mathcal{JCA}((r,s).\varpi_r) \wedge (HAPPENS\ r.\varpi_r)$$

Proof. From the premises, it is mutual belief that s and r believe that they jointly intend β. On receiving ϖ_s, by axioms 2 and 3, r believes that it is mutual belief that s believes that performing ϖ_s is part of $\mathcal{JCA}((s,r).(\varpi_s; \varpi_r))$. From theorem 3, r believes the mutual belief that ϖ_s is s's part of $\mathcal{JCA}((s,r).(\varpi_s; \varpi_r))$. From the premises and the definition of a JCA, r believes that it is mutual belief that r jointly intends β with s. The process β, and from assumption 2, stipulates that agent r should reply with the communicative act ϖ_r after receiving ϖ_s. Since it is the joint intention of both agents for the sequential action to be successful so that $\mathcal{JCA}((s,r).(\varpi_s; \varpi_r))$ succeeds, then r believes that s will perform ϖ_s iff r will perform ϖ_r. Similarly for r, from theorem 2, r intends the joint conversation to achieve his goal and from theorem 3, r believes that it is mutual belief that r will perform ϖ_r as his part in a stepwise execution. Thus r jointly intends to perform ϖ_r as his part if s jointly intends ϖ_s as her part. Since s does indeed perform ϖ_s, then r jointly intends ϖ_r as his part and sends ϖ_r by the definition of intention.

Theorem 5 states that each agent finds it more preferable to perform their part of a JCA as intended while believing that this is so for the other participants also, leading to a Nash equilibrium [10] between the agents' actions.

Theorem 5. *If a group G jointly intends $\mathcal{JCA}(G.\gamma)$ and, if the process γ stipulates that agent r (in G) replies with the communicative act ϖ_r after receiving ϖ_s from agent s (in G), then the actions $r.\varpi_r$ and $s.\varpi_s$ form a Nash equilibrium.*

Proof. To prove the Nash equilibrium here, we need to prove that it is preferable for r and s to perform their allocated parts in accordance with each other. Actions ϖ_r and ϖ_s contribute to the achievement of the goal $(DONE\ \mathcal{JCA}(G.\gamma))$. From the fixed point definition of JCA, r and s jointly intend $(DONE\ \mathcal{JCA}(G.\gamma))$ and they jointly intend $r.\varpi_r$ and $s.\varpi_s$. From axiom 2, r intends ϖ_r and s intends ϖ_s with respect to the overall intention of $(DONE\ \mathcal{JCA}(G..\gamma))$. From theorem 3, it is mutually belief that both r and s should perform their part, ϖ_r and ϖ_s respectively. In fact, by theorem 4, both r and s do indeed choose to perform their part as the best response, with respect the other agent performing his part.

Finally, in theorem 6, we prove that given the assumptions in section 4.1, our framework ensures standard compliance.

Theorem 6. *Given assumptions 1 to 5 in section 4.1, our framework ensures standard compliance in the process $\mathcal{JCA}(G.\gamma)$, in the sense that the mental states of an interacting agent in our framework will be according to the requirements for standard compliance defined in definition 2.*

Proof. To prove standard compliance, we prove that the conditions *STD1* to *STD6* in definition 2 hold.

The definition of $\mathcal{JCA}(G.\gamma)$ states that G has a joint intention to carry out $\mathcal{JCA}(G.\gamma)$, thus proving condition *(STD1)*.

From assumption 2, $\mathcal{JCA}(G.\gamma)$ can be inferred from IP $\Pi(G,\gamma')$ and thus there is a joint intention by each member to perform the possible sequences in $\Pi(G,\gamma')$. This proves the condition *(STD2)*.

Assume that it is i's turn to perform JCA_i after receiving a CA. By applying theorem 4 and axiom 2, i jointly intends to perform JCA_i. By the theory of JI, i also individually intends to perform JCA_i. This proves conditions *(STD3)*.

Assume $(DONE\ \mathcal{JCA}(G.\gamma)) \rightarrow (DONE\ G.\lambda)$. To prove *(STD4)*, we prove $(JI\ G\ G.\lambda\ q)$. This is provable since $\mathcal{JCA}(G.\gamma)$ implies the joint intention in the group to achieve $(DONE\ \mathcal{JCA}(G.\gamma))$ and from deconditionalization.

Theorem 3 proves *(STD5)*, that is that each member jointly intends to perform its share of $\mathcal{JCA}(G.\gamma)$ and this is mutual belief. Condition *(STD6)* requires that the group members retain their joint and individual intentions throughout the joint conversation. This is proved since we use JI theory which incorporates persistency in achieving goals. Thus, because the joint conversation is a joint persistent goal within the group, then the group members exhibits persistency in achieving the goal, which is to carry out the conversation. Furthermore, by theorem 2, they persist in achieving their own goals which is achievable through the joint conversation.

6   Related Work

The work in this paper formulates and analyses the mental states of the agents in an interacting group when they are involved in a joint conversation. There has been past work in the domain of natural language and sociology regarding joint actions and commitments in a group [15].

However in the multi-agent systems domain, it is relatively new in the ACL and IP semantics area to specify and focus on the joint intentions of an interacting group. Kumar et al. 2002 [7] associates semantics to conversation protocols using the JI theory. Their approach is to formulate the beliefs and goals holding after a CA, derived from the semantics of that CA. They remain at the level of what is believed after executing a couple of CAs from the CAs semantics, without delving into the implications of those beliefs on the joint actions of the agents as members of a group. Likewise, kumar et al. 2000 [8] generalise the JI semantics of CAs to apply to groups of agents, but only at the relatively syntactic level of including a group parameter instead of single agents in the CAs. Deriving the semantics of conversations from the semantics of its constituent CAs, as in [7], is not sufficient as discussed in section 1. Thus, their approach lacks the the notion of persistency throughout a joint conversation and they do not investigate compliance to a conversation policy.

Paurobally et al. [12] uses FIPA-like semantics to specify a formal framework for the semantics of agent interactions - ACLs and IPs - but here again only what is believed after executing each CA is analysed. An interactive group's goals to carry out the joint conversation is not investigated. Compliance and persistency in compliance to an interaction protocol are also lacking.

Tuomela [15] investigates joint actions and commitments in communication, but they focus on CAs and do not investigate conversations in detail. Elio and Haddadi [4] propose dialogs for joint tasks that jointly maintain global coherence in a conversation, but there is no concrete specification to their approach.

7   Conclusions

A conversation between a group of agents involves more than simply the exchange of CAs from a sequence dictated by an interaction protocol. When an agent engages with a group in a conversation, there is a joint commitment on that agent's part towards the group to comply and uphold the rules governing the conversation, and to do its share of the conversation when required. Current MAS research in the semantics of conversation policies lacks well defined semantics for such group conversations to show the joint mental states that arise and to enforce compliance to the rules of interaction. To remedy this, we specify a conversation as a joint communicative action between a group of interacting agents and we propose the logic of JCA, $\mathcal{L}_{JCA}$, and a framework in $\mathcal{L}_{JCA}$ to specify the concepts of joint conversations. We formulate and prove the properties of such joint conversations, including an agent's compliance in a joint conversation.

As future work, we are looking into the decomposition and integration of different interaction protocols, and how this affects the notions of joint conversations and compliance.

References

1. Bauer, B., Müller, J.P., Odell, J.: Agent UML: A Formalism for Specifying Multi-agent Software Systems. Agent-Oriented Software Engineering, 91–104 (2000)
2. Cohen, P., Levesque, H.: Intention is choice with commitment. AI 42(3), 213–261 (1990)
3. Cohen, P., Levesque, H.: Teamwork. Nous 25(4), 487–512 (1991)
4. Elio, R., Haddadi, A.: On abstract task models and conversation policies. In: Proc. of the Agents 1999 Work on Specifying and Implementing Conversation Policies (1999)
5. FIPA. FIPA Communicative Act Library Specification. Foundation for Intelligent Physical Agents (2002), http://www.fipa.org
6. Goldblatt, R.: Logics of Time and Computation. CSLI, Stanford (1987)
7. Kumar, S., Huber, M., Cohen, P., McGee, D.: Toward a formalism for conversation protocols using joint intention theory. Computational Intelligence 18(2), 174–228 (2002)
8. Kumar, S., Huber, M.J., McGee, D., Cohen, P.R., Levesque, H.J.: Semantics of agent communication languages for group interaction. In: AAAI/IAAI, pp. 42–47 (2000)
9. Meyer, J.J., Van Der Hoek, W.: Epistemic Logic for AI and Comp. Science. Cambridge Univ. Press, Cambridge (1995)
10. Nash, J.: Two-person cooperative games. Econometrica 21, 128–140 (1953)
11. Nowostawski, M., Purvis, M., Cranefield, S.: A layered approach for modelling agent conversations. In: Proc. 2nd Int. Work. on Infrastructure for Agents, MAS, and Scalable MAS (2001)
12. Paurobally, S., Cunningham, R., Jennings, N.R.: A formal framework for agent interaction semantics. In: Proc. AAMAS, pp. 91–98 (2005)
13. Sandu, G., Tuomela, R.: Joint action and group action made precise. Synthese 105, 319–345 (1996)
14. Smith, I., Cohen, P., Bradshaw, J.: Designing conversation policies using joint intention theory. In: ICMAS, pp. 269–276 (1998)
15. Tuomela, R.: Collective goals and communicative action. Journal of Philosophical Research 27, 29–64 (2002)
16. Wooldridge, M.: Semantic issues in the verification of agent communication languages. Journal of Autonomous Agents and MAS 3(1), 9–31 (2000)
17. Yolum, P., Singh, M.: Flexible protocol specification and execution: Applying event calculus planning using commitments. In: Proc. AAMAS, pp. 527–534 (2002)

Interoperation in Protocol Enactment

Amit K. Chopra and Munindar P. Singh

North Carolina State University
{akchopra,singh}@ncsu.edu

Abstract. Interoperability has been broadly conceptualized as the ability of agents to work together. In open systems, the interoperability of agents is an important concern. A common way of achieving interoperability is by requiring agents to follow prescribed protocols in their interactions with others. In existing systems, agents must follow any protocol to the letter; in other words, they should exchange messages exactly as prescribed by the protocol. This is an overly restrictive constraint; it results in rigid, fragile implementations and curbs the autonomy of agents. For example, a customer agent may send a reminder to a merchant agent to deliver the promised goods. However, if reminders are not supported explicitly in the protocol they are enacting, then the reminder would be considered illegal and the transaction may potentially fail. This paper studies the interoperation of agents, dealing with their autonomy and heterogeneity in computational terms.

1 Introduction

Protocols describe the interactions among autonomous agents. Thus they are crucial to the design and construction of multiagent systems. Previous work on protocols in multiagent systems has dealt with high-level topics such as semantics [8,18], composition [17], and verification [13]. However, protocols are enacted by agents in physical systems. In particular, considerations of the underlying communication models and how distributed agents are able to make compatible choices would greatly affect whether a protocol may in fact be enacted successfully. The objective of this paper is to study the computational underpinnings of protocol enactment in multiagent systems. It seeks to characterize the operationalization of agents so as to determine whether and when agents may be interoperable.

The agents we consider are set in open systems, and they interact with each other based on (typically, published) protocols. An agent may, however, deviate from the protocol because of its internal policies. Such deviations pose certain problems: (1) the agent might no longer be conformant with the protocol, and (2) the agent may no longer be able to interoperate with other agents.

For an agent to be compliant with a protocol, first and foremost it must be conformant with the protocol. Whereas agent compliance can only be checked by monitoring the messages an agent exchanges with its peers at runtime, conformance can be verified from the agent's design. An agent's design is conformant with a protocol if it respects the semantics of the protocol; a useful semantics is obtained when considering the satisfaction of commitments [12]. The distinction between conformance and compliance is

M. Baldoni et al. (Eds.): DALT 2007, LNAI 4897, pp. 36–49, 2008.

important: an agent's design may conform, but its behavior may not comply. This may be because an agent's design may preclude successful interoperation with its peers. In other words, even though an agent is individually conformant, it may not be able to generate compliant computations because of the other agents with whom it interacts, apparently according to the same protocol. Interoperability is distinct from conformance; interoperability is strictly with respect to other agents, whereas conformance is with respect to a protocol.

Protocols provide a way of structuring interactions; however, interoperability is not just a test on agents that adopt roles in the same protocol, and then deviate from their roles. Interoperability is a property of a set of agents. The proposed definition of interoperability declares two agents to be interoperable provided from each joint state that they can enter, they can reach a final state. The essential idea is of determining the states that can be entered. In our approach, these are specified based upon the highly realistic constraint that only messages that have been sent (by an agent) can be received (by another agent). Based on this constraint, some transitions cannot in fact be performed: these transitions correspond to an agent receiving a message before the message has been sent. The transitions that can be performed are termed *causally enabled*.

A communication model sets the physical environment for communication between agents. The parameters of this model include whether communication is synchronous or asynchronous, the number of channels to use, the size of the buffers, and the buffer access mechanism. One cannot simply examine a pair of agents in isolation and decide whether they are interoperable; the agents must be analyzed in light of the communication model in force. Agents that are interoperable in one model may be noninteroperable in another. To analyze interoperability, we capture communication models in terms of causal enablement. Causal enablement is a basic building block that identifies the possible nonblocking actions given the current global state of the interaction. Different models of causal enablement correspond to different communication models.

Our contribution in this work is that we present a formal test for interoperability of agents. The rest of the paper is organized as follows. Section 2 presents agents as transition systems. Section 3 formalizes a test for the interoperability of agents. Section 4 concludes with a discussion of the relevant literature.

2   Agents

We represent agents as transition systems. Informally, a transition system is a graph with states as vertices and actions as edges. A state s is labeled with the propositions that hold in that state; a transition is a triple $\langle s, e, s' \rangle$ where s and s' are states, and the edge e is labeled with the actions that occur in the transition. In addition, the initial and final states are marked. Further, the initial state has no incoming transitions.

Definition 1. *A transition system is a tuple* $\langle \sigma^{fl}, \sigma^{act}, \eta, S, s_0, F, \rho, \delta \rangle$ *where*

- σ^{fl} *is a finite set of propositions*
- σ^{act} *is a finite set of actions*
- $\eta : \sigma^{act} \mapsto \sigma^{fl}$ *is a bijective function*
- S *is a finite set of states*

- $s_0 \in S$ is the initial state
- $F \subseteq S$ is the set of final states
- $\rho : S \mapsto \mathcal{P}(\sigma^{fl})$ is an injective labeling function with the requirement that $\rho(s_0) = \{\}$
- $\delta \subseteq S \times E \times S$ is the set of transitions where $E \subseteq \mathcal{P}(\sigma^{act})$ such that
  - $\forall s \in S : \langle s, \epsilon, s \rangle \in \delta$ where ϵ is the empty set of actions
  - $\forall s, s' \in S : \langle s, \epsilon, s' \rangle \in \delta \Rightarrow s = s'$
  - $\langle s, \{a_0, a_1, \ldots, a_n\}, s' \rangle \in \delta \Rightarrow \rho(s') = \rho(s) \cup \bigcup_{i=0}^{n} \eta(a_i)$

The following description explains the elements of Definition 1. The empty set of actions ϵ corresponds to inaction. For each state s, the set of transitions δ contains the transition $\langle s, \epsilon, s \rangle$ to capture the transition where no action happens. Further, as would be expected, inaction cannot cause a transition in a new state. To capture the occurrence of any action a in the transition, the resulting state is labeled with a unique proposition $\eta(a)$ corresponding to the action. We restrict the transition systems such that the only cycles allowed are those because of inaction. This restriction is placed because η returns the same proposition no matter how many times an action happens, and thus is insufficient to model repeated actions. The propositions a state is labeled with serve as a history of all the actions that have occurred previously.

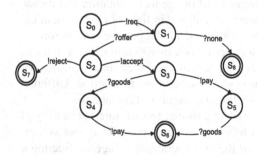

Fig. 1. A customer agent

Table 1. States in Figure 1

State	Fluents
s_0	{}
s_1	req
s_2	req, offer
s_3	req, offer, accept
s_4	req, offer, accept, goods
s_5	req, offer, accept, pay
s_6	req, offer, accept, goods, pay
s_7	req, offer, reject
s_8	req, none

We model two types of actions in agents: sends and receives. Let p be a message. A send is indicated by $!p$, whereas a receive is indicated by a $?p$. The sender and receiver of the message are implicit as the agents under consideration can interact only with one agent at a time. Figure 1 shows the transition system of a customer agent. State s_0 is the start state of this agent; the final states are indicated by concentric circles—in this case they are s_6, s_7, and s_8. This agent can interact with a merchant agent to buy goods. The customer's interactions are described below. Further, we assume that the names of the messages that can be sent by any agent are disjoint from those that any other agent can send.

1. The customer starts the interaction by sending a request for quotes to the merchant.
2. The merchant can respond either by sending an offer, or by indicating that there are no offers in which case the customer terminates.

3. If the merchant sends an offer, the customer can respond to the offer by either sending an accept, or a reject in which case, the customer terminates.
4. After the customer accepts, either the customer may send payment or the merchant may send goods.
5. If the merchant sends goods then the customer sends payment; if the customer sends payment, then the merchant sends goods. In either case, after the exchange the customer terminates.

Table 1 shows the labels of states in the transition system.

3 Interoperability

This section formalizes interoperability, and provides a computational method of verifying the interoperability of two agents.

Interoperability depends crucially on the communication model in force. Communication models may differ along the following dimensions.

Synchrony: The communication mode is synchronous if an agent can send a message only when another is ready is receive it; equivalently, the send of each message coincides with its receipt. The result is that the agents execute in lock-step fashion. The mode is asynchronous if an agent can send a message regardless of the recipient's availability. The mode of communication has important implications for buffer design, as we shall see.

Channels: Channels represent the logical communication medium between agents along which messages are exchanged. A channel can be unidirectional or bidirectional. If it is unidirectional, then it is modeled with a single buffer; if it is bidirectional, then it is modeled with two buffers, one for each direction. A unidirectional channel has two endpoints: one for the sending agent, and another for the receiving agent. A bidirectional channel has four endpoints: two for each agent—one to send, another to receive. Further, the number of channels may vary. For instance, all messages can be exchanged along a single channel, or each message can be exchanged along its own channel. More channels allows for greater concurrency.

Buffers: Synchronous communication corresponds to zero-length buffers, whereas asynchronous communication implies nonzero-length buffers. Further, in the asynchro-nous model buffers may be finite-length or unbounded. Buffers may also differ in how they are accessed. A buffer may be modeled as a FIFO queue, in which case messages are appended to the end of a queue when doing a send, and read from its head when doing a receive. Alternatively, buffers may be modeled as random access memory (RAM), in which case sent messages can be inserted into and read from any location. The sizes of buffers impacts the ways in which an agents can block. If the buffers are unbounded, an attempt to send always succeeds whereas if they are of finite length, then even an attempt to send may block. An attempt to receive, on other hand, may block regardless of buffer size—for an agent to receive a message, another agent must have sent it first.

The proposed definition of interoperability declares two agents to be interoperable provided from each joint state (in the product) that they can enter, they can reach a final state. The essential idea is of determining the states that can be entered. In our approach, these are specified based upon the highly realistic constraint that only messages that have been sent (by an agent) can be received (by another agent). Based on this constraint, some transitions cannot in fact be performed: these transitions correspond to an agent receiving a message before the message has been sent. The transitions that can be performed are termed *causally enabled*. Further, for progress to take place, our definition assumes that if an enabled transition is available then that or another enabled transition is taken.

Operationally, these assumptions can be readily realized in agents that function as follows:

- The agents can perform nonblocking reads on the channels. Thus no agent is stuck attempting to make a transition that is not and will not be enabled.
- The agents try actions corresponding to their various transitions with some sort of a fairness regime. Thus if an agent can perform a send operation in a state, it will not forever stay in that state without performing the send. It may perform some other action to exit that state. Likewise, if an agent can read from a particular channel, it will not forever stay in that state without performing the read.

Although this paper is limited to systems consisting of two agents, it can be expanded to larger systems. For such systems, we would assume the following in addition to the above: the agents have unique incoming channels. That is, the agents do not compete for the messages arriving on their incoming channels.

3.1 Formalization

The interoperability of two agents depends upon the computations that they can jointly generate. The agents may act one by one or in true concurrency (agents can be globally concurrent even if each agent itself is single-threaded). Definition 2 captures the above intuitions for a product transition system of a pair of agents. For any two agents, we assume that their sets of actions as well as their sets of propositions are disjoint.

Definition 2. Given two agents $\alpha := \langle \sigma_\alpha^{fl}, \sigma_\alpha^{act}, \eta_\alpha, S_\alpha, s_{0_\alpha}, F_\alpha, \rho_\alpha, \delta_\alpha \rangle$ and $\beta := \langle \sigma_\beta^{fl}, \sigma_\beta^{act}, \eta_\beta, S_\beta, s_{0_\beta}, F_\beta, \rho_\beta, \delta_\beta \rangle$, their product is $\times_{\alpha,\beta} := \langle \sigma_\times^{fl}, \sigma_\times^{act}, \eta_\times, S_\times, s_{0_\times}, F_\times, \rho_\times, \delta_\times \rangle$ where,

- $\sigma_\times^{fl} = \sigma_\alpha^{fl} \cup \sigma_\beta^{fl}$
- $\sigma_\times^{act} = \sigma_\alpha^{act} \cup \sigma_\beta^{act}$
- $\eta_\times = \eta_\alpha \cup \eta_\beta$
- $S_\times = S_\alpha \times S_\beta$
- $s_{0_\times} = (s_{0_\alpha}, s_{0_\beta})$
- $F_\times = F_\alpha \times F_\beta$
- the labels on a state (s_α, s_β) is given by $\rho_\times(s_\alpha, s_\beta) = \rho_\alpha(s_\alpha) \cup \rho_\beta(s_\beta)$
- $\delta_\times \subseteq S_\times \times E_\times \times S_\times$ such that $\langle s, e, s' \rangle \in \delta_\times$ if and only if $\langle s_\alpha, e_\alpha, s'_\alpha \rangle \in \delta_\alpha$, $\langle s_\beta, e_\beta, s'_\beta \rangle \in \delta_\beta$ and $s = (s_\alpha, s_\beta)$, $s' = (s'_\alpha, s'_\beta)$, $e = e_\alpha \cup e_\beta$

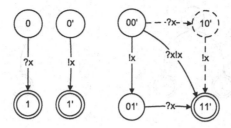

Fig. 2. Simple agents and their causal product (interoperable)

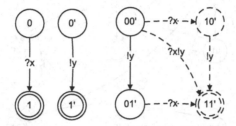

Fig. 3. Simple blocking agents and their causal product. Agents are noninteroperable because no causal final state is reachable from state 01'.

The technical motivation behind Definition 2 is that it accommodates the transitions that would globally result as the agents enact the given protocol. When the agents act one by one, the transitions are labeled with an action from their respective sets of actions. When the agents act concurrently, the transitions are labeled by a pair of actions, one from each agent. Figure 2 shows two agents—one does $!x$, and the other $?x$—and their product. In this product, $00'$ is the initial state and $11'$ is a final state.

Figures 2–8 each contains three transition systems: one for agent α (identified by states labeled with one digit), one for agent β (identified by states labeled with one digit followed by an apostrophe as in $0'$), and their product (identified by states that contain states labeled with two digits—the second with an apostrophe). The start states of the two agents are indicated by 0 and $0'$ respectively. The final states are represented by concentric circles.

Our communication model is one in which agents communicate asynchronously over a bidirectional channel and each agent's buffer is bounded RAM. As explained earlier, the state of an agent serves to capture the history of actions, and since each action can only occur once, the size of an agent's buffer is bounded by the size of its set of actions. For the same reason, an attempt to send a message never blocks. A joint state in a product represents the union of both agents' buffers. The receipt of a message fails if it is attempted before the message is sent. Definition 3 captures these observations formally in terms of causal enablement. Specifically, a state enables a transition if all the actions listed in the transition succeed. Because there is only one channel, it is left implicit in the definition.

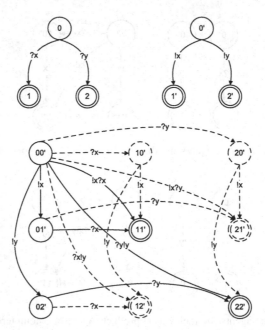

Fig. 4. Agents with a symmetric choice and their product (interoperable)

Definition 3. Given a transition $\langle s_i, e_i, s_{i+1} \rangle \in \delta_\times$ in a product $\times_{\alpha,\beta} := \langle \sigma_\times^{fl}, \sigma_\times^{act}, \eta_\times,$ $S_\times, s_{0_\times}, F_\times, \rho_\times, \delta_\times \rangle$, s_i causally enables e_i, denoted by $s_i \models_{ce} e_i$ if and only if

$$e_i = \epsilon \text{ or,}$$

$$\forall ?p \in e_i (\eta(!p) \in s_i \text{ or } !p \in e_i).$$

Definition 3 means that a transition is enabled if for each receive attempted in it, a corresponding send has been performed previously or is being performed concurrently. For example, in Figure 2

$$01' \models_{ce} \{?x\}$$
$$00' \not\models_{ce} \{?x\}.$$

In Figures 2–8, the solid transitions are causally enabled whereas the dotted ones are not causally enabled. Definition 4 says that if a state is reachable from the initial state by causally enabled transitions, then it is causal.

Definition 4. The set of *causal* states in a product is defined as follows:

  (i) s_0 is causal,
  (ii) s' is causal if $\exists \langle s, e, s' \rangle \in \delta_\times$: s is causal and $s \models_{ce} e$,
  (iii) all states that are not causal according to the above are noncausal.

In Figures 2–8, causal states are indicated with solid circles, whereas the noncausal states are indicated with dashed circles.

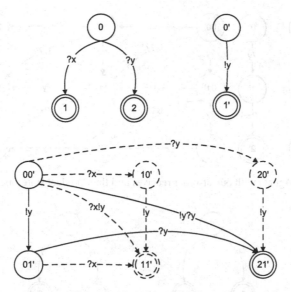

Fig. 5. Agents with limited send choice and their product (interoperable)

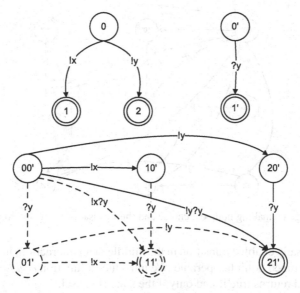

Fig. 6. Agents with no receive choice and their product. Agents are noninteroperable because no final state is reachable from state 10' which itself is causal.

Definition 5 say that two agents α and β are interoperable if and only if for each causal state s, there exists a final state that is reachable from s through causally enabled transitions. Note that the definition does not simply state that there must exists some causally enabled path from the start state to some final state in the product for two agents to be interoperable. It is stronger than that. The definition reflects the fact there

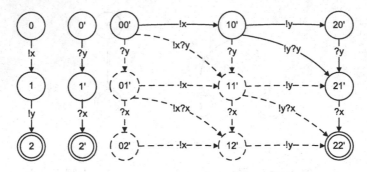

Fig. 7. Agents with out-of-order receives and their product (interoperable)

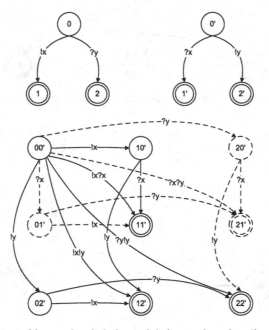

Fig. 8. Agents making nonlocal choice and their causal product (interoperable)

might be no causally enabled transition in the middle of an interaction, in which case the agents are determined noninteroperable. We introduce a function *causal* which takes a product state and returns true if and only if the state is causal.

Definition 5. Let $\times_{\alpha,\beta} := \langle \sigma_{\times}^{fl}, \sigma_{\times}^{act}, \eta_{\times}, S_{\times}, s_{0_{\times}}, F_{\times}, \rho_{\times}, \delta_{\times} \rangle$ be the product of two agents α and β. Agents α and β are interoperable if and only if

$$\forall s_i : causal(s_i)(\exists \langle s_i, e_i, s_{i+1} \rangle, \langle s_{i+1}, e_{i+1}, s_{i+2} \rangle, \ldots, \langle s_{n-1}, e_{n-1}, s_n \rangle :$$

$$\forall j : (i \le j \le n)(causal(s_j) \text{ and } s_n \in F_{\times})).$$

Each pair of agents in the Figures 2–8 is labeled interoperable or noninteroperable based upon the test in Definition 5. The agents in Figure 2 are interoperable as one agent sends

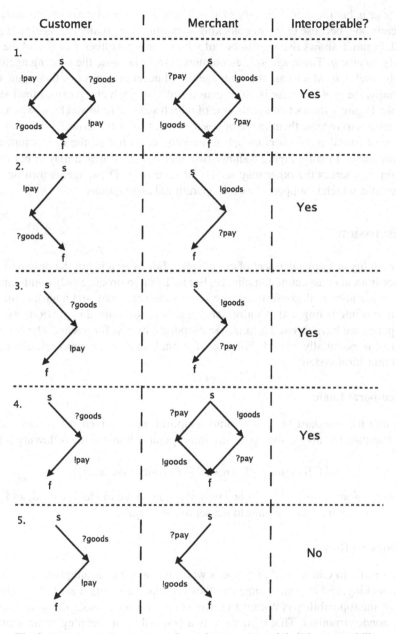

Fig. 9. Variations of customer and merchant agents and their interoperability

x and the other receives x. The agents in Figure 3 are noninteroperable as one agent can only send y, whereas the other may only receive x. Computationally, the problem state is 01', which is a causal state, but no causal final state is reachable from it. The agents in Figure 4 are interoperable—realistic as given the nonblocking receive semantics outlined earlier, eventually some message will be received. In Figure 5, one agent can receive x or y, but the other can only send y. These agents are interoperable and again, realistically so—because of the nonblocking semantics, eventually the receipt of y will succeed. Figure 6 shows two agents, one of which can send either x or y, and the other may only receive y. These agents are noninteroperable because the sending agent may choose to send x, in which case the other agent will never progress to a final state. Computationally, the problem state is 10', a causal state from which no causal final state is reachable. Figure 7 shows two agents, one of which sends x followed by y, whereas the other attempts to receive them in the opposite order, that is y followed by x. Since our definition of causal enablement models a random access buffer, the agents turn out to be interoperable. Finally, Figure 8 shows two agents, one of which may either receive x or send y, whereas the other may send x or receive y. These agents turn out to be interoperable, which is supported by our operational assumptions.

4   Discussion

Interoperability is a crucial aspect of compliance; however, it is not the only one. Conformance is another aspect of compliance. For an agent to produce only compliant executions, it has to be both conformant with some stated protocol, and interoperable with the agent it is interacting with. Conformance has been formalized in previous work [4]. In this paper, we have devised a formal interoperability test for agents. The interoperability test is essentially a reachability test for final states in an appropriately marked product transition system.

4.1   Temporal Logic

We assume the standard branching time temporal logic. Given the product of two agents, computed as above, the agents are interoperable if and if the following formula is true.

$$\text{AG}(causal \rightarrow \text{E}(causal \text{ U } (final \wedge causal)))$$

The proposition $causal$ is true if and only if a state in the model is causal, and $final$ is true if and only if a state belongs to the set of final states.

4.2   Blocking Receives

It is interesting to consider what happens when we drop the assumption that receives are nonblocking, and instead assume that they are blocking. In that case, the above definition of interoperability is optimistic: it makes sense only under the assumption of angelic nondeterminism. That is, if there is a possibility of reaching some joint final state, then the agents will magically take only those actions that necessarily take them there. In essence, the choices are not made by agents, but are made automatically for them. For instance, in Figure 5, our test for interoperability determines the agents interoperable. However, note they are not interoperable in case agent α decides to receive x. They are only interoperable under the assumption that an agent reads whatever is available in its end of the channel. For all practical purposes, at the level of abstraction of the transition system, a "good" choice was made nondeterministically. To consider another example, see Figure 8. If α and β choose to do $?y$ and $?x$ respectively—no matter what, they must each receive first before sending—then the agents would deadlock. (In distributed computing, this problem is commonly referred to as the nonlocal choice problem [14]). But again the choice to send or receive is not made by the agents; it is simply made for them nondeterministically.

The question then is: in the operational assumption that receives are blocking, how do we build agents in practice when angelic nondeterminism is not around to help make choices? The answer is: by encoding additional knowledge required to make the choices in the agent's design. Figure 9 shows variations of the customer and merchant agents with a focus on only the goods-payment exchange. Each row in the Figure depicts a customer-merchant pair and states their interoperability. For each transition system, the labels s and f indicate the start and final states respectively; other states are not made explicit. The interesting thing is that only in case 5—when for both agents there is no choice but to receive first and thus deadlock—are the agents determined noninteroperable by Definition 5. In all other cases, in all stages of the interaction, there is always a causally enabled transition until a joint final state is reached. More importantly, in cases 1 and 4, the agents' choices have to resolved so that they make compatible choices—which is where angelic nondeterminism helps us. In practice, however, the agents' design would have to be amended so that the pairs of agents in cases 1 and 4 would resemble either the pair of case 2 or case 3. In previous work [3], we have specified agents in C+ [10], an action description language with a transition system semantics. C+ is elaboration-tolerant meaning that the addition of new axioms (knowledge) to a C+ theory could possibly invalidate old conclusions; in other words, transitions may be removed by adding new knowledge about the actions. This enables a designer to specify agents in C+ corresponding to the pair of case 1, and then depending upon the context in which the agents are to be deployed, the designer could add additional knowledge to turn them into either the pair of case 2 or case 3. For example, if the customer is not willing to pay first but the merchant is willing to send goods first, then the designer could turn them into the agents of case 3, whereas if they both trust each other, then the could turn them into case 2. An optimistic approach to component composability is that two components are composable if there exists some environment under which they can work together [6]. Under the assumption that receives are blocking, our definition of interoperability may be seen as an optimistic one: two agents can work together in practice, if they are interoperable by our definition, and if new axioms encoding additional knowledge may be appended to their specifications to make them work together.

4.3 Literature

Interoperability leads to a useful notion of compositionality: loosely speaking, two arbitrary agents can be composed if they can interoperate. Our formalization thus tells us which pairs of agents can be composed. We plan to extend our formalization to groups of agents.

Dastani *et al.* [5] describe an approach of composing multiagent systems by composing their coordination specifications, which are modeled as connectors. Omicini *et al.* [15] model composition of distributed workflows through programmable tuple spaces. However, none of these works delve into the question of which agents or workflows are composable.

Fu *et al.* [9] propose conditions for the realizability of protocols—a protocol can be realized if a set of finite agents can generate exactly the conversations in the protocol. Realizability of a protocol is orthogonal to interoperability between agents. A protocol may not be realizable, however agents that follow their respective roles in the protocol could be interoperable. On the other hand, interoperable agents could be following roles in distinct protocols.

Kazhamiakin *et al.* [11] construct a hierarchy of communication models depending on factors such as synchrony and buffers among other, and use this framework to find the best fit communication model for a given service composition such that the cost of further verification is cheapest. However, their method assumes that the services are composable under some model; they present no algorithm that decides composability.

Baldoni *et al.* [2] and Endriss *et al.* [7] present alternative notions of conformance that are closely tied to interoperability, thereby violating the orthogonality of conformance and interoperability. As a result, many agents that should be considered conformant in a practical setting—and are determined to be conformant according to our formalization—are rendered nonconformant in theirs. For example, they would both determine the customer who sends a reminder to the merchant to send goods to be nonconformant.

Approaches based on verifying compliance at runtime [1,16] are important in the context of open systems since agents may behave in unpredictable ways; also it is necessary to have independent arbiters in case of disputes involving agents.

4.4 Directions

Our current formalization supports a useful but limited class of agents: those that interact with only one other agent, and eventually terminate. Our future work involves extending this work to more general agents: specifically, those that interact with multiple other agents and have infinite runs.

References

1. Alberti, M., Daolio, D., Torroni, P., Gavanelli, M., Lamma, E., Mello, P.: Specification and verification of agent interaction protocols in a logic-based system. In: Proceedings of the 19th ACM Symposium on Applied Computing, pp. 72–78 (2004)
2. Baldoni, M., Baroglio, C., Martelli, A., Patti, V.: Verification of protocol conformance and agent interoperability. In: Toni, F., Torroni, P. (eds.) CLIMA VI. LNCS (LNAI), vol. 3900, pp. 265–283. Springer, Heidelberg (2006)
3. Chopra, A.K., Singh, M.P.: Contextualization of commitment protocols. In: Proceedings of the Fifth International Joint Conference on Autonomous Agents and Multiagent Systems (2006)
4. Chopra, A.K., Singh, M.P.: Protocol compliant interactions: Conformance, coverage, and interoperability. In: Baldoni, M., Endriss, U. (eds.) DALT 2006. LNCS (LNAI), vol. 4327, Springer, Heidelberg (2006)

5. Dastani, M., Arbab, F., de Boer, F.: Coordination and composition in multi-agent systems. In: AAMAS 2005. Proceedings of the Fourth International Joint Conference on Autonomous Agents and Multiagent Systems, pp. 439–446 (2005)
6. de Alfaro, L., Henzinger, T.A.: Interface automata. In: Proceedings of the Joint 8th European Software Engineering Conference (ESEC) and 9th ACM SIGSOFT Symposium on the Foundations of Software Engineering (FSE-9), pp. 109–120 (2001)
7. Endriss, U., Maudet, N., Sadri, F., Toni, F.: Protocol conformance for logic-based agents. In: Proceedings of the 18th International Joint Conference on Artificial Intelligence, pp. 679–684 (2003)
8. Fornara, N., Colombetti, M.: Operational specification of a commitment-based agent communication language. In: AAMAS. Proceedings of the 1st International Joint Conference on Autonomous Agents and Multiagent Systems, pp. 535–542. ACM Press, New York (2002)
9. Fu, X., Bultan, T., Su, J.: Conversation protocols: a formalism for specification and verification of reactive electronic services. Theoretical Computer Science 328(1-2), 19–37 (2004)
10. Giunchiglia, E., Lee, J., Lifschitz, V., McCain, N., Turner, H.: Nonmonotonic causal theories. Artificial Intelligence 153(1-2), 49–104 (2004)
11. Kazhamiakin, R., Pistore, M., Santuari, L.: Analysis of communication models in web service compositions. In: Proceedings of the 15th International Conference on World Wide Web, pp. 267–276 (2006)
12. Mallya, A.U., Singh, M.P.: An algebra for commitment protocols. Journal of Autonomous Agents and Multiagent Systems special issue on Agent Communication (JAAMAS) 14(2), 143–163 (2006)
13. Mazouzi, H., Seghrouchni, A.E.F., Haddad, S.: Open protocol design for complex interactions in multi-agent systems. In: Proceedings of the First International Joint Conference on Autonomous Agents and Multiagent Systems, pp. 517–526 (2002)
14. Mooij, A.J., Goga, N.: Dealing with non-local choice in IEEE 1073.2's standard for remote control. In: Amyot, D., Williams, A.W. (eds.) SAM 2004. LNCS, vol. 3319, pp. 257–270. Springer, Heidelberg (2005)
15. Omicini, A., Ricci, A., Zaghini, N.: Distributed workflow upon linkable coordination artifacts. In: Ciancarini, P., Wiklicky, H. (eds.) COORDINATION 2006. LNCS, vol. 4038, pp. 228–246. Springer, Heidelberg (2006)
16. Venkatraman, M., Singh, M.P.: Verifying compliance with commitment protocols: Enabling open Web-based multiagent systems. Journal of Autonomous Agents and Multi-Agent Systems 2(3), 217–236 (1999)
17. Vitteau, B., Huget, M.-P.: Modularity in interaction protocols. In: Dignum, F.P.M. (ed.) ACL 2003. LNCS (LNAI), vol. 2922, pp. 291–309. Springer, Heidelberg (2004)
18. Yolum, P., Singh, M.P.: Flexible protocol specification and execution: Applying event calculus planning using commitments. In: Alonso, E., Kudenko, D., Kazakov, D. (eds.) AAMAS. LNCS (LNAI), vol. 2636, pp. 527–534. Springer, Heidelberg (2003)

Integrating Agent Models and Dynamical Systems

Tibor Bosse, Alexei Sharpanskykh, and Jan Treur

Vrije Universiteit Amsterdam, Department of Artificial Intelligence,
De Boelelaan 1081a, 1081 HV, The Netherlands
{tbosse, sharp, treur}@cs.vu.nl
http://www.cs.vu.nl/~{tbosse, sharp, treur}

Abstract. Agent-based modelling approaches are usually based on logical languages, whereas in many areas dynamical system models based on differential equations are used. This paper shows how to model complex agent systems, integrating quantitative, numerical and qualitative, logical aspects, and how to combine logical and mathematical analysis methods.

1 Introduction

Existing models for complex systems are often based on quantitative, numerical methods such as Dynamical Systems Theory (DST) [23], and more in particular, differential equations. Such approaches often use numerical variables to describe global aspects of the system and how they affect each other over time; for example, how the number of predators affects the number of preys. An advantage of such numerical approaches is that numerical approximation methods and software environments are available for simulation.

The relatively new agent-based modelling approaches to complex systems take into account the local perspective of a possibly large number of separate agents and their specific behaviours in a system; for example, the different individual predator agents and prey agents. These approaches are usually based on qualitative, logical languages. An advantage of such logical approaches is that they allow (automated) logical analysis of the relationships between different parts of a model, for example relationships between global properties of the (multi-agent) system as a whole and local properties of the basic mechanisms within (agents of) the system. Moreover, by means of logic-based approaches, declarative models of complex systems can be specified using knowledge representation languages that are close to the natural language. An advantage of such declarative models is that they can be considered and analysed at a high abstract level. Furthermore, automated support (e.g., programming tools) is provided for manipulation and redesign of models.

Complex systems, for example organisms in biology or organisations in the socio-economic area, often involve both qualitative aspects and quantitative aspects. In particular, in the area of Cognitive Science, the lower-level cognitive processes of agents (e.g., sensory or motor processing) are often modelled using DST-based approaches. Furthermore, at the global level the dynamics of the environment, in which agents are situated, is often described by continuous models (i.e., models based

M. Baldoni et al. (Eds.): DALT 2007, LNAI 4897, pp. 50–68, 2008.

on differential equations); e.g., dynamic models of markets, or natural environmental oscillations. Yet agent-based (logical) languages are often used for describing high-level cognitive processes of agents (e.g., processes related to reasoning) and agent interaction with the environment (e.g., agent actions, execution of tasks).

It is not easy to integrate both types of approaches in one modelling method. On the one hand, it is difficult to incorporate logical aspects in differential equations. For example, qualitative behaviour of an agent that depends on whether the value of a variable is below or above a threshold is difficult to describe by differential equations. On the other hand, quantitative methods based on differential equations are not usable in the context of most logical, agent-based modelling languages, as these languages are not able to handle real numbers and calculations.

This paper shows an integrative approach to simulate and analyse complex systems, integrating quantitative, numerical and qualitative, logical aspects within one expressive temporal specification language. Some initial ideas behind the simulation approach proposed in this paper were described in [5, 6]. The current paper elaborates upon these ideas by proposing more extensive means to design precise, stable, and computationally effective simulation models for hybrid systems (i.e., comprising both quantitative and qualitative aspects). Furthermore, it proposes techniques for analysis of hybrid systems, which were not previously considered elsewhere. The developed simulation and analysis techniques are supported by dedicated tools.

In Section 2, this language (called LEADSTO) is described in detail, and is applied to solve an example differential equation. In Section 3, it is shown how LEADSTO can solve a system of differential equations (for the case of the classical Predator-Prey model), and how it can combine quantitative and qualitative aspects within the same model. Section 4 demonstrates how existing methods for approximation (such as the Runge-Kutta methods) can be incorporated into LEADSTO, and Section 5 shows how existing methods for simulation with dynamic step size can be incorporated. Section 6 demonstrates how interlevel relationships can be established between dynamics of basic mechanisms (described in LEADSTO) and global dynamics of a process (described in a super-language of LEADSTO). Finally, Section 7 is a discussion.

2 Modelling Dynamics in LEADSTO

Dynamics can be modelled in different forms. Based on the area within Mathematics called calculus, the Dynamical Systems Theory [23] advocates to model dynamics by continuous state variables and changes of their values over time, which is also assumed continuous. In particular, systems of differential or difference equations are used. This may work well in applications where the world states are modelled in a quantitative manner by real-valued state variables. The world's dynamics in such application show continuous changes in these state variables that can be modelled by mathematical relationships between real-valued variables. However, not for all applications dynamics can be modelled in a quantitative manner as required for DST. Sometimes qualitative changes form an essential aspect of the dynamics of a process. For example, to model the dynamics of reasoning processes usually a quantitative approach will not work. In such processes states are characterised by qualitative state properties, and changes by transitions between such states. For such applications often qualitative, discrete modelling approaches are advocated, such as variants of modal temporal logic, e.g. [20]. However, using such non-quantitative methods, the more precise timing relations are lost too. For the LEADSTO language described in this paper, the choice has been made to consider the timeline as continuous, described by real values, but for state properties both quantitative and qualitative variants can be used. The approach subsumes approaches based on simulation of differential or difference equations, and discrete qualitative modelling approaches. In addition, the approach makes it possible to combines both types of modelling within one model. For example, it is possible to model the exact (real-valued) time interval for which some qualitative property holds. Moreover, the relationships between states over time are described by either logical or mathematical means, or a combination thereof. This will be explained in more detail in Section 2.1. As an illustration, in Section 2.2 it will be shown how the logistic model for population growth in resource-bounded environments [4] can be modelled and simulated in LEADSTO.

2.1 The LEADSTO Language

Dynamics is considered as evolution of states over time. The notion of state as used here is characterised on the basis of an ontology defining a set of properties that do or do not hold at a certain point in time. For a given (order-sorted predicate logic) ontology Ont, the propositional language signature consisting of all *state ground atoms* (or *atomic state properties*) based on Ont is denoted by APROP(Ont). The *state properties* based on a certain ontology Ont are formalised by the propositions that can be made (using conjunction, negation, disjunction, implication) from the ground atoms. A *state* S is an indication of which atomic state properties are true and which are false, i.e., a mapping S: APROP(Ont) → {true, false}.

To specify simulation models a temporal language has been developed. This language (the LEADSTO language [7]) enables to model direct temporal dependencies between two state properties in successive states, also called *dynamic properties*. A specification of dynamic properties in LEADSTO format has as advantages that it is executable and that it can often easily be depicted graphically. The format is defined as follows. Let α and β be state properties of the form 'conjunction of atoms or negations of atoms', and e, f, g, h non-negative real numbers. In the LEADSTO language the notation $\alpha \twoheadrightarrow_{e, f, g, h} \beta$ (also see Fig. 1), means:

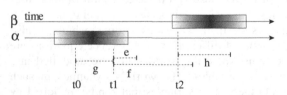

If state property α holds for a certain time interval with duration g, then after some delay (between e and f) state property β will hold for a certain time interval of length h.

Fig. 1. Timing relationships for LEADSTO expressions

An example dynamic property that uses the LEADSTO format defined above is the following: "observes(agent_A, food_present) $\twoheadrightarrow_{2, 3, 1, 1.5}$ beliefs(agent_A, food_present)". Informally, this example expresses the fact that, if agent A observes that food is present during 1 time unit, then after a delay between 2 and 3 time units, agent A will belief that food is present during 1.5 time units. In addition, within the LEADSTO language it is possible to use sorts, variables over sorts, real numbers, and mathematical operations, such as in "has_value(x, v) →$_{e, f, g, h}$ has_value(x, v*0.25)". Next, a *trace* or *trajectory* γ over a state ontology Ont is a time-indexed sequence of states over Ont (where the time frame is formalised by the real numbers). A LEADSTO expression α →$_{e, f, g, h}$ β, holds for a trace γ if:

∀t1 [∀t [t1−g ≤ t < t1 ⇒ α holds in γ at time t] ⇒ ∃d [e ≤ d ≤ f & ∀t' [t1+d ≤ t' < t1+d+h ⇒ β holds in γ at time t']]

To specify the fact that a certain event (i.e., a state property) holds at every state (time point) within a certain time interval a predicate holds_during_interval(event, t1, t2) is introduced. Here event is some state property, t1 is the beginning of the interval and t2 is the end of the interval.

An important use of the LEADSTO language is as a specification language for simulation models. As indicated above, on the one hand LEADSTO expressions can be considered as logical expressions with a declarative, temporal semantics, showing what it means that they hold in a given trace. On the other hand they can be used to specify basic mechanisms of a process and to generate traces, similar to Executable Temporal Logic [3]. More details on the semantics of LEADSTO can be found in [7].

2.2 Solving the Initial Value Problem in LEADSTO: Euler's Method

Often behavioural models in the Dynamical Systems Theory are specified by systems of differential equations with given initial conditions for continuous variables and functions. A problem of finding solutions to such equations is known as an initial value problem in the mathematical analysis. One of the approaches for solving this problem is based on discretisation, i.e., replacing a continuous problem by a discrete one, whose solution is known to approximate that of the continuous problem. For this methods of numerical analysis are usually used [22]. The simplest approach for finding approximations of functional solutions for ordinary differential equations is provided by Euler's method. Euler's method for solving a differential equation of the form dy/dt = f(y) with the initial condition $y(t_0)=y_0$ comprises the difference equation derived from a Taylor series:

$$y(t) = \sum_{n=0}^{\infty} \frac{y^{(n)}(t_0)}{n!} * (t - t_0)^n,$$

where only the first member is taken into account: $y_{i+1}=y_i+h* f(y_i)$, where i≥0 is the step number and h>0 is the integration step size. This equation can be modelled in the LEADSTO language in the following way:

- Each integration step corresponds to a state, in which an intermediate value of y is calculated.
- The difference equation is modelled by a transition rule to the successive state in the LEADSTO format.
- The duration of an interval between states is defined by a step size h.

Thus, for the considered case the LEADSTO simulation model comprises the rule:

has_value(y, v1) →$_{0, 0, h, h}$ has_value(y, v1+h* f(v1))

The initial value for the function y is specified by the following LEADSTO rule:

holds_during_interval(has_value(y, y₀), 0, h)

By performing a simulation of the obtained model in the LEADSTO environment an approximate functional solution to the differential equation can be found.

To illustrate the proposed simulation-based approach based on Euler's method in LEADSTO, the logistic growth model or the Verhulst model [4] which is often used to describe the population growth in resource-bounded environments, is considered: $dP/dt = r*P(1-P/K)$, where P is the population size at time point t; r and K are some constants. This model corresponds to the following LEADSTO simulation model: has_value(y, v1) →₀, ₀, ₕ, ₕ has_value(y, v1+ h*r* v1*(1-v1/K)). The simulation result of this model with the parameters r=0.5 and K=10 and initial value P(0)=1 is given in Figure 2.

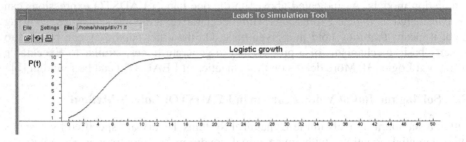

Fig. 2. Logistic growth function modelled in LEADSTO with parameters r=0.5, K=10, P(0)=1

3   Modelling the Predator-Prey Model in LEADSTO

The proposed simulation-based approach can be applied for solving a system of ordinary differential equations. In order to illustrate this, the classical Lotka-Volterra model (also known as a Predator-Prey model) [21] is considered. The Lotka-Volterra describes interactions between two species in an ecosystem, a predator and a prey. The model consists of two equations: the first one describes how the prey population changes and the second one describes how the predator population changes. If x(t) and y(t) represent the number of preys and predators respectively, that are alive in the system at time t, then the Lotka-Volterra model is defined by: $dx/dt = a*x - b*x*y$; $dy/dt = c*b*x*y - e*y$ where the parameters are defined by: a is the per capita birth rate of the prey, b is a per capita attack rate, c is the conversion efficiency of consumed prey into new predators, and e is the rate at which predators die in the absence of prey. To solve this system, numerical methods derived from a Taylor series up to some order can be used. In the following section it will be shown how Euler's (first-order rough) method can be used for creating a LEADSTO simulation model for finding the approximate solutions for the Predator-Prey problem. After that, in Section 3.2 it will be demonstrated how the generated LEADSTO simulation model can be extended by introducing qualitative behavioural aspects in the standard predator-prey model. Section 3.3 briefly presents a more elaborated example of a LEADSTO simulation model combining quantitative and qualitative aspects of behaviour, addressing simulation of human conditioning processes.

3.1 The LEADSTO Language

Using the technique described in Section 2.2, the Lotka-Volterra model is translated into a LEADSTO simulation model as follows:

has_value(x, v1) ∧ has_value(y, v2) →$_{0, 0, h, h}$ has_value(x, v1+h*(a*v1-b*v1*v2))
has_value(x, v1) ∧ has_value(y, v2) →$_{0, 0, h, h}$ has_value(y, v2+h*(c*b*v1*v2-e*v2))

The initial values for variables and functions are specified as for the general case. Although Euler's method offers a stable solution to a stable initial value problem, a choice of initial values can significantly influence the model's behaviour. More specifically, the population size of both species will oscillate if perturbed away from the equilibrium. The amplitude of the oscillation depends on how far the initial values of x and y depart from the equilibrium point. The equilibrium point for the considered model is defined by the values x=e/(c*b) and y=a/b. For example, for the parameter settings a=1.5, b=0.2, c=0.1 and e=0.5 the equilibrium is defined by x=25 and y=7.5. Yet a slight deviation from the equilibrium point in the initial values (x_0=25, y_0=8) results in the oscillated (limit cycle) behaviour.

3.2 Extending the Standard Predator-Prey Model with Qualitative Aspects

In this section, an extension of the standard predator-prey model is considered, with some qualitative aspects of behaviour. Assume that the population size of both predators and preys within a certain eco-system is externally monitored and controlled by humans. Furthermore, both prey and predator species in this eco-system are also consumed by humans. A control policy comprises a number of intervention rules that ensure the viability of both species. Among such rules could be following:

- in order to keep a prey species from extinction, a number of predators should be controlled to stay within a certain range (defined by pred_min and pred_max);
- if a number of a prey species falls below a fixed minimum (prey_min), a number of predators should be also enforced to the prescribed minimum (pred_min);
- if the size of the prey population is greater than a certain prescribed bound (prey_max), then the size of the prey species can be reduced by a certain number prey_quota (cf. a quota for fish catch).

These qualitative rules can be encoded into the LEADSTO simulation model for the standard predator-prey case by adding new dynamic properties and changing the existing ones in the following way:

has_value(x, v1) ∧ has_value(y, v2) ∧ v1< prey_max →$_{0, 0, h, h}$ has_value(x, v1+h*(a*v1-b*v1*v2))
has_value(x, v1) ∧ has_value(y, v2) ∧ v1 ≥ prey_max →$_{0, 0, h, h}$
    has_value(x, v1+h*(a*v1-b*v1*v2) - prey_quota)
has_value(x, v1) ∧ has_value(y, v2) ∧ v1 ≥ prey_min ∧ v2 < pred_max →$_{0, 0, h, h}$
    has_value(y, v2+h* (c*b*v1*v2-e*v2))
has_value(x, v1) ∧ has_value(y, v2) ∧ v2 ≥ pred_max →$_{0, 0, h, h}$ has_value(y, pred_min)
has_value(x, v1) ∧ has_value(y, v2) ∧ v1 < prey_min →$_{0, 0, h, h}$ has_value(y, pred_min)

The result of simulation of this model using Euler's method with the parameter settings: a=4; b=0.2, c=0.1, e=8, pred_min=10, pred_max=30, prey_min=40, prey_max=100, prey_quota=20, x_0=90, y_0=10 is given in Fig. 3.

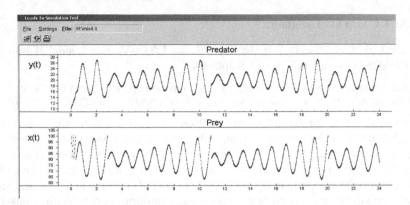

Fig. 3. Simulation results for the Lotka-Volterra model combined some qualitative aspects

3.3 Example Hybrid LEADSTO Specification - Model for Conditioning

Research into conditioning is aimed at revealing the principles that govern associative learning. An important issue in conditioning processes is the adaptive timing of the conditioned response to the appearance of the unconditioned stimulus. This feature is most apparent in an experimental procedure called *trace conditioning*. In this procedure, a trial starts with the presentation of a *warning stimulus* (S1; comparable to a conditioned stimulus). After a blank interval, called the *foreperiod*, an *imperative stimulus* (S2, comparable to an unconditioned stimulus) is presented to which the participant responds as fast as possible. The *reaction time* to S2 is used as an estimate of the conditioned state of preparation at the moment S2 is presented. In this case, the conditioned response obtains its maximal strength, here called *peak level*, at a moment in time, called *peak time*, that closely corresponds to the moment the unconditioned stimulus occurs.

Machado developed a basic model that describes the dynamics of these conditioning processes in terms of differential equations [18]. The structure of this model is shown in Figure 4. The model posits a layer of *timing nodes* and a single *preparation node*. Each timing node is connected both to the next (and previous) timing node and to the preparation node. The connection between each timing node and the preparation node (called *associative link*) has an adjustable weight associated to it. Upon the presentation of a warning stimulus, a cascade of activation propagates through the timing nodes according to a regular pattern. Owing to this regularity, the timing nodes can be likened to an internal clock or pacemaker. At any moment, each timing node contributes to the activation of the preparation node in accordance with its activation X and its corresponding weight W. The activation of the preparation node reflects the participant's preparatory state, and is as such related to reaction time.

The weights reflect the state of conditioning, and are adjusted by learning rules, of which the main principles are as follows. First, *during* the foreperiod extinction takes place, which involves the decrease of weights in real time in proportion to the activation of their corresponding timing nodes. Second, *after* the presentation of the imperative stimulus a process of reinforcement takes over, which involves an increase of the weights in accordance with the current activation of their timing nodes, to preserve the importance of the imperative moment. Machado describes the more detailed dynamics of the process by a mathematical model (based on linear differential equations), representing the (local) temporal relationships between the variables involved. For example, d/dt X(t,n) = λX(t,n-1) - λX(t,n) expresses how the activation level of the n-th timing node X(t+dt,n) at time point t+dt relates to this level X(t,n) at time point t and the activation level X(t,n-1) of the (n-1)-th timing node at time point t. Similarly, as another example, d/dt W(t,n) = -αX(t,n)W(t,n) expresses how the n-th weight W(t+dt,n) at time point t+dt relates to this weight W(t,n) at time point t and the activation level X(t,n) of the n-th timing node at time point t.

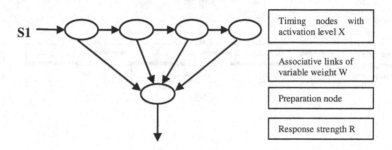

Fig. 4. Structure of Machado's conditioning model (adjusted from [18])

In [6], LEADSTO has been used to specify Machado's mathematical model in a logical, declarative manner. Some of the dynamic properties used are shown below:

LP5 (Extinction of associative links)
LP5 expresses the adaptation of the associative links during extinction, based on their own previous state and the previous state of the corresponding timing node. Here, α is a learning rate parameter. Formalisation:
∀u,v:REAL ∀n:INTEGER
instage(ext) and X(n, u) and W(n, v) →₀,₀,₁,₁ W(n, v*(1-α*u*step))

LP6 (Reinforcement of associative links)
LP6 expresses the adaptation of the associative links during reinforcement, based on their own previous state and the previous state of X. Here, β is a learning rate parameter.
∀u,v:REAL ∀n:INTEGER
instage(reinf) and Xcopy(n, u) and W(n, v) →₀,₀,₁,₁ W(n, v*(1-β*u*step) + β*u*step)

An example simulation trace that has been generated on the basis of this model is shown in Figure 5. The upper part of the figure shows conceptual, qualitative information (e.g., the state properties that indicate the stage of the process); the lower part shows more quantitative concepts, i.e., the state properties involving real numbers with changing values over time (e.g., the preparation level of the person). To limit complexity, only a selection of important state properties was depicted. In the lower part, all instantiations of state property r(X) are shown with different (real) values for X (shown on the vertical axis), indicating the participant's preparation level to respond to a stimulus. For example, from time point 1 to 9, the level of preparation is 0.0, and from time point 9 to 10, the level of preparation is 0.019.

Figure 5 describes the dynamics of a person that is subject to conditioning in an experiment with a foreperiod of 6 time units. As can be seen in the trace, the level of response-related activation increases on each trial. Initially, the subject is not prepared at all: at the moment of the imperative stimulus (S2), the level of response is 0.0. However, already after two trials a peak in response level has developed that coincides exactly with the occurrence of S2. Although this example is relatively simple, it demonstrates the power of LEADSTO to combine (real-valued) quantitative concepts with (conceptual) qualitative concepts.

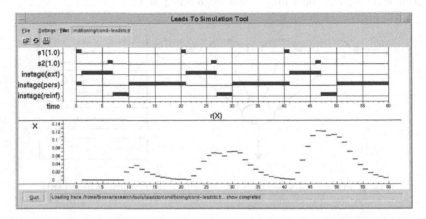

Fig. 5. Example simulation trace of a conditioning process

4 Simulating the Predator-Prey Model by the Runge-Kutta Method

As shown in [22], within Euler's method the local error at each step (of size h) is $O(h^2)$, while the accumulated error is $O(h)$. However, the accumulated error grows exponentially as the integration step size increases. Therefore, in situations in which precision of a solution is required, high order numerical methods are used. For the purpose of illustration of high-order numerical approaches the fourth-order Runge-Kutta method is considered. This method is derived from a Taylor expansion up to the fourth order. It is known to be very accurate (the accumulated error is $O(h^4)$) and stable for a wide range of problems. The Runge-Kutta method for solving a differential equation of the form $dx/dt = f(t, x)$ is described by the following formulae:

$$x_{i+1} = x_i + h/6 *(k_1 + 2*k_2 + 2*k_3 + k_4),$$

where $i \geq 0$ is the step number, $h > 0$ is the integration step size, and

$$k_1 = f(t_i, x_i), k_2 = f(t_i + h/2, x_i + h/2 *k_1), k_3 = f(t_i + h/2, x_i + h/2 *k_2), k_4 = f(t_i + h, x_i + h* k_3).$$

Now, using the Runge-Kutta method, the classical Lotka-Volterra model considered in the previous section is described in the LEADSTO format as follows:

has_value(x, v1) $\wedge$ has_value(y, v2) $\rightarrow_{0, 0, h, h}$ has_value(x, v1 + h/6 *(k_{11} + 2*k_{12} + 2*k_{13} + k_{14}))

has_value(x, v1) $\wedge$ has_value(y, v2) $\rightarrow_{0, 0, h, h}$ has_value(y, v2 + h/6 *(k_{21} + 2*k_{22} + 2*k_{23} + k_{24})), where:

$k_{11} = a*v1-b*v1*v2$, $k_{21} = c*b*v1*v2 - e*v2$, $k_{12} = a*(v1 + h/2 *k_{11}) - b*(v1 + h/2 *k_{11})*(v2 + h/2 *k_{21})$, $k_{22} = c*b*(v1 + h/2 *k_{11})*(v2 + h/2 *k_{21}) - e*(v2 + h/2 *k_{21})$, $k_{13} = a*(v1 + h/2 *k_{12}) - b*(v1 + h/2 *k_{12})*(v2 + h/2 *k_{22})$, $k_{23} = c*b*(v1 + h/2 *k_{12})*(v2 + h/2 *k_{22}) - e*(v2 + h/2 *k_{22})$, $k_{14} = a*(v1 + h *k_{13}) - b*(v1 + h *k_{13})*(v2 + h *k_{23})$, $k_{24} = c*b*(v1 + h *k_{13})*(v2 + h *k_{23}) - e*(v2 + h *k_{23})$.

5 Simulation with Dynamic Step Size

Although for most cases the Runge-Kutta method with a small step size provides accurate approximations of required functions, this method can still be computationally expensive and, in some cases, inaccurate. In order to achieve a higher accuracy together with minimum computational efforts, methods that allow the dynamic (adaptive) regulation of an integration step size are used. This section shows how such methods can be incorporated in LEADSTO.

To illustrate the use of methods for dynamic step size control, the biochemical model of [13], summarised in Table 1, is considered.

Table 1. Glycolysis model by [13]

Variables	Moiety conservation	Rate equations
W: Fructose 6-phosphate X : phosphoenolpyruvate Y : pyruvate N1 : ATP; N2 : ADP; N3 : AMP	N1[t] + N2[t] + N3 = 20	Vxy = 343*N2[t]*X[t]/((0.17 + N2[t])*(0.2 + X[t])) Vak = -(432.9*N3*N1[t] - 133*N2[t]^2)
Differential equations X'[t] == 2*Vpfk - Vxy Y'[t] == Vxy - Vpdc N1'[t] == Vxy + Vak - Vatpase N2'[t] == -Vxy - 2*Vak + Vatpase	Initial conditions N1[0] == 10 N2[0] == 9 Y[0] == 0 X[0] == 0 Fixed metabolites W = 0.0001; Z = 0	Vatpase = 3.2076*N1[t] Vpdc = 53.1328*Y[t]/(0.3 + Y[t]) (*10.0*Y[t]*) Vpfk = 45.4327*W^2/(0.021*(1 + 0.15*N1[t]^2/N3^2 + W^2))

This model describes the process of glycolysis in *Saccharomyces cerevisiae*, a specific species of yeast. This model is interesting to study, because the concentrations of some of the substances involved (in particular ATP and ADP) are changing at a variable rate: sometimes these concentrations change rapidly, and sometimes they change very slowly. Using the technique described in Section 2.2 (based on Euler's method), this model can be translated to the following LEADSTO simulation model:

has_value(x, v1) ∧ has_value(y, v2) ∧ has_value(n1, v3) ∧ has_value(n2, v4) →₀, ₀, ₕ, ₕ
   has_value(x, v1+ (2* (45.4327*w^2/ (0.021* (1+0.15*v3^2/ (20-v3-v4)^2+w^2)))-343*v4*v1/ ((0.17+v4)* (0.2+v1)))*h)

has_value(x, v1) ∧ has_value(y, v2) ∧ has_value(n1, v3) ∧ has_value(n2, v4) →₀, ₀, ₕ, ₕ
   has_value(y, v2+ (343*v4*v1/ ((0.17+v4)* (0.2+v1))-53.1328*v2/ (0.3+v2))*h)

has_value(x, v1) ∧ has_value(y, v2) ∧ has_value(n1, v3) ∧ has_value(n2, v4) →₀, ₀, ₕ, ₕ
   has_value(n1, v3+ (343*v4*v1/ ((0.17+v4)* (0.2+v1))+ (- (432.9* (20-v3-v4)*v3-133*v4^2))-3.2076*v3)*h)

has_value(x, v1) ∧ has_value(y, v2) ∧ has_value(n1, v3) ∧ has_value(n2, v4) →₀, ₀, ₕ, ₕ
   has_value(n2, v4+ (-343*v4*v1/ ((0.17+v4)* (0.2+v1))-2*

   (- (432.9* (20-v3-v4)*v3-133*v4^2))+3.2076*v3)*h)

The simulation results of this model (with a static step size of 0.00001) are shown in Fig. 6. Here the curves for N1 and N2 are initially very steep, but become flat after a while. As demonstrated by Figure 6, for the first part of the simulation, it is necessary to pick a small step size in order to obtain accurate results. However, to reduce computational efforts, for the second part a bigger step size is desirable. To this end, a number of methods exist that allow the dynamic adaptation of the step size in a simulation. Generally, these approaches are based on the fact that the algorithm signals information about its own truncation error. The most straightforward (and most often used) technique for this is *step doubling* and *step halving*, see, e.g. [Gear 1971]. The idea of step doubling is that, whenever a new simulation step should be performed, the algorithm compares the result of applying the current step twice with the result of applying the double step (i.e., the current step * 2) once. If the difference between both solutions is smaller than a certain threshold ε, then the double step is selected. Otherwise, the algorithm determines whether step halving can be applied: it compares the result of applying the current step once with the result of applying the half step (i.e., the current step * 0.5) twice. If the difference between both solutions is smaller than ε, then the current step is selected. Otherwise, the half step is selected.

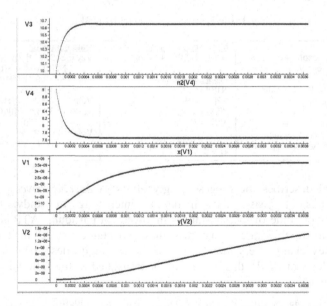

Fig. 6. Simulation results of applying Euler's method to [13]'s glycolysis model

Since its format allows the modeller to include qualitative aspects, it is not difficult to incorporate step doubling and step halving into LEADSTO. To illustrate this, consider the general LEADSTO rule shown in Section 2.2 for solving a differential equation of the form dy/dt = f(y) using Euler's method:

$$\text{has\_value}(y, v1) \rightarrow_{0, 0, h, h} \text{has\_value}(y, v1+h^* f(v1))$$

Adding step doubling and step halving to this rule yields the following three rules:

step(h) ∧ has_value(y, v1) ∧ |(v1+2h* f(v1)) - ((v1+h* f(v1))+h* f(v1+h* f(v1)))| ≤ ε
   →_{0, 0, 2h, 2h} has_value(y, v1+2h* f(v1)) ∧ step(2h)

step(h) ∧ has_value(y, v1) ∧ |(v1+2h* f(v1)) - ((v1+h* f(v1))+h* f(v1+h* f(v1)))| > ε ∧
|(v1+h* f(v1)) - ((v1+0.5h* f(v1))+0.5h* f(v1+0.5h* f(v1)))| ≤ ε
→ₒ, ₀, ₕ, ₕ has_value(y, v1+h* f(v1)) ∧ step(h)

step(h) ∧ has_value(y, v1) ∧ |(v1+h* f(v1)) - ((v1+0.5h* f(v1))+0.5h* f(v1+0.5h* f(v1)))| ≤ ε
→ₒ, ₀, ₀.₅ₕ, ₀.₅ₕ has_value(y, v1+0.5h* f(v1)) ∧ step(0.5h)

Besides step doubling, many other techniques exist in the literature for dynamically controlling the step size in quantitative simulations. Among these are several techniques that are especially aimed at the Runge-Kutta methods, see, e.g., [24], Chapter 16 for an overview. Although it is possible to incorporate such techniques into LEADSTO, they are not addressed here because of space limitations.

6 Analysis in Terms of Local-Global Relations

Within the area of agent-based modelling, one of the means to address complexity is by modelling processes at different levels, from the global level of the process as a whole, to the local level of basic elements and their mechanisms. At each of these levels dynamic properties can be specified, and by interlevel relations they can be logically related to each other; e.g., [14], [27]. These relationships can provide an explanation of properties of a process as a whole in terms of properties of its local elements and mechanisms. Such analyses can be done by hand, but also software tools are available to automatically verify the dynamic properties and their interlevel relations. To specify the dynamic properties at different levels and their interlevel relations, a more expressive language is needed than simulation languages based on causal relationships, such as LEADSTO. The reason for this is that, although the latter types of languages are well suited to express the basic mechanisms of a process, for specifying global properties of a process it is often necessary to formulate complex relationships between states at different time points. To this end, the formal language TTL has been introduced as a super-language of LEADSTO; cf. [8]. It is based on order-sorted predicate logic and, therefore, inherits the standard semantics of this variant of predicate logic. That is, the semantics of TTL is defined in a standard way, by interpretation of sorts, constants, functions and predicates, and variable assignments. Furthermore, TTL allows representing numbers and arithmetical functions. Therefore, most methods used in Calculus are expressible in TTL, including methods based on derivatives and differential equations. In this section, first (in Section 6.1) it is shown how to incorporate differential equations in the predicate-logical language TTL that is used for analysis. Next, in Section 6.2 a number of global dynamic properties are identified, and it is shown how they can be expressed in TTL. In Section 6.3 a number of local dynamic properties are identified and expressed in TTL. Finally, Section 6.4 discusses how the global properties can be logically related to local properties such that a local property implies the global property.

6.1 The LEADSTO Language

As mentioned earlier, traditionally, analysis of dynamical systems is often performed using mathematical techniques such as the Dynamical Systems Theory. The question may arise whether or not such modelling techniques can be expressed in the Temporal Trace Language TTL. In this section it is shown how modelling techniques used in the Dynamical Systems approach, such as difference and differential equations, can be represented in TTL. First the discrete case is considered. As an example consider again the logistic growth model: dP/dt = r*P(1-P/K). This equation can be expressed in TTL on the basis of a discrete time frame (e.g., the natural numbers) in a straightforward manner:

∀t ∀v state(γ, t) ⊨ has_value(P, v) ⇒ state(γ, t+1) ⊨ has_value(P, v + h • r • v • (1 - v/K))

The traces γ satisfying the above dynamic property are the solutions of the difference equation. However, it is also possible to use the dense time frame of the real numbers, and to express the differential equation directly. To this end, the following relation is introduced, expressing that x = dy/dt:

is_diff_of(γ, x, y) :
∀t,w ∀ε>0 ∃δ>0 ∀t',v,v' [0 < dist(t',t) < δ & state(γ, t) ⊨ has_value(x, w) &
state(γ, t) ⊨ has_value(y, v) & state(γ, t') ⊨ has_value(y, v') ⇒ dist((v'-v)/(t'-t),w) < ε]

where γ is the trace that describes the change of values of x and y over time, dist(u,v) is defined as the absolute value of the difference, i.e. u-v if this is ≥ 0, and v-u otherwise. Using this, the differential equation can be expressed by is_diff_of(γ, r • P (1 - P/K), P).

The traces γ for which this statement is true are (or include) solutions for the differential equation. Models consisting of combinations of difference or differential equations can be expressed in a similar manner. This shows how modelling constructs often used in DST can be expressed in TTL. Thus, TTL on the one hand subsumes modelling languages based on differential equations, but on the other hand enables the modeller to express more qualitative, logical concepts as well.

6.2 Mathematical Analysis in TTL: Global Dynamic Properties

Within Dynamical Systems Theory and Calculus, also for global properties of a process more specific analysis methods are known. Examples of such analysis methods include mathematical methods to determine equilibrium points, the behaviour around equilibrium points, and the existence of limit cycles [10]. Suppose a set of differential equations is given, for example a predator prey model: dx/dt = f(x, y) dy/dt = g(x, y), where f(x, y) and g(x, y) are arithmetical expressions in x and y. Within TTL the following abbreviation is introduced as a definable predicate:

point(γ, t, x, v, y, w) ⇔ state(γ, t) |= has_value(x, v) ∧ has_value(y, w)

Using this predicate, the following global properties can for example be specified:

Monotonicity
monotic_increase_after(γ, t, x) ⇔
∀t1, t2 [t ≤ t1 < t2 & point(γ, t1, x, v1, y, w1) & point(γ, t2, x, v2, y, w2) ⇒ v1<v2]

Bounded
upward_bounded_after_by(γ, t, M) ⇔ ∀t1 [t ≤ t1 & point(γ, t1, x, v1, y, w1) ⇒ v1≤M]

Equilibrium points
These are points in the (x, y) plane for which, when they are reached by a solution, the state stays at this point in the plane for all future time points. This can be expressed as a global dynamic property in TTL as follows:

has_equilibrium(γ, x, v, y, w) ⇔ ∀t1 [point(γ, t1, x, v, y, w) ⇒ ∀t2≥t1 point(γ, t2, x, v, y, w)]
occurring_equilibrium(γ, x, v, y, w) ⇔   ∃t point(γ, t, x, v, y, w) & has_equilibrium(γ, x, v, y, w)

Behaviour Around an Equilibrium
attracting(γ, x, v, y, w, ε0) ⇔ has_equilibrium(γ, x, v, y, w) &
ε0>0 ∧ ∀t [point(γ, t, x, v1, y, w1) ∧ dist(v1, w1, v, w) < ε0 ⇒
∀ε>0 ∃t1≥t ∀t2≥t1 [point(γ, t2, x, v2, y, w2) ⇒ dist(v2, w2, v, w) < ε]]

Here, dist(v1, w1, v2, w2) denotes the distance between the points (v1, w1) and (v2, w2) in the (x, y) plane.

Limit cycle
A limit cycle is a set S in the x, y plane such that
∀t, v, w point(γ, t, x, v, y, w) & (v, w) ∈ S ⇒ ∀t'≥t, v', w' [point(γ, t', x, v', y, w') ⇒ (v', w') ∈ S]

In specific cases the set can be expressed in an implicit manner by a logical and/or algebraic formula, e.g., an equation, or in an explicit manner by a parameterisation. For these cases it can be logically expressed that a set S is a limit cycle.

(1) When S is defined in an implicit manner by a formula φ(v, w) with S = { (v, w) | φ(v, w) }, then it is defined that S is a limit cycle as follows:

∀t, v, w point(γ, t, x, v, y, w) & φ(v, w) ⇒ ∀t'≥t, v', w' [point(γ, t', x, v', y, w') ⇒ φ(v', w')]
E.g., when S is a circle defined by a formula of the form S = { (v, w) | $v^2 + w^2 = r^2$ }

(2) When a set S in the plane is parameterised by two functions c1, c2: [0, 1] → ℜ, i.e., S = { (c1(u), c2(u)) | u ∈ [0, 1] }, then S is a limit cycle if

∀t, u point(γ, t, c1(u), c2(u)) ⇒ ∀t'≥t ∃u' point(γ, t', c1(u'), c2(u'))

An example of a parameterising for S in the shape of a circle is as follows:

c1(u) = r cos 2π u, c2(u) = r sin 2π u

In many cases, however, the set S cannot be expressed explicitly in the form of an equation or an explicitly defined parameterisation. What still can be done often is to establish the existence of a limit cycle within a certain area, based on the Poincaré-Bendixson Theorem [16].

6.3 Mathematical Analysis in TTL: Local Dynamic Properties

The global dynamic properties described above can also be addressed from a local perspective. For example, the property of monotonicity (which was expressed above for a whole trace after a certain time point t), can also be expressed for a certain interval (with duration d) around t, as shown below.

Local monotonicity property
monotic_increase_around(γ, t, x, d) ⇔
∀t1, t2 [t-d ≤ t1 < t < t2≤ t+d & point(γ, t1, x, v1, y, w1) & point(γ, t2, x, v2, y, w2) ⇒ v1< v2]

In terms of f and g:
monotic_increase_around(γ, t, x, d) ⇔ point(γ, t, x, v1, y, w1) ⇒ f(v1, w1) > 0

Local bounding property
upward_bounding_around(γ, t, M, δ, d) $\Leftrightarrow$
[point(γ, t, x, v1, y, w1) $\Rightarrow$ $\forall$t' [t$\leq$t'$\leq$t+d & point(γ, t', x, v2, y, w2) $\Rightarrow$ M-v2 $\geq$ (1-δ)*(M-v1)]

In terms of f and g from the equations dx/dt = f(x, y) and dy/dt = g(x, y):
upward_bounding_around(γ, t, M, δ, d) $\Leftrightarrow$ point(γ, t, x, v1, y, w1) $\Rightarrow$ f(v1, w1) $\leq$ δ/d (M - v1)

Local equilibrium property
From the local perspective of the underlying mechanism, equilibrium points are those points for which dx/dt = dy/dt = 0, i.e., in terms of f and g for this case f(x, y) = g(x, y) = 0.
equilibrium_state(v, w) $\Leftrightarrow$ f(v, w) = 0 & g(v, w) = 0

Local property for behaviour around an equilibrium:
attracting(γ, x, v, y, w, δ, ϵ0, d) $\Leftrightarrow$ has_equilibrium(γ, x, v, y, w) &
ϵ0>0 $\wedge$ 0< δ <1 $\wedge$ d$\geq$0 $\wedge$ $\forall$t [point(γ, t, x, v1, y, w1) $\wedge$ dist(v1, w1, v, w) < ϵ0 $\Rightarrow$
$\forall$t' [t+d$\leq$t'$\leq$t+2d & point(γ, t', x, v2, y, w2) $\Rightarrow$ dist(v2, w2, v, w) < δ*dist(v1, w1, v, w)]]

In terms of f and g, this can be expressed by relationships for the eigen values of the matrix of derivatives of f and g.

Local limit cycle property
Let a set S in the plane be parameterised by two explicitly given functions c1, c2: [0, 1] $\rightarrow$ $\Re$, i.e., S = { (c1(u), c2(u)) I u $\in$ [0, 1] }, and d1(u) = dc1(u)/du, d2(u) = dc2(u)/du. Then S is a limit cycle if:

$$\forall t, u \ \text{point}(\gamma, t, c1(u), c2(u)) \Rightarrow d1(u)*g(c1(u), c2(u)) = f(c1(u), c2(u))*d2(u)$$

6.4 Logical Relations Between Local and Global Properties

The properties of local and global level can be logically related to each other by general interlevel relations, for example, the following ones:

$\exists$d>0 $\forall$t'$\geq$t monotic_increase_around(γ, t', x, d)	$\Rightarrow$ monotic_increase_after(γ, t, x)
$\exists$d>0, δ>0 $\forall$t'$\geq$t upward_bounding_around(γ, t, M, δ, d)	$\Rightarrow$ upward_bounded_after_by(γ, t, M)
$\forall$t [state(γ, t) I= equilibrium_state(v, w)	$\Rightarrow$ has_equilibrium(γ, x, v, y, w)
$\exists$d>0, δ>0 attracting(γ, x, v, y, w, δ, ϵ0, d)	$\Rightarrow$ attracting(γ, x, v, y, w, ϵ0)

These interlevel relations are general properties of dynamic systems, as explained, e.g., in [10]. Full proofs for these relations fall outside the scope of this paper. However, to make them a bit more plausible, the following sketch is given. The first interlevel relation involving monotonicity can be based on induction on the number of d-intervals of the time axis between two given time points t1 and t2. The second interlevel relation, involving boundedness is based on the fact that local bounding implies that in any d-interval, if the value at the start of the interval is below M, then it will remain below M in that interval. The third interlevel relation, on equilibrium points, is based on the fact that if at no time point the value changes, then at all time points after this value is reached, the value will be the same. For the fourth interlevel relation, notice that local attractiveness implies that for any d-interval the distance of the value to the equilibrium value at the end point is less than δ times the value at the starting point. By induction over the number of d-intervals the limit definition as used for the global property can be obtained.

7 Discussion

The LEADSTO approach discussed in this paper provides means to simulate models of dynamic systems that combine both quantitative and qualitative aspects. A dynamic system, as it is used here, is a system, which is characterised by states and transitions between these states. As such, dynamic systems as considered in [23], which are described by differential equations, constitute a subclass of the dynamic systems considered in this paper. Systems that incorporate both continuous components and discrete components are sometimes called *hybrid systems*. Hybrid systems are studied in both computer science [9], [19] and control engineering [17]. They incorporate both continuous components, whose dynamics is described by differential equations and discrete components, which are often represented by finite-state automata. Both continuous and discrete dynamics of components influence each other. In particular, the input to the continuous dynamics is the result of some function of the discrete state of a system; whereas the input of the discrete dynamics is determined by the value of the continuous state. In the control engineering area, hybrid systems are often considered as switching systems that represent continuous-time systems with isolated and often simplified discrete switching events. Yet in computer science the main interest in hybrid systems lies in investigating aspects of the discrete behaviour, while the continuous dynamics is often kept simple.

Our LEADSTO approach provides as much place for modelling the continuous constituent of a system, as for modelling the discrete one. In contrast to many studies on hybrid systems in computer science (e.g., [25]), in which a state of a system is described by assignment of values to variables, in the proposed approach a state of a system is defined using a rich ontological basis (i.e., typed constants, variables, functions and predicates). This provides better possibilities for conceptualising and formalising different kinds of systems (including those from natural domains). Furthermore, by applying numerical methods for approximation of the continuous behaviour of a system, all variables in generated model become discrete and are treated equally as finite-state transition system variables. Therefore, it is not needed to specify so-called *control points* [19], at which values of continuous variables are checked and necessary transitions or changes in a mode of a system's functioning are made. Moreover, using TTL, a super-language of LEADSTO, dynamical systems can be analysed by applying formalised standard techniques from mathematical calculus.

Since LEADSTO has a state-based semantics and allows a high ontological expressivity for defining state properties, many action-based languages (*A, B, C* [12], *L* [2] and their extensions) can be represented in (or mapped to) the LEADSTO format. In particular, trajectories that define the world evolution in action languages correspond to traces in LEADSTO, fluents evaluated in each state can be represented by state properties, and transitions between states due to actions can be specified by LEADSTO rules that contain the corresponding actions within the antecedents. Furthermore, to represent actions, observations, and goals of agents and facts about the world, the state ontology of LEADSTO includes corresponding sorts, functions and predicates. LEADSTO allows representing both static and dynamic laws as they are defined in [12], and non-deterministic actions with probabilities. To represent and reason about temporal aspects of actions, LEADSTO includes the sort TIME, which is a set of linearly ordered time points.

The expressions of query languages used to reason about actions [2], [12] can be represented in TTL, of which LEADSTO is a sublanguage. TTL formulae can express causality relations of query languages by implications and may include references to multiple states (e.g., histories of temporally ordered sequences of states). Using a dedicated tool [8], TTL formulae can be automatically checked on traces (or trajectories) that represent the temporal development of agent systems.

Concerning other related work, in [26], a logic-based approach to simulation-based modelling of ecological systems is introduced. Using this approach, continuous dynamic processes in ecological systems are conceptualised by system dynamics models (i.e., sets of compartments with flows between them). For formalising these models and performing simulations, the logical programming language Prolog is used. In contrast to this, the LEADSTO approach provides a more abstract (or high-level) logic-based language for knowledge representation.

Also within the area of cognitive modelling, the idea to combine qualitative and quantitative aspects within one modelling approach is not uncommon. A number of architectures have been developed in that area, e.g., ACT-R [1] and SOAR [15]. Such cognitive architectures basically consist of a number of different modules that reflect specific parts of cognition, such as memory, rule-based processes, and communication. They have in common with LEADSTO that they are hybrid approaches, supporting both qualitative (or *symbolic*) and quantitative (or *subsymbolic*) structures. However, in LEADSTO these qualitative and quantitative concepts can be combined within the same expressions, whereas in ACT-R and SOAR separate modules exist to express them. In these cognitive architectures, often the role of the subsymbolic processes is to control the symbolic processes. For example, the subsymbolic part of ACT-R is represented by a large set of parallel processes that can be summarised by a number of mathematical equations, whereas its symbolic part is fulfilled by a production system. Here, the subsymbolic equations control many of the symbolic processes. For instance, if multiple production rules in ACT-R's symbolic part are candidates to be executed, a subsymbolic utility equation may estimate the relative cost and benefit associated with each rule and select the rule with the highest utility for execution.

Accuracy and efficiency of simulation results for hybrid systems provided by the proposed approach to a great extend depend on the choice of a numerical approximation method. Although the proposed approach does not prescribe usage of any specific approximation method (even the most powerful of them can be modelled in LEADSTO), for most of the cases the fourth-order Runge-Kutta method can be recommended, especially when the highest level of precision is not required. For simulating system models, for which high precision is demanded, higher-order numerical methods with an adaptive step size can be applied.

References

1. Anderson, J.R., Lebiere, C.: The atomic components of thought. Lawrence Erlbaum Associates, Mahwah, NJ (1998)
2. Baral, C., Gelfond, M., Provetti, A.: Representing Actions: Laws, Observation and Hypothesis. Journal of Logic Programming 31(1-3), 201–243 (1997)

3. Barringer, H., Fisher, M., Gabbay, D., Owens, R., Reynolds, M.: The Imperative Future: Principles of Executable Temporal Logic. Research Studies Press Ltd. and John Wiley & Sons (1996)
4. Boccara, N.: Modeling Complex Systems. In: Graduate Texts in Contemporary Physics series, Springer, Heidelberg (2004)
5. Bosse, T., Delfos, M.F., Jonker, C.M., Treur, J.: Modelling Adaptive Dynamical Systems to analyse Eating Regulation Disorders. Simulation Journal: Transactions of the Society for Modeling and Simulation International 82, 159–171 (2006)
6. Bosse, T., Jonker, C.M., Los, S.A., van der Torre, L., Treur, J.: Formalisation and Analysis of the Temporal Dynamics of Conditioning. In: Müller, J.P., Zambonelli, F. (eds.) AOSE 2005. LNCS, vol. 3950, pp. 157–168. Springer, Heidelberg (2006)
7. Bosse, T., Jonker, C.M., Meij, L., van der, L., Treur, J.: LEADSTO: A Language and Environment for Analysis of Dynamics by Simulation. In: Eymann, T., Klügl, F., Lamersdorf, W., Klusch, M., Huhns, M.N. (eds.) MATES 2005. LNCS (LNAI), vol. 3550, pp. 165–178. Springer, Heidelberg (2005) Extended version in: International Journal of Artificial Intelligence Tools (to appear, 2007)
8. Bosse, T., Jonker, C.M., Meij, L., van der Sharpanskykh, A., Treur, J.: Specification and Verification of Dynamics in Cognitive Agent Models. In: Nishida, T. (ed.) IAT 2006, pp. 247–254. IEEE Computer Society Press, Los Alamitos (2006)
9. Davoren, J.M., Nerode, A.: Logics for Hybrid Systems. Proceedings of the IEEE 88(7), 985–1010 (2000)
10. Edwards, C.H., Penney, D.L.: Calculus with Analytic Geometry, 5th edn. Prentice-Hall, London (1998)
11. Gear, C.W.: Numerical Initial Value Problems in Ordinary Differential Equations. Prentice-Hall, Englewood Cliffs (1971)
12. Gelfond, M., Lifschitz, V.: Action languages. Electronic Transactions on AI 3(16) (1998)
13. Hynne, F., Dano, S., Sorensen, P.G.: Full-scale model of glycolysis in Saccharomyces cerevisiae. Biophys. Chem. 94(1-2), 121–163 (2001)
14. Jonker, C.M., Treur, J.: Compositional Verification of Multi-Agent Systems: A Formal Analysis of Pro-activeness and Reactiveness. International Journal of Cooperative Information Systems 11, 51–92 (2002)
15. Laird, J.E., Newell, A., Rosenbloom, P.S.: Soar: An architecture for general intelligence. Artificial Intelligence 33(1), 1–64 (1987)
16. Lefschetz, S.: Differential equations: Geometric theory. Dover Publications, Mineola (2005)
17. Liberzon, D., Morse, A.S.: Basic problems in stability and design of switched systems. IEEE Control Systems Magazine 19(5), 59–70 (1999)
18. Machado, A.: Learning the Temporal Dynamics of Behaviour. Psychological Review 104, 241–265 (1997)
19. Manna, Z., Pnueli, A.: Verifying Hybrid Systems. In: Grossman, R.L., Ravn, A.P., Rischel, H., Nerode, A. (eds.) Hybrid Systems. LNCS, vol. 736, pp. 4–35. Springer, Heidelberg (1993)
20. Meyer, J.J.C., Treur, J.: Agent-based Defeasible Control in Dynamic Environments. In: Gabbay, D., Smets, P. (eds.) Defeasible Reasoning and Uncertainty Management Systems, vol. 7, Kluwer Academic Publishers, Dordrecht (2002)
21. Morin, P.J.: Community Ecology. Blackwell Publishing, USA (1999)
22. Pearson, C.E.: Numerical Methods in Engineering and Science. CRC Press, Boca Raton (1986)

23. Port, R.F., van Gelder, T. (eds.): Mind as Motion: Explorations in the Dynamics of Cognition. MIT Press, Cambridge, Mass (1995)
24. Press, W.H., Teukolsky, S.A., Vetterling, W.T., Flannery, B.P.: Numerical recipes in C: The art of scientific computing, 2nd edn. Cambridge university press, Cambridge (1992)
25. Rajeev, A., Henzinger, T.A., Wong-Toi, H.: Symbolic analysis of hybrid systems. In: CDC. Proceedings of the 36th Annual Conference on Decision and Control, pp. 702–707. IEEE Computer Society Press, Los Alamitos (1997)
26. Robertson, D., Bundy, A., Muetzelfeldt, R., Haggith, M., Ushold, M.: Eco-Logic: Logic-Based Approaches to Ecological Modelling. MIT Press, Cambridge (1991)
27. Sharpanskykh, A., Treur, J.: Verifying Interlevel Relations within Multi-Agent Systems. In: Brewka, G., Coradeschi, S., Perini, A., Traverso, P. (eds.) ECAI 2006. Proc. of the 17th European Conference on Artificial Intelligence, pp. 290–294. IOS Press, Amsterdam (2006)

Composing High-Level Plans
for Declarative Agent Programming

Felipe Meneguzzi and Michael Luck

Department of Computer Science
King's College London
felipe.meneguzzi@kcl.ac.uk,
michael.luck@kcl.ac.uk

Abstract. Research on practical models of autonomous agents has largely focused on a *procedural* view of goal achievement. This allows for efficient implementations, but prevents an agent from reasoning about alternative courses of action for the achievement of its design objectives. In this paper we show how a procedural agent model can be modified to allow an agent to compose existing plans into new ones at runtime to achieve desired world states. This new agent model can be used to implement a declarative goals interpreter, since it allows designers to specify *only* the desired world states in addition to an agent's basic capabilities, enhancing the agent's ability to deal with failures. Moreover our approach allows the new plans to be included in the plan library, effectively enabling the agent to improve its runtime performance over time.

1 Introduction

The notion of autonomous intelligent agents has become increasingly relevant in recent years both in relation to numerous real applications and in drawing together different artificial intelligence techniques. Perhaps the best known and most used family of agent architectures is that based around the notions of beliefs, desires and intentions, which is exemplified by such systems as PRS[1], dMARS[2] and AgentSpeak [3]. For reasons of efficiency and real-time operation, these architectures have been based around the inclusion of a plan library consisting of predefined *encapsulated procedures*, or *plans*, coupled with information about the context in which to use them [3]. However, designing agents in this way severely limits an agent's runtime flexibility, as the agent depends entirely on the designer's previous definition of all possible courses of action associated with proper contextual information to allow the agent to adopt the right plans in the right situations.

Typically, agent interpreters select plans using more or less elaborate algorithms, but these seldom have any knowledge of the contents of the plans, so that plan selection is ultimately achieved using fixed rules, with an agent adopting *black box* plans based solely on the contextual information that accompanies them. Alternatively, some agent interpreters allow for plan modification rules to

M. Baldoni et al. (Eds.): DALT 2007, LNAI 4897, pp. 69–85, 2008.

allow plans to be modified to suit the current situation [4], but this approach still relies on a designer establishing a set of rules that considers all potentially necessary modifications for the agent to achieve its goals. The problem here is that for some domains, an agent description must either be extremely extensive (requiring a designer to foresee every possible situation the agent might find itself in), or will leave the agent unable to respond under certain conditions.

This *procedural* response to goal achievement has been favoured to enable the construction of practical systems that are usable in real-world applications. However, it also causes difficulties in cases of failure. When a procedural agent selects a plan to achieve a given goal it is possible that the selected plan may fail, in which case the agent typically concludes that the goal has also failed, regardless of whether other plans to achieve the same goal might have been successful. By neglecting the *declarative* aspect of goals in not considering the construction of plans on-the-fly, agents lose the ability to reason about alternative means of achieving a goal, making it possible for poor plan selection to lead to an otherwise avoidable failure.

In this paper we describe how a procedural agent model can be modified to allow an agent to build new plans at runtime by chaining existing fine-grained plans from a plan library into high-level plans. We demonstrate the applicability of this approach through a modification to the AgentSpeak architecture, allowing for a combination of declarative and procedural aspects. This modification requires no change to the plan language, allowing designers to specify predefined procedures for known tasks under ideal circumstances, but also allowing the agent to form new plans when unforeseen situations arise. Though we demonstrate this technique for AgentSpeak, it can be easily applied to other agent architectures with an underlying procedural approach to reasoning, such as JADEX or the basic 3APL [5]. The key contribution is a method to augment an agent's runtime flexibility, allowing it to add to its plan library to respond to new situations without the need for the designer to specify all possible combinations of low-level operators in advance.

The paper is organised as follows: in Section 2 we briefly review relevant aspects of AgentSpeak, in order to introduce the planning capability in Section 3; in Section 4 a classic example is provided to contrast our approach to that of traditional AgentSpeak; in Section 5 we compare our work with similar or complementary approaches that also aim to improve agent autonomy; finally, in Section 6 a summary of contributions is provided along with further work that can be carried out to improve our system.

2   AgentSpeak

AgentSpeak [3] is an agent language that allows a designer to specify a set of procedural plans which are then selected by an interpreter to achieve the agent's design goals. It evolved from a series of procedural agent languages originally developed by Rao and Georgeff [6]. In AgentSpeak an agent is defined by a set of beliefs and a set of plans, with each plan encoding a procedure that is assumed to bring about a desired state of affairs, as well as the context in which a plan is relevant. Goals in AgentSpeak are implicit, and plans intended to fulfil them are invoked whenever some triggering condition is met in a certain context, presumably the moment at which this implicit goal becomes relevant.

The control cycle of an AgentSpeak interpreter is driven by events on data structures, including the addition or deletion of goals and beliefs. These events are used as triggering conditions for the adoption of plans, so that adding an achievement goal means that an agent desires to fulfil that goal, and plans whose triggering condition includes that goal (*i.e.* are *relevant* to the goal) should lead to that goal being achieved. Moreover, a plan includes a logical condition that specifies when the plan is *applicable* in any given situation. Whenever a goal addition event is generated (as a result of the currently selected plan having subgoals), the interpreter searches the set of relevant plans for applicable plans; if one (or more) such plan is found, it is pushed onto an intention structure for execution. Elements in the intention structure are popped and handled by the interpreter. If the element is an action it is executed, while if the element is a goal, a new plan is added into the intention structure and processed. During this process, failures may take place either in the execution of actions, or during the processing of subplans. When such a failure takes place, the plan that is currently being processed also fails. Thus, if a plan selected for the achievement of a given goal fails, the default behaviour of an AgentSpeak agent is to conclude that the goal that caused the plan to be adopted is not achievable. This control cycle is illustrated in the diagram of Figure 1,[1] and strongly couples plan execution to goal achievement.

The control cycle of Figure 1 allows for situations in which the poor selection of a plan leads to the failure of a goal that would otherwise be achievable through a different plan in the plan library. While such limitations can be mitigated through meta-level [8] constructs that allow goal addition events to cause the execution of applicable plans in sequence, and the goal to fail only when *all* plans fail, AgentSpeak still regards goal achievement as an implicit side-effect of a plan being executed successfully.

3   Planning in an AgentSpeak Interpreter

In response to these limitations, we have created an extension of AgentSpeak that allows an agent to explicitly specify the world-state that should be achieved by the agent. In order to transform the world to meet the desired state, our extension uses a propositional planner to form high-level plans through the composition of plans already present in the agent's plan library. This propositional planner is invoked by the agent through a regular AgentSpeak action, and therefore requires no change in the language definition. The only assumption we make is the existence of plans that abide by certain restrictions in order to be able to compose higher-level plans, taking advantage of planning capabilities introduced in the interpreter.

---

[1] For a full description of AgentSpeak, refer to d'Inverno *et al.* [7].

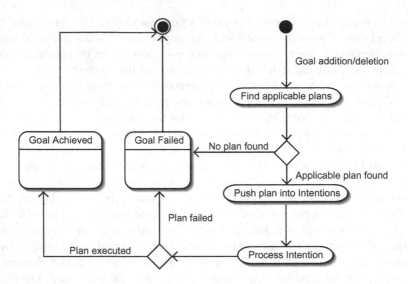

Fig. 1. AgentSpeak control cycle

Whenever an agent needs to achieve a goal that involves planning, it uses a special *planning action* that converts the low-level procedural plans of AgentSpeak into STRIPS operators and invokes the planning module. If the planner succeeds in finding a plan, it is converted back into a high-level AgentSpeak plan and added to the intention structure for execution. Here, we liken the low-level procedural plans of AgentSpeak to STRIPS operators, connecting the agent interpreter to the planner by converting one formalism into the other and *vice versa*. We have chosen to use STRIPS as the planning language in this paper for simplicity reasons, and this approach would not lose applicability if one was to use PDDL [9] (or another language) as the planning language.

3.1 The Planning Action

In order to describe the connection of the planning component with AgentSpeak, we need to review the main constructs of this agent language. As we have seen, an AgentSpeak interpreter is driven by events on the agent's data structures that may trigger the adoption of plans. Additions and deletions of goals and beliefs are represented by the plus (+) and minus (−) sign respectively. Goals are distinguished into *test goals* and *achievement goals*, denoted by a preceding question mark (?), or an exclamation mark (!), respectively. For example, the addition of a goal to achieve g would be represented by $+!g$. Belief additions and deletions arise as the agent perceives the environment, and are therefore outside its control, while goal additions and deletions only arise as part of the execution of an agent's plans.

In our approach, in addition to the traditional way of encoding goals for an AgentSpeak agent implicitly as triggering events consisting of achievement goals

Table 1. Planner invocation plan

$$+goal\_conj(Goals) : true \leftarrow plan(Goals).$$

(!*goal*), we allow desires including multiple beliefs $(b_1, \ldots, b_n)$ describing a desired world-state in the form $goal\_conj([b_1, \ldots, b_n])$. An agent desire description consists of a conjunction of beliefs the agent wishes to be true simultaneously at a given point in time. The execution of the planner component is triggered by an event $+goal\_conj([b_1, \ldots, b_n])$ as shown in Table 1.

Now, the key to our approach to planning in AgentSpeak is the introduction of a special *planning action*, denoted $plan(G)$, where G is a conjunction of desired goals. This action is bound to an implementation of a planning component, and allows all of the process regarding the conversion between formalisms to be encapsulated in the action implementation, making it completely transparent to the remainder of the interpreter.

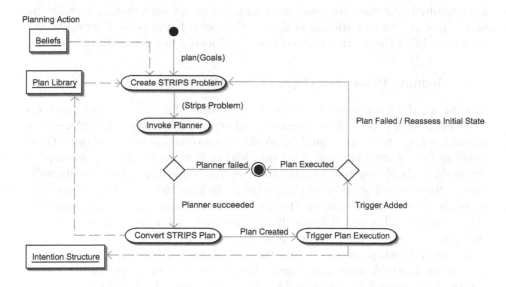

Fig. 2. Operation of the planning action

As illustrated in Figure 2, the internal action to plan takes as an argument the desired world-state, and uses this, along with the current belief database and the plan library, to generate a STRIPS [10] planning problem. This action then invokes a planning algorithm; if a plan is found, the planning action succeeds, otherwise the planning action fails. If the action successfully yields a plan, it converts the resulting STRIPS plan into a new AgentSpeak plan to be added to the plan library, and immediately triggers the adoption of the new plan. If the

Table 2. Movement plans

$$+!move\_to(A, B) \quad : available(car)$$
$$\leftarrow get(car);$$
$$drive(A, B).$$

$$+!move\_to(A, B) : \neg available(car)$$
$$\leftarrow walk(A, B).$$

newly created plan fails, the planner may then be invoked again to try and find another plan to achieve the desired state of affairs, taking into consideration any changes in the agent beliefs.

It is important to note that the planning action is included in a standard AgentSpeak plan with the same triggering condition as the plans generated by it. Moreover, new plans are always added to the plan library *before* the plan that executes the planning action. With this arrangement, previously-created plans are consulted first when the interpreter searches for relevant plans, hence having higher priority for execution, and if no such plan is found to be applicable, the plan containing the planning action is invoked as the last remaining option.

3.2 Chaining Plans into Higher-Level Plans

The design of a traditional AgentSpeak plan library follows a similar approach to programming in procedural languages, where a designer typically defines fine-grained actions to be the building blocks of more complex operations. These building blocks are then assembled into higher-level procedures to accomplish the main goals of a system. Analogously, an AgentSpeak designer traditionally creates fine-grained *plans* to be the building blocks of more complex operations, typically defining more than one plan to satisfy the same goal (*i.e.* sharing the same trigger condition), while specifying the situations in which it is applicable through the context part of each plan. Here, we are likening STRIPS actions to low-level AgentSpeak *plans*, since the effects of primitive AgentSpeak actions are not explicitly defined in an agent description. For example, an agent that has to move around in a city could know many ways of going from one place to another depending on which vehicle is available to it, such as by walking or driving a car, as shown in Table 2.

Modelling STRIPS operators to be supplied to a planning algorithm is similar to the definition of these building-block procedures. In both cases, it is important that operators to be used sequentially *fit*. That is, the results from applying one operator should be compatible with the application of the possible subsequent operators, matching the effects of one operator to the preconditions of the next operator.

Once the building-block procedures are defined, higher-level operations must be defined to fulfil the broader goals of a system by combining these building blocks. In a traditional AgentSpeak plan library, higher-level plans to achieve broader goals contain a series of goals to be achieved by the lower-level operations. This construction of higher-level plans that make use of lower-level ones is analogous to the planning performed by a propositional planning system. By doing the *planning themselves, designers* must cope with every foreseeable situation the agent might find itself in, and generate higher-level plans combining lower-level tasks accordingly. Moreover, the designer must make sure that the subplans being used do not lead to conflicting situations. This is precisely the responsibility we intend to delegate to a STRIPS planner.

Plans resulting from propositional planning can then be converted into sequences of AgentSpeak achievement goals to comprise the body of new plans available within an agent's plan library. In this approach, an agent can still have high-level plans pre-defined by the designer, so that routine tasks can be handled exactly as intended. At the same time, if an unforeseen situation presents itself to the agent, it has the flexibility of finding novel ways to solve problems, while augmenting the agent's plan library in the process.

Clearly, lower-level plans defined by the designer can (and often will) include the invocation of *atomic actions* intended to generate some effect on the environment. Since the effects of these actions are not usually explicitly specified in AgentSpeak (another example of reasoning delegated to the designer), an agent cannot reason about the consequences of these actions. When designing agents using our model, we expect designers to explicitly define the consequences of executing a given AgentSpeak plan in terms of belief additions and deletions in the plan body as well as atomic action invocations. The conversion process can then ignore atomic action invocations when generating a STRIPS specification.

3.3 Translating AgentSpeak into STRIPS

Once the need for planning is detected, the plan in Table 1 is invoked so that the agent can tap into a planner component. The process of linking an agent to a propositional planning algorithm includes converting an AgentSpeak plan library into propositional planning operators, declarative goals into goal-state specifications, and the agent beliefs into the initial-state specification for a planning problem. After the planner yields a solution, the ensuing STRIPS plan is translated into an AgentSpeak plan in which the operators resulting from the planning become subgoals. That is, the execution of each operator listed in the STRIPS plan is analogous to the insertion of the AgentSpeak plan that corresponded to that operator when the STRIPS problem was created.

Plans in AgentSpeak are represented by a header comprising a triggering condition and a context, as well as a body describing the steps the agent takes when a plan is selected for execution. If e is a triggering event, $b_1, \ldots, b_m$ are belief literals, and $h_1, \ldots, h_n$ are goals or actions, then $e : b_1 \& \ldots \& b_m \leftarrow h_1; \ldots; h_n$. is a plan. As an example, let us consider a triggering plan for accomplishing !move(A,B) corresponding to a movement from A to B, where:

- e is !move(A,B);
- at(A) & not at(B) are belief literals; and
- -at(A); +at(B). is the plan body, containing information about belief additions and deletions.

The plan is then as follows:

```
+!move(A,B) : at(A) & not at(B)
    <- -at(A);
       +at(B).
```

When this plan is executed, it results in the agent believing it is no longer in position A, and then believing it is in position B. For an agent to rationally want to move from A to B, it must believe it is at position A and not already at position B.

In the classical STRIPS notation, operators have four components: an identifier, a set of preconditions, a set of predicates to be added (*add*), and a set of predicates to be deleted (*del*). For example, the same move operator can be represented in STRIPS following the correspondence illustrated in Figure 3, in which we convert the AgentSpeak invocation condition into a STRIPS operator header, a context condition into an operator precondition, and the plan body is used to derive add and delete lists.

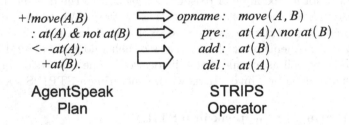

AgentSpeak
Plan

STRIPS
Operator

Fig. 3. Correspondence between an AgentSpeak plan and a STRIPS operator

A relationship between these two definitions is not hard to establish, and we define the following algorithm for converting AgentSpeak plans into STRIPS operators. Let e be a triggering event, $b_1 \& \ldots \& b_m$ a conjunction of belief literals representing a plan's context, and $a_1, \ldots, a_n$ be belief addition actions and $d_1, \ldots, d_o$ be belief deletion actions within a plan's body. All of these elements can be represented in a single AgentSpeak plan. Moreover let *opname* be the operator name and parameters, *pre* be the preconditions of the operator, *add* the predicate addition list and *del* the predicate deletion list. Mapping an AgentSpeak plan into STRIPS operators is accomplished as follows:

1. $opname = e$
2. $pre = b_1 \& \ldots \& b_m$
3. $add = a_1, \ldots, a_n$
4. $del = d_1, \ldots, d_o$

In Section 3.1 we introduced the representation of a conjunction of desired goals as the predicate $goal\_conj([b_1, \ldots, b_n])$. The list $[b_1, \ldots, b_n]$ of desires is directly translated into the goal state of a STRIPS problem. Moreover, the initial state specification for a STRIPS problem is generated directly from the agent's belief database.

3.4 Executing Generated Plans

The STRIPS problem generated from the set of operators, initial state and goal state is then processed by a propositional planner. If the planner fails to generate a propositional plan for that conjunction of literals, the plan in Table 1 fails immediately and this goal is deemed unachievable, otherwise the resulting propositional plan is converted into an AgentSpeak plan and added to the intention structure.

A propositional plan from a STRIPS planner is in the form of a sequence $op_1, \ldots, op_n$ of operator names and instantiated parameters. We define a new AgentSpeak plan in Table 3, where $goal\_conj(Goals)$ is the event that initially caused the planner to be invoked.

Table 3. AgentSpeak plan generated from a STRIPS plan

$$+goal\_conj\ (Goals) : true$$
$$\leftarrow !op_1; \ldots; !op_n.$$

Immediately after adding the new plan to the plan library, the event $goal\_conj(Goals)$ is reposted to the agent's intention structure, causing the generated plan to be executed. Plans generated in this fashion are admittedly simple, since the development of a complete process of plan generalisation is not a trivial matter since, for instance, it involves solving the issue of deriving the context condition adequately. An extremely simple solution for this problem uses the entire belief base of the agent as context for that plan, but this solution includes a great number of beliefs that are probably irrelevant to the goal at hand, severely limiting this plan's future applicability.

Another solution involves replicating the preconditions of the first operator for the new plan, but this could also lead the agent to fail to execute the plan later on. We have developed an algorithm to derive a minimal set of preconditions, which we omit here due to space constraints, showing instead the simple solution of using a constantly true context. Another possible refinement to the conversion of a STRIPS plan into an AgentSpeak plan is to allow the same generated plan to be reused to handle side-effects of the set of goals that led to its generation. For example, a plan for a conjunction of goals g can be used to achieve any subset g' of g.

In the ensuing execution of the generated plan, the fact that multiple concurrent plans might be stacked in an agent's intentions structure must also be addressed. There are multiple ways of addressing this issue, namely:

1. delegate the analysis and resolution of conflicting interaction between plans to the designer;
2. implement provisions to ensure that the plans used by the planner process are executed atomically;
3. drop the entire intention structure before plan adoption, invoking some forward recovery plan, and prevent new intentions from being adopted during plan execution; and
4. analyse the current intention structure and prospective plan steps during planning to ensure they do not interfere with each other.

The first way to resolve concurrency problems, by delegating resolution to the designer, is the traditional solution in an AgentSpeak context, but it is clearly not acceptable, since the main goal of our extension is to diminish the amount of designer tasks. On the other hand, the last alternative, avoiding plan interference, involves the introduction of a complex analysis procedure to solve a very limited number of potential conflicts. In the third option, an agent drops its intentions to prevent concurrently executing plans from interfering with the new plan, which was created without regard for the current intention structure. This alternative requires the existence of forward recovery *abort plans*, such as those described by Thangarajah *et al.* [11].

For our experiments we considered the second and third ways of dealing with concurrency problems and, in the prototype described in Section 4, we opted to enable the agent to execute dynamically generated plans atomically (by preventing other intentions from being selected from the stack while a dynamic plan is being executed).

3.5   Coping with Failure

The possibility of generating new plans at runtime can also be used as an alternative when plans previously selected from the plan library have failed to achieve a certain goal. Constructs for handling these failures are available in Jason [12] and CANPLAN [11], and consist of associating an *abort* plan to be executed when the plan selected to handle an event or goal fails. In Jason this construct is expressed as a goal deletion $(-!g)$. For example, in our system, when a newly generated plan to achieve $!goal\_conj([dg_1, \ldots, dg_N])$ fails, we can attempt to invoke the planner again to find an alternative plan to achieve these declarative goals by including the plan shown in Table 4.

In addition, the application of our planning approach would be beneficial for agents that use a more flexible commitment strategy, such as in the case of CANPLAN2 [13]. In this architecture, multiple plan-library plans are attempted in sequence, until either the agent interpreter concludes that the goal is impossible or all *known* plans have failed. In these situations, an external planner can be

Table 4. Using the planner action to recover from plan failure

$$-!goal\_conj([dg_1, \ldots, dg_N]) : true \leftarrow plan([dg_1, \ldots, dg_N]).$$

invoked to try to generate new plans until it also finds that the desired goals are impossible.

4   Experiments and Results

We have implemented the planning action described in Section 3 using Jason [14], which is an open-source Java implementation of AgentSpeak that includes a number of extensions, such as facilities for communication and distribution. In addition to providing an interpreter for the agent language, Jason has an object-oriented API for the development of *actions* available to the agents being developed. Since planning is to be performed as part of a regular AgentSpeak plan, the planning action encapsulates the conversion process of Section 3.3 using Jason's *internal actions*.

This implementation was used in a number of toy problems, such as the Blocks world used with the original STRIPS planner [10], as well as some examples from the AgentSpeak literature [3]. Solutions for these problems were created using both a procedural approach characteristic of traditional AgentSpeak agents, and a declarative one, in which high-level plans are omitted and left to be derived by the planning system. This switch in the method for describing agents results in a reduction of the plan description size, as it is no longer necessary to enumerate relevant combinations of lower-level plans for the agent to be able to react to different situations.

In terms of complexity the most computationally demanding part of our architecture is the planning process, which can vary significantly depending on the specific planner being used. The complexity of solving propositional planning problems depends on the number of pre-conditions and post-conditions of the operators in a certain domain [15], varying from polynomial to NP-complete and PSPACE-complete complexity. On the other hand, the conversion process into STRIPS is clearly very simple, having linear complexity on the number of pre-conditions and post-conditions of the operators being converted. The same linear complexity applies to the conversion from a STRIPS plan into an AgentSpeak plan.

Rao [3] uses a simple example agent to describe the derivations performed by an AgentSpeak interpreter. This agent detects when waste appears in a particular road lane, and disposes of it in a waste bin. The original plan library for the agent is as follows:

```
% Plan 1
+location(waste, X)
                : location(robot,X) &
                  location(bin,Y)
                <- pick(waste);
                   !location(robot,Y);
                   drop(waste).
% Plan 2
+!location(robot, X)
                : location(robot,X)
                <- true.
% Plan 3
+!location(robot, X)
                : location(robot,Y) &
                  not X = Y &
                  adjacent(Y,Z)&
                  not location(car,Z)
                <- move(Y, Z);
                   !location(robot, X).
```

Using Plan 1, whenever an agent detects waste in its current position, the agent will pick up the waste, move to the location of the waste bin and drop it. In this plan library, the agent's movement is achieved by an internal action, move(Y,Z), and the agent has no way of explicitly reasoning about it. Moreover, if an agent has to perform multiple moves, recursive instantiations of Plan 3 in this library are stacked in the agent's intention structure, until the recursion stop condition is reached in Plan 2.

In order to be able to call a planner we need to modify the portion of the plan library responsible for the agent's movement (*i.e.* the last two plans) into a declarative description yielding the following plan library:

```
+location(waste, X)
        : location(robot, X) &
          location(bin, Y)
        <- pick(waste);
           +goal_conj([location(robot,Y)]);
           drop(waste).

+!move(X,Y)
        : location(robot,X) &
          not X = Y &
          not location(car,Y) &
              adjacent(X,Y)
        <- -location(robot,X);
           +location(robot,Y);
           move(X,Y).
```

The new plan library includes a description of the preconditions and effects of the move(X,Y) action. This is the action that is to be handled by the planning process, and the agent derives the sequence of movements required to reach the waste bin by *desiring* to be in the position of the bin. In order to specify this desire, the plan to dispose of the waste includes a step to add the desire +goal_conj([location(robot,Y)]), which causes the planner to be invoked. Here, the atomic action to move(X,Y) is also included in the plan specification so that when !move(X,Y) is invoked, the agent not only updates its beliefs about the movement, but actually moves in the environment. Unlike the original plan library, however, the agent can plan its movements before starting to execute them, and will only start carrying out these actions if it has found the entire sequence of movements required to reach the desired location.

5   Related Work

Work on the declarative nature of goals as a means to achieve greater autonomy for an agent is being pursued by a number of researchers. Here we consider the approaches to declarative goals currently being investigated, namely those of Hübner *et al.* (Jason) [16], van Riemsdijk *et al.* [17] and Meneguzzi *et al.* [18]. There are multiple interpretations as to the requirements and properties of declarative goals for an agent interpreter, and while some models consist of an agent that performs planning from first principles whenever a goal is selected, others argue that the only crucial aspect of an architecture that handles declarative goals is the specification of target world states that can be reached using the traditional procedural approach.

5.1   Jason

A notion of declarative goals for AgentSpeak that takes advantage of the context part of the plans (representing the moment an implicit goal becomes relevant) was defined by Hübner *et al.* [16], and implemented in Jason [14]. More specifically, plans that share the same triggering condition refer to the achievement of the same goal, so that a goal can only be considered impossible for a given agent if all plans with the same triggering condition have been attempted and failed. In this extended AgentSpeak interpreter, these plans are modified so that the last action of every plan consists of testing for the fulfilment of the declared goal, and then the plans are grouped and executed in sequence until one finishes successfully. A plan only succeeds if at the end of its execution an agent can verify that its intended goal has been achieved. This approach retains the explicitly procedural approach to agent operation (a pre-compiled plan library describing sequences of steps that the agent can perform to accomplish its goals), only adding a more robust layer for handling plan-failure.

5.2   X-BDI

X-BDI [19] was the first agent model that includes a recognisably declarative goal semantics. An X-BDI agent is defined by a set of beliefs, a set of desires, and a set of operators that manipulate the world. The agent refines the set of desires through various constraints on the viability of each desire until it generates a set containing the highest priority desires that are possible and mutually consistent. During this process the agent selects the operators that will be applied to the world in order to fulfil the selected desires in a process that is analogous to planning. The key aspect of X-BDI is that desires express *world-states* rather than triggers for the execution of pre-defined plans, leaving the composition of plans from world-changing operators to the agent interpreter.

5.3   Formalisations of Declarative Goals

Several researchers have worked on a family of declarative agent languages and investigated possible semantics for these languages [20,17]. All of these languages have in common the notion that an agent is defined in terms of beliefs, goals and capabilities, which are interpreted in such a way as to select and apply capabilities in order to fulfil an agent's goals. These approaches have evolved from GOAL [20] into a declarative semantics very similar to that of X-BDI [19], in which an agent's desires express *world-states* which must be achieved by the agent selection and application of capabilities.

5.4   Discussion

In addition to the models described in this section, variations of the way an agent interpreter handles declarative goals have also been described. These approaches advocate the use of fast propositional planners to verify the existence of a sequence of actions that fulfil a declarative goal [18]. The planning process in this setting allows the consideration of the entire set of available operators to create new plans, providing a degree of flexibility to the agent's behaviour. Our research has not dealt with multi-agent issues so far, but the approach taken by Coo-BDI [21] to share plans between agents might provide an interesting extension to our architecture. The exchange of new plans might offset the sometimes significant time needed to create plans from scratch by allowing agents to request the help of other planning-capable agents.

The approaches in Sections 5.1 and 5.3 deal with important aspects of declarative goals in agent systems, such as the verification of accomplishment and logical properties of such systems. However, support for declarative goals in Jason still requires a designer to specify high-level plans, while the formalisms described by van Riemsdijk lack any analysis of the practicality of their implementation. Though X-BDI implements a truly declarative agent specification language, the language is very far from mainstream acceptance, and the underlying logic system used in X-BDI suffers from a stream of efficiency problems.

6   Concluding Remarks

In this paper we have demonstrated how the addition of a planning component can augment the capabilities of a plan library-based agent. In order to exploit the planning capability, the agent uses a special planning action to create high-level plans by composing specially designed plans within an agent's plan library. This assumes no modification in the AgentSpeak language, and allows an agent to be defined so that *built-in* plans can still be defined for common tasks, while allowing for a degree of flexibility for the agent to act in unforseen situations. Our system can also be viewed as a way to extend the declarative goal semantics proposed by Hübner *et al.* [16], in that it allows an agent designer to specify only desired world-states and basic capabilities, relying on the planning component to form plans at runtime. Even though the idea of translating BDI states into STRIPS problems is not new [18], our idea of an encapsulated planning action allows the usage of any other planning formalism sufficiently compatible with the BDI model.

Recent approaches to the programming of agents based on declarative goals rely on mechanisms of plan selection and verification. However, we argue that a declarative model of agent programming must include not only constructs for verifying the accomplishment of an explicit world-state (which is an important capability in any declarative agent), but also a way in which an agent designer can specify *only* the world states the agent has to achieve and the description of atomic operators allowing an underlying *engine* to derive plans at runtime. In this paper we argue that propositional planning can provide one such engine, drawing on agent descriptions that include atomic actions and desired states, and leaving the derivation of actual plans for the agent at runtime.

The addition of a planning component to a BDI agent model has been recently revisited by other researchers, especially by Sardiña *et al.* [22] and Walczak *et al.* [23]. The former describes a BDI programming language that incorporates Hierarchical Task Networks (HTN) planning by exploring the similarities between these two formalisms, but this approach fails to address the fact that designers must specify rules for HTN planning in the same way in which they would decompose multiple plans in a traditional BDI agent. The latter approach is based on a specially adapted planner to support the agent, preventing the model from taking advantage of novel approaches to planning.

The prototype implemented for the evaluation of the extensions described in this paper has been empirically tested for a number of small problems, but, further testing and refinement of this prototype is still required, for instance, to evaluate how interactions between the addition of new plans will affect the existing plan library. The system can also be improved in a number of ways in order to better exploit the underlying planner component. For example, the effort spent on planning can be moderated by a quantitative model of control, so that an agent can decide to spend a set amount of computational effort into the planning process before it concludes the goal is not worth pursuing. This could be implemented by changing the definition of $goal\_conj(Goals)$ to include a representation of motivational model $goal\_conj(Goals, Motivation)$, which can be used to tune the planner and set hard limits to the amount of planning effort devoted to achieving that specific desire.

As indicated above, the key contribution of this paper is a technique that allows procedural agent architectures to use state-space (and hence, declarative) planners to augment flexibility at runtime, thus leveraging advances in planning algorithms. It is important to point out that previous efforts exploring the use of HTN planning do not change the essential procedural mode of reasoning of the corresponding agent architectures, as argued by Sardiña *et al.* [22]. State-space planners operate on a declarative description of the desired goal state, and our conversion process effectively allows a designer to use an AgentSpeak-like language in a declarative way, something which previous planning architectures do not allow. Finally, we are currently working on addressing some of the limitations we have identified regarding the generation and execution of concurrent plans for multiagent scenarios, considering the use of external imported plans such as in Coo-AgentSpeak [24].

Acknowledgments. The first author is supported by Coordenação de Aperfeiçoamento de Pessoal de Nível Superior (CAPES) of the Brazilian Ministry of Education. We would like to thank Rafael Bordini and Jomi Hübner for their support regarding the programming of AgentSpeak agents in their Jason implementation, as well as the discussion of many issues regarding planning and declarative goals.

References

1. Ingrand, F.F., Georgeff, M.P., Rao, A.S.: An architecture for real-time reasoning and system control. IEEE Expert, Knowledge-Based Diagnosis in Process Engineering 7(6), 33–44 (1992)
2. d'Inverno, M., Luck, M., Georgeff, M., Kinny, D., Wooldridge, M.: The dMARS Architecture: A Specification of the Distributed Multi-Agent Reasoning System. Autonomous Agents and Multi-Agent Systems 9(1-2), 5–53 (2004)
3. Rao, A.S.: AgentSpeak(L): BDI agents speak out in a logical computable language. In: Perram, J., Van de Velde, W. (eds.) MAAMAW 1996. LNCS, vol. 1038, pp. 42–55. Springer, Heidelberg (1996)
4. van Riemsdijk, B., van der Hoek, W., Meyer, J.J.C.: Agent programming in dribble: from beliefs to goals using plans. In: Proceedings of the Second International Joint Conference on Autonomous Agents and Multiagent Systems, pp. 393–400. ACM Press, New York (2003)
5. Bordini, R.H., Dastani, M., Dix, J., Fallah-Seghrouchni, A.E.: Multi-Agent Programming: Languages, Platforms and Applications. In: Multiagent Systems, Artificial Societies, and Simulated Organizations, vol. 15, Springer, Heidelberg (2005)
6. Rao, A.S., Georgeff, M.P.: BDI-agents: from theory to practice. In: Proceedings of the First International Conference on Multiagent Systems, San Francisco, pp. 312–319 (1995)
7. d'Inverno, M., Luck, M.: Engineering AgentSpeak(L): A formal computational model. Journal of Logic and Computation 8(3), 233–260 (1998)
8. Georgeff, M.P., Ingrand, F.F.: Monitoring and control of spacecraft systems using procedural reasoning. In: Proceedings of the Space Operations and Robotics Workshop, Houston, USA (1989)

9. Fox, M., Long, D.: PDDL2.1: An Extension to PDDL for Expressing Temporal Planning Domains. Journal of Artificial Intelligence Research 20, 61–124 (2003)
10. Fikes, R., Nilsson, N.: STRIPS: A new approach to the application of theorem proving to problem solving. Artificial Intelligence 2(3-4), 189–208 (1971)
11. Thangarajah, J., Harland, J., Morley, D., Yorke-Smith, N.: Aborting tasks in BDI agents. In: Proceedings of the Sixth International Joint Conference on Autonomous Agents and Multiagent Systems, pp. 8–15 (2007)
12. Bordini, R.H., Hübner, J.F.: Bdi agent programming in agentspeak using jason. In: Toni, F., Torroni, P. (eds.) Computational Logic in Multi-Agent Systems. LNCS (LNAI), vol. 3900, pp. 143–164. Springer, Heidelberg (2006)
13. Sardina, S., Padgham, L.: Goals in the context of BDI plan failure and planning. In: Proceedings of the Sixth International Joint Conference on Autonomous Agents and Multiagent Systems, pp. 16–23 (2007)
14. Bordini, R.H., Hübner, J.F., Vieira, R.: Jason and the golden fleece of agent-oriented programming. In: Bordini, R.H., Dastani, M., Dix, J., Fallah-Seghrouchni, A.E. (eds.) Multi-Agent Programming: Languages, Platforms and Applications, pp. 3–37. Springer, Heidelberg (2005)
15. Bylander, T.: The computational complexity of propositional STRIPS planning. Artificial Intelligence 69(1-2), 165–204 (1994)
16. Hübner, J.F., Bordini, R.H., Wooldridge, M.: Programming declarative goals using plan patterns. In: Baldoni, M., Endriss, U. (eds.) DALT 2006. LNCS (LNAI), vol. 4327, pp. 123–140. Springer, Heidelberg (2006)
17. van Riemsdijk, M.B., Dastani, M., Meyer, J.J.C.: Semantics of declarative goals in agent programming. In: Proceedings of the Fourth International Joint Conference on Autonomous Agents and Multiagent Systems, Utrecht, The Netherlands, pp. 133–140. ACM Press, New York (2005)
18. Meneguzzi, F.R., Zorzo, A.F., Móra, M.D.C.: Propositional planning in BDI agents. In: Proceedings of the 2004 ACM Symposium on Applied Computing, Nicosia, Cyprus, pp. 58–63. ACM Press, New York (2004)
19. Móra, M.d.C., Lopes, J.G.P., Vicari, R.M., Coelho, H.: BDI models and systems: Bridging the gap. In: Rao, A.S., Singh, M.P., Müller, J.P. (eds.) ATAL 1998. LNCS (LNAI), vol. 1555, pp. 11–27. Springer, Heidelberg (1999)
20. Hindriks, K.V., de Boer, F.S., van der Hoek, W., Meyer, J.J.C.: Agent programming with declarative goals. In: Castelfranchi, C., Lespérance, Y. (eds.) ATAL 2000. LNCS (LNAI), vol. 1986, pp. 228–243. Springer, Heidelberg (2001)
21. Ancona, D., Mascardi, V.: Coo-BDI: Extending the BDI Model with Cooperativity. In: Leite, J.A., Omicini, A., Sterling, L., Torroni, P. (eds.) DALT 2003. LNCS (LNAI), vol. 2990, pp. 109–134. Springer, Heidelberg (2004)
22. Sardina, S., de Silva, L., Padgham, L.: Hierarchical Planning in BDI Agent Programming Languages: A Formal Approach. In: Proceedings of the Fifth International Joint Conference on Autonomous Agents and Multiagent Systems, pp. 1001–1008. ACM Press, New York (2006)
23. Walczak, A., Braubach, L., Pokahr, A., Lamersdorf, W.: Augmenting BDI Agents with Deliberative Planning Techniques. In: Programming Multi-Agent Systems, 4th International Workshop. LNCS, vol. 4411, pp. 113–127 (2006)
24. Ancona, D., Mascardi, V., Hübner, J.F., Bordini, R.H.: Coo-agentspeak: Cooperation in agentspeak through plan exchange. In: Proceedings of the Third International Joint Conference on Autonomous Agents and Multiagent Systems, pp. 696–705 (2004)

Satisfying Maintenance Goals

Koen V. Hindriks[1] and M. Birna van Riemsdijk[2]

[1] EEMCS, Delft University of Technology, Delft, The Netherlands
[2] LMU, Munich, Germany

Abstract. A rational agent derives its choice of action from its beliefs and goals. Goals can be distinguished into achievement goals and maintenance goals. The aim of this paper is to define a mechanism which ensures the satisfaction of maintenance goals. We argue that such a mechanism requires the agent to look ahead, in order to make sure that the execution of actions does not lead to a violation of a maintenance goal. That is, maintenance goals may constrain the agent in choosing its actions. We propose a formal semantics of maintenance goals based on the notion of lookahead, and analyze the semantics by proving some properties. Additionally, we discuss the issue of achievement goal revision, in case the maintenance goals are so restrictive that all courses of action for satisfying achievement goals will lead to a violation of maintenance goals.

1 Introduction

The research presented in this paper concerns the role of *maintenance goals* in the selection of actions by a rational agent. A rational agent aims at satisfying its goals, which may include both achievement goals as well as maintenance goals. Achievement goals define states that are to be achieved, whereas maintenance goals define states that must remain true.

The distinction between achievement and maintenance goals is common in the literature about rational agents. However, whereas various proposals for computational semantics and programming frameworks that include achievement goals are available [3,5,11,14,17,18], maintenance goals have received less attention [3,4,6]. In this paper we investigate a semantics for maintenance goals. Our aim is to define a mechanism which ensures the satisfaction of maintenance goals that can be integrated into various agent programming languages.

Achievement goals in agent programming frameworks are typically used in combination with rules that express which action or plan an agent may execute in certain circumstances in order to achieve a particular achievement goal. In such a setting, achievement goals thus trigger the execution of a course of action. A maintenance goal can have a similar role in agent programming frameworks, in the sense that it can trigger an agent to perform actions in order to ensure that a maintenance goal is not violated, or to take action to reestablish the maintenance goal if it is violated.

Implementing maintenance goals using conditions to trigger the execution of actions, however, is not sufficient to guarantee that maintenance goals are

M. Baldoni et al. (Eds.): DALT 2007, LNAI 4897, pp. 86–103, 2008.

not violated. In order to prevent the violation of a maintenance goal, an agent may sometimes have to *refrain* from performing an action that the agent would otherwise have selected, e.g., to satisfy one of its achievement goals [6]. A comprehensive framework for maintenance goals should thus not only incorporate an action selection mechanism based on triggering conditions, but should also take into account the *constraining* role of maintenance goals. As we will show, a selection mechanism that is based on this constraining role can also be used to actively ensure that a maintenance goal is not violated.

We argue that taking into account the constraining role of maintenance goals requires some kind of *lookahead* mechanism, which allows the agent to determine whether certain actions or plans it would like to perform might lead to the violation of one of its maintenance goals. The main aim of this paper is to investigate how the semantics of maintenance goals can be formally defined through such a lookahead mechanism. We analyze the semantics formally by proving several properties. It is important to note that one advantage of giving a formal semantics, is the fact that one can formally prove certain properties. This is important in order to get a clear understanding of the phenomenon under investigation. Besides providing a formal semantics and analysis of maintenance goals, we discuss the issue of achievement goal revision, in case the maintenance goals are so restrictive that all plans for satisfying achievement goals will lead to a violation of maintenance goals.

The paper is organized as follows. In Section 2, a motivating example is introduced to illustrate the main ideas throughout the paper. Our investigations are carried out in the context of the agent programming language GOAL [5], which is briefly introduced in Section 3. The results presented, however, are general and can be integrated into any agent framework. Section 4 formally defines a lookahead mechanism that ensures selected actions do not violate the agent's maintenance goals. The look-ahead mechanism introduced, however, may overconstrain an agent's decision procedure. In Section 5 this problem is discussed and a revision procedure is suggested to resolve it. Section 6 concludes the paper, outlines some directions for future work, and discusses related work.

2 Motivating Example: A Carrier Agent

In this section, a simple scenario involving a carrier agent is presented in order to illustrate the role of maintenance goals in action selection and the reasoning we believe is involved in avoiding violation of maintenance goals.

2.1 The Basic Scenario

The setting is as follows. Consider an agent who wants to bring parcels from some location A to a location B, using its truck. The distance between A and B is too large to make it without refueling, and so, in order not to end up without gas, the agent needs to stop every once in a while to refuel. The fact that the agent does not want to end up without gas, can be modeled as a maintenance goal.[1] This maintenance goal *constrains* the actions of the agent, as it is not supposed to drive on in order to fulfil its goal of delivering the parcels, if driving on would cause it to run out of gas.

The action of driving is an action that the agent can take in order to fulfil its achievement goal of delivering the parcels. Other actions that the agent has at its disposal, may be used to *actively* ensure that the agent's maintenance goals are not violated. In the example scenario, the action of refueling can be viewed as an action of this kind (although, in this example, not violating the maintenance goal is also instrumental for achieving the achievement goal). Maintenance goals thus on the one hand constrain the agent's actions, but may also induce the agent to take preventive actions to make sure maintenance goals are not violated.

An essential reasoning mechanism in order to ensure that the agent does not take actions that would violate the agent's maintenance goals is a *lookahead* mechanism. In the example scenario, the agent should reason about the distance to the next gas station and the amount of fuel it has left, in order to make sure it does not end up without fuel between two gas stations. That is, it should in one way or another, reason about the consequences of possible future sequences of actions in order to be able to choose those actions that will not lead to a violation of maintenance goals at some point in the future.

2.2   Conflicts Between Achievement and Maintenance Goals

In this simple scenario so far, there is no conflict between the agent's maintenance goals and achievement goals. It is perfectly possible for the agent to deliver its parcels without running out of gas, as long as it refuels in time. It may, however, sometimes be the case that conflicts between achievement goals and maintenance goals arise, in the sense that in order to achieve an achievement goal, the agent will have to violate a maintenance goal.

In the example scenario, such a conflict may arise if the agent has the additional maintenance goal of making sure that the weight of truck load stays below a certain threshold. Assuming that the total weight of the parcels exceeds this threshold, and assuming that the agent cannot drive back and forth between A and B (e.g., because the agent has loaned the truck and has to return it after arriving at location B), there is a conflict between the achievement goal of bringing all the parcels from A to B, and not overloading the truck.

Such a situation of conflict may result in the agent not doing anything anymore at a certain point. That is, it may be the case that any action the agent is able to do to achieve its achievement goal is not allowed because this would lead to a violation of the agent's maintenance goal, and, moreover, there is no possibility to actively ensure that the maintenance goal is not violated. In general, there are several possibilities of dealing with such a situation.

The first option is not to do anything about it. The intuition here is that the agent should never violate its maintenance goals, i.e., maintenance goals are *hard constraints*, and the agent wants "all or nothing" when it comes to

---

[1] Other papers [3,4,6] have used a similar maintenance goal in some of their examples.

its achievement goals. In the example scenario, it may be the case that it is of utmost importance that the truck is not overloaded, e.g., because the truck has a device with which the weight of the freight is measured, and if the weight exceeds the threshold the truck cannot start. Moreover, it may be the case that bringing the parcels only makes sense if all parcels are brought, e.g., because the parcels contain parts of a closet and there is no use for bringing only part of the closet. Put differently, the utility of delivering only part of the parcels is zero.

A second option is to allow the agent to *violate its maintenance goals*, if this is absolutely necessary in order to achieve an achievement goal. An intuitive implementation of such a mechanism would have to make sure that the agent really only violates maintenance goals if there is no way around it, and if this is necessary, it should try to "minimize" the violation, e.g., by trying to make sure that the maintenance goal is satisfied again as soon as possible after the achievement goal that was the reason to violate the maintenance goal has been satisified. In the example scenario, it may be the case that overloading the truck does not do too much harm, as long as this does not happen too often. It is then important that the truck is unloaded as soon as the destination is reached.

The third option is to *modify the achievement goal*, such that the modified achievement goal does not conflict anymore with the agent's maintenance goals. The idea here is that there might be achievement goals that can be achieved "to a certain degree", i.e., it might be possible to "weaken" the achievement goal, in case it would conflict with a maintenance goal. In the example scenario, the conflict between the achievement goal of getting all parcels at location A, and the maintenance goal of not overloading the truck, could be resolved by modifying the achievement goal such that the agent settles on bringing only *part* of the parcels to location B. The decision of which parcels to leave behind can be based on the weight of the parcels, i.e., the weight of the parcels to be taken along should not exceed the threshold, and on the utility of getting certain parcels at the destination, i.e., some parcels may be more important than others.

Of course, combinations of these possibilities of dealing with conflicts are also possible. Such combinations might define certain maintenance goals as hard constraints and certain achievement goals as "all or nothing" goals, while other maintenance goals and achievement goals may be violated or modified, respectively. In this paper, however, we focus on the third option, i.e., we view maintenance goals as hard constraints, and opt for the modification or weakening of achievement goals in case a conflict with a maintenance goal arises. In domains in which maintenance goals relate, e.g., to the limited availability of resources and time which cannot easily be lifted the third strategy will typically be valid.

3   The GOAL Language

In this section, the GOAL programming language [5,10] is briefly introduced and a GOAL agent that implements a simplified version of the carrier agent of Section 2.1 is presented. A GOAL agent selects actions on the basis of its beliefs and achievement goals, i.e., maintenance goals were not investigated in the original GOAL language. Whenever goals are mentioned in this section, this should thus be interpreted as meaning achievement goals. The definitions we provide in this section are used to make the notion of an agent computation precise, which we use in Section 4 to define the semantics for maintenance goals.

A GOAL program for the carrier agent is specified in Table 1. The program consists of four sections: (1) a set of initial beliefs, collectively called the (initial) *belief base* of the agent, (2) a set of initial achievement goals, called the (initial) *goal base*, (3) a *program section* which consists of a set of conditional actions, and (4) an *action specification* that consists of a specification of the pre- and post-conditions of *basic actions* of the agent. In the example, variables are used as a means for abbreviation; variables should be thought of as being instantiated with the relevant arguments to yield propositions. The constants used in the example denote locations (a, ab1, ab2, b, assumed to be spatially positioned in this order), parcels (p1,p2) and a truck truck. The order of the locations means that if the agent wants to get from a to b, it first has to pass ab1, and then ab2. We use the comma to denote conjunction.

Table 1. GOAL Carrier Agent

```
:beliefs{ loc(p1,a). loc(p2,a). loc(truck,a). loc(gasstation,ab1).
          fuel(2). next(a,ab1). next(ab1,ab2). next(ab2,b). }
:a-goals{ loc(p1,b), loc(p2,b). }
:program{
    if B(loc(truck,X), loc(P,X), X≠Y), G(loc(P,Y)) then load(P).
    if B(loc(truck,a)), ~(B(loc(P,a)), G(loc(P,b))), G(loc(R,b))
        then adopt(loc(truck,b)).
    if G(loc(truck,b)) then move.
    if B(loc(gasstation,X)) then tank.
    if B(loc(truck,X), in(P,truck)), G(loc(P,X)) then unload(P). }
:action-spec{
    move    { :pre{loc(truck,X), next(X,Y), fuel(Z), Z > 0}
              :post{loc(truck,Y), not loc(truck,X), fuel(Z-1), not fuel(Z)} }
    load(P) { :pre{loc(P,X), loc(truck,X)}      :post{in(P,truck), not loc(P,X)} }
    unload(P){ :pre{in(P,truck), loc(truck,X)} :post{loc(P,X), not in(P,truck)} }
    tank    { :pre{loc(truck,X), loc(gasstation,X), fuel(Y), Y<3}
              :post{fuel(3), not fuel(Y)}} }
```

The belief base, typically denoted by Σ, and the goal base, typically denoted by A, together define the *mental state* of a GOAL agent. Mental states should satisfy a number of rationality constraints, which are introduced next.

Definition 1 *(Mental States)*
Assume a language of propositional logic $\mathcal{L}_0$ with the standard entailment relation $\models$ and typical element ϕ. A mental state of a GOAL agent, typically denoted by s, is a pair $\langle \Sigma, A \rangle$ with $\Sigma, A \subseteq \mathcal{L}_0$ where Σ is the belief base, and A with typical element α is the goal base. Additionally, mental states need to satisfy the following *rationality constraints*:

(i)   The belief base is consistent: $\Sigma \not\models \bot$,
(ii) Individual goals are consistent[2]:   for all $\alpha \in A$: $\not\models \neg\alpha$,
(iii) Goals are not believed to be achieved: for all $\alpha \in A$: $\Sigma \not\models \alpha$.

In the example carrier agent, the two parcels and the truck are initially believed to be at location a, represented by loc(p1,a), loc(p2,a), and loc(truck,a). The agent also believes it has two units of fuel, and that the gas station is at location ab1. The initial achievement goal of the agent is to have both parcels at location b, represented by loc(p1,b), loc(p2,b). Note that the carrier agent satisfies the rationality constraints on mental states.

A GOAL agent derives its choice of action from its beliefs and goals. In order to do so, a GOAL agent inspects its mental state by evaluating so-called *mental state conditions*. The syntax and semantics of these conditions is defined next.

Definition 2 *(Mental State Conditions)*
The language $\mathcal{L}_M$ of mental state conditions, typically denoted by ψ, is inductively defined by the two clauses:

- if $\phi \in \mathcal{L}_0$, then $\mathbf{B}\phi, \mathbf{G}\phi \in \mathcal{L}_M$,
- if $\psi_1, \psi_2 \in \mathcal{L}_M$, then $\neg\psi_1, \psi_1 \wedge \psi_2 \in \mathcal{L}_M$.

The truth conditions of mental state conditions ψ, relative to a mental state $s = \langle \Sigma, A \rangle$, are defined by the following four clauses:

$$
\begin{aligned}
s \models_m \mathbf{B}\phi &\quad \text{iff} \quad \Sigma \models \phi, \\
s \models_m \mathbf{G}\phi &\quad \text{iff} \quad \text{there is } \alpha \in A \text{ such that } \alpha \models \phi \text{ and } \Sigma \not\models \phi, \\
s \models_m \neg\psi &\quad \text{iff} \quad s \not\models_m \psi, \\
s \models_m \psi_1 \wedge \psi_2 &\quad \text{iff} \quad s \models_m \psi_1 \text{ and } s \models_m \psi_2.
\end{aligned}
$$

The semantics of $\mathbf{B}\phi$ defines that this holds iff ϕ follows from the belief base under a standard proposition logic entailment relation. The definition of the semantics of $\mathbf{G}\phi$ is somewhat more involved. It specifies that $\mathbf{G}\phi$ holds, iff ϕ is not already believed by the agent, and there is a formula in the goal base from which ϕ follows. Also multiple goals are not required to be consistent which reflects the fact that each goal may be realized at a different moment in time.

In GOAL, two types of actions are distinguished: basic actions and goal update actions. The execution of basic actions updates and modifies the agent's beliefs, apart from changing the agent's environment. Indirectly, a basic action may also affect the goal base of an agent. That is, in case a goal is believed to be achieved after action execution the goal is dropped by the agent and may be removed from the agent's goal base.

In the example program, the way in which the execution of basic actions changes the beliefs of the agent is specified using pre- and post-conditions. The example agent has four basic actions at its disposal, i.e., the actions move, load(P), unload(P), and tank. Through the action move, it can move one position towards location b. Using unload(P) and load(P), it can unload and load the parcel P, respectively, if the agent is at the same location as the parcel. The action tank can be executed if the agent is at location ab1, resulting in the amount of fuel becoming 3.

In the formal definition of GOAL, we use a *transition function* $\mathcal{T}$ to model the effects of basic actions. This function maps a basic action a and a belief base Σ to an updated belief base $\mathcal{T}(\mathbf{a}, \Sigma) = \Sigma'$. The transition function is undefined if an action is not enabled in a mental state. In a GOAL agent, the action specification section of that agent specifies this transition function. In the example agent in Table 1 a STRIPS-like notation is used, where positive literals define the add list and negative literals define the delete list (cf. [12]). (Other, extended action formalisms could be used but for the purpose of this paper a more extended formalism is not needed.) GOAL has two built-in goal update actions: the **adopt**(ϕ) action to adopt a goal, and the **drop**(ϕ) to drop goals from the agent's goal base. An **adopt**(ϕ) action has to satisfy the rationality constraints on mental states, i.e. ϕ must be consistent and not believed by the agent. The **drop**(ϕ) action removes all goals from the goal base that imply ϕ.

Definition 3 *(Mental State Transformer $\mathcal{M}$)*
Let $\mathbf{a}$ be a basic action, $\phi \in \mathcal{L}_0$ and $\mathcal{T}$ be a transition function for basic actions. Then the *mental state transformer function* $\mathcal{M}$ is defined as a mapping from actions and mental states to updated mental states as follows:

$$\mathcal{M}(\mathbf{a}, \langle \Sigma, A \rangle) \qquad = \begin{cases} \langle \Sigma', A \setminus \{\psi \mid \Sigma' \models \psi\} \rangle & \text{if } \mathcal{T}(\mathbf{a}, \Sigma) = \Sigma' \\ \text{undefined} & \text{otherwise} \end{cases}$$

$$\mathcal{M}(\mathbf{adopt}(\phi), \langle \Sigma, A \rangle) = \begin{cases} \langle \Sigma, A \cup \{\phi\} \rangle & \text{if } \not\models \neg\phi \text{ and } \Sigma \not\models \phi \\ \text{undefined} & \text{otherwise} \end{cases}$$

$$\mathcal{M}(\mathbf{drop}(\phi), \langle \Sigma, A \rangle) \ = \langle \Sigma, A \setminus \{\psi \in A \mid \psi \models \phi\} \rangle$$

In order to select the appropriate actions to achieve the goal of having the two parcels at location **b**, our example carrier agent has five conditional actions as listed in the program section of Table 1. A conditional action c has the form **if** ψ **then** $\mathbf{a}$, with $\mathbf{a}$ either a basic action or a goal update action. This conditional action specifies that $\mathbf{a}$ may be performed if the mental state condition ψ and the preconditions of $\mathbf{a}$ hold. In that case we say that conditional action c is *enabled*.

During execution, a GOAL agent selects non-deterministically any of its enabled conditional actions. This is expressed in the following transition rule, describing how an agent gets from one mental state to another.

Definition 4 *(Conditional Action Semantics)*
Let s be a mental state, and $c = $ **if** ψ **then** $\mathbf{a}$ be a conditional action. The transition relation $\xrightarrow{c}$ is the smallest relation induced by the following transition rule.

$$\frac{s \models \psi \quad \mathcal{M}(\mathbf{a}, s) \text{ is defined}}{s \xrightarrow{c} \mathcal{M}(\mathbf{a}, s)}$$

The execution of a GOAL agent results in a *computation*. We define a computation as a sequence of mental states, such that each mental state can be obtained from the previous by applying the transition rule of Definition 4. As GOAL agents are non-deterministic, the semantics of a GOAL agent is defined as the *set* of possible computations of the GOAL agent, where all computations start in the initial mental state of the agent.

Definition 5 *(Agent Computation)*
A computation, typically denoted by t, is an infinite sequence of mental states $s_0, s_1, s_2, \ldots$ such that for each i there is an action c_i and $s_i \xrightarrow{c_i} s_{i+1}$ can be derived using the transition rule of Definition 4, or $s_i \not\xrightarrow{c_i}$ and for all $j > i$, $s_j = s_i$. The meaning $S_{\mathcal{A}}$ of a GOAL agent named $\mathcal{A}$ with initial mental state $\langle \Sigma_0, A_0 \rangle$ is the set of all computations starting in that state.

Observe that a computation is infinite by definition, even if the agent is not able to perform any action anymore from some point in time on. Also note that the concept of an agent computation is a general notion in program semantics that is not particular to GOAL. The notion of a computation can be defined for any agent programming language that is provided with a well-defined operational semantics. For such languages, it is possible to transfer the analysis of maintenance goals in this paper that is based on the notion of a computation and to incorporate the proposed maintenance goal semantics.

Our example carrier agent may execute the following computations. In the initial mental state, the conditional action for loading a parcel is executed, and the agent non-deterministically picks up one of the parcels, followed by another execution of this conditional action to load the other parcel. Consecutively, the only enabled conditional action is the one for adopting the goal loc(truck,b), by which the example agent adopts the goal to be at location b. As the agent now has the goal to be at location b it will execute the enabled action move. After executing the move action, the agent is at location ab1, and has one unit of fuel left.

In this situation, there are two possibilities. The agent can execute another move action, after which the agent will be at location ab2 without any fuel. The other option is that the agent executes the tank action, after which the agent will have three units of fuel while still being at location ab1. If the agent chooses the first option, it will get stuck at ab2, as it has no fuel and there is no possibility to tank. If the agent chooses the second option, it can execute two move actions after tanking and get to location b. Then the only option is to execute the conditional action for unloading parcels two times, after which the achievement goal of having the parcels at location b is reached.

4   Semantics of Maintenance Goals

In this section, we define the semantics of a GOAL agent if this agent is given a set of maintenance goals to satisfy. In defining the operational semantics for maintenance goals, the idea is that agents reason about the result of the execution of their actions, in order to make sure that only those actions are chosen that do not violate the agent's maintenance goals. That is, agents *look ahead* in order to foresee the consequences of their actions. Adding maintenance goals that may have a constraining role makes sense only if the original agent is underspecified, that is, if alternative courses of action are available, as in the case of GOAL agents. Only then can the agent actually *choose* to take actions that do not violate maintenance goals. Intuitively, the idea is thus that the incorporation of maintenance goals leads to the exclusion of (parts of) computations that were allowed in the agent semantics of Definition 5 without maintenance goals.

In the example program of Section 3, we have seen that the carrier agent gets stuck at location ab2 if it does not tank at location ab1. The idea is that such behavior can be prevented by introducing a maintenance goal that expresses that the agent should not be in a situation where it has no fuel left (Table 2).

Table 2. Extension With Maintenance Goals

```
:m-goals{ fuel(X), X > 0. }
```

Syntactically, the introduction of maintenance goals thus poses no problems. Incorporating maintenance goals in the semantics, however, is more involved and is the subject of the remainder of this section. In Section 5 we look at the case that maintenance and achievement goals cannot be satisfied simultaneously.

4.1 Operational Semantics of Maintenance Goals

Ideally, an agent should look ahead infinitely far into the future, in order to be absolutely sure that it does not choose a path that will lead to the violation of a maintenance goal. In practice, however, infinite lookahead cannot be implemented, and presumably it will neither be necessary. We propose a general definition of lookahead, that takes the *number of steps* that an agent may look ahead as a parameter. This parameter is called the *lookahead range*.

In the following, $\Omega \subseteq \mathcal{L}_0$ will denote a set of maintenance goals. A set of maintenance goals will be assumed to be consistent, i.e., $\Omega \not\models \bot$. If maintenance goals are hard constraints, it is not rational to have two maintenance goals that are inconsistent, as it will never be possible to satisfy both maintenance goals. Moreover, we assume that maintenance goals are satisfied initially, i.e., it should be the case that for the initial belief base Σ_0 we have $\Sigma_0 \models \Omega$ (where $\Sigma_0 \models \Omega$ abbreviates $\forall \omega \in \Omega : \Sigma \models \omega$). Also, we take the set of maintenance goals as being static. That is, an agent cannot drop or adopt new maintenance goals. Although there might be situations where one would want to consider dropping or adopting maintenance goals, we think that maintenance goals are intuitively more stable than achievement goals as the former express a kind of background requirements that an agent should always fulfill.

In order to provide a formal definition of the effect of n-step lookahead on the computations of an agent, we first introduce some additional terminology and notation. A *prefix* of a computation t is an initial finite sequence of t or t itself. A prefix of length n of a computation t is denoted by $t^{\langle n \rangle}$ with $n \in \mathbb{N} \cup \{\infty\}$, where $t^{\langle \infty \rangle}$ is defined as t. $\mathbb{N}$ is the set of natural numbers including 0, and ∞ is the first infinite ordinal. We write $p \preceq p'$ to denote that p is a prefix of p'. The order $\preceq$ is lifted to sets as follows: $S \preceq S'$ iff each $p \in S$ is a prefix of some $p' \in S'$. A set S of sequences is called a *chain* if for all $p, p' \in S$ we have either

$p \preccurlyeq p'$ or $p' \preccurlyeq p$. The *least upper bound* of a chain S is denoted by $\sqcup S$. In case of a set S of prefixes of a computation t, $\sqcup S$ is either a maximal element in S (i.e. a prefix that has the greatest finite length), or the computation t itself (which need not be in S); moreover, $\sqcup \emptyset = \epsilon$ with ϵ the empty sequence. Finally, $s \in p$ for s a mental state and p a prefix of a computation abbreviates that s is a state on the prefix p; sometimes s_i is used to denote the ith state in the sequence.

Now we are in a position to formally define how maintenance goals, given an n-step lookahead operator $\lceil_n$, restrict the possible computations of an agent $\mathcal{A}$. First, we define the notion of a *safe prefix* of a computation t, given a set of maintenance goals Ω and the capability to do a lookahead of n steps. The predicate $safe_n(p, \Omega)$, with $n \in \mathbb{N} \cup \{\infty\}$, is true if all states of the prefix p of computation t satisfy the maintenance goals Ω and, in the next n steps of computation t no violation of such a goal will occur, except possibly for the last state. (Note that we leave the computation t implicit in $safe_n(p, \Omega)$.) This corresponds with the behavior of a very cautious agent that will avoid to go in a direction that may lead towards a violation of a maintenance goal. Formally, we define $safe_n(\epsilon, \Omega)$ to be false for technical reasons, and we define $safe_n(t^{\langle k \rangle}, \Omega)$ for prefixes of non-zero length $k > 0$ as follows:

$$safe_n(t^{\langle k \rangle}, \Omega) \text{ iff } \forall s \in t^{\langle k+n-1 \rangle}(\Sigma_s \models \Omega).$$

When the set of maintenance goals Ω is clear from the context, we also simply write $safe_n(t^{\langle k \rangle})$. All states on a safe prefix of a computation t based on n-step lookahead have the property that lookahead does not predict any violations of a maintenance goal in Ω in less then n steps. Note that there is at least one non-empty safe prefix including the initial state using 0-step lookahead since a goal agent initially must believe that its maintenance goals are satisfied. The set of all safe prefixes of computation t is denoted by $Safe_n(t, \Omega)$. Note that the set $Safe_n(t, \Omega)$ is a chain and has a least upper bound, which is the computation t itself when all prefixes of t are safe.

The n-step lookahead operator $\lceil_n$ applied to a computation t and a set of maintenance goals Ω can now be defined in terms of safe prefixes. Using this operator it is easy to define the effect of maintenance goals as hard constraints on the behavior of an agent with an n-step lookahead capability: The semantics $S_{\mathcal{A}}$ of an agent without such goals, i.e. its associated set of computations, is restricted by applying the lookahead operator to each computation in $S_{\mathcal{A}}$ to ensure that an agent with such lookahead capabilities will act cautiously and will never head towards a predicted violation of one of its maintenance goals.

Definition 6 (Lookahead Operator and Semantics of Maintenance Goals)
The n-step lookahead operator $\lceil_n$, applied to a computation t and a set of maintenance goals Ω, is defined as the least upper bound of the set of safe prefixes of t with respect to Ω, and is also lifted to sets of computations.

- The n-step lookahead operator $\lceil_n$ is defined as: $t \lceil_n \Omega = \sqcup Safe_n(t, \Omega)$.
- The lift of $\lceil_n$ to a set S is defined by:

$$S \lceil_n \Omega = \bigcup_{t \in S} \{t \lceil_n \Omega \mid \forall t' \in S : t \lceil_n \Omega \preccurlyeq t' \lceil_n \Omega \Rightarrow t \lceil_n \Omega = t' \lceil_n \Omega\}$$

– Let $\mathcal{A}$ be an agent with an n-step lookahead capability. Then the semantics of $\mathcal{A}$ with a set of maintenance goals Ω is defined as: $S_\mathcal{A}\!\restriction_n\!\Omega$.

The lift of $\restriction_n$ to a set S is the set of all maximal elements of the set $\bigcup_{t \in S} t\!\restriction_n\!\Omega$. Only the maximal elements are taken in order to exclude prefixes p that are a strict prefix of another prefix p' in this set, i.e., $p \prec p'$. The semantics $S_\mathcal{A}\!\restriction_n\!\Omega$ for an agent $\mathcal{A}$ with maintenance goals Ω thus specifies that the agent continues until all further action would lead to a violation within n steps. Note that the set $S_\mathcal{A}\!\restriction_n\!\Omega$ may be empty when the set of maintenance goals Ω is so restrictive that each computation would violate a maintenance goal within n steps.

4.2 Properties

The following proposition says that a lookahead capability with a bigger lookahead range than another one is more restrictive than the latter. Since the semantics implements a cautious strategy towards possible violations of maintenance goals, an agent that detects such potential violations sooner, will act cautiously and will not follow a course of action that may lead to this violation.

Proposition 1. *If $n > m$, then $S_\mathcal{A}\!\restriction_n\!\Omega \preccurlyeq S_\mathcal{A}\!\restriction_m\!\Omega$.*

The proposition suggests that agents with a more powerful lookahead capability, i.e. with a greater lookahead range, possibly are able to satisfy fewer achievement goals than they would be able to satisfy with a less powerful lookahead capability. That is, an agent that does everything to avoid maintenance goal violation will not allow itself to achieve a highly valued goal on a path that will lead to such a violation. Such computation paths may be excluded by the the more powerful lookahead capability while still being allowed by the weaker one.

For the idealized situation where an agent has infinite lookahead, we have the following proposition.

Proposition 2. (Infinite Lookahead Maintenance Goal Semantics)

$$S_\mathcal{A}\!\restriction_\infty\!\Omega = \{t \in S_\mathcal{A} \mid \forall s \in t : \Sigma_s \models \Omega\}$$

This proposition states that an agent with infinite lookahead will only execute a computation that is completely free of maintenance goal violations. For the example carrier agent, if we assume infinite lookahead, any computation where the agent does not tank at location **ab1** are excluded from the semantics. The reason is that in these computations the agent will violate its maintenance goal as it will be at location **ab2** without any fuel.

Although the infinite lookahead semantics is elegant and captures intuitions in a simple manner, such lookahead cannot be implemented. In the next proposition we look at *bounded lookahead* where lookahead ranges are less than ∞.

Proposition 3. (Bounded Lookahead Maintenance Goal Semantics)
Let $n \in \mathbb{N}$. The n-step lookahead semantics $S_\mathcal{A}\!\restriction_n\!\Omega$ is equal to:

$$\bigcup_{t \in S_\mathcal{A}} \{p \prec t \mid safe_n(p)\ \&\ (\forall p', t' : p \preccurlyeq p' \prec t'\ \&\ safe_n(p') \Rightarrow p = p')\} \cup S_\mathcal{A}\!\restriction_\infty\!\Omega$$

Corollary 1. (One-Step Lookahead Maintenance Goal Semantics)
The one-step lookahead semantics $S_\mathcal{A}\lceil_1\Omega$ of an agent $\mathcal{A}$ is equal to:

$$\bigcup_{t\in S_\mathcal{A}} \{p \prec t \mid (\forall s \in p : \Sigma_s \models \Omega) \ \& \ (\forall t' : p \prec t' \ \& \ s_{k+1} \in t' \Rightarrow \Sigma_{s_{k+1}} \not\models \Omega)\}$$
$$\cup \ S_\mathcal{A}\lceil_\infty\Omega$$

Bounded lookahead implies that the agent may choose a path which inevitably will violate a maintenance goal because potential violations of the maintenance goal lie outside of the agent's lookahead range. As discussed above, it might be the case that on such a path an achievement goal is achieved that would never have been achieved if the agent would have had a greater lookahead range that would have predicted these violations. Note, however, that the fact that an agent takes a path on which it would violate a maintenance goal if it would continue still does *not* lead to violation of a maintenance goal. The reason is that the agent will be required to stop acting as soon as there are only actions enabled that would lead to a violation of a maintenance goal. This is in line with our assumption that maintenance goals are hard constraints.

In our example carrier agent it is sufficient to have a lookahead of one. As stated in Corollary 1, an agent with a lookahead range of one continues acting until it recognizes that by doing so at all possible next states it violates a maintenance goal. The carrier agent with a lookahead of one will be able to detect that if it executes a `move` action at location `ab1` before tanking, it will immediately violate its maintenance goal and will select the alternative action of tanking as a result. This illustrates that the lookahead mechanism, which primarily *constrains* the actions of the agent, may also induce the agent to *actively* prevent the violation of maintenance goals (in the example realized through tanking). To be more accurate, our mechanism does not distinguish between preventive actions that should prevent the violation of an achievement goal, and actions that are executed to fulfill achievement goals. As we can see in this example, in practice a very limited lookahead range may already be sufficient to prevent the agent from taking a path that would lead to violation of maintenance goals. To be more specific, the semantics of the example agent with lookahead range of one is equal to the semantics with lookahead range ∞. In general, the minimally needed lookahead range should be derived from available domain knowledge.

In this simple example, it is not difficult to modify the GOAL program in such a way that the desired behavior is obtained without explicitly incorporating maintenance goals. One could, e.g., add a condition to the conditional action for moving, specifying that if the agent is at location `ab1`, it may not move unless its tank is full. We argue, however, that the explicit incorporation of maintenance goals in the GOAL program provides a separation of concerns, and thereby potentially yields more transparent and easier to verify agent programs.

It is interesting to investigate under what circumstances bounded lookahead is guaranteed to be sufficient to avoid violation of maintenance goals. One particular such case is the case that an agent can *undo* actions, that is, if it has a *rollback mechanism* to go back to a previous state. In the presence of such a rollback mechanism, a bounded lookahead of 1 is sufficient to satisfy all maintenance goals. Obviously, the ability to rollback combined with 1 step looka-head will not be sufficient in all cases to realize the agent's achievement goals. The combination does allow the agent, however, to continue any computation given that at least one action is enabled. For our purposes, we model such a rollback mechanism simply by adding for each transition $s \rightarrow s'$ the inverse transition $s' \rightarrow s$ to the agent semantics.

Theorem 1. (Lookahead of One Sufficient with Rollback Mechanism)
For agents that can do at least one action initially without violating a mainte-nance goal, and that have a rollback mechanism to undo arbitrary actions, that is, are able to reverse a computation step $s \rightarrow s'$ by performing the step $s' \rightarrow s$, we have the following:

$$S_A \restriction_1 \Omega = S_A \restriction_\infty \Omega$$

Proof. The main observation needed in the proof is that any finite, safe prefix can be continued without violating a maintenance goal by doing either a "regular" action or otherwise by doing an "undo" action. By assumption, the agent can at least do one action initially, and so any finite safe prefix can be extended to a complete computation that does not violate a maintenance goal.

Although Theorem 1 shows that an agent will always be able to continue pur-suing its goals, it does not state that it will also achieve these goals if possible. In the presence of a rollback mechanism, computations that make no progress but instead repeatedly have to recover from performing an action that leads to a violation of a maintenance goal are included in the set $S_A \restriction_\infty \Omega$. What is missing is a notion of fairness that would prevent such repeated execution of a part of the computation (cf. [7]). Fairness is included in the original GOAL semantics but is not discussed further in this paper (cf. [5]). Intuitively, moreover, by us-ing lookahead of more than one step computations that require rollback can be detected sooner which will reduce the need for such rollbacks.

5   Detecting and Revising Goal Conflicts

In this section an algorithm is presented that implements the maintenance goal semantics and, additionally, it includes an extension that provides the agent with the option to revise its achievement goals in case no achievement goal is reachable without choosing a path that would lead to violation of a maintenance goal.   As discussed in Section 2.2, revising achievement goals is a way of dealing with conflicts between maintenance goals and achievement goals, if maintenance goals are taken as hard constraints. Revision of achievement goals is not the main subject of this paper (see e.g. [9]), but we will illustrate the main ideas using the carrier agent example.

    The first step to implement the semantics for maintenance goals based on lookahead is to define an algorithm which is able to *detect* potential future maintenance goal violations. The algorithm depicted in Table 3 implements the detection of such violations as well as the cautious strategy of an agent that

Table 3. Action Selection Algorithm Including Maintenance Goals

```
Function SELECTACTION(E, s, n)
Input: A set of enabled conditional actions E, a state s, a lookahead range n
Output: A selected conditional action c, or skip
1.    actionOkSet ← ∅
2.    for each c ∈ E
3.        do conflict[c] ← CONFLICTSETS(c, s, n)
4.            if ∅ ∈ conflict[c] then actionOkSet ← actionOkSet ∪ {c}
5.    if actionOkSet ≠ ∅
6.    then return CHOOSEACTION(actionOkSet)
7.    else  c' ← SELECTACTIONWITHMINIMALCONFLICTS(E, conflict)
8.          REVISECONFLICTINGACHIEVEMENTGOALS(conflict[c'])
9.          (* do nothing and recompute enabled actions using revised achievement goal(s) *)
10.         return skip

Function CONFLICTSETS(c, s, n)
Input: A conditional action c, a state s, and a lookahead range n
Output: The conflict sets of c
1.    if n ≤ 0
2.    then return {∅} (* Indicates that at least one path is ok. *)
3.    else   S ← SUCCESSORSTATES(c, s)
4.        for each s' ∈ S
5.            do cset ← ∅ (* Conflict set *)
6.                if Σ_{s'} ⊭ Ω
7.                    then cset ← cset ∪ {REASONCONFLICT(c)}
8.                    else  E ← COMPUTEENABLEDACTIONS(s')
9.                        for each c' ∈ E
10.                            do cset ← cset ∪ CONFLICTSETS(c', s', n − 1)
11.        return cset
```

avoids taking a path that would lead to violation of a maintenance goal. The function SELECTACTION computes for each enabled conditional action whether it might result in any conflicts with or violations of maintenance goals for a given lookahead range n. In case executing an action does not inevitably lead to such a conflict, it is added to the set of actions that are *ok* to select for execution. Only if there are no actions that are "safe" in this sense, the action selection algorithm will select an achievement goal in order to revise it. The detection of these conflicts is done through the function CONFLICTSETS. This function recursively computes the so-called conflict sets, which will be explained in more detail below. An empty conflict set indicates that no future violation of a maintenance goal within lookahead range is detected.

As discussed in Section 2.2, detected conflicts between achievement goals and maintenance goals may cause the agent not to do anything at a certain point, as it might be the case that any action would lead to a future violation of a maintenance goal. In the example scenario, adding a weight constraint that expresses that the truck cannot carry a load that weighs more than a certain threshold, has this effect if the sum of the weight of the two parcels is higher than the threshold (see Table 4, where `weightTotal(N)` computes the total weight of the parcels in the truck).

If at least a lookahead of two is used, the agent will not be able to execute any action in the initial mental state. After loading either one of the parcels, loading the other one would lead to a violation of the weight maintenance goal. With the

Table 4. GOAL Carrier Agent

```
:beliefs{ ... weight(p1,3). weight(p2,2). threshold(4). weightTotal(N) :- ... }
:a-goals{ loc(p1,b), loc(p2,b). }
:m-goals{ fuel(X), X > 0. weightTotal(T), threshold(W), T<W. }
```

cautious strategy, taking a path on which the violation of a maintenance goal is foreseen within two steps, is not an option (note that the agent can only unload parcels at location b).

In this case where the agent cannot execute any action as this would lead to violation of maintenance goals, the algorithm of Table 3 allows the revision of achievement goals by means of lowering ones ambitions. The idea here is that actions are induced by achievement goals and these actions thus may be prevented from being taken by revising those goals (we disregard the possibility of incorrect beliefs, which might instead require an agent to revise its beliefs). In order to revise its achievement goals the agent needs more information to base the revision on and to this end the notion of a *conflict set* is introduced. A *conflict set* is an achievement goal α which has been identified as a potential reason for the violation of a maintenance goal. In general, identifying such a reason may involve complicated diagnostic reasoning, but in GOAL a more pragmatic solution is available. In GOAL, goal conditions are typically associated with the selection of actions and we can simply take these conditions as the reason why a maintenance goal is violated. In our example agent, the function REASONCONFLICT(c) extracts *an instance* of the goal condition loc(P,b) as a reason for the violation of the maximum weight loaded. The function REVISE-CONFLICTINGACHIEVEMENTGOALS then may revise the achievement goal in the goal base and drop one of the conjuncts to avoid the violation. Consecutively, the agent verifies again if the maintenance goal violation has been eliminated. If no reason can be identified in this way, # is returned to indicate a violation of a maintenance goal.

6   Conclusion and Related Work

In this paper, we have looked at a mechanism for agents to handle maintenance goals. In particular, we have proposed a formal semantics of maintenance goals based on the notion of lookahead, and we have analyzed the semantics by proving some properties, in order to gain a better understanding of the role of maintenance goals in action selection. We presented an algorithm for detecting maintenance goal violation, parametrized by a variable lookahead range in order to be able to control computational costs. Additionally, we have discussed the issue of achievement goal revision, in case the maintenance goals are so restrictive that all courses of action for satisfying achievement goals will lead to a violation of maintenance goals.

There are several interesting directions for future research. Regarding the revision of achievement goals, several issues have remained unexplored. For example, we have suggested one possible way of determining that an achievement goal conflicts with a maintenance goal. In future research, we plan to investigate this approach and possible alternatives in more detail. One research direction in this respect is the investigation of existing techniques for determining whether achievement goals conflict with each other [16,15,13]. It will need to be investigated whether the issue of conflicts between maintenance goals and achievement goals is the same as or similar to the issue of conflicts between achievement goals.

Existing approaches for defining preferences over goals, such as in utility theory [1], may be useful to refine the strategy for revising achievement goals. Intuitively, an agent should revise its achievement goals in such a way that they are reachable without violating maintenance goals, and the revision should maximize the agents expected utility. Moreover, in this paper we have taken maintenance goals as hard constraints, and have suggested to revise achievement goals in case they conflict with the agent's maintenance goals. Alternatively, it could be allowed to violate maintenance goals under certain circumstances. Again utility theory could be useful here, in order to weigh the violation of a maintenance goal against the realization of an achievement goal. For example, negative utility could be associated with the violation of a maintenance goal assigning a maintenance goal that defines a hard constraint e.g. as having infinitely negative utility. The work in [8] on qualitative preferences in agent programming could also be relevant here. There are also some similarities with the planning literature on oversubscription (e.g. [2]), but as with planning approaches in general the main difference is that GOAL agents check violations of maintenance goals while executing actions.

Regarding related work on maintenance goals, we discuss the approach followed in the Jadex framework [3], the language presented by Dastani et al. [4], and the work of Duff et al. [6]. These approaches can be categorized into approaches that use maintenance goals as a *trigger* for the execution of actions, and approaches that use some mechanism for *reasoning* about the result of action execution in order to prevent maintenance goals from being violated. Jadex uses maintenance goals to trigger the execution of actions in case the maintenance goal is violated. In the framework of Dastani et al., a trigger condition is used to determine when action is needed to prevent the violation of maintenance goals. In our approach and in the framework of Duff et al., a reasoning mechanism is used in order to prevent maintenance goals from being violated.

One of the main differences between the work of Duff et al. and our work is that in Duff et al. it is determined *before* an achievement goal is pursued whether the plans for achieving this achievement goal may conflict with one of the agent's maintenance goals. In our work, by contrast, we propose to use a lookahead mechanism for keeping maintenance goals from being violated *during* pursuit of achievement goals. We also suggested the possibility to revise achievement goals when they cannot be realized without violating maintenance goals, while Duff et al. propose to not adopt such achievement goals to avoid the risk of violating maintenance goals. The approaches also differ in that in this paper a mechanism to ensure satisfaction of maintenance goals is based on a semantic analysis and Duff et al. validate their work using an experimental approach.

Finally, an advantage of doing lookahead during achievement goal pursuit, we believe, is that it may provide for more flexible agent behavior. An approach based on executing a preventive plan that is associated with the maintenance goal in case an achievement goal might conflict with a maintenance goal, as proposed in Duff et al., does not seem to leave the agent with as many options as are possible. Moreover, such an approach still does not guarantee that the consecutive pursuit of the achievement goal will not violate the maintenance goal. The approach of Duff et al. can be compared with planning approaches, in the sense that reasoning takes place before execution. If something is about to go wrong during execution, this is not detected. In our approach, the agent pursues achievement goals, but takes any measures that it has at its disposal if this is necessary to prevent a maintenance goal from being violated.

References

1. Boutilier, C., Dean, T., Hanks, S.: Decision-theoretic planning: Structural assumptions and computational leverage. Journal of AI Research 11, 1–94 (1999)
2. Brafman, R.I., Chernyavsky, Y.: Planning with goal preferences and constraints. In: Proceedings of ICAPS 2005 (2006)
3. Braubach, L., Pokahr, A., Moldt, D., Lamersdorf, W.: Goal representation for BDI agent systems. In: Bordini, R.H., Dastani, M., Dix, J., Seghrouchni, A.E.F. (eds.) ProMAS 2004. LNCS (LNAI), vol. 3346, pp. 44–65. Springer, Heidelberg (2005)
4. Dastani, M., van Riemsdijk, M.B., Meyer, J.-J.C.: Goal types in agent programming. In: Mehdi Dastani, M. (ed.) ECAI 2006. Proceedings of the 17th European Conference on Artifical Intelligence. Frontiers in Artificial Intelligence and Applications, vol. 141, pp. 220–224. IOS Press, Amsterdam (2006)
5. de Boer, F.S., Hindriks, K.V., van der Hoek, W., Meyer, J.-J.C.: A Verification Framework for Agent Programming with Declarative Goals. Journal of Applied Logic (2006)
6. Duff, S., Harland, J., Thangarajah, J.: On Proactivity and Maintenance Goals. In: AAMAS 2006. Proceedings of the fifth international joint conference on autonomous agents and multiagent systems, Hakodate, pp. 1033–1040 (2006)
7. Francez, N.: Fairness. Springer, Heidelberg (1986)
8. Fritz, C., McIlraith, S.A.: Decision-theoretic golog with qualitative preferences. In: KR, pp. 153–163 (2006)
9. Gardenfors, P.: Belief Revision. In: Cambridge Computer Tracts, Cambridge University Press, Cambridge (1992)
10. Hindriks, K.V., de Boer, F.S., van der Hoek, W., Meyer, J.-J.C.: Agent Programming with Declarative Goals. In: Castelfranchi, C., Lespérance, Y. (eds.) ATAL 2000. LNCS (LNAI), vol. 1986, pp. 228–243. Springer, Heidelberg (2001)
11. Hübner, J.F., Bordini, R.H., Wooldridge, M.: Declarative goal patterns for AgentSpeak. In: Baldoni, M., Endriss, U. (eds.) DALT 2006. LNCS (LNAI), vol. 4327, Springer, Heidelberg (2006)
12. Lifschitz, V.: On the semantics of strips. In: Georgeff, M.P., Lansky, A.L. (eds.) Reasoning about Actions and Plans, pp. 1–9. Morgan Kaufmann, San Francisco (1986)

13. Pokahr, A., Braubach, L., Lamersdorf, W.: A goal deliberation strategy for BDI agent systems. In: Eymann, T., Klügl, F., Lamersdorf, W., Klusch, M., Huhns, M.N. (eds.) MATES 2005. LNCS (LNAI), vol. 3550, pp. 82–93. Springer, Heidelberg (2005)
14. Sardina, S., Shapiro, S.: Rational action in agent programs with prioritized goals. In: AAMAS 2003. Proceedings of the second international joint conference on autonomous agents and multiagent systems, Melbourne, pp. 417–424 (2003)
15. Thangarajah, J., Padgham, L., Winikoff, M.: Detecting and avoiding interference between goals in intelligent agents. In: IJCAI 2003. Proceedings of the 18th International Joint Conference on Artificial Intelligence (2003)
16. Thangarajah, J., Winikoff, M., Padgham, L., Fischer, K.: Avoiding resource conflicts in intelligent agents. In: van Harmelen, F. (ed.) ECAI 2002. Proceedings of the 15th European Conference on Artifical Intelligence, Lyon, France (2002)
17. van Riemsdijk, M.B., Dastani, M., Meyer, J.-J.C., de Boer, F.S.: Goal-oriented modularity in agent programming. In: Birna van, M. (ed.) AAMAS 2006. Proceedings of the fifth international joint conference on autonomous agents and multiagent systems, Hakodate, pp. 1271–1278 (2006)
18. Winikoff, M., Padgham, L., Harland, J., Thangarajah, J.: Declarative and procedural goals in intelligent agent systems. In: KR2002. Proceedings of the eighth international conference on principles of knowledge respresentation and reasoning, Toulouse (2002)

Towards Alternative Approaches to Reasoning About Goals

Patricia H. Shaw and Rafael H. Bordini

Department of Computer Science,
University of Durham, U.K.
{p.h.shaw,r.bordini}@durham.ac.uk

Abstract. Agent-oriented programming languages have gone a long way in the level of sophistication offered to programmers, and there has also been much progress in tools to support multi-agent systems development using such languages. However, much work is still required in mechanisms that can reduce the burden, typically placed on programmers, of ensuring that agents behave *rationally*, hence being effective and as efficient as possible. One such mechanisms is *reasoning about declarative goals*, which is increasingly appearing in the agents literature; it allows agents to make better use of resources, to avoid plans hindering the execution of other plans, and to be able to take advantage of opportunities for reducing the number of plans that have to be executed to achieve certain combinations of goals. In this paper, we introduce a Petri-net based approach to such reasoning, and we report on experimental results showing that this technique can obtain comparable improvements on an agent's behaviour to other existing approaches (our experiments do not yet cover reasoning about resource usage). Our long-term goal is to provide a number of alternative approaches for such reasoning, evaluate and compare their performances under different configurations, and incorporate them into interpreters for agent-oriented programming languages in such a way that the most appropriate approach is used at given circumstances.

1 Introduction

Recent years have seen an astonishing progress in the level of sophistication and practical use of various different agent-oriented programming languages [3]. These languages provide constructs that were specifically created for the implementation of systems designed on the basis of the typical abstractions used in the area of autonomous agents and multi-agent systems, therefore of much help for the development of large-scale multi-agent systems. However, the burden of ensuring that an agent behaves *rationally* in a given application is left to programmers (even though the languages do offer some support for that task).

Clearly, it would make the work of multi-agent systems developers much easier if we could provide (semi-) automatic mechanisms to facilitate the task of ensuring such rationality, provided, of course, that they are sufficiently fast to be used in *practical* agent programming languages. One important issue for a

M. Baldoni et al. (Eds.): DALT 2007, LNAI 4897, pp. 104–121, 2008.
© Springer-Verlag Berlin Heidelberg 2008

rational agent is that of *deliberation* — that is, deciding *which goals to adopt* in the first place (see [15,9,2] for some approaches to agent deliberation in the context of agent programming languages). Besides, once certain goals have been adopted, the particular choice of plans to achieve them can cause a significant impact in the agent's behaviour and performance, as particular plans may interfere with one another (e.g., through the use of particular resources, or through the effects they have in the environment). The general term that has been used to refer to the reasoning that addresses these issues, which requires *declarative goal* representations [25,24], is *reasoning about goals*.

Much work has been published recently introducing various approaches which contribute to addressing this problem [7,21,22,23,11,16]. In most cases, in particular in the work by Thangarajah *et al.* and Clement *et al.*, the idea of "summary information" is used in the proposed techniques for reasoning about goals. However, the size of such summary information can potentially grow exponentially on the number of goals and plans the agent happens to be committed to achieve/execute [8]. It remains to be seen how practical those approaches will be for real-world problems.

In our work, we are interested in mechanisms for goal reasoning which do not require such summary information, yet can reproduce the reasoning that has been proposed in the literature. Avoiding the use of summary information, of course, does not guarantee that those alternative techniques will be more efficient than the existing approaches. In fact, our approach is to try and use well-known formalisms with which to attempt to model the goal reasoning problem, then experimentally evaluating the various different approaches. We aim, in future work, to combine those approaches in such a way that agents can use one mechanism or another in the circumstances where each works best, if that turns out to be practically determinable.

So far, we have been able to model the goal reasoning problem using two different approaches, neither of which requires summary information as in the existing literature on the topic (the next section gives a detailed description of such work). First, we have modelled goal-adoption decision making as a reachability problem in a Petri net [14]. Then, using the idea and method suggested in [18,17] for translating a Hierarchical Task Network (HTN) plan into a Constraint Satisfaction Problem (CSP), we have also developed a method for, given an agent's current goals and plans (possibly including a goal the agent is considering adopting), generating an instance of a CSP which can produce a valid ordering of plans — if one exists — to help the agent avoid conflicts (and take advantage of opportunities) when attempting to achieve all its goals.

For reasons of space, in this paper we focus on presenting the Petri-net based technique only, and we also give initial experimental analysis of an agent's performance when using such goal reasoning in two different scenarios; the results of the CSP-based technique will be reported in a separate paper. The remainder of this paper is organised as follows. Section 2 gives an overview of the types of goal reasoning and various approaches to that problem that have appeared in the literature. Then, in Section 3, we look at how such reasoning can be

represented as a Petri net. Section 4 provides an experimental analysis of the
Petri-net based reasoning. Finally, we give conclusions and a summary of future
work in Section 5.

2   Reasoning About Goals

There are multiple types of conflicts that rational agents need to be aware of;
these can be internal to the individual agent, or external between two or more
agents [10]. While conflicts can occur in social interactions, when attempting to
delegate or collaborate over a set of given tasks [5], the main focus of this paper
is to look at conflicts between goals within an individual agent.

The conflicts arise within a single agent when it has taken on two or more
goals that are not entirely compatible [10]. The conflicts may be caused if there
is a limited amount of resources available [23,16], or it may be due to the effects
the actions involved in achieving the goals have on the environment; the actions
in the plans being executed to achieve concurrent goals can cause effects which
can hinder, or even prevent altogether, the successful completion of some of those
plans [21,22].

In all the work by Thangarajah *et al.* referred above, a Goal-Plan Tree (GPT)
is used to represent the structure of the various plans and sub-goals related to
each goal (see Figure 1). In order for a plan within the tree to be completed,
all of its sub-goals must first be completed. However, to achieve a goal or a
sub-goal, only one of its possible plans needs to be executed. At each node
on the tree, *summary information* is used to represent the various constraints
under consideration. The reasoning done in their approach is solely internal to
an individual agent.

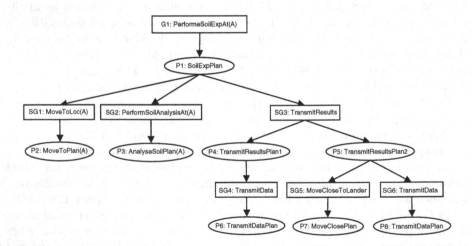

Fig. 1. Goal-Plan Tree for a Mars rover as used by Thangarajah *et al.* Goals and
sub-goals are represented by rectangles, while plans are represented by ovals.

Reasoning about effects of actions needs to consider both positive and negative impacts in relation to other plans, and causal links that may exist between goals. In the first paper by Thangarajah *et al.* where reasoning about effects is considered, they show how to detect and avoid negative interference between goals [21]. By using additional types of summary information, similar to those developed in [7], such as summaries for definite or potential pre-conditions and in-conditions along with post-conditions or effects, they monitor the causal links between effects produced by a plan which are used as pre-conditions of another to ensure these are not interfered with. To derive these effects, a formal notation based on set theory is defined, to allow agents to produce the summary information in order to reason about conflicting actions between its current goals and any new goals the agent might consider adopting.

When conflicts occur, often they can be handled by scheduling the plan execution so as to protect the causal links until they are no longer required. Also in [21], the authors determine a sequence of steps for an agent to schedule plan execution so as to avoid interference, including checks that need to be performed before an agent can accept to adopt a new goal. Empirical results from experiments using the reasoning described in that paper are given in [19], comparing the performance of an agent with and without such reasoning, varying the level of interaction between goals and the amount of parallelism. The results show the improvement in number of goals successfully achieved, and only slight increase in time taken to perform the additional reasoning.

In [22], Thangarajah *et al.* focus on exploiting positive interaction between goals. This is where two or more plans cause the same effect, so rather than executing both, it might be possible to merge the two plans, thereby improving the agents' performance. To represent this form of reasoning, they again use the goal-plan tree with summary information including *definite* and *potential* effects of the plans and goals; they also define a particular method to derive such summaries. They then describe how an agent can decide if it is feasible to merge the plans, and how to avoid waiting too long if one of the two plans selected for merging is reached considerably sooner than the other or the second plan is never reached, in case it was a "potential" merge rather than a "definite" merge. Results from experiments using this type of reasoning are once again presented in [19].

Horty and Pollack also consider positive interaction between plans [11]. In their work, an agent evaluates the various options it has between its goals within the context of its existing plans. They use estimates for the costs of plans, and where there is some commonality between some plans, those plans will be considered for merging. If the estimated merged cost is less than the sum of the two separate estimated costs, then the plans are actually merged. The example they give to illustrate this is an "important" plan for going to a shopping centre to buy a shirt, while also having a less important goal of buying a tie. Both plans involve getting money and travelling to a shopping centre, so if the overall cost of buying the tie at the same time as the shirt is less than that of buying the tie separately, then the plans will be merged, even though the goal of having a tie is not as important. In this way, they look for the least expensive execution of plans involved in achieving the goals.

When referring to reasoning about resource usage in a GPT [23], Thangarajah *et al.* consider both reusable and consumable resources. For example, a communication channel is a reusable resource, while energy or time is consumed so they cannot be reused. Summaries of the resource requirements are passed up the tree towards the goal, describing which resources are *necessary* in order to achieve the goals, and also which resources are used only *potentially*. They introduce a notation, based on set theory, allowing the derivation of summaries for the resource requirements of each goal and plan with sub-goals. These can then be used to reason about where conflicts might occur, so that they can be avoided by choosing suitable alternative plans or appropriately ordering plan execution. An algorithm is given to compute whether it is feasible to add a new goal to the existing set of goals without rendering them unachievable. The initial formulation of the goal-plan tree and summary information for an agent is produced at compile time, and the highlighted conflicts are then monitored at runtime in an attempt to avoid conflict.

Empirical results from experiments done using such reasoning are given in [20]. They consider goal-plan trees of depth 2 and depth 5, varying the amount of parallelism between multiple goals, and the amount of competition for the resources either by reducing their availability or increasing the number of goals competing for the same resources. The reasoning is implemented as an extension to the JACK agent development system [4]; the extended system is called X-JACK. The performance of X-JACK is compared against the performance of JACK without any of the additional reasoning, and shows an improvement in performance regarding the number of goals successfully achieved, typically with only a half-second time increase in the computation cost.

In comparison, [16] consider the use of limited resources when deliberating and performing actions in a multi-agent environment, where coordination and negotiation with the other agents is required. In their attempt to address the problem of limited resources within meta-level control, they make use of reinforcement learning to improve the agents' performance over time.

To our knowledge, while Thangarajah *et al.* have reported on experimental results for reasoning separately about each of the types of interactions between plans and goals as well as resource usage, no results appear in the literature showing what is the performance obtained when an agent is doing all those forms of reasoning simultaneously. All results are given for the individual types, to demonstrate the sole effects from the individual reasoning and the (typically very small) amount of added computational costs associated with it. The lack of combined results seem to suggest the possibility of there being interference between the different forms of reasoning presented in their approach. For example, if one reasoning suggests that performing a particular plan will cause one type of conflict (say, lack or resources), while another reasoning suggests that the only alternative plan for that goal will also cause a conflict (say, a negative interference with another goal), the agent may be unable to decide between the two without some additional overriding reasoning. It also remains unknown if their approach is still equally efficient when the various types of reasoning are combined.

The results were also limited in the depth of trees tested. In the real world, it is likely the plans (and hence the goals) would be far more complex, leading to trees of significantly greater sizes. However, using the summary information, as a goal-plan tree grows, the amount of summary information to handle could potentially grow exponentially [8], which would have a significant impact on the performance of the agent for larger problems.

Prior to the time that the work by Thangarajah *et al.* was published, the Distributed Intelligent Agents Group led by Edmund Durfee, produced some similar research for modelling — and reasoning about — plan effects, extending their work to cover multi-agent systems rather than individual agents [6,7,8]. In their work, they were interested in reasoning about conflicts to coordinate the actions of agents that use HTN planning, while the work by Thangarajah was based around BDI agents (focusing on individual agents instead). In [7], Clement *et al.* present the summary information for pre-, in-, and post-conditions of plans, which is adopted by Thangarajah *et al.* and used within goal-plan trees to reason about both resources and effects.

3   Reasoning About Goals Using Petri Nets

Petri nets are mathematical models, with an intuitive diagrammatic representation, used for describing and studying concurrent systems [14]. They consist of *places* that are connected by *arcs* to *transitions*, with *tokens* that are passed from place to place through transitions. Transitions can only *fire* when there are sufficient tokens in each of the input places, acting as pre-conditions for the transition. A token is then removed from each input place, and one is placed in each of the output places. Places are graphically represented as circles, while transitions are represented as rectangles.

There are many variations on the basic Petri net representation, and many of these have been used in a variety of agent systems [13,1]. Arcs can have weights associated with them, the default weight being one. Greater weights on arcs either require the place to have at least that many tokens for the transition to fire, or the transition adds to the output place that number of tokens as its output. Coloured Petri Nets are able to hold tokens of different types, representing for example different data types. The weightings on the arcs then match up and select the relevant tokens to fire. Reference nets allow nets to contain sub-nets. *Renew* is a Petri net editor and simulator that is able to support high-level Petri nets such as coloured and reference nets [12].

We have developed a method to represent an agents' goals and plans using Petri nets. Essentially, we are able to represent the same problems as expressed by goal-plan trees in the work by Thangarajah *et al.* (see Figure 2 for an example). According to the method we have devised, goals and plans are represented by a series of places and transitions. A plan consists of a sequence of actions that starts with a place, and has a transition to another place to represent each of the atomic actions that occur in sequence within that plan. Goals and subgoals are also set up as places with transitions linked to the available plans for each goal. In Figure 2, the plans are enclosed in dark boxes, while the goals and subgoals are in light boxes. The plans and subgoals are nested within each other, matching the hierarchical tree structure of the GPT.

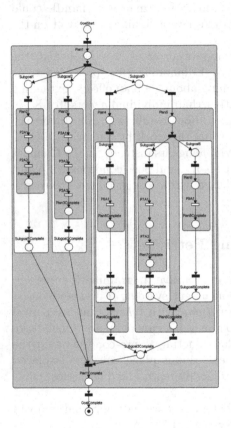

Fig. 2. Petri Net Representation of the Mars Rover GPT in Figure 1

The goal reasoning that we have incorporated into the Petri nets is to allow an agent to handle both positive and negative interactions between multiple goals; we are in the process of incorporating reasoning about resources on top of these. Our aim is to be able to reason about these three aspects together whilst also avoiding the use of any "summary information" as in the work by Thangarajah *et al.* and Clement *et al.*. This reasoning and the representation of the plans and goals themselves can each be seen as an interlinked module, as will be discussed below. This modularisation of the method we use to represent goals and plans as (sub) Petri nets allows an agent to dynamically produce Petri-net representations of goals and plans (and their relationship to existing goals and plans) that can then be used by an agent to reason on-the-fly about its ability to adopt a new goal given its current commitments towards existing goals.

Currently, the Petri nets are being generated manually, but they have been designed in such modular way with the aim of being able to automate this process. An agent will then be able to generate new Petri nets to model new goals as the agent generates them or receive requests to achieve goals, allowing it to reason about whether it is reasonable to accept the new goal. If the goal is accepted then the Petri nets can be used to advise plan selection to avoid interference and to benefit from positive interactions. Figure 3 shows the main modules being used in the Petri nets. Some of the notation used in the Petri nets is specific to the *Renew* Petri net editor.

The negative interference reasoning protects the effects that have been caused in the environment until they are no longer required by the goal that caused the change. When an agent executes a plan that produces an effect in the

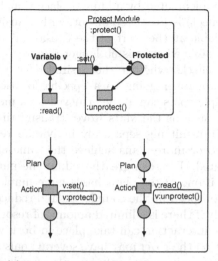
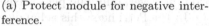

(a) Protect module for negative interference.

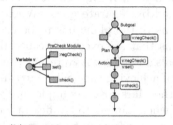

(b) Pre-check module for positive interaction.

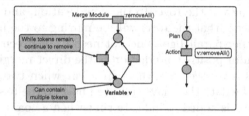

(c) Merge module for positive interaction.

Fig. 3. Petri-Net Representation of Modules for Reasoning about Goals

environment, and that effect will be required by a later plan, the effect is immediately marked as protected until it is no longer required. This is done by using a protect module (Figure 3(a)) that adds a set of transitions and places to the Petri nets so that when the relevant effect takes place, a transition is fired to protect it, then when it is no longer needed another transition is fired to release the protected effect. If another plan attempts to change something that will impact on the protected effects, then it will be blocked and forced to wait until the effects are no longer protected (i.e., until the release transition fires).

In the Mars Rover example, negative interference occurs when two or more goals require taking samples at different locations and after having moved to the first location, a second goal interferes to take the rover to another location before the sample is taken to satisfy the fist goal. To avoid this, the causal link is identified based on the effects and preconditions of the plans when Petri nets are generated, and a protect module is added to ensure other goals and plans cannot interfere with the casual link until the necessary plans have executed. In the Petri nets, the protect module is implemented by adding a place that holds a token to indicate if a variable (i.e., effect) is protected or not, with transitions that the plan fires to protect the variable at the start of the causal link, then another transition to unprotect the variable when it is no longer required.

The positive interaction reasoning checks whether the desired effects have already been achieved (such as a Mars rover going to a specific location to perform some tests), or whether multiple goals can all be achieved by a merged plan rather than a plan for each goal, such as the Mars Rover transmitting all the data back in one go instead of transmitting separately individual results obtained by separate goals. When two or more plans achieve the same effect, only one of the plans has to be executed. This can greatly reduce the number of plans that are executed, especially if one of the plans has a large number of subgoals and plans. As a result, this can speed up the completion and reduce the costs of achieving the goals, particularly if there is a limited amount of resources.

In the Mars rover example, positive interaction can take place in both ways. First, when moving to a different location the rover may have several goals all of which required going to the same location; however, only one plan needs to be actually executed to take the rover there. In the Petri nets, this is handled by a pre-check module (Figure 3(b)) that first checks whether another plan is about to, or has already, moved the rover to the new location, and if not it then fires a transition to indicate that the rover will be moving to the new location so the similar plans for other parallel goals do not need to be executed.

The second form of positive interaction is the direct merging of two or more plans. In the Mars rover scenario, this can occur when two or more goals are ready to transmit the data they have collected back to the base station. A merge module (Figure 3(c)) is added to indicate that when a goal is ready to transmit data back, it also checks to see if other goals are also ready to transmit their data. If so, all data that is ready is transmitted by the one plan rather than each goal separately executing individual plans to transmit the data.

4   Experimental Results and Analysis

We have used two different scenarios in our evaluation: the first is an abstract example and the other is the simple Mars rover example.

Scenario 1: Abstract Example

In this scenario, the goal structure in Figure 4 was used for each of the goals that were initiated. In the experiments reported here, we have opted for not considering varying structures, but this will be considered in future experiments. The experiments we conducted with Scenario 1 aimed to match, to the extent we could understand and reproduce, the settings of the experiments conducted in [19] to evaluate the GPT and summary information method that they introduced, in particular their experiments to compare the performance of JACK and X-JACK.

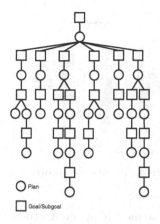

Fig. 4. Goal-Plan Tree Used for all Goals in Scenario 1

In our experiments using Scenario 1, ten goal types were defined adjusting the selection of plans within the goal plan tree that would interact with those of other goals. The interaction was modelled through a set of common variables to which each goal was able to assign values. The variables and values are used to represent the different effects that plans can have in the environment.

To stress-test the Petri nets, tests were set up that involved high levels of interaction, using a set of 5 variables, or low levels of interaction, using a set of 10 variables. Out of the 10 goal types, 5 of the goal types used 3 variables, while the remaining 5 goals types only altered 1 variable. During testing, 20 instantiations of the 10 possible goal types were created at random intervals and running concurrently. The Petri nets were implemented using Renew 2.1 [12], and each experiment was repeated 50 times.

Four experimental setups were used, with "High & Long" in the graphs (see Figure 5) corresponding to High Levels of Negative Interference for Long Periods, down to "Normal & Random" corresponding to Normal Levels of Negative Interference for Random Length Periods. The periods are controlled by defining the levels within the GPT that the interaction occurs at; so, for example, in the positive interaction, the duration over which the positive interaction takes place can be maximised by making plans in the top levels of the GPT with the greatest depth to interact.

A dummy Petri net was set up using the same goal structure and set of goal types, but without any of the reasoning for positive or negative interaction. The results from running this against the Petri net where such reasoning was included could then be compared to show the improvements obtained by the reasoning.

Negative Interference. Each goal was given a set of 1 or 3 variables to which it was to assign a given value and then use it (recall that this represents the effects of plan execution in the environment). The positions in the goals where the variables were set and then used were varied either randomly or set to require the variables to be protected for the longest possible periods (meaning the state of the world caused by a plan is required to be preserved for longer periods before the interfering plans can be executed). The selections of plans in each goal are designed to cause interference for other goals being pursued simultaneously. This is done by ensuring a significant overlap in the variables which the goals are setting, particularly under high levels of interaction. The effect of the reasoning is measured by counting the number of goals achieved both by the "dummy" and by the "reasoning" Petri nets.

The results are shown in Figure 5(a). The graphs show the averages for the number of goals achieved by the reasoning Petri net and the dummy Petri net from the 50 runs for each of the experiment settings, also showing the standard

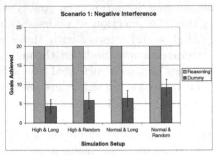

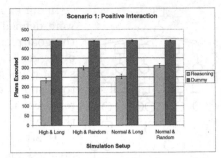

(a) Experimental results for negative interference.

(b) Experimental results for positive interaction.

Fig. 5. Results for Negative Interference and Positive Interaction in an Abstract Scenario

deviation. The effects of the negative reasoning are immediately obvious by the fact that the Petri nets with goal reasoning were consistently able to achieve all the goals, while the dummy Petri nets achieved, on average, very few goals, particularly when there were high levels of interference and variables that had to be protected for a long time, where it was only able to achieve approximately 21% of the goals, on average. Even at normal levels of interaction and random depth positioning, it was still only able to achieve, on average, 46% of the goals. The standard deviation shows that the performance of the dummy Petri nets was highly variable within the 50 runs of this experiment.

Positive Interaction. To measure the effects of reasoning about positive interactions, each goal was again given a set of 1 or 3 variables, with overlap between the goals, so that we can determine a selection of plans for each goal which can potentially be achieved by just executing one of the plans. Each goal contains 25 plans (in its GPT), of which at least 21 would have to be executed if the goal was being pursued on its own. This is due to two subgoals having a choice of plans to execute in the GPT. The scenario was set up to ensure all the goals are achievable without any reasoning, so the effects of the reasoning are measured by the number of plans that are required to execute in order to achieve all the goals.

As with the negative interference, the depth of the plans within the goal-plan structure at which merging can occur is varied. Plans with more subgoals will have a greater impact on the number of plans executed when merged than plans with no or very few subgoals. The tests were set with mergeable plans either high up in the GPT, or randomly placed within the tree.

The results are shown in Figure 5(b). The graphs show the averages for the number of plans executed by an agent using the Petri net with goal reasoning and a dummy agent; the averages are taken from the 50 runs for each of the experiment setups, and the graphs also show the standard deviations. There is clearly a major improvement between the dummy and the reasoning agents in all of the simulation settings, with the reasoning agent requiring significantly fewer plans to be executed than the dummy, whilst still achieving the same goals. For high levels of interaction and mergeable plans at high levels in the GPT, there is an average drop of 47% in the number of plans being executed. Even with lower levels of interaction, and randomly placed mergeable plans, there is still a decrease of 30% on average. This could lead to large savings in the time and resources required by an agent to achieve its goals. While the standard deviation shows there is more variance in the performance of the reasoning agent than the dummy, this is due to the variations in depth and GPT of the merged plans. Even with the variance, the reasoning consistently caused a significant improvement in the performance in comparison to the dummy agent.

Negative and Positive Interaction. In this section, the two types of reasoning have been combined into one Petri net with a scenario that causes negative interference as well as it provides opportunities for positive interaction. To maintain exactly the same levels of interaction, both positively and negatively, the same GPT has been used again and the variables are duplicated for this abstract scenario. One set of variables is used for positive interaction, while the other is used for negative interference. This has been done, in the abstract scenario, to maintain the levels of interaction to allow for a clear comparison, but in the second scenario both forms of reasoning are applied to the same variables to represent a more realistic scenario.

Each goal is given 1 or 3 variables to assign values to for the negative interference, and we use the same number of variables for positive interaction. The number of goals achieved and the plans required are then measured to compare the expected performance of an agent that uses the Petri-net based reasoning against a dummy agent (i.e., an agent without any goal reasoning).

The four sets of tests were combined, in particular the negative interference at high levels of interaction over long periods was combined with the positive interference at high levels of interaction and at high levels within the GPT, while the negative interference at high levels of interaction over random periods was combined with the positive interference at high levels of interaction and at random levels within the GPT. The experiment for interaction at normal levels was combined in the same way.

The results are shown in Figure 6. These are broken down into three groups: 6(a) goals achieved, 6(b) plans executed, and 6(c) the ratio between plans executed and goals achieved. The standard deviations are also included in each of these graphs.

The reasoning agent is once again able to achieve all of its goals, while the dummy agent is still only able to achieve 57–83% of its goals. Not only is the dummy agent failing to achieve all its goals, it is also attempting to execute almost all its plans in an effort to achieve those goals. This means the effects of the positive interaction reasoning are also very obvious with a drop of 50% in the number of plans executed by the reasoning agent for high levels of negative interference with positive interaction for long periods in the GPT, while still maintaining a 32% decrease in plans at lower levels of interference. The *plan*

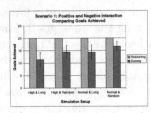 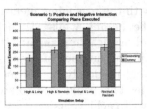 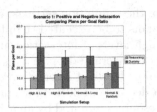

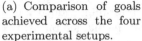

(a) Comparison of goals achieved across the four experimental setups.

(b) Comparison of plans executed across the four experimental setups.

(c) Comparison of ratio between plans executed and goals achieved.

Fig. 6. Experimental Results for Combined Positive and Negative Interaction in an Abstract Scenario

to goal ratio shows that the reasoning agent only had to execute on average 10 plans at high levels of interaction, and 14 plans at lower levels of interaction, to achieve its goals, while the dummy agent had to execute on average 39 plans at high levels of interaction and 25 at normal levels. Recall that while in the GPT there are only 25 plans available to achieve the main goal on its own, the dummy agent was still executing plans in goals that failed, and the ratio shows all the plans executed compared to the goals actually achieved. The standard deviation shows that, in general, the performance of the reasoning agent is very consistent, whereas the dummy agent is highly erratic, particularly when there are high levels of interaction for long periods.

Scenario 2: Mars Rover

To show the reasoning being used in a more concrete example, a Mars rover scenario has also been used. In this scenario, the rover is given a set of locations and a set of tests (or tasks) to perform at each location. Each task at each location is represented by a separate goal, as shown in Figure 2, offering much opportunity for both negative and positive interactions. All of the plans contain a set of preconditions that must be true for it to be able to execute, and these preconditions are satisfied by the effects of other plans. So while there may be less plans involved than in Scenario 1, there is still a lot of interaction taking place. The preconditions lead to a partial ordering of the plans for the goal to be achieved. In our experiments, 2, 4, and 6 locations were used, with 5 tests carried out at each location, in order to evaluate the performance of the reasoning over different levels of concurrency, specifically 10, 20, or 30 goals being simultaneously pursued.

For the interests of comparison, the negative and positive reasoning have again been separated out before being combined together in the final set of experiments.

Negative Interference. Negative interference is caused when the rover goes to a location ready to perform its tasks, but is then interrupted by another goal that required going to a different location before the tasks required at the first location by the previous goal had been completed. The effects of the reasoning is again measured by the number of goals achieved. The results are shown in Figure 7(a).

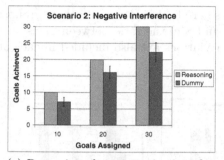

(a) Reasoning about negative interference.

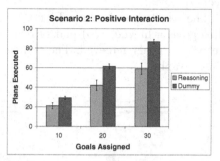

(b) Reasoning about positive interaction.

Fig. 7. Results for Negative Interference and Positive Interaction in the Mars Rover Example

The results again show a definite improvement obtained by adding the reasoning about negative interference, whereby all goals were achieved, while the dummy agent is still only able to achieve on average 75% of its goals, across all the levels of goal concurrency, even at the lowest levels.

Positive Interaction. In the Mars Rover example, there are two main places for positive interaction. The first is when multiple goals all require the rover to perform tests/tasks at the same location, while the second is when the goals require transmitting their results back to the mission control team, after having performed the tests. When the goals have all obtained their test results, these can either be transmitted back to the base individually, or one goal can assume the responsibility of transmitting all the results back at the same time. This means only one plan has to be executed whereas without the reasoning an agent ends up executing one plan per goal.

The negative interference was removed from this setup to ensure all goals could be achieved without any reasoning. This meant the number of plans executed could be compared more fairly. The results are shown in Figure 7(b).

A clear reduction in the average number of plans executed can again be observed in these results, with higher levels of concurrency giving a 32% reduction in the number of plans executed to achieve the same goals. Even the lowest level of concurrency offers a 28% reduction that could be highly beneficial when there are many constraints imposed on an agent, such as time and resource availability.

Combined Negative and Positive Interaction. While both types of reasoning can be effectively used on their own, the combined effects of both types of reasoning give the best results, particularly in highly constrained conditions. In the final set of results reported here, we show the results of the combined reasoning about negative interference and positive interaction in the Mars rover scenario.

The results are shown in Figure 8. These are broken down into three groups: 8(a) goals achieved, 8(b) plans executed, and 8(c) the ratio between plans executed and goals achieved. The standard deviations are also included in each of these graphs.

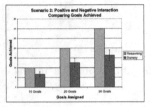

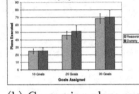

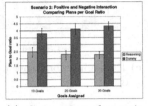

(a) Comparing goals achieved.

(b) Comparing plans executed.

(c) Comparing the ratio between plans executed and goals achieved.

Fig. 8. Experimental Results for Reasoning about Negative and Positive Interaction in the Mars Rover Example

While the results all show that there is only a slight improvement in the number of plans executed, the number of goals achieved by the reasoning agent is significantly more, and the *plan to goal ratio* is almost half that of the agent without any reasoning, increasing from a 34% reduction in the number of plans per goal to a 47% reduction as the level of goal concurrency increases. The reasoning agent is again consistently achieving all the goals it has been given, while the proportion the dummy agent was able to achieve dropped from 67% to 54% as the amount of concurrency increased. The standard deviation also shows that the reasoning agent is more consistent in its results in this scenario, with a lower range of variation.

5   Conclusions and Future Work

In this paper we have presented an alternative approach to reasoning about negative and positive interactions between goals. The results clearly show a significant improvement in the number of goals being achieved, and the number of plans required to achieve them. To the best of our knowledge, this is the first time the two types of reasoning have been combined together to show the joint effects of reasoning about both positive and negative goal interactions working in tandem for an individual agent. As only a small extra computing cost is expected to result from the added reasoning, the benefits are very likely to outweigh any costs. However, in future work, we aim to analyse in detail the costs associated with the reasoning and compare this cost with alternative approaches such as a CSP representation and existing approaches such as the approach by Thangarajah *et al.* using a GPT [21,22,23]. In all experiments reported in this paper, such costs appeared to be negligible.

Preliminary work has been done in representing the same type of reasoning approached in this paper as a CSP, in order to provide further sources of comparison. A further type of reasoning that can be used to improve an agent's performance is reasoning about resources, particularly when there is a limited supply of consumable resources available. We are currently in the process of including that type of reasoning in both our Petri-net and CSP-based techniques for reasoning about goals.

Currently, the Petri nets are being produced manually, but their modular design provides scope for automating this process, so that it can be incorporated into an agent architecture for on-the-fly reasoning about new goals to be potentially adopted. This will also be possible for the CSP-based approach, offering the agents a choice of reasoners if one proves to be better suited for particular situations (e.g., the structure/scale of the agent's GPT, or specific properties of the environment) than the others. Our long-term objective is to incorporate such reasoners into the interpreters of agent-oriented programming languages.

Acknowledgements

We gratefully acknowledge the support of EPSRC's DTA scheme. Many thanks to Berndt Farwer for recommending the Renew tool and the help in using it.

References

1. Bonnet-Torrès, O., Tessier, C.: From team plan to individual plans: a petri net-based approach. In: AAMAS 2005. 4th International Joint Conference on Autonomous Agents and Multiagent Systems, pp. 797–804. ACM Press, New York (2005)
2. Bordini, R.H., Bazzan, A.L.C., de Oliveira Jannone, R., Basso, D.M., Viccari, R.M., Lesser, V.R.: AgentSpeak(XL): Efficient intention selection in BDI agents via decision-theoretic task scheduling. In: Castelfranchi, C., Johnson, W. (eds.) AAMAS 2002, pp. 1294–1302. ACM Press, New York (2002)
3. Bordini, R.H., Dastani, M., Dix, J., El Fallah Seghrouchni, A.: Multi-Agent Programming: Languages, Platforms and Applications. In: Number 15 in Multiagent Systems, Artificial Societies, and Simulated Organizations, Springer, Heidelberg (2005)
4. Busetta, P., Rönnquist, R., Hodgson, A., Lucas, A.: JACK intelligent agents - components for intelligent agents in java. Technical report, Technical report, Agent Oriented Software Pty. Ltd, Melbourne, Australia (1998)

5. Castelfranchi, C., Falcone, R.: Conflicts within and for collaboration. In: Tessier, C., Chaudron, L., Müller, H.-J. (eds.) Conflicting Agents: Conflict Management in Multiagent Systems, Multiagent systems, Artificial societies, and Simulated organizations, ch. 2, pp. 33–62. Kluwer Academic Publishers, Dordrecht (2001)
6. Clement, B.J., Durfee, E.H.: Identifying and resolving conflicts among agents with hierarchical plans. In: Proceedings of AAAI Workshop on Negotiation: Settling Conflicts and Identifying Opportunities, Technical Report WS-99-12, pp. 6–11. AAAI Press (1999)
7. Clement, B.J., Durfee, E.H.: Theory for coordinating concurrent hierarchical planning agents using summary information. In: AAAI 1999/IAAI 1999. Proceedings of the sixteenth national conference on Artificial intelligence and the eleventh Innovative applications of artificial intelligence conference innovative applications of artificial intelligence, pp. 495–502. AAAI Press, California (1999)
8. Clement, B.J., Durfee, E.H.: Performance of coordinating concurrent hierarchical planning agents using summary information. In: ICMAS. Proceedings of 4th International Conference on Multi-Agent Systems, pp. 373–374. IEEE Computer Society Press, Los Alamitos (2000)
9. Dastani, M., de Boer, F., Dignum, F., Meyer, J.-J.: Programming agent deliberation: an approach illustrated using the 3apl language. In: AAMAS 2003. Proceedings of the second international joint conference on Autonomous agents and multiagent systems, pp. 97–104. ACM Press, New York (2003)
10. Hannebauer, M.: Their problems are my problems - the transition between internal and external conflict. In: Tessier, C., Chaudron, L., Müller, H.-J. (eds.) Conflicting Agents: Conflict Management in Multiagent Systems, Multiagent systems, Artificial societies, and Simulated organizations, ch. 3, pp. 63–110. Kluwer Academic Publishers, Dordrecht (2001)
11. Horty, J.F., Pollack, M.E.: Evaluating new options in the context of existing plans. Artificial Intelligence 127(2), 199–220 (2004)
12. Kummer, O., Wienberg, F., Duvigneau, M.: Renew – the Reference Net Workshop(Release 2.1) (May 2006), http://www.renew.de/
13. Mazouzi, H., El Fallah Seghrouchni, A., Haddad, S.: Open protocol design for complex interactions in multi-agent systems. In: AAMAS 2002, pp. 517–526. ACM Press, New York (2002)
14. Peterson, J.L.: Petri Net Theory and the modeling of Systems. Prentice-Hall, Englewood Cliffs (1981)
15. Pokahr, A., Braubach, L., Lamersdorf, W.: A goal deliberation strategy for bdi agent systems. In: Eymann, T., Klügl, F., Lamersdorf, W., Klusch, M., Huhns, M.N. (eds.) MATES 2005. LNCS (LNAI), vol. 3550, pp. 82–94. Springer, Heidelberg (2005)
16. Raja, A., Lesser, V.: Reasoning about coordination costs in resource-bounded multi-agent systems. In: Proceedings of AAAI 2004 Spring Symposium on Bridging the multiagent and multi robotic research gap, pp. 25–40 (March 2004)
17. Surynek, P.: On state management in plan-space planning from CP perspective. In: ICAPS. Proceedings of Workshop on Constraint Satisfaction Techniques for Planning and Scheduling Problems, International Conference on Automated Planning and Scheduling, AAAI Press, Stanford (2006)
18. Surynek, P., Barták, R.: Encoding HTN planning as a dynamic CSP. In: van Beek, P. (ed.) CP 2005. LNCS, vol. 3709, p. 868. Springer, Heidelberg (2005)
19. Thangarajah, J.: Managing the Concurrent Execution of Goals in Intelligent Agents. PhD thesis, School of Computer Science and Informaiton Technology, RMIT University, Melbourne, Victoria, Australia (December 2004)

20. Thangarajah, J., Padgham, L.: An empirical evaluation of reasoning about resource conflicts in intelligent agents. In: Kudenko, D., Kazakov, D., Alonso, E. (eds.) AAMAS 2004. LNCS (LNAI), vol. 3394, pp. 1298–1299. Springer, Heidelberg (2005)
21. Thangarajah, J., Padgham, L., Winikoff, M.: Detecting and avoiding interference between goals in intelligent agents. In: IJCAI. Proceedings of 18th International Joint Conference on Artificial Intelligence, pp. 721–726. Morgan Kaufmann, San Francisco (2003)
22. Thangarajah, J., Padgham, L., Winikoff, M.: Detecting and exploiting positive goal interaction in intelligent agents. In: AAMAS 2003. Proceedings of the second international joint conference on Autonomous agents and multiagent systems, pp. 401–408. ACM Press, New York (2003)
23. Thangarajah, J., Winikoff, M., Padgham, L.: Avoiding resource conflicts in intelligent agents. In: van Harmelen, F. (ed.) ECAI 2002. Proceedings of 15th European Conference on Artifical Intelligence, IOS Press, Amsterdam (2002)
24. van Riemsdijk, M.B., Dastani, M., Meyer, J.-J.C.: Semantics of declarative goals in agent programming. In: AAMAS 2005. Proceedings of the fourth international joint conference on Autonomous agents and multiagent systems, pp. 133–140. ACM Press, New York (2005)
25. Winikoff, M., Padgham, L., Harland, J., Thangarajah, J.: Declarative and procedural goals in intelligent agent systems. In: KR2002. Proceedings of the Eighth International Conference on Principles of Knowledge Representation and Reasoning, 22–25 April, Toulouse, France, pp. 470–481(2002)

Reflections on Agent Beliefs

J.W. Lloyd[1] and K.S. Ng[2]

[1] College of Engineering and Computer Science
The Australian National University
jwl@cecs.anu.edu.au
[2] National ICT Australia
kee.siong@nicta.com.au

Abstract. Some issues concerning beliefs of agents are discussed. These issues are the general syntactic form of beliefs, the logic underlying beliefs, acquiring beliefs, and reasoning with beliefs. The logical setting is more expressive and aspects of the reasoning and acquisition processes are more general than are usually considered.

1 Introduction

Beliefs are an important component of every agent system that assist in the selection of actions. Because of their importance, there is a huge literature on representing, reasoning with, and acquiring beliefs. This paper contributes to this literature with a setting for beliefs that employs an unusually expressive logic.

We argue that since the purpose of beliefs is to help select actions, the general syntactic form for beliefs matters and that this form should be function definitions. We also argue that it is desirable that the logic in which these definitions are written be as expressive as possible. For this reason, we admit higher-order functions so that functions may take other functions as arguments. This means that the programming idioms of functional programming are available, and that sets and multisets can be represented by abstractions. Also it is common for beliefs to have a modal nature, usually temporal or epistemic. For example, on the temporal side, it might be important that at the last time or at some time in the past, some situation held and, therefore, a certain action is now appropriate. Similarly, on the epistemic side, beliefs about the beliefs of other agents may be used to determine which action to perform. The usefulness of modal beliefs for agents is now well established, in [1] and [2], for example. Besides, introspection reveals that people use temporal and epistemic considerations when deciding what to do. These considerations lead to the choice of multi-modal, higher-order logic as the logic for the beliefs.

While many beliefs can be built into agents beforehand by their designers, it is also common for beliefs to be acquired by some kind of learning process during deployment. We discuss an approach to belief acquisition that includes as special cases simple updating, belief revision [3], and learning [4].

M. Baldoni et al. (Eds.): DALT 2007, LNAI 4897, pp. 122–139, 2008.

During action selection, it is necessary to reason about beliefs or, more accurately in our case, compute with beliefs. We discuss a computation system for the logic that greatly extends existing modal and temporal logic programming systems, and give examples to illustrate how computation works. For most applications, computation is efficient enough that it could be used to select actions in real time.

In summary, the main contribution of this paper is a setting for agent beliefs in an expressive logic. A computation system that forms the core of a modal functional logic programming language is provided to reason about beliefs. All the facilities described here have been implemented.

The next section contains a discussion of the necessary logical machinery. Section 3 motivates the idea that beliefs should be function definitions. Section 4 shows how agents can acquire beliefs. Section 5 discusses how reasoning with beliefs is handled. Section 6 gives some conclusions.

2 Logic

In this section, we outline the most relevant aspects of the logic, focussing to begin with on the monomorphic version. We define types and terms, and give an introduction to the modalities that will be most useful in this paper. Full details of the logic, including its reasoning capabilities, can be found in [5].

Definition 1. *An* alphabet *consists of three sets:*

1. *A set $\mathfrak{T}$ of type constructors.*
2. *A set $\mathfrak{C}$ of constants.*
3. *A set $\mathfrak{V}$ of variables.*

Each type constructor in $\mathfrak{T}$ has an arity. The set $\mathfrak{T}$ always includes the type constructor Ω of arity 0. Ω is the type of the booleans. Each constant in $\mathfrak{C}$ has a signature. The set $\mathfrak{V}$ is denumerable. Variables are typically denoted by $x, y, z, \ldots$. Types are built up from the set of type constructors, using the symbols $\rightarrow$ and $\times$.

Definition 2. *A* type *is defined inductively as follows.*

1. *If T is a type constructor of arity k and $\alpha_1, \ldots, \alpha_k$ are types, then $T\,\alpha_1 \ldots \alpha_k$ is a type. (Thus a type constructor of arity 0 is a type.)*
2. *If α and β are types, then $\alpha \rightarrow \beta$ is a type.*
3. *If $\alpha_1, \ldots, \alpha_n$ are types, then $\alpha_1 \times \cdots \times \alpha_n$ is a type.*

The set $\mathfrak{C}$ always includes the following constants.

1. $\top$ and $\bot$, having signature Ω.
2. $=_\alpha$, having signature $\alpha \rightarrow \alpha \rightarrow \Omega$, for each type α.
3. $\neg$, having signature $\Omega \rightarrow \Omega$.
4. $\wedge$, $\vee$, $\longrightarrow$, $\longleftarrow$, and $\longleftrightarrow$, having signature $\Omega \rightarrow \Omega \rightarrow \Omega$.
5. Σ_α and Π_α, having signature $(\alpha \rightarrow \Omega) \rightarrow \Omega$, for each type α.

The intended meaning of $=_\alpha$ is identity (that is, $=_\alpha x\ y$ is $\top$ iff x and y are identical), the intended meaning of $\top$ is true, the intended meaning of $\bot$ is false, and the intended meanings of the connectives $\neg$, $\wedge$, $\vee$, $\longrightarrow$, $\longleftarrow$, and $\longleftrightarrow$ are as usual. The intended meanings of Σ_α and Π_α are that Σ_α maps a predicate to $\top$ iff the predicate maps at least one element to $\top$ and Π_α maps a predicate to $\top$ iff the predicate maps all elements to $\top$.

We assume there are necessity modality operators $\Box_i$, for $i = 1, \ldots, m$.

Definition 3. *A term, together with its type, is defined inductively as follows.*

1. *A variable in $\mathfrak{V}$ of type α is a term of type α.*
2. *A constant in $\mathfrak{C}$ having signature α is a term of type α.*
3. *If t is a term of type β and x a variable of type α, then $\lambda x.t$ is a term of type $\alpha \to \beta$.*
4. *If s is a term of type $\alpha \to \beta$ and t a term of type α, then $(s\ t)$ is a term of type β.*
5. *If $t_1, \ldots, t_n$ are terms of type $\alpha_1, \ldots, \alpha_n$, respectively, then $(t_1, \ldots, t_n)$ is a term of type $\alpha_1 \times \cdots \times \alpha_n$.*
6. *If t is a term of type α and $i \in \{1, \ldots, m\}$, then $\Box_i t$ is a term of type α.*

Terms of the form $(\Sigma_\alpha\ \lambda x.t)$ are written as $\exists_\alpha x.t$ and terms of the form $(\Pi_\alpha\ \lambda x.t)$ are written as $\forall_\alpha x.t$ (in accord with the intended meaning of Σ_α and Π_α). Thus, in higher-order logic, each quantifier is obtained as a combination of an abstraction acted on by a suitable function (Σ_α or Π_α).

Constants can be declared to be *rigid*; they then have the same meaning in each world (in the semantics). A term is *rigid* if every constant in it is rigid.

If α is a type, then $\mathfrak{B}_\alpha$ is the set of basic terms of type α [6]. Basic terms represent individuals. For example, $\mathfrak{B}_\Omega$ is $\{\top, \bot\}$. Also $\mathfrak{B}_{Int}$ is $\{\ldots, -2, -1, 0, 1, 2, \ldots\}$.

The polymorphic version of the logic extends what is given above by also having available parameters which are type variables (denoted by $a, b, c, \ldots$). The definition of a type as above is then extended to polymorphic types that may contain parameters and the definition of a term as above is extended to terms that may have polymorphic types. We work in the polymorphic version of the logic in the remainder of the paper. In this case, we drop the α in $\exists_\alpha$, $\forall_\alpha$, and $=_\alpha$, since the types associated with $\exists$, $\forall$, and $=$ are now inferred from the context. The universal closure of a formula φ is denoted by $\forall(\varphi)$.

An important feature of higher-order logic is that it admits functions that can take other functions as arguments. (First-order logic does not admit these so-called higher-order functions). This fact can be exploited in applications, through the use of predicates to represent sets and predicate rewrite systems that are used for learning, for example.

Theories in the logic consist of two kinds of assumptions, global and local. The essential difference is that global assumptions are true in each world in the intended interpretation, while local assumptions only have to be true in the actual world in the intended interpretation. Each kind of assumption has a certain role to play when proving a theorem. A theory is denoted by a pair $(\mathcal{G}, \mathcal{L})$, where $\mathcal{G}$ is the set of global assumptions and $\mathcal{L}$ is the set of local assumptions.

As is well known, modalities can have a variety of meanings, depending on the application. Some of these are indicated here; much more detail can be found in [1], [2] and [5], for example.

In multi-agent applications, one meaning for $\square_i \varphi$ is that 'agent i knows φ'. In this case, the modality $\square_i$ is written as $\boldsymbol{K}_i$.

A weaker notion is that of belief. In this case, $\square_i \varphi$ means that 'agent i believes φ' and the modality $\square_i$ is written as $\boldsymbol{B}_i$.

The modalities also have a variety of temporal readings. We will make use of the (past) temporal modalities ● ('last') and ■ ('always in the past'). We also use the modality ◆ ('sometime in the past'), which is dual to ■.

Modalities can be applied to terms that are not formulas. Thus terms such as $\boldsymbol{B}_i 42$ and ●A, where A is a constant, are admitted. We will find to be particularly useful terms that have the form $\square_{j_1} \cdots \square_{j_r} f$, where f is a function and $\square_{j_1} \cdots \square_{j_r}$ is a sequence of modalities.

Throughout, it is assumed that all belief bases contain the standard equality theory given in [5] which includes definitions for equality, the connectives, the quantifiers, the if_then_else function, an assumption that gives β-reduction, and some assumptions concerning modalities.

One of these modal assumptions is the following schema that can be used as a global assumption.

$$(\square_i \mathbf{s}\ \mathbf{t}) = \square_i(\mathbf{s}\ \mathbf{t}),$$

where $\mathbf{s}$ is a syntactical variable ranging over terms of type $\alpha \to \beta$ and $\mathbf{t}$ is a syntactical variable ranging over $rigid$ terms of type α. Specialised to some of the epistemic and temporal modalities discussed so far, this means, for example, that

$$(\boldsymbol{B}_i \mathbf{s}\ \mathbf{t}) = \boldsymbol{B}_i(\mathbf{s}\ \mathbf{t}) \quad \text{and} \quad (●\mathbf{s}\ \mathbf{t}) = ●(\mathbf{s}\ \mathbf{t})$$

are global assumptions (under the rigidity assumption on $\mathbf{t}$).

Another useful global assumption in the standard equality theory is

$$\square_i \boldsymbol{t} = \boldsymbol{t},$$

where $\boldsymbol{t}$ is a syntactical variable ranging over $rigid$ terms and $i \in \{1, \ldots, m\}$. Instances of this schema that could be used as global assumptions include the following.

$$\boldsymbol{B}_i 42 = 42, \quad \boldsymbol{B}_i \top = \top \quad \text{and} \quad ●\bot = \bot.$$

Let $(X, \mathcal{A}, \mu)$ be a measure space. A $density$ (with respect to the measure μ) is a non-negative, integrable function h on X such that $\int_X h\, d\mu = 1$. We let $Density\ \sigma$ denote the type of densities defined on sets whose elements have type σ.

3   Beliefs as Function Definitions

In this section, we discuss suitable syntactic forms for beliefs. There are no generally agreed forms for beliefs in the literature, other than the basic requirement that they be formulas. For the purpose of constructing multi-agent systems, we propose the following definition.

Definition 4. *A belief is the definition of a function* $f : \sigma \to \tau$ *having the form*

$$\Box \forall x.((f\ x) = t),$$

where $\Box$ *is a (possibly empty) sequence of modalities and* t *is a term of type* τ.
   A belief base is a set of beliefs.

Typically, for agent j, beliefs have the form $\boldsymbol{B}_j \varphi$, with the intuitive meaning 'agent j believes φ', where φ is $\forall x.((f\ x) = t)$. Other typical beliefs have the form $\boldsymbol{B}_j \boldsymbol{B}_i \varphi$, meaning 'agent j believes that agent i believes φ'. If there is a temporal component to beliefs, this is often manifested by temporal modalities at the front of beliefs. Then, for example, there could be a belief of the form $\bullet^2 \boldsymbol{B}_j \boldsymbol{B}_i \varphi$, whose intuitive meaning is 'at the second last time, agent j believed that agent i believed φ'. (Here, $\bullet^2$ is a shorthand for $\bullet\bullet$).

We will now use the rational agent architecture described in [7] to motivate the introduction of Definition 4 and illustrate its usefulness. The arguments used are sufficiently general to be applicable to more general (PO)MDP-based agent architectures. Consider an agent application for which σ is the type of (internal) states of the agent and α is the type of actions. The dynamics of the agent can thus be modelled with a density $f : Density\ \sigma \times \alpha \times \sigma$. By conditioning on the first two arguments, we get a (conditional) density $f' : \sigma \times \alpha \to Density\ \sigma$. If the agent is in a certain state and a certain action is applied, this function gives a distribution over the states the agent could end up in as a result of applying that action. In principle, knowing this transition distribution and the utility of states is enough to make a rational choice of action, where rational means choosing the action with the maximum expected utility.

The problem is that, in practice, there are usually a very large number of states which makes the direct use of this approach infeasible. To reduce the difficulty, an obvious idea is to define features on the state space in order to partition it into (a much smaller number of) equivalence classes of states that can be treated uniformly. This idea is illustrated in Figure 1, where *initial* projects onto the initial state, *action* projects onto the action, and *final* projects onto the state that is reached as a result of applying that action. The features are the evidence features e_i, for $i = 1, \ldots, n$, and the result features r_j, for $j = 1, \ldots, m$. Each class of features serves a different purpose. The evidence features are chosen so as to assist the selection of a good action, whereas the result features are chosen so as to provide a good evaluation of the resulting state.

Now consider the function

$$transition : \epsilon_1 \times \cdots \times \epsilon_n \times \alpha \to Density\ \rho_1 \times \cdots \times \rho_m$$

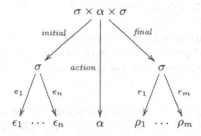

Fig. 1. Evidence and result features

that could be learned by an agent using training examples which indicate the state that results (possibly non-deterministically) from applying a particular action to a particular state. Given the function *transition*, the policy function *policy* : $\sigma \to \alpha$ is then defined by

$$(policy\ s) = \underset{a}{\arg\max}\ \mathbb{E}_{(transition\ ((e_1\ s),...,(e_n\ s),a))}(utility),$$

where s ranges over states, a ranges over actions, and *utility* is a (real-valued) random variable over a product space of type $\rho_1 \times \cdots \times \rho_m$ that defines the utility of each tuple in this space. Here $\mathbb{E}_{(transition\ ((e_1\ s),...,(e_n\ s),a))}$ denotes the expectation with respect to the density $(transition\ ((e_1\ s),\ldots,(e_n\ s),a))$.

Now consider this question: what makes up the belief base of such an agent? Clearly, the definitions of the evidence and (some of the) result features should be in the belief base. Further, the definitions of the functions *transition*, *utility* and *policy* should also be in the belief base. And these are all the beliefs the agent needs to maintain about the environment in order to act rationally. This concludes our motivation for Definition 4.

We now examine the form that beliefs can take in more detail. Some beliefs can be specified directly by the programmer and the body of the definition can be any term of the appropriate type. Some beliefs, however, need to be acquired from training examples, usually during deployment. We propose a particular form for beliefs of this latter type. We consider beliefs that, for a function $f : \sigma \to \tau$, are definitions of the following form.

$\Box \forall x.((f\ x) =$

    if $(p_1\ x)$ *then* v_1

    else if $(p_2\ x)$ *then* v_2

    $\vdots$

    else if $(p_n\ x)$ *then* v_n

    else v_0),

where $\Box$ is a (possibly empty) sequence of modalities, $p_1, \ldots, p_n$ are predicates that can be modal and/or higher order, and $v_0, v_1, \ldots, v_n$ are suitable values.

Such a belief is a definition for the function f in the context of the modal sequence $\square$.

While the above form for beliefs may appear to be rather specialised, it turns out to be convenient and general, and easily encompasses beliefs in more conventional form. Here is an example to illustrate how one can represent a (relational) database.

Example 1. Consider an agent that recommends TV programs. Amongst other things the agent will need to have access to a TV guide as part of its belief base. Represented as a relational database, the TV guide would consist of a set of tuples, where each tuple gave details of the program that is on at a certain date, time, and channel. Similarly, as a Prolog program, the TV guide would be the corresponding set of facts. Actually, neither of these representations is a good one because each ignores a functional dependency in the data: each date, time and channel triple uniquely determines a program. Here we represent the TV guide as a function definition that correctly models this functional dependency.

For this, we require the following type synonyms.

$Occurrence = Date \times Time \times Channel$

$Date = Day \times Month \times Year$

$Time = Hour \times Minute$

$Program = Title \times Duration \times (List\ Genre) \times Classification \times Synopsis.$

Now we can give (a typical instance of) the definition of the function

$tv\_guide : Occurrence \rightarrow Program$

that models the TV guide.

$\boldsymbol{B_t}\ \forall x.((tv\_guide\ x) =$

$\quad\quad if\ ((= ((21, 7, 2004), (19, 30), WIN))\ x)$

$\quad\quad\quad\quad\quad\quad then\ (\text{``}Seinfeld\text{''}, 30, [Sitcom], PG, \text{``}Kramer\ldots\text{''})$

$\quad\quad else\ if\ ((= ((20, 7, 2004), (20, 30), ABC))\ x)$

$\quad\quad\quad\quad\quad\quad then\ (\text{``}The\ Bill\text{''}, 50, [Drama], M, \text{``}Sun\ Hill\ldots\text{''})$

$\quad\quad\quad\vdots$

$\quad\quad else\ (\text{`` ''}, 0, [], NA, \text{`` ''})),$

where $\boldsymbol{B_t}$ is the belief modality for the TV recommender and (`` ''}, 0, [], NA, \text{`` '') is the default program (where 'default' has a technical meaning [6]). It is worth noting that all the queries that one might want to pose to the relational database (or Prolog) version of the TV guide can be just as easily posed to, and answered by, the function definition form (using computation, as discussed in Section 5).

It is also straightforward to rewrite Horn clause theories, a common way of representing beliefs, as function definitions in the form above.

Example 2. Consider an agent with belief modality B that has beliefs of the form

$$B((p\ t_1) \longleftarrow W_1)$$
$$\vdots$$
$$B((p\ t_n) \longleftarrow W_n).$$

This form of belief base includes Horn clause theories and logic programs. By adding equations to the bodies and existentially quantifying free local variables in the bodies, the beliefs can be written in the form

$$B((p\ x) \longleftarrow V_1)$$
$$\vdots$$
$$B((p\ x) \longleftarrow V_n).$$

This set of beliefs can then be written in the function definition form

$$B\ \forall x.((p\ x) =$$
$$\quad if\ (\lambda x.V_1\ x)\ then\ \top$$
$$\qquad \vdots$$
$$\quad else\ if\ (\lambda x.V_n\ x)\ then\ \top$$
$$\quad else\ \bot),$$

which is equivalent to the original set of beliefs under the closed world assumption. (The latter formula is essentially the completion of the original set of beliefs, probably the semantics intended anyway.)

4   Acquiring Beliefs

Now we turn to belief acquisition. Belief bases are generally dynamic, that is, they change from time to time during deployment of the agent. It follows that agents need to have some method by which they can acquire new beliefs. We use the phrase 'belief acquisition' to name this process. The term 'acquire' is intended to be understood in a general sense that includes 'update', 'revise' and 'learn' as special cases. 'Update' refers to the simplest form of belief acquisition in which facts are added to or deleted from a simple database, 'revise' refers to the form of acquisition that is studied in the literature on belief revision [3], and 'learning' refers to machine learning [4]. Belief acquisition thus covers the spectrum from simple updating at one end to the generalisation that is characteristic of learning at the other end.

The approach we take to belief acquisition starts from the machine learning perspective in that it extends decision-list learning in [8]. In machine learning, one wants to learn a function definition. The input to the learning process is a collection of training examples that give the value of the function for some points in its domain. A space of hypotheses is searched to find a definition for the function that agrees 'as well as possible' with the training examples, according to some measure. The hypothesis learned is intended to generalise, in the sense that it should give the correct value on unseen examples.

We extend the learning process in several ways so that it also includes update and belief revision. The first extension is that training examples can give the value of the function not just on a single point of the domain but on a subset of it given by some predicate. This allows us to capture some aspects of what happens in theory revision. In addition, the predicate can include modalities. Then, in order to control where on the spectrum from updating to learning we want to be, we make a careful choice of hypothesis language. If we want simple updating, then the hypothesis language is chosen to be very specific; if we want learning, then the hypothesis language is chosen to be general; for intermediate points on the spectrum, the hypothesis language is chosen accordingly.

A major ingredient for belief acquisition is a method of generating predicates. For this, we use predicate rewrite systems which we describe informally as follows. A predicate rewrite is an expression of the form $p \rightarrowtail q$, where p and q are predicates (in a particular syntactic form). The predicate p is called the *head* and q is the *body* of the rewrite. A predicate rewrite system is a finite set of predicate rewrites. One should think of a predicate rewrite system as a kind of grammar for generating a particular class of predicates. Roughly speaking, this works as follows. Starting from the weakest predicate *top* (defined below), all predicate rewrites that have *top* (of the appropriate type) in the head are selected to make up child predicates that consist of the bodies of these predicate rewrites. Then, for each child predicate and each redex in that predicate, all child predicates are generated by replacing each redex by the body of the predicate rewrite whose head is identical to the redex. This generation of predicates continues to produce the entire space of predicates given by the predicate rewrite system. The details of the non-modal version of this can be found in [6] and the modal version in [5].

A particular predicate language, called the basic language, often arises in applications.

Definition 5. *Let α be a type. A* basic predicate *for the type α is one of the form $(= t)$, for some $t \in \mathfrak{B}_\alpha$.*

The set $\mathbf{B}_\alpha = \{(= t) \mid t \in \mathfrak{B}_\alpha\}$ of basic predicates for the type α is called the basic language *for the type α.*

We distinguish two predicate languages that are used in belief acquisition. One is the *training predicate language* that is used in training examples. The general form of a training example for a function f is

$$\Box \forall x.((p\ x) \rightarrow (f\ x) = v),$$

where p is a predicate from the training predicate language and v is a value. It is common for training predicate languages to include the corresponding basic language (of the appropriate type).

The other language is the *hypothesis predicate language* that is used in hypotheses. The predicates appearing in a belief come from the hypothesis predicate language. In the case of learning, it would be very unlikely that the hypothesis predicate language would include any basic predicates at all (because in learning one wants to generalise beyond the training examples).

Here are two examples that illustrate some of the issues for belief acquisition.

Example 3. This example illustrates database updating which is the simplest form of belief acquisition. We show how to acquire the database of Example 1.

First, we set up the training examples. The training predicate language is the basic language $\mathbf{B}_{Occurrence}$. A typical predicate in this language is

$$(= ((21, 7, 2004), (19, 30), WIN)).$$

The set of values is the set of basic terms $\mathfrak{B}_{Program}$. A typical value is

$$(\text{``Seinfeld''}, 30, [Sitcom], PG, \text{``Kramer} \ldots \text{''}).$$

Training examples have the form

$$\mathbf{B}_t \ \forall x.(((= ((21, 7, 2004), (19, 30), WIN)) \ x) \longrightarrow$$
$$(tv\_guide \ x) = (\text{``Seinfeld''}, 30, [Sitcom], PG, \text{``Kramer} \ldots \text{''}))$$
$$\mathbf{B}_t \ \forall x.(((= ((20, 7, 2004), (20, 30), ABC)) \ x) \longrightarrow$$
$$(tv\_guide \ x) = (\text{``The Bill''}, 50, [Drama], M, \text{``Sun Hill} \ldots \text{''}))$$

and so on.

Now we choose the hypothesis predicate language. For database updating, one wants predicates in the hypothesis predicate language to pick out individuals. Thus $\mathbf{B}_{Occurrence}$ is also chosen as the hypothesis predicate language. With this choice, the belief acquisition algorithm returns the definition for the function *tv_guide* given in Example 1.

Example 4. (This example appears in [9].) Consider a majordomo agent that manages a household. There are many tasks for such an agent to carry out including keeping track of occupants, turning appliances on and off, ordering food for the refrigerator, and so on.

Here we concentrate on one small aspect of the majordomo's tasks which is to recommend television programs for viewing by the occupants of the house. Suppose the current occupants are Alice, Bob, and Cathy, and that the agent knows the television preferences of each of them. Methods for acquiring these preferences were studied in [10]. Suppose that each occupant has a personal agent that has acquired (amongst many other functions) the function *likes* : *Program* $\rightarrow \Omega$, where *likes* is true for a program iff the person likes the program. We also suppose that the majordomo has access to the definitions of this function for each occupant, for the present time and for some suitable period into the past. Let $\mathbf{B}_m$ be the belief modality for the majordomo agent, $\mathbf{B}_a$ the belief modality for Alice, B_b the belief modality for Bob, and B_c the belief modality for Cathy. Thus part of the majordomo's belief base has the following form:

$B_m B_a \forall x.((likes\ x) = \varphi_0)$

$\bullet B_m B_a \forall x.((likes\ x) = \varphi_1)$

$\vdots$

$\bullet^{n-1} B_m B_a \forall x.((likes\ x) = \varphi_{n-1})$

$\bullet^n B_m \forall x.(\blacklozenge B_a(likes\ x) = \bot)$

$B_m B_b \forall x.((likes\ x) = \psi_0)$

$\bullet B_m B_b \forall x.((likes\ x) = \psi_1)$

$\vdots$

$\bullet^{k-1} B_m B_b \forall x.((likes\ x) = \psi_{k-1})$

$\bullet^k B_m \forall x.(\blacklozenge B_b(likes\ x) = \bot)$

$B_m B_c \forall x.((likes\ x) = \xi_0)$

$\bullet B_m B_c \forall x.((likes\ x) = \xi_1)$

$\vdots$

$\bullet^{l-1} B_m B_c \forall x.((likes\ x) = \xi_{l-1})$

$\bullet^l B_m \forall x.(\blacklozenge B_c(likes\ x) = \bot),$

for suitable φ_i, ψ_i, and ξ_i. The form these can take is explained in [10].

In the beginning, the belief base contains the formula

$B_m \forall x.(\blacklozenge B_a(likes\ x) = \bot),$

whose purpose is to prevent runaway computations into the infinite past for certain formulas of the form $\blacklozenge \varphi$. The meaning of this formula is "the agent believes that for all programs it is not true that at some time in the past Alice likes the program". After n time steps, this formula has been transformed into

$\bullet^n B_m \forall x.(\blacklozenge B_a(likes\ x) = \bot).$

In general, at each time step, the beliefs about *likes* at the previous time steps each have another $\bullet$ placed at their front to push them one step further back into the past, and a new current belief about *likes* is acquired. (For this application, a time step could occupy hours, days, or even longer, depending on how often the beliefs need to be updated.)

Based on these beliefs about the occupant preferences for TV programs, the task for the agent is to recommend programs that all three occupants would be interested in watching together. The simplest idea is that the agent should only recommend programs that all three occupants currently like. But it is possible that less stringent conditions might also be acceptable; for example, it might be sufficient that two of the occupants currently like a program but that the third has liked the program in the past (even if they do not like it at the present time). A (simplified) predicate rewrite system suitable for giving an hypothesis predicate language for such an acquisition task is as follows.

$top \rightarrowtail \wedge_3\ top\ top\ top$

$top \rightarrowtail \vee_2\ top\ top$

$top \rightarrowtail \boldsymbol{B}_i likes \quad \%$ for each $i \in \{a, b, c\}$

$top \rightarrowtail \blacklozenge \boldsymbol{B}_i likes \quad \%$ for each $i \in \{a, b, c\}.$

Here, the function $top : a \rightarrow \Omega$ is defined by $(top\ x) = \top$, for each x. The function

$$\wedge_3 : (a \rightarrow \Omega) \rightarrow (a \rightarrow \Omega) \rightarrow (a \rightarrow \Omega) \rightarrow a \rightarrow \Omega$$

is defined by $\wedge_3\ p_1\ p_2\ p_3\ x = (p_1\ x) \wedge (p_2\ x) \wedge (p_3\ x)$, for each x. The function $\vee_2$, which defines 'disjunction' at the predicate level for two arguments, is defined analogously.

Let $group\_likes : Program \rightarrow \Omega$ be the function that the agent needs to acquire. Thus the informal meaning of $group\_likes$ is that it is true for a program iff the occupants collectively like the program. (This may involve a degree of compromise by some of the occupants.) The training predicate language is $\boldsymbol{B}_{Program}$, so that training examples for this task look like

$\boldsymbol{B}_m \forall x.(((= P_1)\ x) \longrightarrow (group\_likes\ x) = \top)$

$\boldsymbol{B}_m \forall x.(((= P_2)\ x) \longrightarrow (group\_likes\ x) = \bot),$

where P_1 and P_2 are particular programs. The definition of a typical function that might be acquired from training examples and the hypothesis predicate language given by the above predicate rewrite system is as follows.

$\boldsymbol{B}_m \forall x.\,((group\_likes\ x) =$

$\quad\quad if\ ((\wedge_3\ \blacklozenge\boldsymbol{B}_a likes\ \boldsymbol{B}_b likes\ \boldsymbol{B}_c likes)\ x)\ then\ \top$

$\quad\quad else\ if\ ((\wedge_3\ \boldsymbol{B}_c likes\ (\vee_2\ \boldsymbol{B}_a likes\ \boldsymbol{B}_b likes)\ top)\ x)\ then\ \top$

$\quad\quad else\ \bot).$

Now let P be some specific program. Suppose that a computation shows that $\boldsymbol{B}_m((group\_likes\ P) = \bot)$ is a consequence of the belief base of the agent. On this basis, the agent will presumably not recommend to the occupants that they watch program P together.

5   Reasoning with Beliefs

As well as representing knowledge, it is necessary to reason with it. The reasoning system for the logic combines a theorem prover and an equational reasoning system. The theorem prover is a fairly conventional tableau theorem prover for modal higher-order logic similar to what is proposed in [11]. The equational reasoning system is, in effect, a computational system that significantly extends existing declarative programming languages by adding facilities for computing with modalities. The proof component and the computational component are tightly integrated, in the sense that either can call the other. Furthermore, this synergy between the two makes possible all kinds of interesting reasoning tasks. For agent applications, the most common reasoning task is a computational one, that of evaluating a function call. In this case, the theorem-prover plays a subsidiary role, usually that of performing some rather straightforward modal theorem-proving tasks. However, in other applications it can just as easily be the other way around with the computational system performing subsidiary equational reasoning tasks for the theorem prover.

Here we concentrate on computation. As motivation for what computation actually means, consider the problem of determining the meaning of a term t in the intended interpretation (for some application). If a formal definition of the intended interpretation is available, then this problem can be solved (under some finiteness assumptions). However, we assume here that the intended interpretation is not available, as is usually the case, so that the problem cannot be solved directly. Nevertheless, there is still a lot that can be done if the theory $\mathcal{T}$ of the application is available and enough of it is in equational form. Intuitively, if t can be 'simplified' sufficiently using $\mathcal{T}$, its meaning may become apparent even in the absence of detailed knowledge of the intended interpretation. For example, if t can be simplified to a term containing only data constructors, then the meaning of t will generally be obvious.

More formally, the *computation problem* is as follows.

Given a theory $\mathcal{T}$, a term t, and a sequence $\Box_{j_1} \cdots \Box_{j_r}$ of modalities, find a 'simpler' term t' such that $\Box_{j_1} \cdots \Box_{j_r} \forall (t = t')$ is a consequence of $\mathcal{T}$.

Thus t and t' have the same meaning in all worlds accessible from the point world in the intended interpretation according to the modalities $\Box_{j_1} \cdots \Box_{j_r}$.

Here now is the definition of a mechanism that addresses the computational problem by employing equational reasoning to rewrite terms to 'simpler' terms that have the same meaning. To simplify matters, we only consider the case when the computation does not need to call on the theorem prover. (This is the rank 0 case in [5].) In the following definition, a modal path to a subterm is the sequence of indices of modalities whose scope one passes through when going down to the subterm. A substitution is admissible if any term that replaces a free occurrence of a variable that is in the scope of a modality is rigid.

Definition 6. *Let $\mathcal{T} \equiv (\mathcal{G}, \mathcal{L})$ be a theory. A computation using $\Box_{j_1} \cdots \Box_{j_r}$ with respect to $\mathcal{T}$ is a sequence $\{t_i\}_{i=1}^{n}$ of terms such that the following conditions are satisfied.*

1. *For $i = 1, \ldots, n-1$, there is*
   (a) *a subterm s_i of t_i at occurrence o_i, where the modal path to o_i in t_i is $k_1 \ldots k_{m_i}$,*

(b)   i. a formula $\Box_{j_1} \cdots \Box_{j_r} \Box_{k_1} \cdots \Box_{k_{m_i}} \forall(u_i = v_i)$ in $\mathcal{L}$, or
ii. a formula $\forall(u_i = v_i)$ in $\mathcal{G}$, and
(c) a substitution θ_i that is admissible with respect to $u_i = v_i$

such that $u_i \theta_i$ is α-equivalent to s_i and t_{i+1} is $t_i[s_i/v_i \theta_i]_{o_i}$.

The term t_1 is called the goal of the computation and t_n is called the answer. Each subterm s_i is called a redex.

Each formula $\Box_{j_1} \cdots \Box_{j_r} \Box_{k_1} \cdots \Box_{k_{m_i}} \forall(u_i = v_i)$ or $\forall(u_i = v_i)$ is called an input equation.

The formula $\Box_{j_1} \cdots \Box_{j_r} \forall(t_1 = t_n)$ is called the result of the computation.

The treatment of modalities in a computation has to be carefully handled. The reason is that even such a simple concept as applying a substitution is greatly complicated in the modal setting by the fact that constants generally have different meanings in different worlds and therefore the act of applying a substitution may not result in a term with the desired meaning. This explains the restriction to admissible substitutions in the definition of computation. It also explains why, for input equations that are local assumptions, the sequence of modalities $\Box_{k_1} \cdots \Box_{k_{m_i}}$ whose scopes are entered going down to the redex must appear in the modalities at the front of the input equation. (For input equations that are global assumptions, in effect, every sequence of modalities that we might need is implicitly at the front of the input equation).

In the general case, an input equation can also be a theorem that was proved by the theorem-proving component of the reasoning system, as the examples below show.

Here are two examples to illustrate various aspects of computation.

Example 5. Consider a belief base for an agent that contains the definition

$\boldsymbol{B}\ \forall x.((f\ x) =$
if $x = A$ then 42 else if $x = B$ then 21 else if $x = C$ then 42 else 0),

where $A, B, C : \sigma$, $f : \sigma \to Nat$ and $\boldsymbol{B}$ is the belief modality for the agent. With such a definition, it is straightforward to compute in the 'forward' direction. Thus $(f\ B)$ can be computed in the obvious way to produce the answer 21 and the result $\boldsymbol{B}((f\ B) = 21)$.

Less obviously, the definition can be used to compute in the 'reverse' direction. For example, consider the computation of $\{x \mid (f\ x) = 42\}$ in Figure 2, which produces the answer $\{A, C\}$. The redexes selected are underlined. This computation makes essential use of the equations

$(w\ $ if x then y else $z) =$ if x then $(w\ y)$ else $(w\ z)$
$($ if x then y else $z\ w) =$ if x then $(y\ w)$ else $(z\ w)$

from the standard equality theory.

$\{x \mid \underline{(f\ x)} = 42\}$

$\{x \mid ((= \quad \textit{if } x = A \textit{ then } 42 \textit{ else if } x = B \textit{ then } 21 \textit{ else if } x = C \textit{ then } 42 \textit{ else } 0)\ 42)\}$

$\{x \mid \underline{(\textit{if } x = A \textit{ then } (= \quad 42) \textit{ else } (= \quad \textit{if } x = B \textit{ then } 21 \textit{ else if } x = C \textit{ then } 42 \textit{ else } 0)\ 42)}\}$

$\{x \mid \textit{if } x = A \textit{ then } \underline{(42 = 42)} \textit{ else } ((= \quad \textit{if } x = B \textit{ then } 21 \textit{ else if } x = C \textit{ then } 42 \textit{ else } 0)\ 42)\}$

$\{x \mid \textit{if } x = A \textit{ then } \top \textit{ else } ((= \quad \underline{\textit{if } x = B \textit{ then } 21 \textit{ else if } x = C \textit{ then } 42 \textit{ else } 0})\ 42)\}$

$\{x \mid \textit{if } x = A \textit{ then } \top \textit{ else } \underline{(\textit{if } x = B \textit{ then } (= \quad 21) \textit{ else } (= \quad \textit{if } x = C \textit{ then } 42 \textit{ else } 0)\ 42)}\}$

$\{x \mid \textit{if } x = A \textit{ then } \top \textit{ else if } x = B \textit{ then } \underline{(21 = 42)} \textit{ else } ((= \quad \textit{if } x = C \textit{ then } 42 \textit{ else } 0)\ 42)\}$

$\{x \mid \textit{if } x = A \textit{ then } \top \textit{ else if } x = B \textit{ then } \bot \textit{ else } ((= \quad \underline{\textit{if } x = C \textit{ then } 42 \textit{ else } 0})\ 42)\}$

$\{x \mid \textit{if } x = A \textit{ then } \top \textit{ else if } x = B \textit{ then } \bot \textit{ else } \underline{(\textit{if } x = C \textit{ then } (= \quad 42) \textit{ else } (= \quad 0)\ 42)}\}$

$\{x \mid \textit{if } x = A \textit{ then } \top \textit{ else if } x = B \textit{ then } \bot \textit{ else if } x = C \textit{ then } \underline{(42 = 42)} \textit{ else } (0 = 42)\}$

$\{x \mid \textit{if } x = A \textit{ then } \top \textit{ else if } x = B \textit{ then } \bot \textit{ else if } x = C \textit{ then } \top \textit{ else } \underline{(0 = 42)}\}$

$\{x \mid \textit{if } x = A \textit{ then } \top \textit{ else if } x = B \textit{ then } \bot \textit{ else if } x = C \textit{ then } \top \textit{ else } \bot\}$

Fig. 2. Computation using $\boldsymbol{B}$ of $\{x \mid (f\ x) = 42\}$

Example 6. This example illustrates computation using a belief base that has been obtained by incremental belief acquisition and that exploits modalities acting on arbitrary terms. Consider an agent with belief modality $\boldsymbol{B}$ and a belief base that includes definitions of the function $f : \sigma \to Nat$ at the current time and some recent times. Suppose at the current time the part of the belief base concerning f is as follows.

$\boldsymbol{B}\ \forall x.((f\ x) = \textit{if } (p_4\ x) \textit{ then } (\bullet f\ x) \textit{ else if } (p_5\ x) \textit{ then } 84 \textit{ else } 0)$

$\bullet\boldsymbol{B}\ \forall x.((f\ x) = \textit{if } (p_3\ x) \textit{ then } (\bullet f\ x) \textit{ else } 0)$

$\bullet^2\boldsymbol{B}\ \forall x.((f\ x) = \textit{if } (p_1\ x) \textit{ then } 42 \textit{ else if } (p_2\ x) \textit{ then } 21 \textit{ else } 0)$

$\bullet^3\boldsymbol{B}\ \forall x.((f\ x) = 0).$

Three time steps ago, the function f was 0 everywhere. Two time steps ago, the definition

$\boldsymbol{B}\ \forall x.((f\ x) = \textit{if } (p_1\ x) \textit{ then } 42 \textit{ else if } (p_2\ x) \textit{ then } 21 \textit{ else } 0)$

for f was acquired. Then, one time step ago, the definition

$\boldsymbol{B}\ \forall x.((f\ x) = \textit{if } (p_3\ x) \textit{ then } (\bullet f\ x) \textit{ else } 0)$

for f was acquired. This definition states that, on the region defined by p_3, f is the same as the f at the last time step; and, otherwise, f is 0. Finally, we come to the current definition, which on the region defined by p_4 is the same as the f at the last time step; on the region defined by p_5 is 84; and, otherwise, f is 0. Definitions like these which use earlier definitions arise naturally in incremental belief acquisition. A technical device needed to achieve incrementality is to admit values of the form ($\bullet^k f\ x$), so that earlier definitions become available for use. In turn this depends crucially on being able to apply modalities to arbitrary terms, in this case, functions.

Now suppose t is a rigid term of type σ and consider the computation using B of ($f\ t$) in Figure 3. Note how earlier definitions for f get used in the computation: at the step $\bullet\underline{(f\ t)}$, the definition at the last time step gets used, and at the step $\bullet^2\underline{(f\ t)}$, the definition from two time steps ago gets used.

$\underline{(f\ t)}$

if $\underline{(p_4\ t)}$ then ($\bullet f\ t$) else if $(p_5\ t)$ then 84 else 0

$\vdots$

if $\top$ then ($\bullet f\ t$) else if $(p_5\ t)$ then 84 else 0
$\underline{(\bullet f\ t)}$
$\bullet\underline{(f\ t)}$
$\bullet\underline{(if\ (p_3\ t)\ then\ (\bullet f\ t)\ else\ 0)}$

$\vdots$

$\bullet\underline{(if\ \top\ then\ (\bullet f\ t)\ else\ 0)}$
$\bullet\underline{(\bullet f\ t)}$
$\bullet^2\underline{(f\ t)}$
$\bullet^2\underline{(if\ (p_1\ t)\ then\ 42\ else\ if\ (p_2\ t)\ then\ 21\ else\ 0)}$

$\vdots$

$\bullet^2\underline{(if\ \top\ then\ 42\ else\ if\ (p_2\ t)\ then\ 21\ else\ 0)}$
$\bullet^2\underline{42}$
$\bullet\underline{42}$
42

Fig. 3. Computation using B of ($f\ t$)

Also needed in this computation is the instance ($\bullet f\ t$) $=$ $\bullet(f\ t)$ of the global assumption discussed in Section 2. Incidentally, the assumption that the argument to a function like f is rigid is a weak one; in typical applications, the argument will naturally be rigid.

It is assumed that the belief base of the agent contains the global assumption

$\bullet B\varphi \longrightarrow B\bullet\varphi.$

Using this assumption, it can be proved that

$$\boldsymbol{B}\bullet \; \forall x.((f \; x) = \textit{if} \; (p_3 \; x) \; \textit{then} \; (\bullet f \; x) \; \textit{else} \; 0)$$

and

$$\boldsymbol{B}\bullet^2 \; \forall x.((f \; x) = \textit{if} \; (p_1 \; x) \; \textit{then} \; 42 \; \textit{else if} \; (p_2 \; x) \; \textit{then} \; 21 \; \textit{else} \; 0)$$

are consequences of the belief base. These can then be used as input equations in the computation.

The computation shows that $\boldsymbol{B}((f \; t) = 42)$ is a consequence of the belief base. Thus the agent believes that the value of $(f \; t)$ is 42; on the basis of this and other similar information, it will select an appropriate action.

6   Conclusion

In this paper, we have reflected on some issues concerning beliefs for agents. The main conclusion we draw from this is the value of using a highly expressive logic for representing beliefs. Temporal and epistemic modalities allow beliefs to capture information about an environment that can be crucial when an agent is trying to select an appropriate action. For beliefs, propositional logic is not particularly useful and so it is necessary to move beyond the propositional case; we argue for the use of higher-order logic because of its extra expressive power. In spite of the expressive power of the logic (which is of course undecidable), a reasoning system in the form of a modal functional logic programming language means that agents can effectively compute using their beliefs when selecting actions. Thus reasoning during deployment of agents is substantially a programming task rather than a theorem-proving task. We are currently working on some challenging application domains for these ideas.

Acknowledgement

NICTA is funded through the Australian Government's Backing Australia's Ability initiative, in part through the Australian Research Council.

References

1. Fagin, R., Halpern, J., Moses, Y., Vardi, M.: Reasoning about Knowledge. MIT Press, Cambridge (1995)
2. Gabbay, D., Kurucz, A., Wolter, F., Zakharyaschev, M.: Many-Dimensional Modal Logics: Theory and Applications. In: Studies in Logic and The Foundations of Mathematics, vol. 148, Elsevier, Amsterdam (2003)
3. Alchourrón, C., Gärdenfors, P., Makinson, D.: On the logic of theory change: Partial meet contraction and revision functions. Journal of Symbolic Logic 50, 510–530 (1985)
4. Mitchell, T.: Machine Learning. McGraw-Hill, New York (1997)

5. Lloyd, J.: Knowledge representation and reasoning in modal higher-order logic (2007), http://users.rsise.anu.edu.au/~jwl
6. Lloyd, J.: Logic for Learning. In: Cognitive Technologies, Springer, Heidelberg (2003)
7. Lloyd, J., Sears, T.: An architecture for rational agents. In: Baldoni, M., Endriss, U., Omicini, A., Torroni, P. (eds.) DALT 2005. LNCS (LNAI), vol. 3904, pp. 51–71. Springer, Heidelberg (2006)
8. Rivest, R.: Learning decision lists. Machine Learning 2, 229–246 (1987)
9. Lloyd, J., Ng, K.S.: Learning modal theories. In: Muggleton, S., Otero, R., Tamaddoni-Nezhad, A. (eds.) ILP 2006. LNCS (LNAI), vol. 4455, pp. 320–334. Springer, Heidelberg (2007)
10. Cole, J., Gray, M., Lloyd, J., Ng, K.S.: Personalisation for user agents. In: Dignum, F., et al (eds.) AAMAS 2005. Fourth International Conference on Autonomous Agents and Multiagent Systems, pp. 603–610 (2005)
11. Fitting, M.: Types, Tableaus, and Gödel's God. Kluwer Academic Publishers, Dordrecht (2002)

Modeling Agents' Choices in Temporal Linear Logic

Duc Q. Pham, James Harland, and Michael Winikoff

School of Computer Science and Information Technology
RMIT University
GPO Box 2476V, Melbourne, 3001, Australia
{qupham,jah,winikoff}@cs.rmit.edu.au

Abstract. Decision-making is a fundamental feature of agent systems. Agents need to respond to requests from other agents, to react to environmental changes, and to prioritize and pursue their goals. Such decisions can have ongoing effects, as the future behavior of an agent may be heavily dependent on choices made earlier. In this paper we investigate a formal framework for modeling the choices of an agent. In particular, we show how the use of a choices calculus based on *temporal linear logic* can be used to capture distribution, temporal and dependency aspects of choices.

1 Introduction

Agents are increasingly becoming accepted as a suitable paradigm for conceptualizing, designing, and implementing the sorts of distributed complex dynamic systems that can be found in a range of domains, such as telecommunications, banking, crisis management, and business transactions [1].

A fundamental theme in agent systems is *decision-making*. Agents have to decide which resources to use, which actions to perform, and which goals and commitments to attend to in order to fulfill their design objectives as well as to respond to other agents in an open and dynamic operating environment. Choices made now may very well affect future achievement of goals or other threads of interactions. Accordingly, agents need to be able to reflect on how their choices may affect future actions and interactions.

Moreover, in open and dynamic environments, changes from the environment occur frequently and often are unpredictable, which can hinder the accomplishment of agents' goals. How agents cope with changes remains an open and challenging problem. On the one hand, agents should be able to reason about changes and act flexibly. On the other hand, agents should be equipped with a reasoning ability to anticipate changes and act accordingly.

These characteristics are desirable for a single agent. However, no agent is an island, and decisions of an agent are not made in isolation, but in the context of decisions made by other agents, and as part of interactions between agents. Thus, the challenging setting here is that in negotiation and other forms of agent interaction, decision making is *distributed*. In particular, key challenges in modeling decision making in agent interaction are:

- *Distribution:* choices are distributed among agents, and changes from the environment affect each agent in different ways. How to capture these choices, their

M. Baldoni et al. (Eds.): DALT 2007, LNAI 4897, pp. 140–157, 2008.

dependencies and the effects of different strategies for their decisions as well as to reason about the global changes at the individual level in agent systems are important.
- *Time:* decision making by agents occurs over time, as do the choices to be made and the changes in the environment. Hence it is necessary to deal with them in a time-dependent manner.
- *Dependencies:* i.e. capturing that certain decisions depend on other decisions.

The central importance of decision-making in agent systems makes it natural to use logic as a basis for a formal framework for agents. This means that we can model the current state of an agent as a collection of formulas, and the consequences of a particular action on a given state can be explored via standard reasoning methods. In this paper, we explore how to extend this approach to include decisions as well as actions. Hence, for logic-based agents, whose reasoning and decision making is based on a declarative logical formalism, it is important to model the decision making about choices and about environment changes.

This paper tackles the modeling of agent decisions in a way that allows distribution, dependencies, and time of choices to be captured. We discuss specific desirable properties of a formal model of agent choices (section 3) and present a formal *choice calculus* (section 5). We then consider an application of the choice calculus. Specifically, by ensuring that the choices are made in multiple different formulas consistently, the choice calculus allows us to turn an interaction concerning a goal into multiple concurrent and distributed threads of interaction on its subgoals. This is also based on a mechanism to split a formula Γ which contains A into two formulas, one of which contains A, the other contains the results of "subtracting" A from Γ.

In [2], it was shown how *Temporal Linear Logic* (TLL) can be used to model agent interactions to achieve flexibility, particularly due to its ability to model resources and choices, as well as temporal constraints. This paper can be seen as further developing this line of work to include explicit considerations of the choices of each agent and the strategies of dealing with them.

The remainder of this paper is structured as follows. Section 2 briefly reviews temporal linear logic, and the agent interaction framework. The following three sections motivate and present the choice calculus. Section 6 presents an application of the choice calculus to distributed concurrent problem solving. We then conclude in section 7.

2   Background

2.1   Temporal Linear Logic

Temporal Linear Logic (**TLL**) [3] is the result of introducing temporal logic into linear logic. While linear logic provides advantages for modeling and reasoning about resources, temporal logic addresses the description and reasoning about the changes of truth values of logic expressions over time [4]. Hence, TLL is resource-conscious as well as dealing with time.

In particular, linear logic [5] is well-known for modeling resources as well as updating processes. It has been considered in agent systems to support agent negotiation and planning by means of proof search [6,7].

In multi-agent systems, resource production and consumption processes are fundamental. In a logic such as classical or temporal logic, however, a direct mapping of resources onto formulas is troublesome. If we model resources like A as "one dollar" and B as "a chocolate bar", then $A, A \Rightarrow B$ in classical logic is read as "given one dollar we can get a chocolate bar". The problem is that A - one dollar - remains afterward. In order to resolve such resource - formula mapping issues, Girard proposed treating formulas as resources and hence they will be used exactly once in derivations.

As a result, classical conjunction (and) and disjunction (or) are recast over different uses of contexts - multiplicative as combining and additive as sharing to come up with four connectives. In particular, A $\otimes$ A (*multiplicative conjunction*) means that one has two As at the same time, which is different from $A \wedge A = A$. Hence, $\otimes$ allows a natural expression of proportion. A $\wp$ B (*multiplicative disjunction*) means that if not A then B or vice versa but not both A and B.

The ability to specify choices via the additive connectives is also a particularly useful feature of linear logic. If we consider formulas on the left hand side of $\vdash$ as what are provided (program formulas), then A & B (*additive conjunction*) stands for one's own choice, either of A or B but not both. A $\oplus$ B (*additive disjunction*) stands for the possibility of either A or B, but we don't know which. In other words, while & refers to inner determinism, $\oplus$ refers to inner non-determinism. Hence, & can be used to model an agent's own choices (*internal choices*) whereas $\oplus$ can be used to model *indeterminate possibilities* (or external choices) in the environment. The duality between & and $\oplus$, being respectively an internal and an external choice, is a well-known feature of linear logic [5]. Indeed, internal choices and external choices have been modeled previously using Linear Logic [6,8] and TLL [9,2].

Due to the duality between formulas on two sides of $\vdash$, formulas on the right side can be regarded as goal formulas, i.e. what is to be derived. A goal A & B means that after deriving this goal, one can choose between A or B. In order to have this ability to choose, one must prepare for both cases - being able to derive A and derive B. On the other hand, a goal $A \oplus B$ means a goal A or a goal B and which one is not yet determined. Hence, one can choose to derive either of them. In terms of deriving goals, & and $\oplus$ among goal formulas act as introducing indeterminate possibilities and introducing an internal choice respectively.

The temporal operators used are $\bigcirc$ (next), $\Box$ (anytime), and $\Diamond$ (sometime) [3]. Formulas with no temporal operators can be considered as being available only at present. Adding $\bigcirc$ to a formula A, i.e. $\bigcirc A$, means that A can be used only at the next time point and exactly once. Similarly, $\Box A$ means that A can be used at any time (exactly once, since it is linear). $\Diamond A$ means that A can be at some time (also exactly once). Whilst the temporal operators have their standard meanings, the notions of internal and external choice can be applied here as well, in that $\Box A$ means that A can be used at any time (but exactly once) with the choice of time being internal to the agent, and $\Diamond A$ means that A can be used at some time with the choice of time being external to the agent.

The semantics of TLL connectives and operators as above are given via its sequent calculus, since we take a proof-theoretic approach in modeling agent interaction. The rules for $\bigcirc$ and $\Box L$ are below. The full set of rules for TLL includes rules for $\Box R$ and $\Diamond$ (which are not used in this paper), and all of the rules for linear logic [3].

$$\frac{!\Gamma, \Box\Delta, \Xi \vdash A, \Phi, \Diamond\Lambda, ?\Pi}{!\Gamma, \Box\Delta, \bigcirc\Xi \vdash \bigcirc A, \overline{\bigcirc}\,\Phi, \Diamond\Lambda, ?\Pi} \; \bigcirc \qquad \frac{A, \Gamma \vdash \Delta}{\Box A, \Gamma \vdash \Delta} \; \Box L$$

2.2 A Model for Agent Interaction

In [9], an interaction modeling framework which uses Temporal Linear Logic (TLL) as a means of specifying interaction protocols is used as TLL is natural to model resources, internal choices and indeterminate possibilities with respect to time. Various concepts such as resource, capability and commitment/goal are encoded in TLL. The symmetry between a formula and its negation in TLL is explored as a way to model resources and commitments/goals. In particular, formulas to be located on the left hand side of $\vdash$ can be regarded as formulas in supply (resources) while formulas to be located on the right hand side of $\vdash$ as formulas in demand (goals).

A unit of consumable *resources* is then modeled as a proposition in linear logic and can be preceded by temporal operators to address time dependency. For example, listening to music after (exactly) three time points is denoted as $\bigcirc \bigcirc \bigcirc music$. A shorthand is $\bigcirc^3 music$.

The *capabilities* of agents refer to producing, consuming, relocating and changing ownership of resources. Capabilities are represented by describing the states before and after performing them. The general representation form is $\Gamma \multimap \Delta$, in which Γ describes the conditions before and Δ describes the conditions after. The linear implication $\multimap$ ensures that the conditions before will be transformed into the conditions after.

To take an example, consider a capability of producing music using a music player to play music files. There are two options available at the agent's own choice, one is using an mp3 player to play mp3 files, the other is using a CD player to play CD files. The encoding is:

$$\Box[[(mp3 \otimes mp3\_player) \oplus (CD \otimes CD\_player)] \multimap music]^1$$

where $\Box$ means that the capability can be applied at any time, $\oplus$ indicates an internal choice (not &, as it is located on the left hand side of $\multimap$).

3 Desiderata for a Choice Calculus

Unpredictable changes in the environment can be regarded as a set of possibilities for which the agents do not know the outcomes. There are several strategies for dealing with unpredictable changes. A safe approach is to prepare for all the possible scenarios, at the cost of extra reservation and/or consumption of resources. Other approaches are more risky in which agents make a prediction of which possibilities will occur and act accordingly. If the predictions are correct, agents achieve the goals with resource efficiency. Here, there is a trade-off between resource efficiency and safety.

---

[1] In the modeling, formulas representing media players are consumed away, which does not reflect the persistence of physical objects. However, we focus on modeling how resources are utilized for interaction, not their physical existences and hence simplify the encoding since it is not necessary to have the media players retained for later use.

In contrast to indeterminate possibilities, internal choices can decided by the agents themselves. Decisions on internal choices can be based on what is best for the agents' current and local needs. However, it is desirable that they consider internal choices in the context of other internal choices that have been or will be made. This requires an ability to make an informed decision on internal choices. If we put information for decision making on internal choices as constraints associated with those internal choices then what required is a modeling of internal choices with their associated constraints such that agents can reason about them and decide accordingly.

In addition, as agents act in time, decisions can be made precisely at the required time or can be well prepared in advance. When to decide and act on internal choices should be at the agents' autonomy. The advantages of deciding internal choices in advance can be seen in an example as resolving a goal of $\bigcirc^3(A \oplus B)$. This goal involves an internal choice ($\oplus$) to be determined at the third next time point ($\bigcirc^3$). If the agent decides now to choose A and commits to making the same decision at the third next time point, then from now, the agent only has to focus on the goal of $\bigcirc^3 A$. This also means that resources used for other goals can be guaranteed to be exclusive from the requirements of $\bigcirc^3(A \oplus B)$.

The following example illustrates various desirable strategies of agents.

Peter intends to organize an outdoor party in two days time. He has a goal of providing music at the party. He also has a blank CD which he can use with his CD burner to burn music in CD format or mp3 format. His friend, John, can help by bringing a CD player or an mp3 player to the party but Peter does not know which until tomorrow. In addition, there is an external request that David wants to borrow Peter's CD burner today. Peter needs to consider achieving his goal and whether to let David borrow the CD burner.

In this situation, to Peter, there is an internal choice on the music format and an indeterminate possibility regarding the player. We consider two strategies for Peter. If Peter does not let David borrow the CD Burner, he can wait until tomorrow to learn what John will bring to the party and choose the music format to burn accordingly at that time. Otherwise, if he wants to let David borrow the CD Burner, he can not delay burning the CD until tomorrow and so has to make a prediction on which player John will bring to the party, then decide the choice on the music format and burn the CD early (now). This corresponds to the second strategy. The question is then how to make such strategies available for agent Peter to explore.

An important observation to make is that although (temporal) linear logic captures the notions of internal choice and indeterminate possibility, its sequent rules constrain decision making on them to certain strategies and to be done in isolation (subject only to local information). Specifically, consider the following rules of standard sequent calculus:

$$\frac{\Gamma, A \vdash \Delta \quad \Gamma, B \vdash \Delta}{\Gamma, A \oplus B \vdash \Delta} \quad \frac{\Gamma \vdash A, \Delta \quad \Gamma \vdash B, \Delta}{\Gamma \vdash A \,\&\, B, \Delta} \qquad (set1)$$

$$\frac{\Gamma, A \vdash \Delta}{\Gamma, A \,\&\, B \vdash \Delta} \quad \frac{\Gamma, B \vdash \Delta}{\Gamma, A \,\&\, B \vdash \Delta} \quad \frac{\Gamma \vdash A, \Delta}{\Gamma \vdash A \oplus B, \Delta} \quad \frac{\Gamma \vdash B, \Delta}{\Gamma \vdash A \oplus B, \Delta} \qquad (set2)$$

The first set of rules (set 1) reflects the strategy that agents prepare for all outcomes of indeterminate possibilities. Though applying the strategy is safe, it requires extra and unnecessary resources and actions. Moreover, the strategy does not take into account agents' predictions of the outcomes of some indeterminate possibilities in the environment (in our example it is Peter's prediction of the player) and whether agents are willing to take some risks by following their predictions. This also means that the notion of proof needs to be extended to allow for cases where it is not necessary for the proof to cover all possible outcomes of indeterminate possibilities but only their actual outcomes.

The second set of rules (set 2) reflects agents' decisions on internal choices at their associated times. According to these rules, internal choices are determined freely, without any guidance or constraints. Hence, such decisions on these choices may not be optimal. For example, if an agent decides an internal choice $A \& B$ to be A, and later realizes there are some goals that requires B then it misses the chance to obtain the necessary resource B. Hence, it is important how information such as possible future goals or information on any constraints or dependencies among choices should be included in agents' consideration of decisions on internal choices. However, the sequent rules do not allow agents to explore the strategy of deciding choices in advance.

Referring to our running example, in the first strategy, Peter does not let David borrow the CD burner, and so Peter can then find a proof using standard sequent rules to achieve the goal of providing music at the party two days later. However, in the second strategy, the search using standard TLL sequent calculus for a proof of the goal fails as it requires Peter to have music in both formats (mp3 and CD) so as to be matched with the future possibility of the media player.

Hence, in this paper, we investigate how we can use TLL not only to model the difference between internal choice and indeterminate possibility with respect to time, but also to capture *dependencies* among choices, constraints on how choices can be made and predictions and decisions of indeterminate possibilities. Such constraints may also reflect global consideration of other goals and other threads of interaction. We further consider strategies that can be used to deal with choices with respect to time, reflecting how cautious the agents are and whether the agents deal with them in advance. However, we will not discuss how agents can predict the environment outcomes correctly.

4   Modeling Decisions on Choices

In this section, we consider the modeling of choice decisions, how to express constraints on choice decisions, and their dependency on other choices' decisions.

If we assume that the order of the operants is unchanged throughout the process of formula manipulation, then the decision on choices and indeterminate possibilities can be regarded as selecting the left hand side or the right hand side of the connective. For simplicity of discussion, we shall refer to both internal choices and indeterminate possibilities simply as choices unless it is important to mention them distinctly.

Each choice is associated with a particular time point. Due to the inherent property of TLL that formulas denoted at a specific time point exist only at that time point and becomes invalid after that time point, we assume that outcomes of choices must be revealed at their associated times. Regarding internal choices, to support agents being able to decide them in advance we assume that agents can make decisions early and keep those decisions unchanged until the decisions become effective. Regarding indeterminate possibilities, we assume that their outcomes are determined by the environment (or external factors) at their associated times and only at these times, the outcomes become known to agents. For example, given an indeterminate possibility $\bigcirc^3(A \oplus B)$, at the third next time point, the environment determines the possibility such that $\bigcirc^3(A \oplus B)$ becomes $\bigcirc^3 A$ or becomes $\bigcirc^3 B$.

Hence, for a given choice at the time $\bigcirc^x$, $x > 0$, there are three distinct states — not determined, decided on left, and decided on right.

In what follows, we have restricted the use of the temporal operators to be $\bigcirc$ only. This is due to some technical issues with the formal results about the choice calculus when $\square$ and $\lozenge$ are included. A full exploration of this issue is beyond the scope of this paper. Here we note that whilst we restrict the choice calculus to exclude $\square$ and $\lozenge$ in this paper, we can regain some of their functionality by the use of $\bigcirc^x$, for an appropriate term x.

We use the notation $\overset{\&_x}{\hookrightarrow}$ or $\overset{\oplus_x}{\hookrightarrow}$ to record the results of agents' decision making or outcomes on the choices $\&_x$ and $\oplus_x$ respectively. The subscript indicates the ID of the connective. Base values for choice decisions can be encoded by TLL propositions as L for deciding on the left, and R for deciding on the right. For example, the base value for a decision on $A \& B$ is L (denoted as $\overset{\&}{\hookrightarrow} = L$) if A results from deciding the choice $A \& B$ (by agents or by the environment) and is R ($\overset{\&}{\hookrightarrow} = R$) if B results. Formally, we write $\vdash \overset{\&_1}{\hookrightarrow} \multimap L$ or $\overset{\&_1}{\hookrightarrow} \vdash L$ to denote that the left sub-formula of $\&_1$ was selected.

Regarding internal choices, their decisions can be regarded as variables on which agents can decide the assignment of values. On the other hand, outcomes of indeterminate possibilities are not determined by agents but by external factors.

By modeling choices' decisions explicitly, we can state constraints between them. For example, if two choices, $\overset{\&_x}{\hookrightarrow}$ and $\overset{\&_y}{\hookrightarrow}$, need to be made consistently — either both right or both left — then this can be stated as $\overset{\&_x}{\hookrightarrow} = \overset{\&_y}{\hookrightarrow}$ or in logic encoding, $\overset{\&_x}{\hookrightarrow} \vdash \overset{\&_y}{\hookrightarrow}$, $\overset{\&_x}{\hookrightarrow} \dashv \overset{\&_y}{\hookrightarrow}$.

More generally, we can state that a given internal choice $\&_x$ (or $\oplus_x$) should depend on a combination of other choices or some external constraints. We use $condL_x$ (respectively $condR_x$) to denote the condition that should hold for the left side (respectively right side) of the internal choice to be taken. Clearly, satisfaction of $condL_x$ means $condR_x$ cannot be satisfied and vice versa. In other words, they should always be mutually exclusive. These conditions completely determine the results of the choices' decisions. We encode these conditions as TLL sequents so that sub-conditions (sequents) can be found via proof search.

Moreover, composite formulas, in general, contain sub-formulas that are interrelated, such as independently co-existing or mutually exclusive due to the choices between them. A sub-formula may be removed or retained after choices in the composite formula are decided. It is then important to make readily available the conditions on which a sub-formula of interest is retained or removed. Based on such information, agents would be able to judge the significance of a compound formula w.r.t retaining the sub-formula of interest and exercise various strategies in dealing with the compound formula.

In particular, given a formula Γ which contains a sub-formula A, we can compress the sequence of decisions that need to be made in order to obtain A from Γ into a single *representative choice*. For example, if $\Gamma = B \mathbin{\&_1} \bigcirc^a(\bigcirc^b(A \oplus_2 C) \mathbin{\&_3} D)$ then, in order to obtain A from Γ we need to decide on the right side of $\&_1$, then, a time units later, decide on the left side of $\&_3$, and b time units after that, have the left side of $\oplus_2$ be selected by the environment (an indeterminate possibility). Formally, the notion of representative choice is defined as below.

Definition 1 (Representative Choice). *A representative choice $\&_r$ with respect to a formula A in a compound program formula (respectively goal formula) Γ is a choice $\bigcirc^x A \mathbin{\&_r} \bigcirc^y 1$ (respectively $\bigcirc^x A \oplus_r \bigcirc^y 1$) whose decision is L if $\bigcirc^x A$ is retained from Γ after choices in Γ are decided and is R otherwise (where $\bigcirc^y 1$ is retained instead), where $x \geq 0$ is the time associated with A in Γ and $y \geq 0$ is the time point associated with 1.*

Note that at the time of representing the choice $\&_r$ (or $\oplus_r$), the value of y is not known. It will be known after all the decisions of internal choices and indeterminate possibilities in Γ are revealed.

In the previous example, such a sequence of decisions on internal choices and indeterminate possibilities on Γ to obtain A can be captured by the sequent:

$$\vdash (\overset{\&_1}{\longleftrightarrow} \multimap R) \otimes \bigcirc^a(\overset{\&_3}{\longleftrightarrow} \multimap L) \otimes \bigcirc^{a+b}(\overset{\oplus_2}{\longleftrightarrow} \multimap L).$$

This is the determining condition for A to be obtained from Γ. Observe that we can compress Γ into a representative choice for A of the form $(\bigcirc^{a+b} A \mathbin{\&_r} \bigcirc^y)$ such that the choice $\&_r$ is decided left if $\bigcirc^{a+b} A$ results from Γ and is decided right otherwise. The condition above then corresponds to $condL_r$ of $\&_r$. Being mutually exclusive, $condR_r$ is captured as: $\vdash (\overset{\&_1}{\longleftrightarrow} \multimap L) \oplus \bigcirc^a(\overset{\&_3}{\longleftrightarrow} \multimap R) \oplus \bigcirc^{a+b}(\overset{\oplus_2}{\longleftrightarrow} \multimap R).$

We now come to determine sequent calculus rules for various strategies on choices.

5   A Choice Calculus

When it comes to indeterminate possibilities, proof searches using standard sequent calculus rules reflect the strategy of preparing all possible cases and do not allow agents to take risks by preparing only the anticipated cases. We need to extend the sequent calculus rules to accommodate such a strategy of risk taking.

In particular, we need to provide the proof steps in which agents can make predictions on the outcomes of indeterminate possibilities and follow only the search paths corresponding to the predicted ones. In other words, we need to provide inference rules for dealing with indeterminate possibilities such that the agents can decide on a particular branch to follow in proof search rather than preparing for all branches. We also need to keep track of the predictions that agents make. Such sequent rules are of the following forms:

$$\frac{\Gamma \vdash_{cc} F, \Delta \quad [\vdash \overset{\&_n}{\longleftrightarrow} \multimap L]}{\Gamma \vdash_{cc} F \&_n G, \Delta} \qquad \frac{\Gamma \vdash_{cc} G, \Delta \quad [\vdash \overset{\&_n}{\longleftrightarrow} \multimap R]}{\Gamma \vdash_{cc} F \&_n G, \Delta}$$

$$\frac{\Gamma, F \vdash_{cc} \Delta \quad [\vdash \overset{\oplus_n}{\multimap} L]}{\Gamma, F \oplus_n G \vdash_{cc} \Delta} \qquad \frac{\Gamma, G \vdash_{cc} \Delta \quad [\vdash \overset{\oplus_n}{\multimap} R]}{\Gamma, F \oplus_n G \vdash_{cc} \Delta}$$

Note that $\vdash_{cc}$ means $\vdash$ in the choice calculus context, and that a prediction on the outcome of an indeterminate possibility is expressed in square brackets. A prediction can be thought as an assumption that the search technique relies on and it needs to be checked with the actual outcome(s). If the assumptions are correct then successful searches on the corresponding branches that rely on them constitute a proof. If the assumptions are not correct, even though the searches are successful, then the corresponding plan is not sound. Here, we take the notion of proof as that the search using these extended inference rules above is successful and hence soundness of the proof depends on the assumptions (agents' predictions). We will further discuss how such proofs using extended inference rules are related to those proofs using only standard sequent calculus rules in theorems 1 and 2.

Moreover, we consider allowing agents to decide upon an indeterminate possibility beforehand, which is not available if using only the standard sequent rules of TLL. What is needed is inference rules that permit agents to follow only the branches that correspond to their predictions on the indeterminate possibilities. Such rules are of the following forms. As above, predictions are kept aside in square brackets.

$$\frac{\Gamma \vdash_{cc} \bigcirc^n F, \Delta \quad [\vdash \bigcirc^n(\overset{\&_n}{\multimap} L)]}{\Gamma \vdash_{cc} \bigcirc^n(F \&_n G), \Delta} \qquad \frac{\Gamma \vdash_{cc} \bigcirc^n G, \Delta \quad [\vdash \bigcirc^n(\overset{\&_n}{\multimap} R)]}{\Gamma \vdash_{cc} \bigcirc^n(F \&_n G), \Delta}$$

$$\frac{\Gamma, \bigcirc^n F \vdash_{cc} \Delta \quad [\vdash \bigcirc^n(\overset{\oplus_n}{\multimap} L)]}{\Gamma, \bigcirc^n(F \oplus_n G) \vdash_{cc} \Delta} \qquad \frac{\Gamma, \bigcirc^n G \vdash_{cc} \Delta \quad [\vdash \bigcirc^n(\overset{\oplus_n}{\multimap} R)]}{\Gamma, \bigcirc^n(F \oplus_n G) \vdash_{cc} \Delta}$$

Internal choices can be decided by the owner agent at the time associated with the choices, subject to any constraints ($condL_n$ or $condR_n$) imposed on them. Accordingly, we derive new sequent rules for internal choices to reflect that such constraints need to be followed by attaching the corresponding conditions to the proof search steps. The new sequent rules are:

$$\frac{\Gamma, F \vdash_{cc} \Delta \quad (condL_n)}{\Gamma, F \&_n G \vdash_{cc} \Delta} \qquad \frac{\Gamma, G \vdash_{cc} \Delta \quad (condR_n)}{\Gamma, F \&_n G \vdash_{cc} \Delta}$$

$$\frac{\Gamma \vdash_{cc} F, \Delta \quad (condL_n)}{\Gamma \vdash_{cc} F \oplus_n G, \Delta} \qquad \frac{\Gamma \vdash_{cc} G, \Delta \quad (condR_n)}{\Gamma \vdash_{cc} F \oplus_n G, \Delta}$$

where $condL_n$ (respectively $condR_n$) are conditions imposed on the internal choice n for the choice to be decided left (respectively right). These conditions may be absent. In their absence, the internal choices are truly free choices and the standard inference rules are used.

Moreover, if the agent is to decide the choice in advance, it can bring out the choice's outcome earlier in the search. Similarly to those rules that allow agents to deal with indeterminate possibilities ahead of time, the rules needed should permit the agents to follow a branch of choice while keeping track of the associated conditions. They are of the forms:

$$\frac{\Gamma, \bigcirc^n F \vdash_{cc} \Delta \quad (condL_n)}{\Gamma, \bigcirc^n (F \,\&_n G) \vdash_{cc} \Delta} \qquad \frac{\Gamma, \bigcirc^n G \vdash_{cc} \bigcirc^n \Delta \quad (condR_n)}{\Gamma, \bigcirc^n (F \,\&_n G) \vdash_{cc} \bigcirc^n \Delta}$$

$$\frac{\Gamma \vdash_{cc} \bigcirc^n F, \Delta \quad (condL_n)}{\Gamma \vdash_{cc} \bigcirc^n (F \oplus_n G), \Delta} \qquad \frac{\Gamma \vdash_{cc} \bigcirc^n G, \Delta \quad (condR_n)}{\Gamma \vdash_{cc} \bigcirc^n (F \oplus_n G), \Delta}$$

These above new sequent rules, together with standard TLL sequent rules, form the *choice calculus*.

Considering our running example, recall that if Peter is to let David borrow the CD burner now, then he needs to make a prediction on the player that John will possibly bring and based on the prediction, decides on the indeterminate possibility early. For instance, Peter predicts that John will provide an mp3 player (i.e. $\vdash \bigcirc(\overset{\oplus_3}{\hookrightarrow} \multimap L)$). Using the choice calculus, this is captured by the following inference:

$$\frac{\Gamma, \bigcirc^2 mp3p \vdash_{cc} \bigcirc^2 m \quad [\vdash \bigcirc(\overset{\oplus_3}{\hookrightarrow} \multimap L)]}{\Gamma, \bigcirc(\bigcirc mp3p \oplus_3 \bigcirc cdp) \vdash_{cc} \bigcirc^2 m}$$

where Γ is some formula in the proof, $mp3p$ = mp3 player, cdp = CD player, and m = music.

Based on this prediction, Peter decides on the choice of mp3 music format now and burns the blank CD accordingly. The imposed condition for the choice $\&_1$ is $\vdash \bigcirc(\overset{\oplus_3}{\hookrightarrow} \multimap L)$. Such decision with a constraint is reflected in the following proof step in the choice calculus.

$$\frac{\Gamma, \square mp3 \vdash \Delta \quad (\vdash \bigcirc(\overset{\oplus_3}{\hookrightarrow} \multimap L))}{\Gamma, \square mp3 \,\&_1 \square cd \vdash \Delta}$$

where Γ and Δ are some formulas in the proof.

By taking the risk in following his prediction, Peter then successfully obtains a proof of $CD\_Burner \otimes \bigcirc^2 m$. If his prediction is correct then a successful plan is obtained to achieve his goal. The proof is given in figure 1, where some inferences combine a number of rule applications.

In this example we begin (bottom-most inference) by making an "in-advance" decision of the indeterminate possibility $\oplus_3$, specifically we predict that John will provide an mp3 player. We then decide on the format mp3. When the time comes to make a decision for $\oplus_2$ we can select to use the mp3 player to produce music. As the condition for these choices, $\vdash \bigcirc(\overset{\oplus_3}{\hookrightarrow} \multimap L)$, is the same as the condition of the prediction on $\oplus_3$, we omit it for readability.

As can be seen from the example, internal choices and indeterminate possibilities are properly modeled with respect to time. Moreover, several strategies are enabled for Peter due to the use of the choice calculus. If Peter is to take a safe approach, he should delay deciding the music format until tomorrow and ignore David's request. If Peter is willing to take risks, he can predict the indeterminate possibility of which player John will bring to the party and act accordingly. Peter can then decide the choice on music early so as to lend David the CD burner.

Hence, these sequent calculus rules are in place to equip agents with various strategies for reasoning to deal with indeterminate possibilities and internal choices. These

$$
\dfrac{
  \dfrac{
    \dfrac{
      \dfrac{
        \dfrac{mp3 \vdash mp3 \quad mp3p \vdash mp3p}{mp3, mp3p \vdash mp3 \otimes mp3p}\ \otimes
      }{mp3, mp3p \vdash (mp3 \otimes mp3p) \oplus_2 (cd \otimes cdp)}\ \oplus_2
    }{\square mp3, PP, \bigcirc^2 mp3p \vdash \bigcirc^2 m}\ \bigcirc^2,\square,\multimap
    \qquad cdb \vdash cdb
  }{\dfrac{cdb, \square mp3, PP, \bigcirc^2 mp3p \vdash cdb \otimes \bigcirc^2 m}{\dfrac{cdb, \square mp3\ \&_1\ \square cd, PP, \bigcirc^2 mp3p \vdash cdb \otimes \bigcirc^2 m}{PR, PP, PB, \bigcirc^2 mp3p \vdash cdb \otimes \bigcirc^2 m}\ \otimes,\multimap,\square}\ \&_1}\ \otimes
}{JR, PP, PR, PB \vdash cdb \otimes \bigcirc^2 m}\ \oplus_3
\qquad [\vdash \bigcirc(\overset{\oplus_3}{\rightarrow}\multimap L)]
$$

where $JR = \bigcirc[\bigcirc mp3p \oplus_3 \bigcirc cdp]$
$PP = \square[[(mp3 \otimes mp3p) \oplus_2 (cd \otimes cdp)] \multimap m]$
$PR = \square Blank\_CD \otimes \square CD\_Burner$
$PB = \square[Blank\_CD \otimes CD\_Burner \multimap CD\_Burner \otimes (\square mp3\ \&_1\ \square cd)]$
$cdb = CD\_Burner$

Fig. 1. Proof of $CD\_Burner \otimes \bigcirc^2 music$

strategies make it more flexible to deal with changes and handle exceptions with global awareness and dependencies among choices. In the next section, we explore an application of such modeling of choices and their coping strategies, especially dependencies among choices, to distributed problem solving in a flexible interaction modeling TLL framework [9]. But first, we show that proofs using the additional rules are, in a sense, equivalent to proofs in the original TLL sequent calculus.

The intuition behind the soundness and completeness properties of proofs using these additional rules with respect to proofs which only use original TLL sequent calculus is that eventually indeterminate possibilities like between A and B will be revealed as the outcome turns out to be A or B. Hence, if the agents have made the right predictions and followed them then they have successfully dealt with these indeterminate possibilities.

The soundness and completeness properties are then evaluated and proved in this context. In particular, we introduce the concept of a revealed proof, which has all the internal choices and indeterminate possibilities replaced by their actual outcomes. Proofs under the choice calculus are then examined in relation to their corresponding revealed proofs. They are sound if all the assumptions they rely on turn out to be correct. If the assumptions turn out to be unfounded, then the proofs under the choice calculus are not valid.

Definition 2 (Revealed Proof). *The **revealed proof** corresponding to a given proof of $\Gamma \vdash \Delta$ is the proof resulting from replacing all occurrences of choices with the actual outcomes of these choices. That is, any formula $F \oplus G$ corresponding to an indeterminate possibility is replaced by either F or G, corresponding to the decision that was made by the environment; and any formula $F\,\&\,G$ corresponding to an internal choice is replaced by either F or G, corresponding to the choice that was made by the agent.*

Theorem 1 (Soundness). *Let P be a proof of $\Gamma \vdash_{cc} \Delta$ under the choice calculus where Γ and Δ are multisets of TLL formulas. Let $rev(\Gamma)$, $rev(\Delta)$ and $rev(P)$ be the outcomes of replacing all the choices in Γ, Δ and the proof P by their actual outcomes respectively. If all the conditions associated with the additional inference rules on choices in P are correct,*

$$rev(\Gamma) \vdash rev(\Delta)$$

is then provable under standard TLL sequent calculus by the proof $rev(P)$.

Proof sketch: *All of the additional rules introduced by the choice calculus disappear when the proof is made into a revealed proof. For example, consider the rules (on the left) which are replaced in a revealed proof, where $F \& G$ is replaced by F, by the identities on the right.*

$$\frac{\Gamma \vdash_{cc} F, \Delta \quad [L \vdash L \&_n R]}{\Gamma \vdash_{cc} F \&_n G, \Delta} \qquad \frac{\Gamma \vdash F, \Delta}{\Gamma \vdash F, \Delta}$$

$$\frac{\Gamma \vdash_{cc} \bigcirc^x F, \Delta \quad [L \vdash L \&_n R]}{\Gamma \vdash_{cc} \bigcirc^x (F \&_n G), \Delta} \qquad \frac{\Gamma \vdash \bigcirc^x F, \Delta}{\Gamma \vdash \bigcirc^x F, \Delta}$$

$$\frac{\Gamma, F \vdash_{cc} \Delta}{\Gamma, F \&_n G \vdash_{cc} \Delta} \qquad \frac{\Gamma, F \vdash \Delta}{\Gamma, F \vdash \Delta}$$

Once these identity rules are eliminated, a standard TLL proof results. □

Theorem 2 (Completeness). *A proof using standard TLL sequent calculus rules is also a proof under the choice calculus.*

Proof: *As the choice calculus also contains all of the standard TLL sequent calculus rules, the completeness property holds trivially.* □

6 Splitting a Formula

Interaction between agents is often necessary for the achievement of their goals. In the above example with Peter and John, if Peter had a CD player of his own, he would not need to interact with John in order to have music at the party. In general, it will be necessary for an agent to co-ordinate interaction with many different agents while the precise number and identity of which may not be known in advance. In order to achieve this, in this section we investigate a mechanism for partial achievement of a goal. In particular, this is a process of decomposing a given TLL goal formula into concurrent subgoals.

For example, assume that Peter now has the additional goal of having either Chinese or Thai food at the party. Deriving which goal - Chinese food (abbreviated as C) or Thai food (abbreviated as T) - is an internal choice ($\oplus_3$). Peter's goal is then

$$CD\_Burner \otimes \bigcirc^2 [music \otimes (C \oplus_3 T)]$$

However, Peter can not provide food, but his friends, Ming and Chaeng, can make Chinese food and Thai food respectively. Hence, this goal can not be fulfilled by Peter alone but involves interaction with John and David as above and also Ming or Chaeng.

If this goal is sent as a request to any one of them, none would be able to fulfill the goal in its entirety. Hence, it is important that the goal can be split up and achieved partially via concurrent threads of interaction. In this case, we would split this into the sub-goal $CD\_Burner \otimes \bigcirc^2 music$, which is processed as above, the sub-goal $\bigcirc^2 C \oplus_4 \bigcirc^2 1$, which is sent as a request to Ming, and the sub-goal $\bigcirc^2 1 \oplus_4 \bigcirc^2 T$, which is sent as a request to Chaeng. The choice $\oplus_4$ will be later determined consistently with $\oplus_3$.

Hence we need to be able to split a goal into sub-goals, and to keep track of which parts have been achieved. In particular, it is useful to isolate a sub-goal from the rest of the goal. We do this by taking the overall formula Γ and separating from it a particular sub-formula A. We show how this can be done in the fragment, denoted as MCA, which contains the connectives $\otimes, \oplus, \&, \bigcirc$ and the units $1, \perp$.

The split-ups of a formula Γ with respect to the formula A that Γ contains are the two formulas $\widehat{\Gamma - A}$ and $\widehat{A}$, which are defined below.

$\widehat{\Gamma - A}$ is the formula Γ which has undergone a single removal or substitution of (one occurrence of) A by 1 while the rest is kept unchanged. Specifically, where A resides in the structure of Γ, the following mapping is applied to A and its directly connected formulas Δ. Δ is any TLL formula and $x \geq 0$.

1. $A \mapsto 1$
2. $\bigcirc^x A \mapsto \bigcirc^x 1$
3. $\bigcirc^x A \ op \ \Delta \mapsto \bigcirc^x 1 \ op \ \Delta$ for $op \in \{\otimes, \&, \oplus\}$

Here, we further apply the equivalence $1 \otimes \Delta \equiv \Delta$ so that $\bigcirc^x A \otimes \Delta \mapsto \Delta$.

The formula $\widehat{A}$ is determined recursively as a result of a split up process. $\widehat{A} = \mathrm{SPLITUP}(\Gamma, A)$, where $\mathrm{SPLITUP}(\Gamma, A)$ is defined as follows:

- if $\Gamma = A$, then $\mathrm{SPLITUP}(\Gamma, A) = A$
- if $\Gamma = \bigcirc \Gamma'$, then $\mathrm{SPLITUP}(\Gamma, A) = \bigcirc \ \mathrm{SPLITUP}(\Gamma', A)$
- if $\Gamma = \Gamma' \otimes \Delta$, then $\mathrm{SPLITUP}(\Gamma, A) = \mathrm{SPLITUP}(\Gamma', A)$
- if $\Gamma = \Gamma' \ \&_n \ \Delta$, then $\mathrm{SPLITUP}(\Gamma, A) = \mathrm{SPLITUP}(\Gamma', A) \ \&_n \ 1$
- if $\Gamma = \Gamma' \ \oplus_m \ \Delta$, then $\mathrm{SPLITUP}(\Gamma, A) = \mathrm{SPLITUP}(\Gamma', A) \ \oplus_m \ 1$

where n, m are some numbers representing IDs of choices, Γ' is a sub-formula of Γ, A occurs in Γ' but does not occur in Δ.

Another view is that $\widehat{A}$ is obtained by recursively replacing formulas that rest on the other side of connective (to the formula that contains A) by 1 if the connective is $\oplus$ or $\&$ and removing them if the connective is $\otimes$.

It can be seen from the formulation of $\widehat{\Gamma - A}$ and $\widehat{A}$ that there are requirements of choice dependencies among the split ups. Indeed, all the corresponding choices and possibilities in them must be consistent. In particular, decisions made on the corresponding choices and possibilities in $\widehat{\Gamma - A}$, and $\widehat{A}$ should be the same as those that would have been made on the corresponding ones in Γ. Indeed, if A ever results from Γ by a sequence of choices and possibilities in Γ being decided, then those decisions also make $\widehat{A}$ become A.

As an example, we return to our running example and consider Peter's goal formula. The goal $G = CD\_Burner \otimes \bigcirc^2 [music \otimes (C \oplus_3 T)]$ can be split into: $[\widehat{G - C}] = CD\_Burner \otimes \bigcirc^2 [music \otimes (1 \oplus_3 T)]$ and $\widehat{C} = \bigcirc^2 (C \oplus_3 1)$.

Subsequently, $\widehat{G - C}$ can be split into:

$[\widehat{G - C - T}] = CD\_Burner \otimes \bigcirc^2 music$ and $\hat{T}$ of $\widehat{G - C}$ is $\bigcirc^2(1 \oplus_3 T)$.

In general, $\hat{A}$ can result in $\bigcirc^x A$ or $\bigcirc^y 1$, $x, y \geq 0$, as a result of having all the choices in $\hat{A}$ decided. In the following theorem, we show that $\hat{A}$ can be compressed into a representative choice (of A in $\hat{A}$) of the form $\bigcirc^x A \&_r \bigcirc^y 1$.

Theorem 3. *Let Γ be a formula in the fragment MCA and $\hat{A}$ be its split up w.r.t A in Γ. We have that $\hat{A}$ is equivalent to the representative choice w.r.t. A, i.e. that*

$$\hat{A} \vdash_{cc} \bigcirc^a A \&_r \bigcirc^b 1$$

and

$$\bigcirc^a A \&_r \bigcirc^b 1 \vdash_{cc} \hat{A}$$

where a indicates the corresponding time of the existence of A, and b is an appropriate time depending on the outcomes of choices in $\hat{A}$.

Proof: *by induction on the structure of $\hat{A}$. We highlight a few cases of the proof for $\hat{A} \vdash_{cc} \bigcirc^x A \&_r \bigcirc^y 1$. The others are similar.*

Base step: *$\hat{A} = A$, hence $x = 0$, the choice is decided left, and we have $A \vdash_{cc} A$.*

Induction step: *Assume the hypothesis is true for n, so that $\widehat{A^n} \vdash_{cc} \bigcirc^n A \&_n \bigcirc^y 1$ is provable, which means that we have either of the following proofs:*

$$\frac{\vdots \qquad\qquad \widehat{A^n} \vdash_{cc} \bigcirc^n A \, [\vdash condL_n]}{\widehat{A^n} \vdash_{cc} \bigcirc^n A \&_n \bigcirc^y 1} \&n \qquad \frac{\vdots \qquad\qquad \widehat{A^n} \vdash_{cc} \bigcirc^y 1 \, [\vdash condR_n]}{\widehat{A^n} \vdash_{cc} \bigcirc^n A \&_n \bigcirc^y 1} \&n$$

We show the case for $\widehat{A^{n+1}} = \widehat{A^n} \&_1 1$ below, the other cases $\bigcirc\widehat{A^n}$, and $\widehat{A^n} \oplus_2 1$ are similar. In this case, we need to prove $\widehat{A^n} \&_1 1 \vdash_{cc} \bigcirc^n A \&_{n+1} \bigcirc^y 1$, where $condL_{n+1} = condL_n \otimes (\overset{\&_1}{\hookrightarrow} \multimap L)$; and $condR_{n+1} = condR_n \oplus (\overset{\&_1}{\hookrightarrow} \multimap R)$.

$$\frac{\frac{\vdots \quad \widehat{A^n} \vdash_{cc} \bigcirc^n A \, [\vdash condL_n]}{\widehat{A^n} \&_1 1 \vdash_{cc} \bigcirc^n A \, [\vdash condL_n \otimes (\overset{\&_1}{\hookrightarrow} \multimap L)]} \&1}{\widehat{A^n} \&_1 1 \vdash_{cc} \bigcirc^n A \&_{n+1} \bigcirc^y 1} \&n+1 \qquad \frac{\frac{\vdots \quad \widehat{A^n} \vdash_{cc} \bigcirc^y 1 \, [\vdash condR_n] \quad \frac{1 \vdash_{cc} 1(y=0)}{1 \vdash_{cc} \bigcirc^y 1}}{\widehat{A^n} \&_1 1 \vdash_{cc} \bigcirc^y 1 \, [\vdash condR_n \oplus (\overset{\&_1}{\hookrightarrow} \multimap R)]} \&1}{\widehat{A^n} \&_1 1 \vdash_{cc} \bigcirc^n A \&_{n+1} \bigcirc^y 1} \&n+1$$

where the value of y is assigned as appropriately in the proof. Note that both cases of the decision on $\&_1$ are proved. □

Applying this theorem to the above example, we can obtain further results:

$\hat{C} = \bigcirc^2(C \oplus_3 1) = \bigcirc^2 C \oplus_4 \bigcirc^2 1$,

$\hat{T}$ (of $\widehat{G - C}$) $= \bigcirc^2(1 \oplus_3 T) = \bigcirc^2 1 \oplus_4 \bigcirc^2 T$, where $\oplus_4$ is the representative choice and is of the same decision as $\oplus_3$ at the second next time point.

The equivalence relationship between Γ and its split ups, $\widehat{\Gamma - A}$ and $\hat{A}$, is established by the following theorems. The first theorem shows that $\widehat{\Gamma - A}, \hat{A} \vdash \Gamma$, and the subsequent two theorems show, roughly speaking, the reverse direction, i.e. that $\Gamma \vdash \widehat{\Gamma - A} \otimes \hat{A}$.

Theorem 4. *Let Γ be a formula in the fragment MCA that contains A, where Γ is split up into $\widehat{A}$ and $\widehat{\Gamma - A}$ w.r.t A, where $\widehat{A}$ contains A and $\widehat{\Gamma - A}$ is the remainder. Then*

$$\widehat{A}, \widehat{\Gamma - A} \vdash_{cc} \Gamma.$$

That is, the multiplicative conjunction of the split ups of Γ via A can derive Γ.

Proof (sketch): *by induction on the size of Γ. We highlight a few cases of the proof. The others are similar.*

Base step: *$\Gamma = A$. We need to prove $A, 1 \vdash_{cc} A$, which is obvious.*

Induction step: *Assume the hypothesis is true for Γ of size n, so that $\widehat{A^n}, [\widehat{\Gamma - A}]^n \vdash_{cc} \Gamma^n$.*

We need to prove that this holds for the size $n + 1$ by reducing the $n + 1$ case to the hypothesis using relevant proof steps. We show the case for $\Gamma^{n+1} = \Gamma^n \mathbin{\&_1} \Delta$ below; the other cases ($\bigcirc^x \Gamma^n$, $\Gamma^n \otimes \Delta$ and $\Gamma^n \oplus_2 \Delta$) are all similar. In this case we have $[\widehat{\Gamma - A}]^{n+1} = [\widehat{\Gamma - A}]^n \mathbin{\&_1} \Delta$, and $\widehat{A^{n+1}} = \widehat{A^n} \mathbin{\&_1} 1$. Denote the conditions of $\&_1$ for being decided left as $condL_1$ and (respectively the condition for being decided right as $condR_1$).

$$\frac{\widehat{A^n}, [\widehat{\Gamma - A}]^n \vdash_{cc} \Gamma^n \quad [condL_1]}{\widehat{A^n} \mathbin{\&_1} 1, [\widehat{\Gamma - A}]^n \mathbin{\&_1} \Delta \vdash_{cc} \Gamma^n \mathbin{\&_1} \Delta} \&R, \&L \qquad \frac{\dfrac{\Delta \vdash_{cc} \Delta}{1, \Delta \vdash_{cc} \Delta} \quad [condR_1]}{\widehat{A^n} \mathbin{\&_1} 1, [\widehat{\Gamma - A}]^n \mathbin{\&_1} \Delta \vdash_{cc} \Gamma^n \mathbin{\&_1} \Delta} \&R, \&L$$

Hence, both cases of the decision on $\&_1$ are proved, in which the first case is reduced to the hypothesis. □

The next two theorems establish a relationship between Γ and its split ups. We do this in two steps because we only have that $A, B \equiv A \otimes B$ on the left of $\vdash$. We thus firstly show that $\Gamma, \widehat{A^\perp} \vdash {}^*\widehat{\Gamma - A}$, which in a sense can be thought of as replacing $G = (G - A) + A$ with $G + (-A) = (G - A)$. Here we note that because we are placing $\widehat{\Gamma - A}$ on the right of $\vdash$, we need to replace 1 by $\perp$ (denoted ${}^*\widehat{\Gamma - A}$). We then show that $\widehat{A}, \widehat{A^\perp} \vdash$, which can be thought of in a sense as $A + (-A) = 0$. These two results then together give us a form of $\Gamma \vdash \widehat{\Gamma - A} \otimes \widehat{A}$ as desired.

Theorem 5. *Let Γ be a formula in the fragment MCA that contains A. Γ is split up into $\widehat{A}$ and $\widehat{\Gamma - A}$ w.r.t A, where $\widehat{A}$ contains A and $\widehat{\Gamma - A}$ is the remainder. Let $\widehat{A^\perp}$ be the result of replacing the single copy of A in $\widehat{A}$ by $A^\perp$. Let ${}^*\widehat{\Gamma - A}$ be defined as $\widehat{\Gamma - A}$ except that where A is replaced by 1 in $\widehat{\Gamma - A}$, it is replaced by $\perp$ instead. Then*

$$\Gamma, \widehat{A^\perp} \vdash_{cc} {}^*\widehat{\Gamma - A}.$$

Proof (sketch): *by induction on the size of Γ. The proof can be obtained similarly from the proof of theorem 4 and is omitted here for space reasons.* □

It follows from the theorem that $\Gamma, \widehat{A^\perp}, \widehat{A} \vdash_{cc} {}^*\widehat{\Gamma - A} \otimes \widehat{A}$. Combining this result with theorem 4, we have $\Gamma, \widehat{A^\perp}, \widehat{A} \vdash_{cc} \widehat{\Gamma - A} \otimes \widehat{A} \vdash_{cc} \Gamma$.

Regarding $\widehat{A}$ and $\widehat{A^\perp}$, we further have the theorem.

Theorem 6. *Let Γ be a formula in the fragment MCA, and A be a sub-formula of Γ. Let $\widehat{A}$ be a split up of Γ that contains A and $\widehat{A^\perp}$ be the result of replacing the single copy of A in $\widehat{A}$ by $A^\perp$. If A and $A^\perp$ are chosen in all the choices in $\widehat{A}$ and $\widehat{A^\perp}$ respectively, then the following sequent is provable in TLL:*

$$\widehat{A} \otimes \widehat{A^\perp} \vdash$$

Proof (sketch): *the theorem can be proved by induction on the size of $\widehat{A}$ in a similar manner as the proof of theorem 4 and is omitted here for space reason.*   □

As a result of theorem 6, the concurrent presence of both $\widehat{A}$ and its consumption $\widehat{A^\perp}$ does not produce anything in terms of resources and actions. Therefore, the resources and actions $(\Gamma, \widehat{A^\perp}, \widehat{A})$ required to produce $^*\widehat{\Gamma - A} \otimes \widehat{A}$ are essentially Γ. In other words, $\Gamma, \widehat{A}, \widehat{A^\perp} \vdash_{cc} {}^*\widehat{\Gamma - A} \otimes \widehat{A}$ is essentially

$$\Gamma \vdash_{cc} {}^*\widehat{\Gamma - A} \otimes \widehat{A}.$$

Theorems 4 and 5 lay an important foundation for splitting up resources and goals in agent interaction. Particularly, if a goal Γ contains a formula A that the current interaction can derive, then Γ can be split into $\widehat{A}$ and $\widehat{\Gamma - A}$. If A is ever chosen in Γ, then the goal $\widehat{A}$ becomes a goal of A which can be achieved immediately by the current interaction. Similarly, if a resource Γ, which contains A, is available for use in an interaction that only uses A than the resource Γ can be split into two resources $\widehat{\Gamma - A}$ and $\widehat{A}$, of which $\widehat{A}$ can be used right away if A is ever chosen in Γ.

Returning to our example, the above theorems can be applied so that Peter can turn his goal into concurrent sub-goals $CD\_Burner \otimes \bigcirc^2 music \otimes (\bigcirc^2 C \oplus_4 \bigcirc^2 1) \otimes (\bigcirc^2 1 \oplus_4 \bigcirc^2 T)$, where the decision on $\oplus_4$ now is the same as that of $\oplus_3$ (recall that in Peter's original goal in this section, $\oplus_3$ was the choice between Chinese and Thai food). Therefore, agent Peter can achieve the two sub-goals $CD\_Burner \otimes \bigcirc^2 music$ as above and sends the subgoal $(\bigcirc^2 C \oplus_4 \bigcirc^2 1)$ as a request to Ming and the subgoal $(\bigcirc^2 1 \oplus_4 \bigcirc^2 T)$ as a request to Chaeng.

If Ming makes Chinese food, then $\bigcirc^2 C \ [\overset{\oplus_4}{\hookrightarrow} \vdash L]$ results. As the choice $\oplus_4$ is decided left, the other subgoal $(\bigcirc^2 1 \oplus_4 \bigcirc^2 T)$ becomes $\bigcirc^2 1$, which is also readily achievable.

If Ming does not make Chinese food, there is a proof of $\bigcirc^2 1$, where $[\overset{\oplus_4}{\hookrightarrow} \vdash R]$. This decision on the choice $\oplus_4$ (choosing right) makes the subgoal $(\bigcirc^2 1 \oplus_4 \bigcirc^2 T)$ becomes $\bigcirc^2 T$. Thus, if all the subgoals are successful, this mechanism ensures that only one kind of food is made.

Hence, such splitting up of formulas allows Peter to concurrently and partially achieve his goal via different threads of interaction.

7   Discussion and Conclusion

This paper addresses issues in agents' decision making when it comes to agents' choices and indeterminate possibilities in a distributed environment. A modeling of internal choices and indeterminate possibilities as well as their decisions is presented via choice calculus. The modeling supports decisions across time, decisions based on predictions of changes in the environment, as well as dependencies and distribution among choices with respect to time.

Temporal linear logic has been used in our modeling due to its natural role in supporting agent planning in concurrent and resource-conscious agent systems. Its limitation that the standard sequent calculus rules only provide a strategy of being safe by always taking all future options into account is overcome. Indeed, our choice calculus provides agents with various strategies at each decision making point when it comes to internal choices and future possibilities. In particular, agents can make predictions of future events and/or can make early decisions and act accordingly. The combinations of these strategies reflect how cautious the agents are when dealing with future changes, how agents strike a balance between safety and resource efficiency, how agents match up their plans with the future via predictions and how agents shape their future actions by early decisions. Moreover, as these strategies add flexibility into agents' decision making to deal with choices and changes, this is a step forward in providing flexible agent interaction.

Furthermore, the ability to deal with dependencies among distributed choices opens up another area for enhancing the quality of agents' decision making. Indeed, consideration of other or future choices or events can be specified as constraints to be satisfied on current choices. Hence, decision making by agents on choices is not carried out locally but with global and temporal awareness, and in a distributed manner.

Our second contribution is deriving a mechanism for agent reasoning to divide tasks into multiple subtasks which can be attempted concurrently in a distributed manner. In other words, rather than having human designers specify the distribution of concurrent tasks for agents, we can have agents construct a distributed model of task resolution by themselves. The mechanism is based on transferring inner dependencies into outer dependencies among distributed formulas. This is well suited to the nature of systems composed of multiple independent agents interacting with each other.

The mechanism also supports the notion of arbitrary partial achievement of goals and partial utilization of resources. This removes the need to pre-specify subgoals for various threads of interaction and lets agents work out the partial achievement of the goals and what remain. Interaction then can take place at agents' discretion, so long as it is beneficial to agents' goals. This further provides agents with an autonomy in interacting in open systems.

Our further work includes extending the choice calculus to other temporal operators like $\Box$ and $\Diamond$. We will also explore variations of the splitting up of formulas which directly encode various strategies of agents in dealing with choices. Furthermore, deriving an implementation platform using choice calculus and splitting up mechanisms for such a modeling of flexible agent interaction using TLL as [2] is also considered. Finally, there is scope for investigating the relationship between our approach for modeling choices, and the use of Computational Tree Logic (CTL).

Acknowledgments

We would like to acknowledge the support of the Australian Research Council under grant DP0663147 and also thank the reviewers for their helpful comments.

References

1. Munroe, S., Miller, T., Belecheanu, R.A., Pechoucek, M., McBurney, P., Luck, M.: Crossing the agent technology chasm: Experiences and challenges in commercial applications of agents. Knowledge Engineering Review 21(4) (2006)
2. Pham, D.Q., Harland, J.: Temporal linear logic as a basis for flexible agent interactions. In: AAMAS 2007. Proceedings of the Sixth International Joint Conference on Autonomous Agents and Multi-Agent Systems, pp. 124–131 (May 2007)
3. Hirai, T.: Temporal Linear Logic and Its Applications. PhD thesis, Graduate School of Science and Technology, Kobe University (2000)
4. Emerson, E.A.: Temporal and modal logic. Handbook of theoretical computer science (vol. B): formal models and semantics, 995–1072 (1990)
5. Girard, J.Y.: Linear logic. Theoretical Computer Science 50, 1–102 (1987)
6. Harland, J., Winikoff, M.: Agent negotiation as proof search in linear logic. In: AAMAS 2002. Proceedings of the first international joint conference on Autonomous agents and Multi-Agent Systems, pp. 938–939. ACM Press, New York (2002)
7. Küngas, P.: Linear logic, partial deduction and cooperative problem solving. In: Leite, J.A., Omicini, A., Sterling, L., Torroni, P. (eds.) DALT 2003. LNCS (LNAI), vol. 2990, pp. 97–112. Springer, Heidelberg (2004)
8. Küngas, P., Matskin, M.: Symbolic negotiation with linear logic. In: Dix, J., Leite, J.A. (eds.) CLIMA IV. LNCS (LNAI), vol. 3259, pp. 71–88. Springer, Heidelberg (2004)
9. Pham, D.Q., Harland, J.: Flexible agent protocols via temporal and resource-based reasoning. In: AAMAS 2006. Proceedings of the fifth international joint conference on Autonomous agents and Multi-Agent Systems, pp. 235–237. ACM Press, New York (2006)

Conflict Resolution in Norm-Regulated Environments Via Unification and Constraints

M.J. Kollingbaum[1], W.W. Vasconcelos[1],
A. García-Camino[2], and T.J. Norman[1]

[1] Dept. of Computing Science, Univ. of Aberdeen, Aberdeen AB24 3UE, UK
{mkolling, wvasconc, tnorman}@csd.abdn.ac.uk
[2] IIIA-CSIC, Campus UAB 08193 Bellaterra, Spain
andres@iiia.csic.es

Abstract. We present a mechanism to detect and resolve conflicts in virtual environments, populated by agents whose behaviours are regulated by norms, that is, explicit representations of obligations, permissions and prohibitions. A *conflict* arises when an action is simultaneously prohibited and obliged/permitted. We use first-order unification and constraint satisfaction to detect and resolve such conflicts, introducing a concept of *norm curtailment*. We present an algorithm for norm adoption which preserves conflict-freedom. Our approach allows us to address indirect conflicts and conflicts arising from the delegation of actions between agents.

1 Introduction

Norm-regulated virtual organisations (VOs) use obligations, permissions and prohibitions to constrain and influence the behaviour of self-interested, heterogeneous software agents. Norms are important for VOs, as they allow a generic albeit precise specification of social structures in terms of rights and duties of agents. Norm-regulated VOs, however, may experience problems when norms assigned to agents are in *conflict* – actions may be simultaneously forbidden and obliged/permitted. For example, a norm "agent X is permitted to $send\_bid(ag_1, 20)$" and "agent ag_2 is forbidden to $send\_bid(Y, Z)$" (where X, Y and Z are variables and ag_1, ag_2 and 20 are constants) show two norms that are in conflict regarding action $send\_bid$.

In order to detect and resolve norm conflicts and to check norm-compliance of actions, we propose a mechanism based on first-order unification [1] and constraint satisfaction [2]. We have generalised the work presented in [3] allowing for arbitrary constraints to be added to norms, and the conflict resolution itself has been reformulated as a manipulation of constraints associated with norms.

This paper is organised as follows. In the following section we introduce a "lightweight" definition of virtual organisations and their enactments. In Section 3 we define norms, constraints and global normative states. Section 4 describes in detail a mechanism for conflict detection and resolution. In Section 5, we describe how agents check the norm-compliance of their actions with the use

M. Baldoni et al. (Eds.): DALT 2007, LNAI 4897, pp. 158–174, 2008.

of unification and constraint satisfaction. Section 6 describes *indirect* conflicts occurring via domain-specific relationships between actions and via the delegation of actions among roles. Section 7 describes the application of the conflict resolution mechanism in a detailed example. Section 8 surveys related work and Section 9 concludes this paper.

2   Virtual Organisations

Following [3], we base our discussion of norm conflicts on a simple representation of a virtual organisation [4] as a finite-state machine where actions of individual agents lead to state transitions. Figure 1 shows a graphical representation of one

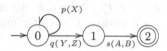

Fig. 1. Sample VO as a Finite-State Machine

such finite-state machine, whose edges between states are labelled with first-order formulae representing actions to be performed by individual agents[1]. Although there are more sophisticated and expressive ways to represent agent activity and interaction (*e.g.*, AUML [6] and electronic institutions [7], to name a few) we shall assume any higher-level formalism can be mapped onto a finite-state machine (possibly with some loss of expressiveness). A virtual organisation is defined as follows:

Definition 1. *A virtual organisation $\mathcal{I}$ is a tuple $\langle S, s_0, E, T \rangle$, where $S = \{s_1, \ldots, s_n\}$ is a finite and non-empty set of states, $s_0 \in S$ is the initial state, E is a finite set of edges (s, s', φ) with $s, s' \in S$ connecting s to s' and labelled with a first-order atomic formula φ, and $T \subseteq S$ is a set of final states.*

Notice that edges are directed, so $(s, t, \varphi) \neq (t, s, \varphi)$. The sample VO of Figure 1 is formally represented as $\mathcal{I} = \langle \{0, 1, 2\}, 0, \{(0, 0, p(X)), (0, 1, q(Y, Z)), (1, 2, s(A, B)\}, \{2\} \rangle$. We assume an implicit existential quantification on any variables in φ, so that, for instance, $s(A, B)$ stands for $\exists A, B\ s(A, B)$.

Roles, as exploited in, for instance, [8] and [7], define a pattern of behaviour to which any agent that adopts a particular role ought to conform. Moreover, all agents with the same role are guaranteed the same rights, duties and opportunities. We shall make use of two finite, non-empty sets, $Agents = \{ag_1, \ldots, ag_n\}$ and $Roles = \{r_1, \ldots, r_m\}$, representing, respectively, the sets of agent identifiers and role labels.

The specification of a VO as a finite-state machine gives rise to a possibly infinite set of histories of computational behaviours, in which the actions labelling the paths from the initial state to a final state are recorded. Although

---

[1] We adopt Prolog's convention [5] and use strings starting with a capital letter to represent variables and strings starting with a small letter to represent constants.

the actions comprising a VO are carried out in a distributed fashion, we propose an explicit global account of all events. In practice, this can be achieved if we require individual agents to declare/inform whatever actions they have carried out; this assumes trustworthy agents, naturally[2].

In order to record the authorship of actions, we annotate the formulae with the agents' unique identification. Our explicit global account of all events is a set of ground atomic formulae $\bar{\varphi}$, that is, we do not allow variables in formulae. Each formula is a truthful record of an action specified in the VO. Notice, however, that in the VO specification generality and flexibility are attained via the variables that may appear in formulae: when an agent performs an actual action then any variables of the specified action are assigned values. We thus define:

Definition 2. *A global execution state of a VO, denoted as Ξ, is a finite, possibly empty, set of tuples $\langle a : r, \bar{\varphi}, t \rangle$ where $a \in Agents$ is an agent identifier, $r \in Roles$ is a role label, $\bar{\varphi}$ is a ground first-order atomic formula, and $t \in I\!N$ is a time stamp.*

For instance, $\langle ag_1\!:\!buyer, p(a, 34), 20 \rangle$ states that agent ag_1 adopting role *buyer* performed action $p(a, 34)$ at instant 20. Given a VO $\mathcal{I} = \langle S, s_0, E, T \rangle$, an execution state Ξ and a state $s \in S$, we can define a function which obtains a possible next execution state, *viz.*, $h(\mathcal{I}, \Xi, s) = \Xi \cup \{\langle a\!:\!r, \bar{\varphi}, t \rangle\}$, for one $(s, s', \varphi) \in E$. Such a function h must address two kinds of non-determinism found in VOs: non-determinism arising from more than one edge leaving a state, and non-determinism arising from the possible values the variables of the formulae labelling edges may get; additionally, there are the choices on the possible agents that can carry out actions and their roles. We also define a function to compute the set of all possible execution states, $h^*(\mathcal{I}, \Xi, s) = \{\Xi \cup \{\langle a\!:\!r, \bar{\varphi}, t \rangle\} \mid (s, s', \varphi) \in E\}$.

The VO specification introduced previously must be augmented to accommodate the agent identification as well as its associated role. We thus have edges specified as $(s, s', \langle a, r, \varphi, t \rangle)$. More expressiveness can be achieved if we allow constraints (as introduced below) to be added to edges, as in, for instance, $(s, s', \langle a, r, (p(X, Y) \wedge X > Y), t \rangle)$, showing that $p(X, Y)$ causes the progress of the VO, provided $X > Y$. Such VOs are as expressive as the logic-based electronic institutions proposed in [10].

3 Norms

Norms are central to our discussion. We assume that agents adopt specific roles and, with that, a set of norms that regulate their actions within a virtual organisation. We extend our previous work [3], and introduce a more expressive norm definition, accommodating constraints. We, again, adopt the notation of [8] for specifying norms and complement it with *constraints* [2]. By using constraints,

---

[2] Non-trustworthy agents can be accommodated in this proposal, if we assign to each of them a *governor agent* which supervises the actions of the external agent and reports on them. This approach was introduced in [9] and is explained in section 5.

we can *restrict* the influence of norms on specific parameters of actions. Our building blocks are first-order terms τ, that is, constants, variables and functions (applied to terms). We shall make use of numbers and arithmetic functions to build those terms. Arithmetic functions may appear infix, following their usual conventions. Constraints are defined as follows:

Definition 3. *Constraints, generically represented as γ, are any constructs of the form $\tau \lhd \tau'$, where $\lhd \in \{=, \neq, >, \geq, <, \leq\}$.*

The syntax of our norms are as follows:

Definition 4. *A norm ω is a tuple $\langle \nu, t_d, t_a, t_e \rangle$, where ν is any construct of the form $\mathsf{O}_{\tau_1:\tau_2}\varphi \wedge \bigwedge_{i=0}^{n} \gamma_i$ (an obligation), $\mathsf{P}_{\tau_1:\tau_2}\varphi \wedge \bigwedge_{i=0}^{n} \gamma_i$ (a permission) or $\mathsf{F}_{\tau_1:\tau_2}\varphi \wedge \bigwedge_{i=0}^{n} \gamma_i$ (a prohibition), where τ_1, τ_2 are terms, φ is a first-order atomic formula and γ_i, $0 \leq i \leq n$, are constraints. The parameters $t_d, t_a, t_e \in I\!\!N$ are, respectively, the time when ν was declared (introduced), when ν becomes active and when ν expires, $t_d \leq t_a \leq t_e$.*

Term τ_1 identifies the agent(s) to whom the norm is applicable and τ_2 is the role of such agent(s). $\mathsf{O}_{\tau_1:\tau_2}\varphi \wedge \bigwedge_{i=0}^{n} \gamma_i$ thus represents an obligation on agent τ_1 taking up role τ_2 to bring about φ, subject to constraints γ_i, $0 \leq i \leq n$. The γ_i's express constraints on those variables occurring in φ.

In the definition above, we only cater for conjunctions of constraints. If disjunctions are required then a norm must be established for each disjunct. For instance, if we required the norm $\mathsf{P}_{A:R}move(X) \wedge (X < 10 \vee X = 15)$ then we must break it into two norms $\mathsf{P}_{A:R}move(X) \wedge X < 10$ and $\mathsf{P}_{A:R}move(X) \wedge X = 15$. We assume an implicit universal quantification over variables in ν; for instance, $\mathsf{P}_{A:R}p(X, b, c)$ stands for $\forall A \in Agents. \forall R \in Roles. \forall X. \mathsf{P}_{A:R}p(X, b, c)$. We comment on the existential quantification in the final section of this paper.

We propose to formally represent the normative positions of all agents taking part in a virtual society from a global perspective. By "normative position" we mean the "social burden" associated with individuals [9], that is, their obligations, permissions and prohibitions:

Definition 5. *A global normative state Ω is a finite and possibly empty set of tuples $\omega = \langle \nu, t_d, t_a, t_e \rangle$.*

As a simplification, we assume a single global normative state Ω for a virtual organisation. However, this can be further developed into a fully distributed form, with each agent maintaining its own Ω, thus allowing the scaling up of our mechanism.

Global normative states complement the execution states of VOs with information on the normative positions of individual agents. We can relate them via a function to obtain a norm-regulated next execution state of a VO, that is, $g(\mathcal{I}, \Xi, s, \Omega, t) = \Xi'$, t standing for the time of the update. For instance, we might want all prohibited actions to be excluded from the next execution state, that is, $g(\mathcal{I}, \Xi, s, \Omega, t) = \Xi \cup \{\langle a{:}r, \bar{\varphi}, t \rangle\}$, $(s, s', \varphi) \in E$ and $\langle \mathsf{F}_{a:r}\varphi, t_d, t_a, t_e \rangle \notin \Omega, t_a \leq t \leq t_e$. We might equally wish that only permitted actions be chosen for the next execution state. We do not legislate, or indeed recommend, any particular way to regulate VOs. We do, however, offer simple underpinnings to allow arbitrary policies to be put in place. In the same way that a normative state is useful to obtain the next execution state of a VO, we can use an execution state to update a normative state. For instance, we might want to remove any obligation specific to an agent and role, which has been carried out by that specific agent and role, that is, $f(\Xi, \Omega) = \Omega - Obls$, $Obls = \{\langle O_{a:r}\varphi, t_d, t_a, t_e \rangle \in \Omega \mid \langle a : r, \bar{\varphi}, t \rangle \in \Xi\}$. The management (*i.e.*, creation and updating) of global normative states is an interesting area of research. A simple and useful approach is reported in [11]: production rules generically depict how norms should be updated to reflect what agents have done and which norms currently hold. In this paper our focus is not proposing how Ωs should be managed, and assume some mechanism which does it.

4   Norm Conflicts

A conflict between two norms occurs if a formula representing an action is simultaneously *under the influence* of a prohibition and an obligation/permission for the same agent (or set of agents). In such situations, norm-compliant agents will experience a "paralysis" as whatever they do (or do not do) violates a norm. A norm *influences* who (what agent/set of agents in a specific role) is permitted, prohibited or obliged to perform a specific action (or set of actions). We regard norms as having a *scope of influence*: the agent/role to which the norm is associated, the action referred to in the norm, its variables (and the constraints of the norm) all define the scope of influence (or simply scope) a norm.

Figure 2 shows the scope of influence of a prohibition and a permission on instantiations of the action $shift(X, Y, Z)$, $X \in \{a, b\}$, $Y \in \{r, s\}$, $Z \in \{u, v\}$, in a block world scenario, representing that block X is shifted from the top of block Y to the top of block Z. The prohibition $\mathsf{F}_{A:R}shift(X, Y, Z) \wedge X = a$ prevents any agent A in any role R from shifting a specific block $X = a$ from any block Y to any block Z (we explain below why we use a constraint $X = a$ and not simply a constant a in the formula). The scope of this prohibition is the action's space of possibilities enclosed within the larger irregular polygon. The diagram also shows the scope of a permission $\mathsf{P}_{A:R}shift(X, Y, Z) \wedge X = a \wedge Y = r$ conflicting with the prohibition – it permits any agent A in any role R to shift a specific block $X = a$ from a specific block $Y = r$ to any other block Z. The scope of influence of the permission is $shift$'s space of possibilities enclosed within the smaller grey irregular polygon, contained within the scope of the prohibition. This is a typical situation of conflict – the scopes of influence of the norms overlap.

We use first-order *unification* [5,1] to detect and resolve conflicts between norms. Unification allows us *i)* to detect whether norms are in conflict and *ii)* to detect the set of actions that are under the influence of a norm. Unification is a fundamental problem in automated theorem proving [1] and many algorithms have been proposed; recent work propose means to obtain unifiers efficiently. Unification is based on the concept of substitution:

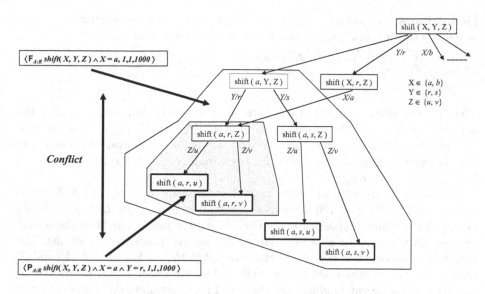

Fig. 2. Conflict between a Permission and a Prohibition

Definition 6. *A substitution σ is a finite and possibly empty set of pairs x/τ, where x is a variable and τ is a term.*

We define the application of a substitution in accordance with [1] – a substitution σ is a *unifier* of two terms τ_1 and τ_2, if $\tau_1 \cdot \sigma = \tau_2 \cdot \sigma$. Additionally, we describe how substitutions are applied to obligations, permissions and prohibitions. Below, X stands for either O, P or F:

1. $c \cdot \sigma = c$ for a constant c.
2. $x \cdot \sigma = \tau \cdot \sigma$ if $x/\tau \in \sigma$; otherwise $x \cdot \sigma = x$.
3. $p^n(\tau_0, \ldots, \tau_n) \cdot \sigma = p^n(\tau_0 \cdot \sigma, \ldots, \tau_n \cdot \sigma)$.
4. $(\mathsf{X}_{\tau_1 : \tau_2} \varphi \wedge \bigwedge_{i=0}^{n} \gamma_i) \cdot \sigma = (\mathsf{X}_{(\tau_1 \cdot \sigma):(\tau_2 \cdot \sigma)} \varphi \cdot \sigma) \wedge \bigwedge_{i=0}^{n} \gamma_i \cdot \sigma)$.
5. $\langle \nu, t_d, t_a, t_e \rangle \cdot \sigma = \langle (\nu \cdot \sigma), t_d, t_a, t_e \rangle$

We shall use unification in the following way:

Definition 7. *$unify(\tau_1, \tau_2, \sigma)$ holds for two terms τ_1, τ_2, iff $\tau_1 \cdot \sigma = \tau_2 \cdot \sigma$ holds, for some σ; $unify(p^n(\tau_0, \ldots, \tau_n), p^n(\tau_0', \ldots, \tau_n'), \sigma)$ holds, for two atomic formulae $p^n(\tau_0, \ldots, \tau_n), p^n(\tau_0', \ldots, \tau_n')$, iff $unify(\tau_i, \tau_i', \sigma), 0 \leq i \leq n$, for some σ.*

We assume that $unify$ is based on a suitable implementation of a unification algorithm that *i)* always terminates (possibly failing, if a unifier cannot be found), *ii)* is correct and *iii)* is of linear computational complexity. The $unify$ relationship checks that substitution σ is a unifier, but can also be used to find σ.

4.1 Conflict Detection

With unification, we can detect whether norms are in conflict. We define formally a conflict between norms as follows:

Definition 8. *A conflict arises between* $\omega, \omega' \in \Omega$ *under a substitution* σ, *denoted as* **conflict**$(\omega, \omega', \sigma)$, *iff the following conditions hold:*

1. $\omega = \langle (\mathsf{F}_{\tau_1:\tau_2}\varphi \wedge \bigwedge_{i=0}^{n}\gamma_i), t_d, t_a, t_e \rangle$, $\omega' = \langle (\mathsf{O}_{\tau_1':\tau_2'}\varphi' \wedge \bigwedge_{i=0}^{n}\gamma_i'), t_d', t_a', t_e' \rangle$,
2. $unify(\langle \tau_1, \tau_2, \varphi \rangle, \langle \tau_1', \tau_2', \varphi' \rangle, \sigma)$, $satisfy(\bigwedge_{i=0}^{n}\gamma_i \wedge (\bigwedge_{i=0}^{m}\gamma_i' \cdot \sigma))$
3. $overlap(t_a, t_e, t_a', t_e')$.

That is, a conflict occurs if *i)* a substitution σ can be found that unifies the variables of two norms[3], and *ii)* the conjunction $\bigwedge_{i=0}^{n}\gamma_i \wedge (\bigwedge_{i=0}^{m}\gamma_i') \cdot \sigma)$ of constraints from both norms can be satisfied[4] (taking σ under consideration), and *iii)* the activation period of the norms overlap. The *overlap* relationship holds if *i)* $t_a \leq t_a' \leq t_e$; or *ii)* $t_a' \leq t_a \leq t_e'$.

For instance, we can unify the variables of norms $\mathsf{P}_{A:R}p(c, X) \wedge X > 50$ and $\mathsf{F}_{a:b}p(Y, Z) \wedge Z < 100$ if we use substitution $\sigma = \{A/a, R/b, Y/c, X/Z\}$ Being able to find a substitution/unifier is a first indication that there may be a conflict, expressed as an overlap of the norms' influence on actions. The unifier guarantees that the two norms conflict if the variables A, R, Y and X obtain the values contained in the unifier. On the other hand, there will be no conflict if different bindings are chosen. The constraints on the norms may restrict this overlap and, therefore, leave actions under certain variable bindings free of conflict. The constraints of both norms have to be investigated to see if an overlap of the values indeed occurs. In our example, the permission has a constraint $X > 50$ and the prohibition has $Z < 100$. By using the substitution X/Z, we see that $50 < X < 100$ and $50 < Z < 100$ represent ranges of values for variables X and Z where a conflict will occur.

For convenience (and without any loss of generality) we assume that our norms are in a special format: any non-variable term τ occurring in ν is replaced by a fresh variable X (not occurring anywhere in ν) and a constraint $X = \tau$ is added to ν. This transformation can be easily automated by scanning ν from left to right, collecting all non-variable terms $\{\tau_1, \ldots, \tau_n\}$; then we add $\bigwedge_{i=1}^{n}X_i = \tau_i$ to ν. For example, norm $\mathsf{P}_{A:R}p(c, X) \wedge X > 50$ is transformed into $\mathsf{P}_{A:R}p(C, X) \wedge X > 50 \wedge C = c$.

4.2   Conflict Resolution

In order to resolve a norm conflict, law enforcers have to decide which of the two conflicting norms should be ignored in favour of the other. For a software agent, a mechanism should resolve the conflict – the set of norms Ω has to be transformed into a set Ω' that does not contain any conflicting norms so that the agent can proceed with its execution. In [3], we defined the *curtailment* of norms – one of the norms is manipulated so that its scope of influence is retracted from

---

[3] A similar definition is required to address the case of conflict between a prohibition and a permission – the first condition should be changed to $\omega' = \langle (\mathsf{P}_{\tau_1':\tau_2'}\varphi' \wedge \bigwedge_{i=0}^{n}\gamma_i'), t_d', t_a', t_e' \rangle$. The rest of the definition remains the same.

[4] We assume an implementation of the *satisfy* relationship based on "off the shelf" constraint satisfaction libraries such as those provided by SICStus Prolog [12,13,14]; it holds if the conjunction of constraints is satisfiable.

specific instantiations of actions. By curtailing the scope of influence of a norm, its overlap with another norm is eliminated.

Extending [3], we achieve curtailment by manipulating the constraints of the norms. In Figure 3, we show how a curtailment of the prohibition changes its

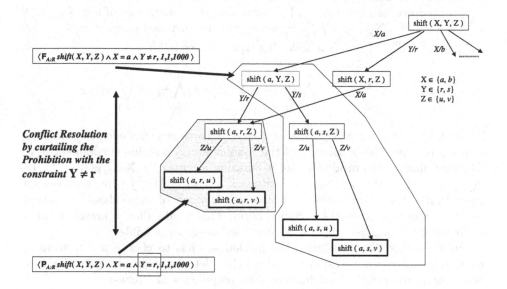

Fig. 3. Conflict Resolution via Curtailment

scope of influence and thus eliminates the overlap between the two norms. Specific constraints are added to the prohibition thus curtailing it – these constraints are derived from the other conflicting norm, that is, the permission. The scope of the permission is determined by the constraints $X = a$ and $Y = r$, restricting the set of bindings for variables X and Y to values a and r. Adding a constraint $Y \neq r$ to the prohibition curtails its scope of influence thus eliminating the overlap with the scope of influence of the permission.

We now formally define how the curtailment of norms takes place. It is important to notice that the curtailment of a norm creates a new (possibly empty) set of curtailed norms:

Definition 9. *Relationship* **curtail**$(\omega, \omega', \Omega)$, *where* $\omega = \langle X_{\tau_1:\tau_2}\varphi \wedge \bigwedge_{i=0}^{n} \gamma_i$, $t_d, t_a, t_e \rangle$ *and* $\omega' = \langle X'_{\tau'_1:\tau'_2}\varphi' \wedge \bigwedge_{j=0}^{m} \gamma'_j, t'_d, t'_a, t'_e \rangle$ *(X and X' being either* O, F *or* P*) holds iff* Ω *is a possibly empty and finite set of norms obtained by curtailing* ω *with respect to* ω'. *The following cases arise:*

1. *If* **conflict**$(\omega, \omega', \sigma)$ *does not hold then* $\Omega = \{\omega\}$, *that is, the set of curtailments of a non-conflicting norm* ω *is* ω *itself.*
2. *If* **conflict**$(\omega, \omega', \sigma)$ *holds, then* $\Omega = \{\omega_0^c, \dots, \omega_m^c\}$, *where* $\omega_j^c = \langle X_{\tau_1:\tau_2}\varphi \wedge \bigwedge_{i=0}^{n} \gamma_i \wedge (\neg\gamma'_j \cdot \sigma), t_d, t_a, t_e \rangle$, $0 \leq j \leq m$.

The rationale for the definition above is as follows. In order to curtail ω thus avoiding any overlapping of values its variables may have with those variables of ω', we must "merge" the negated constraints of ω' with those of ω. Additionally, in order to ensure the appropriate correspondence of variables between ω and ω' is captured, we must apply the substitution σ obtained via $\mathbf{conflict}(\omega, \omega', \sigma)$ on the merged negated constraints. By combining the constraints of $\nu = X_{\tau_1:\tau_2}\varphi \wedge \bigwedge_{i=0}^{n}\gamma_i$ and $\nu' = X'_{\tau_1':\tau_2'}\varphi' \wedge \bigwedge_{j=0}^{m}\gamma_j'$, we obtain the curtailed norm $\nu^c = X_{\tau_1:\tau_2}\varphi \wedge \bigwedge_{i=0}^{n}\gamma_i \wedge \neg(\bigwedge_{j=0}^{m}\gamma_j' \cdot \sigma)$. The following equivalences hold:

$$X_{\tau_1:\tau_2}\varphi \wedge \bigwedge_{i=0}^{n}\gamma_i \wedge \neg(\bigwedge_{j=0}^{m}\gamma_j' \cdot \sigma) \equiv X_{\tau_1:\tau_2}\varphi \wedge \bigwedge_{i=0}^{n}\gamma_i \wedge (\bigvee_{j=0}^{m}\neg\gamma_j' \cdot \sigma)$$

That is, $\bigvee_{j=0}^{m}(X_{\tau_1:\tau_2}\varphi \wedge \bigwedge_{i=0}^{n}\gamma_i \wedge \neg(\gamma_j' \cdot \sigma))$. This shows that each constraint of ν' leads to a possible resolution of the conflict and a possible curtailment of ν. The curtailment thus produces a set of curtailed norms $\nu_j^c = X_{\tau_1:\tau_2}p(t_1, \ldots, t_n) \wedge \bigwedge_{i=0}^{n}\gamma_i \wedge \neg\gamma_j' \cdot \sigma, 0 \leq j \leq m$. Although each of the ν_j^c, $0 \leq j \leq m$, represents a resolution of the norm conflict, we advocate that *all* of them should be added to Ω in order to replace the curtailed norm. This would allow a preservation of as much of the original scope of the curtailed norm as possible.

During the conflict resolution the mechanism has to choose which norm to curtail. We introduce curtailment *policies* that determine, given a pair of norms, which norm to curtail. We define curtailment policies as follows:

Definition 10. *A policy π is a tuple $\langle \omega, \omega', (\bigwedge_{i=0}^{n}\gamma_i) \rangle$ establishing that ω should be curtailed (and ω' should be preserved), if $(\bigwedge_{i=0}^{n}\gamma_i)$ hold.*

For example, a policy $\langle \langle F_{A:R}p(X, Y), T_d, T_a, T_e \rangle, \langle P_{A:R}p(X, Y), T_d', T_a', T_e' \rangle, (T_d < T_d') \rangle$ represents that a prohibition $F_{A:R}p(X, Y)$ has to be curtailed, if the additional constraint, ensuring that the prohibition's time of declaration T_d precedes that of the permission's T_d', holds. Adding constraints to policies allows us a fine-grained control of conflict resolution, capturing classic forms of resolving deontic conflicts – the constraint in the example establishes a precedence relationship between the two norms that is known as *legis posterioris* (see section 8 for more details). We shall represent a set of such policies as Π.

The algorithm shown in figure 4 describes how an originally conflict-free (possibly empty) set Ω can be extended in a fashion that resolves any emerging conflicts during norm adoption. With that, a conflict-free Ω is always transformed into a conflict-free Ω' that may contain curtailments. The algorithm makes use of a set Π of policies determining how the curtailment of conflicting norms should be achieved.

When a norm is curtailed, a set of new norms replaces the original norm. This set of norms is collected into Ω'' by $\mathbf{curtail}(\omega, \omega', \Omega'')$. A curtailment takes place if there is a conflict between ω and ω'. The conflict test creates a unifier σ re-used in the policy test. When checking for a policy that is applicable, the algorithm uses unification to check *(a)* whether ω matches/unifies with ω_π and ω' with ω_π'; and *(b)* whether the policy constraints hold under the given σ. If a

```
algorithm adoptNorm(ω, Ω, Π, Ω′)
input ω, Ω, Π
output Ω′
begin
    Ω′ := ∅
    if Ω = ∅ then Ω′ := Ω ∪ {ω}
    else
        for each ω′ ∈ Ω do
            if conflict(ω, ω′, σ) then // test for conflict
                if ⟨ωπ, ω′π, (⋀ⁿᵢ₌₀ γᵢ)⟩ ∈ Π and // test policy
                    unify(ω, ωπ, σ) and unify(ω′, ω′π, σ) and satisfy(⋀ⁿᵢ₌₀(γᵢ · σ))
                then
                    curtail(ω, ω′, Ω″)
                    Ω′ := Ω ∪ Ω″
                else
                    if ⟨ω′π, ωπ, (⋀ⁿᵢ₌₀ γᵢ)⟩ ∈ Π and // test policy
                        unify(ω, ωπ, σ) and unify(ω′, ω′π, σ) and satisfy(⋀ⁿᵢ₌₀(γᵢ · σ))
                    then
                        curtail(ω′, ω, Ω″)
                        Ω′ := (Ω − {ω′}) ∪ ({ω} ∪ Ω″)
        endfor
end
```

Fig. 4. Norm Adoption Algorithm

previously agreed policy in Π determines that the newly adopted norm ω is to be curtailed in case of a conflict with an existing $\omega' \in \Omega$, then the new set Ω' is created by adding Ω'' (the curtailed norms) to Ω. If the policy determines a curtailment of an existing $\omega' \in \Omega$ when a conflict arises with the new norm ω, then a new set Ω' is formed by $a)$ removing ω' from Ω and $b)$ adding ω and the set Ω'' to Ω.

5   Norm-Aware Agent Societies

With a conflict-free set of norms Ω, agents can test whether their actions are norm-compliant. In order to check actions for norm-compliance, we use unification, again. If an action unifies with a norm, then it is within its scope of influence:

Definition 11. $\langle a : r, \bar{\varphi}, t \rangle$, is within the scope of influence of $\langle X_{\tau_1 : \tau_2} \varphi \wedge \bigwedge_{i=0}^{n} \gamma_i, t_d, t_a, t_e \rangle$ (where X is either O, P or F) iff the following conditions hold:
1. $unify(\langle a, r, \bar{\varphi} \rangle, \langle \tau_1, \tau_2, \varphi' \rangle, \sigma)$ and $satisfy(\bigwedge_{i=0}^{n} \gamma_i \cdot \sigma)$
2. $t_a \leq t \leq t_e$

This definition naturally defines a predicate check/2, which holds if its first argument, a candidate action (in the format of the elements of Ξ of Def. 2), is within the influence of an prohibition ω, its second parameter. Figure 5 shows the definition of this relationship as a logic program. Similarly to the check of conflicts between norms, it tests $i)$ if the agent performing the action and its role unify with the appropriate terms τ_1, τ_2 of ω; $ii)$ if the actions $\bar{\varphi}, \varphi$ themselves unify; and $iii)$ the conjunction of the constraints of both norms can be satisfied, all under the same unifier σ. Lastly, it checks if the time of the action is within the norm temporal influence.

$$\textbf{check}(Action, \omega) \leftarrow$$
$$Action = \langle a : r, \bar{\varphi}, t \rangle \wedge$$
$$\omega = \langle (\mathsf{F}_{\tau_1:\tau_2}\varphi' \wedge \bigwedge_{i=0}^{n} \gamma_i), t_d, t_a, t_e \rangle \wedge$$
$$unify(\langle a, r, \bar{\varphi} \rangle, \langle \tau_1, \tau_2, \varphi' \rangle, \sigma) \wedge satisfy(\bigwedge_{i=0}^{n} \gamma_i \cdot \sigma) \wedge$$
$$t_a \leq t \leq t_e$$

Fig. 5. Check if Action is within Influence of a Prohibition

6   Indirect Conflicts

In our previous discussion, norm conflicts were detected via a direct comparison of atomic formulae representing actions. However, conflicts and inconsistencies may also arise *indirectly* via relationships among actions. For instance, if we consider an with norms $\mathsf{P}_{A:R}p(X)$ and $\mathsf{F}_{A:R}q(X, X)$ and if we assume that $p(X)$ amounts $q(X, X)$, then we can rewrite the permission as $\mathsf{P}_{A:R}q(X, X)$ and identify an *indirect* conflict between these agent's norms. We use a set of *domain axioms* in order to declare such domain-specific relationships between actions:

Definition 12. *A set of domain axioms, denoted as Δ, is a finite and possibly empty set of formulae $\varphi \to (\varphi_1' \wedge \cdots \wedge \varphi_n')$ where $\varphi, \varphi_i', 1 \leq i \leq n$, are atomic first-order formulae.*

In order to accommodate indirect conflicts between norms based on domain-specific relationships of actions, we have to adapt our curtailment mechanism. A curtailment occurs if there is a conflict, that is, if for two norms ω and ω', their variables unify, the conjunction of their constraints can be satisfied and their activation periods overlap. With the introduction of domain axioms, this test has to be performed for each of the conjuncts in the relationship. For example, if we have a set of domain axioms $\Delta = \{(p(X) \to q(X, X) \wedge r(X, Y))\}$ and a permission $\langle \mathsf{P}_{A:R}p(X), t_d, t_a, t_e \rangle$ then $q(X, X)$ and $r(X, Y)$ are also permitted. There is thus an indirect conflict between $\langle \mathsf{P}_{A:R}p(X), t_d, t_a, t_e \rangle$ and $\langle \mathsf{F}_{A:R}q(X, X), t_d, t_a, t_e \rangle$ and $\langle \mathsf{F}_{A:R}r(X, Y), t_d, t_a, t_e \rangle$.

Domain axioms may also accommodate the delegation of actions between agents. Such a delegation transfers norms across the agent community, possibly creating conflicts. We introduce a special logical operator $\varphi \xrightarrow{\tau_1:\tau_2\ \tau_1':\tau_2'} (\varphi_1' \wedge \cdots \wedge \varphi_n')$ to represent that agent τ_1 adopting role τ_2 can transfer any norms on action φ to agent τ_1' adopting role τ_2', which should carry out actions $\varphi_1' \wedge \cdots \wedge \varphi_n'$ instead.

7   Example: Agents for the Grid

We address a scenario taken from the e-Science/Grid domain in which a service provider may request payment that introduces a financial obligation for users, but, at the same time commits them to the provision of the service that represents a right for the user to access the service.

In this scenario, a Principal Investigator (PI) of a research project has to perform a specific research task that involves the analysis of data. We assume that a contract exists between the PI and the funding body that introduces certain permissions, prohibitions and obligations for the contracting partners. We regard both the PI and the funding body as being represented as agents operating

$$\left\{ \begin{array}{l} \langle \mathsf{F}_{rsa:pi}\, claim(X), 1, 1, 1000 \rangle \\ \langle \mathsf{P}_{rsa:pi}\, claim(staff\_costs), 1, 1, 1000 \rangle \\ \langle \mathsf{P}_{rsa:pi}\, claim(travel), 1, 1, 1000 \rangle \\ \langle \mathsf{O}_{rsa:pi}\, report\_experiment(rsa, D), 1, 1, 1000 \rangle \\ \langle \mathsf{F}_{X:Y}\, publish(D), 1, 1, 1000 \rangle \end{array} \right\}$$

Fig. 6. Contract C

on the Grid and assume that this contract is available in an electronic form and followed by the agents in their actions.

A possible initial contract C is shown in Fig. 6. The first three norms represent financial requirements of the agent taking on the principal investigator role. All claims are prohibited (norm 1) with the exception of a number of specific types of item: staff costs (norm 2) and travel costs (norm 3) are itemised here. In addition, an obligation is stated that requires the PI to report about the experiment as well as a

$$\left\{ \begin{array}{l} \langle \mathsf{F}_{A:R}\ claim(X) \wedge \left(\begin{array}{c} A = rsa \wedge \\ R = pi \end{array} \right), 1, 1, 1000 \rangle \\ \langle \mathsf{P}_{A:R}\ claim(X) \wedge \left(\begin{array}{c} A = rsa \wedge R = pi \wedge \\ X = staff\_costs \end{array} \right), 1, 1, 1000 \rangle \\ \langle \mathsf{P}_{A:R}\ claim(X) \wedge \left(\begin{array}{c} A = rsa \wedge \\ R = pi \wedge \\ X = travel \end{array} \right), 1, 1, 1000 \rangle \\ \langle \mathsf{O}_{A:R}\ report\_experiment(A, D) \wedge \left(\begin{array}{c} A = rsa \wedge \\ R = pi \wedge \end{array} \right), 1, 1, 1000 \rangle \\ \langle \mathsf{F}_{X:Y}\ publish(D), 1, 1, 1000 \rangle \end{array} \right\}$$

Fig. 7. Alternative Format of Contract C

prohibition for anybody to publish data. The last norm is a basic prohibition, prohibiting any agent in any role from publishing data. Contract C in its alternative (equivalent) format in which constants are replaced by variables and constraints is shown in Fig. 7.

7.1 Conflict Resolution

Contract C has conflicting norms. We use our mechanism to obtain a conflict-free version C' of it, in which only the first prohibition is curtailed. C' is shown in Fig. 8. In our example, two Grid services are made available by two potential subcontractors for the execution of the data analysis task. These are: *i)* a public non-profit organisation provides a free service, but requires the disclosure of data in a public repository; and *ii)* a private commercial organisation provides the service without the need for disclosure, but re-

$$\left\{ \begin{array}{l} \langle \mathsf{F}_{A:R}\ claim(X) \wedge \left(\begin{array}{c} A = rsa \wedge R = pi \wedge \\ X \neq staff\_costs \wedge \\ X \neq travel \end{array} \right), 1, 1, 1000 \rangle \\ \langle \mathsf{P}_{A:R}\ claim(X) \wedge \ldots, 1, 1, 1000 \rangle \\ \vdots \\ \langle \mathsf{F}_{X:Y}\ publish(D), 1, 1, 1000 \rangle \end{array} \right\}$$

Fig. 8. Contract C' with Curtailed Norm

quests a payment. These conditions of use can be expressed as norms in our formalism. The terms of the service, provided by the public non-profit organisation, are $N_1 = \{\langle O_{A:R} \; publish(D'), 1, 1, 1000\rangle\}$, that is, according to the terms of conditions of the public service, the input data have to be published. The terms of the service of the private commercial organisation, on the other hand, are $\langle O_{A:R} \; pay(fee), 1, 1, 1000\rangle$ or, alternatively, $N_2 = \{\langle O_{A:R} \; pay(X) \wedge X = fee, 1, 1, 1000\rangle\}$ That is, whoever uses the service is obliged to pay a fee. The Research Assistant Agent (*rsa*) has to choose which service to use. Each of them introduces a new obligation with associated conflicts, explained below.

If the public Grid service is chosen, then the set N_1, containing a new obligation, is introduced. The set $C' \cup N_1$ contains a conflict: the obligation to publish overlaps with the prohibition to publish. Our mechanism handles this, completely curtailing the prohibition and giving rise to a new set C'', shown in Fig. 9. The constraint $D \neq D'$ ensures that variable D cannot be bound to anything (since D' is a free variable) – the prohi-

$$\left\{\begin{array}{l} \langle \mathsf{F}_{A:R} \; claim(X) \wedge \dots, 1, 1, 1000 \rangle \\ \langle \mathsf{P}_{A:R} \; claim(X) \wedge \dots, 1, 1, 1000 \rangle \\ \langle \mathsf{P}_{A:R} \; claim(X) \wedge \dots, 1, 1, 1000 \rangle \\ \langle \mathsf{O}_{A:R} \; report\_experiment(A, D) \dots, 1, 1, 1000 \rangle \\ \langle \mathsf{F}_{X:Y} \; publish(D) \wedge D \neq D', 1, 1, 1000 \rangle \\ \langle \mathsf{O}_{A:R} \; publish(D'), 1, 1, 1000 \rangle \end{array}\right\}$$

Fig. 9. Contract $C'' = C' \cup N_1$

bition, therefore, becomes completely curtailed and has no further effect and, hence, it is as if it had been removed.

A conflict within the set $C' \cup N_2$ is not immediately obvious. Intuitively, in terms of paying expenses for research (the domain of discussion here), the action *pay* is related to the action *claim*. Our mechanism copes with such *indirect* conflicts as explained below.

7.2 Indirect Conflict Resolution

In choosing the private service, the obligation $N_2 = \{\langle O_{A:R} \; pay(X) \wedge X = fee, 1, 1, 1000\rangle\}$ is introduced and a contract $C'' = C' \cup N_2$ created. Intuitively, we know that this introduces an *indirect* conflict, as the original contract does not allow such a claim. With a domain axiom, we can express that to pay for something eventually amounts to claiming it: $\Delta = \{pay(X) \xrightarrow{A:R\ A:R} claim(X)\}$. In contract C'', we have permissions that allow staff to claim costs and travel, but not fees. According to the given

$$\left\{\begin{array}{l} \langle \mathsf{F}_{A:R} \; claim(X) \wedge \dots, 1, 1, 1000 \rangle \\ \langle \mathsf{P}_{A:R} \; claim(X) \wedge \dots, 1, 1, 1000 \rangle \\ \langle \mathsf{P}_{A:R} \; claim(X) \wedge \dots, 1, 1, 1000 \rangle \\ \langle \mathsf{O}_{A:R} \; report\_experiment(A, D) \dots, 1, 1, 1000 \rangle \\ \langle \mathsf{F}_{X:Y} \; publish(D) \wedge D \neq D', 1, 1, 1000 \rangle \\ \langle \mathsf{O}_{A:R} \; claim(X) \wedge X = fee, 1, 1, 1000 \rangle \end{array}\right\}$$

Fig. 10. Contract $C'' = C' \cup N_2^\Delta$

domain axiom, obligation N_2 can be transformed into $N_2^\Delta = O_{A:R} \; claim(X) \wedge X = fee, 1, 1, 1000\rangle\}$. By forming a new contract $C'' = C' \cup N_2^\Delta$, a direct conflict between the first prohibition regarding claims and obligation N_2^Δ arises (Fig. 10). The conflict resolution can now take place as shown in the case of *direct* conflicts (see contract C' in Fig. 8).

7.3 Solving Conflicts Arising from Delegation

Conflicts can also arise from delegation among agents/roles. Let there be the set of domain axioms Δ of Fig. 11: it contains axioms describing how the

Research Assistant Agent can fulfil its obligation to report the result of an experiment. As the domain axioms show, there is a relationship between the action *report_experiment* and *do_exp*. An additional axiom tells us that the action *do_exp* leads to the sending of experimental data to one of the chosen Grid services of subcontractors. The domain axiom $send(A, R', E, D)\xrightarrow{A:R\ A':R'} receive(A', R', A, E, D)$ shows

the delegation of activities from the agent responsible for the data analysis to a subcontractor for actually performing the experiment. The remaining domain axioms describe how a subcontractor performs an experiment and sends back results upon receiving such a

$$\left\{ \begin{array}{l} pay(X)\xrightarrow{A:R\ A:R} claim(X) \\ report\_experiment(A, E, D)\xrightarrow{A:R\ A:R} do\_exp(A, E, D) \\ do\_exp(A, e_1, D)\xrightarrow{A:pi\ A:pi} send(A, exp, e_1, D) \\ send(A, R', E, D)\xrightarrow{A:R\ A':R'} receive(A', R', A, E, D) \\ receive(A', R', A, E, D)\xrightarrow{A':R'\ A':R'} \left(\begin{array}{c} analyse(A', E, D, S)\wedge \\ send(A, A', S) \end{array} \right) \end{array} \right\}$$

Fig. 11. Set of Domain Axioms Δ

request. For example, the obligation to report experimental results gives rise to an obligation to perform the action *do_exp* and, continuing in this transitive fashion, obligations for all the related actions as described before. Due to the delegation step, obligations also arise for the partner agents. These obligations on their turn may interfere with prohibitions held by the collaborating agents and should be dealt with in the same way.

8 Related Work

The work presented in this paper is an extension of the work presented in [3,15,16]. It is also a logic-theoretic investigation into ways to represent normative modalities along with their paradoxes [17,18]. In [3], we introduced conflict detection and resolution based on unification. In this paper, we re-visited that research and introduced constraints to the conflict detection/resolution mechanism. The result is a generic mechanism for conflict detection/resolution.

Efforts to keep law systems conflict-free can be traced back to the jurisprudential practice in human society. Inconsistency in law is an important issue and legal theorists use a diverse set of terms such as, for example, normative inconsistencies/conflicts, antinomies, discordance, etc., in order to describe this phenomenon. There are three classic strategies for resolving deontic conflicts by establishing a precedence relationship between norms: *legis posterioris* – the most recent norm takes precedence, *legis superioris* – the norm imposed by the strongest power takes precedence, and *legis specialis* – the most specific norm takes precedence [19]. The work presented in [15] discusses a set of conflict scenarios and conflict resolution strategies, among them the classic strategies mentioned above. For example, one of these conflict resolution strategies achieves a resolution of a conflict via negotiation with a norm issuer. In [20], an analysis of different normative conflicts is provided. The authors suggest that a deontic inconsistency arises when an action is simultaneously permitted and prohibited. In [21], three forms of conflict/inconsistency are described as *total-total, total-partial* and *intersection*. These are special cases of the intersection of norms as described in figure 2 and in [15] – a permission entailing the prohibition, a prohibition entailing the permission or an overlap of both norms.

The SCIFF framework [22] is related to our work in that it also uses constraint satisfaction to reduce the scope of expectations to avoid conflict – expectation is a concept closely related to norms [23]. For instance, in that work, $\mathbf{E}(p, X), 0 \leq X \leq 10$ means that p is expected to hold true between 0 and 10, and $\mathbf{EN}(p, Y), Y > 5$ means that p is expected not to hold true when Y is greater than 5; positive expectations are related to obligations (and are implicitly existentially quantified) and negative expectations are related to prohibitions (and are implicitly universally quantified). The SCIFF proof procedure uses constraint resolution to reduce the domain of the expectations (and non-expectations). However, SCIFF always gives higher priority to negative expectations over positive ones.

9   Conclusions, Discussion and Future Work

We have presented a novel mechanism to detect and resolve conflicts in norm-regulated environment. Such conflicts arise when an action is simultaneously obliged and prohibited or, alternatively, when an action is permitted and prohibited. We introduce norms as first-order atomic formulae whose variables can have arbitrary constraints – this allows for more expressive norms, with a finer granularity and greater precision. The proposed mechanism is based on first-order unification and constraint satisfaction algorithms, extending our previous work [3], addressing a more expressive class of norms.

Our conflict resolution mechanism amounts to manipulating the constraints of norms to avoid overlapping values of variables – this is called the "curtailment" of variables/norms. We have also introduced a robust and flexible algorithm to manage the adoption of possibly conflicting norms, whereby explicit policies depict how the curtailment should take place. Our proposed formalism enables the detection of indirect normative conflicts, arising when an action is broken down into composite actions appearing in conflicting norms.

In this paper we only considered universally quantified norms, leaving out important cases of existential quantifications. If existential quantification is allowed, then disjunction of constraints must be preserved. In this case, replacing a norm that has a disjunction of constraints with a conjunction of separate norms does not work any more. If we allow existential quantification then we must preserve disjunctions of constraints and the set of norms Ω should be managed differently, in particular, disjunctions of norms should be allowed. We are currently working to address these issues.

The policies establishing which of two conflicting norms should be curtailed confers generality on our approach, being neatly accommodated in our algorithm. We observe, however, that it would also be possible to make policies part of the virtual organisation (VO) specification, giving higher priority to those norms that allow the progress of the organisation. For instance, if $p(X)$ is forbidden and $p(Y)$ is permitted (both for the same group of agents/roles), that is, there is a complete overlap on the norms' scope of influence, then a policy on the VO could specify which of the two should be "removed" (by adding the constraint $X \neq Y$ onto it), based on which of them would allow the VO to progress. For example, if the VO progresses when an agent performs $p(a)$, then the prohibition could be lifted.

We want to extend our work to also address the removal of norms: when a norm is removed, any curtailments it may have caused must be undone. We envisage a roll-back/roll-forward mechanism, whereby a history of normative states allows us to retrieve the state prior to the introduction of the norm to be removed (roll-back) and apply to this state all the updates which took place after the norm was introduced, skipping the actual norm to be removed (roll-forward). Additionally, we want to integrate our mechanisms with norm-updating approaches such as [11] and to investigate if it is possible (and in which circumstances) to detect conflicts at the design stage of norm updates (as opposed to run-time).

Acknowledgements. This research is continuing through participation in the International Technology Alliance sponsored by the U.S. Army Research Laboratory and the U.K. Ministry of Defence (http://www.usukita.org).

References

1. Fitting, M.: First-Order Logic and Automated Theorem Proving. Springer, New York (1990)
2. Jaffar, J., Maher, M.J.: Constraint Logic Programming: A Survey. Journal of Logic Progr. 19/20, 503–581 (1994)
3. Vasconcelos, W., Kollingbaum, M., Norman, T., García-Camino, A.: Resolving Conflict and Inconsistency in Norm-Regulated Virtual Organizations. In: AAMAS. Procs. 6th Int'l Joint Conf. on Autnomous Agents and Multi-Agent Systems, Honoloulu, Hawai'i (2007)
4. O'Leary, D.E., Kuokka, D., Plant, R.: Artificial Intelligence and Virtual Organizations. Commun. ACM 40(1) (1997)
5. Apt, K.R.: From Logic Programming to Prolog. Prentice-Hall, U.K (1997)
6. Parunak, H.V.D., Odell, J.: Representing Social Structures in UML. In: Procs 5th Int'l Conf. on Autonomous Agents, pp. 100–101. ACM Press, New York (2001)
7. Rodríguez-Aguilar, J.A.: On the Design and Construction of Agent-mediated Electronic Institutions. PhD thesis, IIIA-CSIC, Spain (2001)
8. Pacheco, O., Carmo, J.: A Role Based Model for the Normative Specification of Organized Collective Agency and Agents Interaction. Autonomous Agents and Multi-Agent Systems 6(2), 145–184 (2003)
9. Garcia-Camino, A., Rodriguez-Aguilar, J.A., Sierra, C., Vasconcelos, W.W.: A Distributed Architecture for Norm-Aware Agent Societies. In: Baldoni, M., Endriss, U., Omicini, A., Torroni, P. (eds.) DALT 2005. LNCS (LNAI), vol. 3904, Springer, Heidelberg (2006)
10. Vasconcelos, W.W.: Expressive Global Protocols via Logic-Based Electronic Institutions. In: AAMAS 2003. Proc. 2nd Int'l Joint Conf. on Autonomous Agents & Multi-Agent Systems, ACM Press, New York (2003)
11. García-Camino, A., Rodríguez-Aguilar, J.A., Sierra, C., Vasconcelos, W.: A Rule-based Approach to Norm-Oriented Programming of Electronic Institutions. ACM SIGecom Exchanges 5(5), 33–40 (2006)

12. Swedish Institute of Computer Science: SICStus Prolog (2005),
    http://www.sics.se/isl/sicstuswww/site/index.html
13. Jaffar, J., Maher, M.J., Marriott, K., Stuckey, P.J.: The Semantics of Constraint
    Logic Programs. Journal of Logic Programming 37(1-3), 1–46 (1998)
14. Holzbaur, C.: ÖFAI clp(q,r) Manual, Edition 1.3.3. TR-95-09, Austrian Research
    Institute for A. I., Vienna, Austria (1995)
15. Kollingbaum, M., Norman, T., Preece, A., Sleeman, D.: Norm Refinement: Inform-
    ing the Re-negotiation of Contracts. In: COIN@ECAI 2006. Workshop on Coordi-
    nation, Organization, Institutions and Norms in Agent Systems, Riva del Garda,
    Italy (2006)
16. García-Camino, A., Noriega, P., Rodríguez-Aguilar, J.A.: An Algorithm for Con-
    flict Resolution in Regulated Compound Activities. In: O'Hare, G.M.P., Ricci, A.,
    O'Grady, M.J., Dikenelli, O. (eds.) ESAW 2006. LNCS, vol. 4457, pp. 193–208.
    Springer, Heidelberg (2006)
17. Dignum, F.: Autonomous Agents with Norms. Artificial Intelligence and Law 7,
    69–79 (1999)
18. Sergot, M.: A Computational Theory of Normative Positions. ACM Transactions
    on Computational Logic 2(4), 581–622 (2001)
19. Leite, J.A., Alferes, J.J., Pereira, L.M.: Multi-Dimensional Dynamic Knowledge
    Representation. In: Eiter, T., Faber, W., Truszczyński, M. (eds.) LPNMR 2001.
    LNCS (LNAI), vol. 2173, Springer, Heidelberg (2001)
20. Elhag, A., Breuker, J., Brouwer, P.: On the Formal Analysis of Normative Conflicts.
    Information & Comms. Techn. Law 9(3), 207–217 (2000)
21. Ross, A.: On Law and Justice. Stevens & Sons (1958)
22. Alberti, M., Gavanelli, M., Lamma, E., Mello, P., Torroni, P.: The SCIFF Ab-
    ductive Proof Procedure. In: Bandini, S., Manzoni, S. (eds.) AI*IA 2005. LNCS
    (LNAI), vol. 3673, Springer, Heidelberg (2005)
23. Alberti, M., Gavanelli, M., Lamma, E., Mello, P., Sartor, G., Torroni, P.: Mapping
    Deontic Operators to Abductive Expectations. Computational & Mathematical
    Organization 12(2-3), 205–225 (2006)

On the Complexity Monotonicity Thesis for Environment, Behaviour and Cognition

Tibor Bosse, Alexei Sharpanskykh, and Jan Treur

Vrije Universiteit Amsterdam, Department of Artificial Intelligence,
De Boelelaan 1081a, 1081 HV, The Netherlands
{tbosse, sharp, treur}@cs.vu.nl
http://www.cs.vu.nl/~{tbosse, sharp, treur}

Abstract. Development of more complex cognitive systems during evolution is sometimes viewed in relation to environmental complexity. In more detail, growth of complexity during evolution can be considered for the dynamics of externally observable behaviour of agents, for their internal cognitive systems, and for the environment. This paper explores temporal complexity for these three aspects, and their mutual dependencies. A number of example scenarios have been formalised in a declarative temporal language, and the complexity of the structure of the different formalisations was measured. Thus, some empirical evidence was provided for the thesis that for more complex environments, more complex behaviour and more complex mental capabilities are needed.

1 Introduction

Behaviour of agents (both living organisms and artificial (software or hardware) agents) can occur in different types and complexities, varying from very simple behaviour to more sophisticated forms. Depending on the complexity of the externally observable behaviour, the internal mental representations and capabilities required to generate the behaviour also show a large variety in complexity. From an evolutionary viewpoint, for example, Wilson [16], p. 187 and Darwin [3], p. 163 point out how the development of behaviour relates to the development of more complex cognitive capabilities. Godfrey-Smith [4], p. 3 assumes a relationship between the complexity of the environment and the development of mental representations and capabilities. He formulates the main theme of his book in condensed form as follows: 'The function of cognition is to enable the agent to deal with environmental complexity' (the *Environmental Complexity Thesis*). In this paper, this thesis is refined as follows:

- the more complex the environment, the more sophisticated is the behaviour required to deal with this environment,
- the more sophisticated the behaviour, the more complex are the mental representations and capabilities needed

This refined thesis will be called the *Complexity Monotonicity Thesis*. The idea is that to deal with the physical environment, the evolution process has generated and

M. Baldoni et al. (Eds.): DALT 2007, LNAI 4897, pp. 175–192, 2008.
© Springer-Verlag Berlin Heidelberg 2008

still generates a variety of organisms that show new forms of behaviour. These new forms of behaviour are the result of new architectures of organisms, including cognitive systems with mental representations and capabilities of various degrees of complexity. The occurrence of such more complex architectures for organisms and the induced more complex behaviour itself increases the complexity of the environment during the evolution process. New organisms that have to deal with the behaviour of such already occurring organisms live in a more complex environment, and therefore need more complex behaviour to deal with this environment, (to be) realised by an architecture with again more complex mental capabilities. In particular, more complex environments often ask for taking into account more complex histories, which requires more complex internal cognitive representations and dynamics, by which more complex behaviour is generated.

This perspective generates a number of questions. First, how can the Complexity Monotonicity Thesis be formalised, and in particular how can the 'more complex' relation be formalised for (1) the environment, (2) externally observable agent behaviour and (3) internal cognitive dynamics? Second, connecting the three items, how to formalise (a) when does a behaviour fit an environment: which types of externally observable behaviours are sufficient to cope with which types of environments, and (b) when does a cognitive system generate a certain behaviour: which types of internal cognitive dynamics are sufficient to generate which types of externally observable agent behaviour?

In this paper these questions are addressed from a dynamics perspective, and formalised by a declarative temporal logical approach. Four cases of an environment, suitable behaviour and realising cognitive system are described, with an increasing complexity over the cases. Next, for each case, complexity of the dynamics of environment, externally observable agent behaviour and internal cognitive system are formalised in terms of structure of the formalised temporal specifications describing them, thus answering (1) to (3). Moreover, (a) and (b) are addressed by establishing formalised logical (entailment) relations between the respective temporal specifications. By comparing the four cases with respect to complexity, the Complexity Monotonicity Thesis is tested.

2   Evolutionary Perspective

The environment imposes certain requirements that an agent's behaviour needs to satisfy; these requirements change due to changing environmental circumstances. The general pattern is as follows. Suppose a certain goal G for an agent (e.g., sufficient food uptake over time) is reached under certain environmental conditions ES1 (Environmental Specification 1), due to its Behavioural Specification BS1, realised by its internal (architecture) CS1 (Cognitive Specification 1). In other words, the behavioural properties BS1 are sufficient to guarantee G under environmental conditions ES1, formally ES1 & BS1 $\Rightarrow$ G, and the internal dynamics CS1 are sufficient to guarantee BS1, formally CS1 $\Rightarrow$ BS1. In other environmental circumstances, described by environmental specification ES2 (for example, more complex) the old circumstances ES1 may no longer hold, so that the goal G may no longer be reached by behavioural properties BS1. An environmental change from ES1 to ES2 may entail that behaviour BS1 becomes insufficient. It has to be replaced by new behavioural properties BS2 (also more complex) which express how under environment ES2 goal G can be achieved, i.e., ES2 & BS2 $\Rightarrow$ G.

Thus, a population is challenged to realise such behaviour BS2 by changing its internal architecture and its dynamics, and as a consequence fulfill goal G again. This challenge expresses a redesign problem: the given architecture of the agent as described by CS1 (which entails the old behavioural specification BS1) is insufficient to entail the new behavioural requirements BS2 imposed by the new environmental circumstances ES2; the evolution process has to redesign the architecture into one with internal dynamics described by some CS2 (also more complex), with CS2 $\Rightarrow$ BS2, to realise the new requirements on behaviour.

Based on these ideas, the Complexity Monotonicity Thesis can be formalised in the following manner. Suppose $< E_1, B_1, C_1 >$ and $< E_2, B_2, C_2 >$ are triples of environment, behaviour and cognitive system, respectively, such that the behaviours B_i are adequate for the respective environment E_i and realised by the cognitive system C_i. Then the Complexity Monotonicity Thesis states that

$$E_1 \leq_c E_2 \Rightarrow B_1 \leq_c B_2 \quad \& \quad B_1 \leq_c B_2 \Rightarrow C_1 \leq_c C_2$$

Here $\leq_c$ is a partial ordering in complexity, where $X \leq_c Y$ indicates that Y is more complex than X. A special case is when the complexity ordering is assumed to be a total ordering where for every two elements X, Y either $X \leq_c Y$ or $Y \leq_c X$ (i.e., they are comparable), and when some complexity measure cm is available, assigning degrees of complexity to environments, behaviours and cognitive systems, such that

$$X \leq_c Y \Leftrightarrow cm(X) \leq cm(Y)$$

where $\leq$ is the standard ordering relation on (real or natural) numbers. In this case the Complexity Monotonicity Thesis can be reformulated as

$$cm(E_1) \leq cm(E_2) \Rightarrow cm(B_1) \leq cm(B_2) \quad \&$$
$$cm(B_1) \leq cm(B_2) \Rightarrow cm(C_1) \leq cm(C_2)$$

The Temporal Complexity Monotonicity Thesis can be used to explain increase of complexity during evolution in the following manner. Make the following assumption on Addition of Environmental Complexity by Adaptation, as described above:

- adaptation of a species to an environment adds complexity to this environment

Suppose an initial environment is described by ES0, and the adapted species by BS0. Then this transforms ES0 into a more complex environmental description ES1. Based on ES1, the adapted species will have description BS1. As ES1 is more complex than ES0, by the Complexity Monotonicity Thesis it follows that this BS1 is more complex than BS0: ES0 $\leq$ ES1 $\Rightarrow$ BS0 $\leq$ BS1. Therefore BS1 again adds complexity to the environment, leading to ES2, which is more complex than ES1, et cetera:

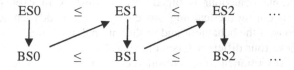

Note that this argument can also be applied to multiple species at the same time, i.e., species A increases the complexity of the environment, which causes another species B to adapt to this more complex environment.

This argument shows that the increase of complexity during evolution can be related to and explained by two assumptions: the Complexity Monotonicity Thesis, and the Addition of Environmental Complexity by Adaptation assumption. This paper focuses on the former assumption.

3 Variations in Behaviour and Environment

To evaluate the approach put forward, a number of cases of increasing complexity are analysed, starting from very simple *stimulus-response behaviour* solely depending on stimuli the agent gets as input at a given point in time. This can be described by a very simple temporal structure: direct associations between the input state at one time point and the (behavioural) output state at a next time point. A next class of behaviours, with slightly higher complexity, analysed is *delayed response behaviour*: behaviour that not only depends on the current stimuli, but also may depend on input of the agent in the past. This pattern of behaviour cannot be described by direct functional associations between one input state and one output state; it increases temporal complexity compared to stimulus-response behaviour. For this case, the description relating input states and output states necessarily needs a reference to inputs received in the past. Viewed from an internal perspective, to describe mental capabilities generating such a behaviour, often it is assumed that it involves a memory in the form of an internal model of the world state. Elements of this world state model mediate between the agent's input and output states.

Other types of behaviour go beyond the types of reactive behaviour sketched above. For example, behaviour that depends in a more indirect manner on the agent's input in the present or in the past. Observed from the outside, this behaviour seems to come from within the agent itself, since no direct relation to current inputs is recognised. It may suggest that the agent is motivated by itself or acts in a goal-directed manner. For a study in *goal-directed behaviour* and foraging, see, for example, [5]. Goal-directed behaviour to search for invisible food is a next case of behaviour analysed. In this case the temporal description of the externally observable behavioural dynamics may become still more complex, as it has to take into account more complex temporal relations to (more) events in the past, such as the positions already visited during a search process. Also the internal dynamics may become more complex. To describe mental capabilities generating such a type of behaviour from an internal perspective, a mental state property *goal* can be used. A goal may depend on a history of inputs. Finally, a fourth class of behaviour analysed, which also goes beyond reactive behaviour, is *learning behaviour* (e.g., conditioning). In this case, depending on its history comprising a (possibly large) number of events, the agent's externally observable behaviour is tuned. As this history of events may relate to several time points during the learning process, this again adds temporal complexity to the specifications of the behaviour and of the internal dynamics.

To analyse these four different types of behaviour in more detail, four cases of a food supplying environment are considered in which suitable food gathering behaviours are needed. These cases are chosen in such a way that they correspond to the types of behaviour mentioned above. For example, in case 1 it is expected that stimulus-response behaviour is sufficient to cope with the environment, whilst in case 2, 3 and 4, respectively, delayed response behaviour, goal-directed behaviour, and learning behaviour is needed). The basic setup is inspired by experimental literature in animal behaviour such as [6], [14], [15]. The world consists of a number of positions which have distances to each other. The agent can walk over these positions. Time is partitioned in fixed periods (days) of a duration of d time units (hours). Every day the environment generates food at certain positions, but this food may or may not be visible, accessible and persistent at given points in time. The four different types of environment with increasing temporal complexity considered are:

(1) Food is always visible and accessible. It persists until it is taken.
(2) Food is visible at least at one point in time and accessible at least at one later time point. It persists until it is taken.
(3) Food either is visible at least at one point in time and accessible at least at one later time point, or it is invisible and accessible the whole day. It persists until it is taken.
(4) One of the following cases holds:
    a) Food is visible at least at one point in time and accessible at least at one later time point. It persists until it is taken.
    b) Food is invisible and accessible the whole day. It persists until it is taken.
    c) Food pieces can disappear, and new pieces can appear, possibly at different positions. For every position where food appears, there are at least three different pieces in one day. Each piece that is present is visible. Each position is accessible at least after the second food piece disappeared.

Note that there is an accumulating effect in the increase of complexity of these types of environment. For example, the behaviour of environment (3) is described as the disjunction of the behaviour of environment (2) and another type of behaviour. For this reason, it is expected that agents that survive in environment n will also survive in environment n-1.

4   Modelling Approach

To express formal specifications for environmental, behavioural and cognitive dynamics for agents, the Temporal Trace Language (TTL, see [2]) is used. This language is a variant of order-sorted predicate logic. In dynamic property expressions, TTL allows explicit references to time points and traces. If a is a state property, then, for example state(γ, t, input(agent)) |= a denotes that this state property holds in trace γ at time point t in the input state of the agent. Here, a *trace* (or trajectory) is defined as a time-indexed sequence of states, where time points can be expressed, for example, by real or integer values. If these states are input states, such a trace is called an *input trace*. Similarly for an *output trace*. Moreover, an *input-output correlation* is defined as a binary relation C : Input_traces x Output_traces between the set of possible input traces and the set of possible output traces.

In the following sections, the four variations in behaviour and environment as introduced above are investigated in more detail. For formalising dynamic properties in TTL that will be used to specify these cases, the following state properties are used:

at(o, p)   object o is at position p
visible(sp)   an object occurring in the state property sp is visible
                          (e.g. as it is not covered by a large object)
accessible(p)   position p is accessible (e.g., because there is no enemy at the
                          position)
distance(p1, p2, i)   the distance between positions p1 and p2 is i
max_dist   a constant indicating the maximum distance the agent can
                          travel in one step
observed(sp)   the agent observes state property sp
performing_action(a)   the agent performs action a

For example, a property that describes stimulus-response behaviour of an agent that goes to food, observed in the past can be expressed and formalised as follows:

At any point in time t,
    if   the agent observes itself at position p
    and   it observes an amount of food x at position p'
    and   position p' is accessible
    then   at the next time point after t the agent will go to position p'

Formalisation:

$\forall t \, \forall x \, \forall p \, \forall p'$
[state(γ, t, input(agent)) |= observed(at(agent, p)) $\wedge$ observed(at(food(x), p')) $\wedge$
  observed(accessible(p')) $\Rightarrow$ state(γ, t+1, output(agent)) |= performing_action(goto(p'))]

5   Behavioural Cases

Using the introduced approach to formalise dynamic properties, the four variations in behaviour and environment are addressed in this section: stimulus-response, delayed-response, goal-directed, and learning behaviour.

5.1   Stimulus-Response Behaviour

As a first, most simple type of behaviour, stimulus-response behaviour is analysed in more detail. For this and the following cases of behaviour the following basis properties EP1-EP5 are used to describe the behaviour of the environment. They are specified both in a structured semi-formal temporal language, and in the formal temporal language TTL. Additionally, for every case specific properties of the environment will be specified.

Environmental properties

EP1 Sufficient food within reach
At the beginning of every day n (d is the duration of a day), the agent is positioned at a position p, and a sufficient amount x of food (c is the minimum) is provided at some position p' within reachable distance from p.

$\forall$n $\exists$p $\exists$p' $\exists$x $\exists$i x>c & i≤max_dist &
state(γ, n*d, environment) |= at(agent, p) $\wedge$ at(food(x), p') $\wedge$ distance(p, p', i)

EP2 Complete observability
If the agent is at position p, and a(p, p') is a visible state property involving p and a position p' within reachable distance, then this is observed by the agent. This property is to be applied to food, distance, accessibility, agent position, and the absence of these.

$\forall$t $\forall$x $\forall$p $\forall$p' $\forall$i
[[i≤max_dist & state(γ, t, environment) |= at(agent, p) $\wedge$ a(p, p') $\wedge$ visible(a(p, p')) $\wedge$
    distance(p, p', i)] $\Rightarrow$ state(γ, t, input(agent)) |= observed(a(p, p')))]

EP3 Guaranteed effect of movement
At any point in time t, if the agent goes to position p, then it will be at position p.

$\forall$t $\forall$p state(γ, t, output(agent)) |= performing_action(goto(p))
    $\Rightarrow$ state(γ, t+1, environment) |= at(agent, p)

EP4 Guaranteed effect of eating
At any point in time t, if the agent takes food and the amount of food is sufficient for the agent then the agent will be well fed

$\forall$t [[$\forall$x state(γ, t, output(agent))|= performing_action(take(food(x))) & x≥c]
    $\Rightarrow$ state(γ, t+1, environment) |= agent_well_fed]

EP5 Reachability of environment
The distances between all positions p in the agent's territory are smaller than max_dist. Here, p and p' are variables over the type TERRITORY_POSITION, which is a subtype of POSITION.

$\forall$t $\forall$p $\forall$p' $\forall$l state(γ, t, environment) |= distance(p, p', i) $\Rightarrow$ i ≤ max_dist

The following environmental properties hold for the stimulus-response case and some of the other cases considered.

EP6 Food persistence
Food persists until taken by the agent.

$\forall$t1 $\forall$t2 $\forall$x $\forall$p [t1<t2 & state(γ, t1, environment) |= at(food(x), p) &
[$\forall$t t1 ≤ t ≤ t2 $\Rightarrow$ state(γ, t, output(agent)) |= not(performing_action(take(food(x))))]
    $\Rightarrow$ state(γ, t2, environment) |= at(food(x), p)]

EP7 Food on one position
Per day, food only appears on one position.

$\forall$n $\forall$x $\forall$p $\forall$p' $\forall$t state(γ, n*d, environment) |= at(food(x), p) &
state(γ, t, environment) |= at(food(x), p') & n*d < t ≤ (n+1)*d $\Rightarrow$ p = p'

EP8 Complete accessibility
Each position is accessible for the agent (i.e., never blocked by enemies).

∀t ∀p state(γ, t, environment) |= accessible(p)

EP9 Complete visibility
All state properties a(p, p') that are true, are visible (which means that they will be observed by agents that are close enough, according to EP2). This property is to be applied to food, distance, accessibility, agent position, and the absence of these.

∀t ∀p ∀p' state(γ, t, environment) |= a(p, p') ⇒ state(γ, t, environment(agent)) |= visible(a(p, p'))

Note that the property of an agent being well fed is assumed to be a state property of the environment, since it refers to the agent's body state.

For the case of stimulus-response behaviour the environment is characterised by the following conjunction ES1 of a subset of the environmental properties given above:

$$ES1 \equiv EP1 \ \& \ EP2 \ \& \ EP3 \ \& \ EP4 \ \& \ EP5 \ \& \ EP6 \ \& \ EP7 \ \& \ EP8 \ \& \ EP9$$

Behavioural Properties
The agent's stimulus-response behaviour is characterised by the following behavioural properties.

BP1 Going to observed food
At any point in time t, if the agent observes itself at position p and it observes no food at position p and it observes that an amount of food x is present at position p' and it observes that position p' is accessible and it observes that position p' is within reachable distance then it will go to position p'.

∀t ∀x ∀p ∀p' [[state(γ, t, input(agent)) |= observed(at(agent, p)) ∧ observed(not(at(food(x), p))) ∧
observed(at(food(x), p')) ∧ observed(accessible(p')) ∧ observed(distance(p, p', i)) & i≤max_dist]
  ⇒ state(γ, t+1, output(agent)) |= performing_action(goto(p'))]

BP2 Food uptake
At any point in time t, if the agent observes itself at position p and the agent observes food at p then it will take the food

∀t ∀x ∀p [[state(γ, t, input(agent)) |= observed(at(agent, p)) ∧ observed(at(food(x), p))]
  ⇒ state(γ, t+1, output(agent))|= performing_action(take(food(x)))]

Vitality property VP
The animal gets sufficient food within any given day.

∀n ∃t1 [n*d ≤ t1 ≤ (n+1)*d & state(γ, t1, environment) |= agent_well_fed]

Logical relations
Given the dynamic properties specified above, the *environmental* and *behavioural* specifications (in short, ES1 and BS1) for case 1 (stimulus-response behaviour) are as follows:

ES1 ≡ EP1 & EP2 & EP3 & EP4 & EP5 &EP6 & EP7 & EP8 & EP9
BS1 ≡ BP1 & BP2

Given these specifications, the question is whether they are logically related in the sense that this behaviour is adequate for this environment, i.e., whether indeed the following implication holds:

BS1 & ES1 $\Rightarrow$ VP

To automatically check such implications between dynamic properties at different levels, model checking techniques can be used. To this end, first the dynamic properties should be converted from TTL format to a finite state transition format. This can be done using an automated procedure, as described in [11]. After that, for checking the implications between the converted properties, the model checker SMV is appropriate (see URL: http://www.cs.cmu.edu/~modelcheck/smv.html; see also [8]). SMV has been used to verify (and confirm) the above implication, as well as a number of other implications shown in this paper.

Concerning the relation between the specification of the *cognitive* and the *behavioural* dynamics: in this case CS1 = BS1. Thus, CS1 $\Rightarrow$ BS1 also holds.

5.2 Delayed Response Behaviour

In delayed response behaviour, previous observations may have led to maintenance of some form of memory of the world state: a model or representation of the (current) world state (for short, *world state model*). This form of memory can be used at any point in time as an additional source (in addition to the direct observations). In that case, at a given time point the same input of stimuli can lead to different behavioural output, since the world state models based on observations in the past can be different. This makes that agent behaviours do not fit in the setting of an input-output correlation based on a direct functional association between (current) input states and output states. Viewed from an external viewpoint, this type of behaviour, which just like stimulus-response behaviour occurs quite often in nature, is just a bit more complex than stimulus-response behaviour, in the sense that it adds complexity to the temporal dimension by referring not only to current observations but also to observations that took place in the past.

This leads to the question what kind of complexity in the environment is coped with this kind of behaviour that is not coped with by stimulus-response behaviour. An answer on this question can be found in a type of environment with aspects which are important for the animal (e.g., food or predators), and which cannot be completely observed all the time; e.g., food or predators are sometimes hidden by other objects:

Environmental properties
For this case the environment described sometimes shows the food, but not always as in the previous case. It is characterised by the following conjunction ES2 of a subset of the environmental properties given above, extended with the properties EP10, EP11 and EP12 given below:

ES2 $\equiv$ EP1 & EP2 & EP3 & EP4 & EP5 & EP6 & EP7 & EP10 & EP11 & EP12

EP10 Temporary visibility of food
Per day, all food that is present is visible for at least one time point, and is accessible for at least one later time point[1].

EP11 Complete visibility of non-food
All state properties that are true, except the presence of food, are visible. Thus, this property is applied to distance, accessibility, and agent position.

EP12 Complete local observability of food
For all time points, if the agent is at the position p with food then the agent observes the food (no matter if it is visible, e.g., by smell)

Behavioural properties
Next, dynamic properties are identified that characterise the input-output correlation of delayed response behaviour, observed from an external viewpoint. Such a dynamic property has a temporal nature; it can refer to the agent's input and output in the present, the past and/or the future. In semi-formal and formal notation, for the case considered, the input-output correlation for delayed response behaviour can be characterised by:

BP3 Going to food observed in the past
At any point in time t, if the agent observes itself at position p and it observes no food at position p and it observes that position p' is accessible and it observes that position p' is within reachable distance and at some earlier point in time t1 the agent observed that an amount of food x was present at position p' and at every point in time t2 after t1 up to t, the agent did not observe that no food was present at p' then at the next time point after t the agent will go to position p'

$\forall t \; \forall x \; \forall i \; \forall p \; \forall p'$
[[state(γ, t, input(agent)) |= observed(at(agent, p)) $\land$ observed(not(at(food(x), p))) $\land$
    observed(accessible(p')) $\land$ observed(distance(p, p', i)) & i$\leq$max_dist] &
    $\exists$t1<t [state(γ, t1, input(agent)) |= observed(at(food(x), p')) &
        $\forall$t2 [t $\geq$ t2 > t1 $\Rightarrow$ state(γ, t2, input(agent))|= not(observed(not(at(food(x), p'))))]]
        $\Rightarrow$ state(γ, t+1, output(agent)) |= performing_action(goto(p'))]

Cognitive properties
Since the external characterisations of delayed response behaviour refer to the agent's input in the past, it is assumed that internally the agent maintains past observations by means of persisting internal state properties, i.e., some form of memory. These persisting state properties are sometimes called *beliefs*. For the example case, it is assumed that an internal state property b1(p) is available, with the following dynamics:

CP1 Belief formation on food presence
At any point in time t, if the agent observes that food is present at position p then internal state property b1(p) will hold (i.e., a belief that food is present at p)

---

[1] Formal expressions for all properties can be found in the Appendix at http://www.cs.vu.nl/~tbosse/complexity.

CP2 Belief b1 persistence
At any point in time t, if internal state property b1(p) holds and the agent does not observe the absence of food at position p then at the next time point internal state property b1(p) still holds

CP3 Going to food believed present
At any point in time t, if the agent observes itself at position p and it observes no food at position p and it observes that position p' is accessible and it observes that position p' is within reachable distance and p ≠ p' and internal state property b1(p') holds then the agent will go to position p'

Logical relations
  ES2 ≡ EP1 & EP2 & EP3 & EP4 & EP5 & EP6 & EP7 & EP10 & EP11 & EP12
  BS2 ≡ BP2 & BP3
  CS2 ≡ BP2 & CP1 & CP2 & CP3
  BS2 & ES2 ⇒ VP
  CS2 ⇒ BS2

5.3 Goal-Directed Behaviour

A next, more complex type of behaviour considered is goal-directed behaviour. This behaviour is able to cope with environments where visibility can be more limited than in the environments considered before.

Environmental properties
For this case the environment is characterised by the following expression ES3 based on a subset of the environmental properties given earlier, extended with property EP13, given below:

  ES3 ≡ EP1 & EP2 & EP3 & EP4 & EP5 & EP6 & EP7 & EP11 & EP12 &
      (EP10 OR (EP8 & EP13))

EP13 Complete invisibility of food
Food is always invisible for the agent (e.g., always covered), unless the agent is at the same position as the food.

Behavioural properties
The agent's behaviour exploring positions in order to discover food is characterised by the following behavioural property:

BP4 Searching for food
At any point in time t, if the agent observes itself at position p and it observes that position p' is accessible and it observes that position p' is within reachable distance and it did not visit position p' yet and p' is the position closest to p which the agent did not visit and it did not observe any food at all yet then at the next time point after t the agent will go to position p'

∀t ∀p ∀p'
state(γ, t, input(agent)) |= observed(at(agent, p)) ∧ observed(accessible(p')) ∧
observed(distance(p, p', i)) & i≤max_dist &
   not [∃t' t'<t & state(γ, t', input(agent)) |= observed_at(agent, p')] &
  ∀p" [[not [∃t' t'<t & state(γ, t', input(agent)) |= observed_at(agent, p")]]
    ⇒ ∃d1 ∃d2 state(γ, t, input(agent)) |= observed(distance(p, p', d1)) ∧
    observed(distance(p, p", d2)) & d1<d2] &
    not [∃t' ∃p" ∃x t'≤t & state(γ, t', input(agent)) |= observed(at(food(x), p"))]
     ⇒ state(γ, t+1, output(agent)) |= performing_action(goto(p'))

Cognitive properties
To describe the internal cognitive process generating this type of behaviour, the
mental state property *goal* is used. In particular, for the case addressed here, when the
agent has no beliefs about the presence of food, it will generate the goal to find food.
If it has this goal, it will pro-actively search for food in unexplored positions. This is
characterised by the following dynamic properties:

CP4 Goal formation
At any point in time t, if the agent does not believe that food is present at any position
p then it will have the goal to find food

CP5 Non-goal formation
At any point in time t, if the agent believes that food is present at position p then it
will not have the goal to find food

CP6 Belief formation on visited position
At any point in time t, if the agent observes itself at position p then internal state
property b2(p) will hold (i.e., the belief that it visited p)

CP7 Belief b2 persistence
At any point in time t, if internal state property b2(p) holds then at the next time point
internal state property b2(p) still holds

CP8 Belief formation on distances
At any point in time t, if the agent observes that the distance between position p and p'
is d then internal state property belief(p, p', d) will hold

CP9 Belief persistence on distances
At any point in time t, if internal state property belief(p, p', d) holds then at the next
time point internal state property belief(p, p', d) still holds

CP10 Going to closest position
At any point in time t, if the agent observes itself at position p and it observes that
position p' is accessible and it observes that position p' is within reachable distance
and it has the goal to find food and it believes it did not visit p' yet and p' is the
position closest to p of which the agent believes it did not visit it then at the next time
point after t the agent will go to position p'

Logical relations
    ES3 ≡ EP1 & EP2 & EP3 & EP4 & EP5 & EP6 & EP7 & EP11 & EP12 &
        (EP10 OR (EP8 & EP13))
    BS3 ≡ BP2 & BP3 & BP4
    CS3 ≡ BP2 & CP1 & CP2 & CP3 & CP4 & CP5 & CP6 & CP7 & CP8 & CP9 & CP10
    BS3 & ES3 ⇒ VP
    CS3 ⇒ BS3

5.4 Learning Behaviour

A final class of behaviour analysed is learning behaviour. In this case, depending on its history comprising a (possibly large) number of events, the agent's externally observable behaviour is tuned to the environment's dynamics. In the case addressed here, in contrast to the earlier cases, the environment has no guaranteed persistence of food for all positions. Instead, at certain positions food may come and go (e.g., because it is eaten by competitors). The agent has to learn that, when food often appears (and disappears) at a certain position, then this is an interesting position to be, because food may re-appear at that position (but soon disappear again).

Environmental properties
For this case the environment is characterised by the following expression ES4 based on a subset of the environmental properties given earlier, extended with property EP14, given below.

    ES4 ≡ EP1 & EP2 & EP3 & EP4 & EP5 & ((EP6 & EP7 & EP10 & EP11 & EP12)
        OR (EP6 & EP7 & EP8 & EP11 & EP12 & EP13) OR (EP9 & EP14))

EP14 Food reoccurrence
Every piece of food disappears and reappears at least 2 times per day, of which at least after the second disappearance its position will be accessible.

Behavioural properties
The agent's behaviour for this case should take into account which positions show reoccurence of food. The following behavioural property characterises this.

BP5 Being at useful positions
At any point in time t, if the agent observes itself at position p and it observes that position p' is accessible and it observes that position p' is within reachable distance and for all positions p" that the agent observed food in the past, the agent later observed that the food disappeared and at some earlier point in time t1 the agent observed that food was present at position p' and after that at time point t2 before t the agent observed no food present at position p' and after that at time point t3 before t the agent again observed the presence of food at position p' and after that at a time point t4 before t the agent again observed no food present at position p' and p' is the closest reachable position for which the above four conditions hold then at the next time point after t the agent will go to position p'

∀t ∀p ∀p' ∀x
state(γ, t, input(agent)) |= observed(at(agent, p)) ∧

observed(accessible(p')) ∧ observed(distance(p, p', i)) & i≤max_dist &
∀t' ∀p" ∀x' [t'<t & state(γ, t', input(agent)) |= observed(at(food(x'), p"))
⇒ ∃t" t'<t"≤t &
  state(γ, t", input(agent)) |= observed(not(at(food(x'), p"))))]
  & ∃t1 ∃t2 ∃t3 ∃t4 [t1<t2<t3<t4<t &
  state(γ, t1, input(agent)) |= observed(at(food(x), p')) &
  state(γ, t2, input(agent)) |= observed(not(at(food(x), p'))) &
  state(γ, t3, input(agent)) |= observed(at(food(x), p')) &
  state(γ, t4, input(agent)) |= observed(not(at(food(x), p')))]
  & ∀p" [∃t1 ∃t2 ∃t3 ∃t4 [t1<t2<t3<t4 &
  state(γ, t1, input(agent)) |= observed(at(food(x), p")) &
  state(γ, t2, input(agent)) |= observed(not(at(food(x), p"))) &
  state(γ, t3, input(agent)) |= observed(at(food(x), p")) &
  state(γ, t4, input(agent)) |= observed(not(at(food(x), p")))] ⇒
    ∃d1 ∃d2
    state(γ, t, input(agent)) |= observed(distance(p, p', d1)) ∧
    observed(distance(p, p", d2)) & d1<d2]
    ⇒ state(γ, t+1, output(agent)) |= performing_action(goto(p'))

Cognitive properties

The internal cognitive dynamics has to take into account longer histories of positions and food (re)appearing there. This is realised by representations that are built up for more complex world properties, in particular, not properties of single states but of histories of states of the world. For example, at a certain time point, it has to be represented that for a certain position in the past food has appeared twice and in between disappeared. The state properties $b3(p, q)$ play the role of representations of world histories on food (re)occurrence.

CP11 Initial mental state
At the beginning of every day n, for all positions p, internal state property $b3(p, 0)$ holds (i.e. a belief that there is no food at p)

CP12 Belief update on food presence
At any point in time t, for $q \in \{0,2\}$, if internal state property $b3(p, q)$ holds and the agent observes food at position p then internal state property $b3b(p, q+1)$ will hold

CP13 Belief update on food absence
At any point in time t, for $q \in \{1,3\}$, if internal state property $b3(p,q)$ holds and the agent observes no food at position p then internal state property $b3(p,q+1)$ will hold

CP14 Belief b3 persistence
At any point in time t, for all q, if internal state property $b3(p,q)$ holds then at the next time point internal state property $b3(p,q)$ still holds

CP15 Going to interesting position
At any point in time t, if the agent observes itself at position p and it observes that position p' is accessible and it observes that position p' is within reachable distance and it has the goal to find food and p' is the position closest to p of which the agent believes that it is an attractive position then at the next time point after t the agent will go to position p'

Here, b3(p,4) represents the belief that food was twice present at p, and subsequently disappeared (in other words, a belief that p is an attractive position, since food might show up again). Note that, although the mechanism described here is quite different from, e.g., machine learning, this type of behaviour nevertheless can be qualified as learning behaviour. The reason for this is that the behaviour can be split into two distinct phases: one in which nothing was learned, and one in which the agent has learned which positions are useful by maintaining a history of previous observations.

Logical relations
ES4 ≡ EP1 & EP2 & EP3 & EP4 & EP5 & ((EP6 & EP7 & EP10 & EP11 & EP12)
    OR (EP6 & EP7 & EP8 & EP11 & EP12 & EP13) OR (EP9 & EP14))
BS4 ≡ BP2 & BP3 & BP4 & BP5
CS4 ≡ BP2 & CP1 & CP2 & CP3 & CP4 & CP5 & CP6 & CP7 & CP8 & CP9 & CP10 &
    CP11 & CP12 & CP13 & CP14 & CP15
BS4 & ES4 ⇒ VP
CS4 ⇒ BS4

6 Formalisation of Temporal Complexity

The Complexity Monotonicity Thesis discussed earlier involves environmental, behavioural and cognitive dynamics of living systems. In Section 2 it was shown that based on a given complexity measure cm this thesis can be formalised by:

$$cm(E_1) \leq cm(E_2) \Rightarrow cm(B_1) \leq cm(B_2) \ \& $$
$$cm(B_1) \leq cm(B_2) \Rightarrow cm(C_1) \leq cm(C_2)$$

What remains is the existence or choice of the complexity measure function cm. To measure degrees of complexity for the three aspects considered, a temporal perspective is chosen: complexity in terms of the temporal relationships describing them. For example, if references have to be made to a larger number of events that happened at different time points in the past, the temporal complexity is higher. The temporal relationships have been formalised in the temporal language TTL based on predicate logic. This translates the question how to measure complexity to the question how to define complexity of syntactical expressions in such a language. In the literature an approach is available to define complexity of expressions in predicate logic in general by defining a function that assigns a *size* to every expression [7]. To measure complexity, this approach was adopted and specialised to the case of the temporal language TTL. Roughly spoken, the complexity (or size) of an expression is (recursively) calculated as the sum of the complexities of its components plus 1 for the composing operator. In more details it runs as follows.

Similarly to the standard predicate logic, predicates in the TTL are defined as relations on terms. The size of a TTL-term t is a positive natural number s(t) recursively defined as follows:

(1) s(x)=1, for all variables x.
(2) s(c)=1, for all constant symbols c.
(3) $s(f(t1,..., t_n))= s(t1) + ... + s(t_n) + 1$, for all function symbols f.

For example, the size of the term observed(not(at(food(x), p))) from the property BP1 (see the Appendix) is equal to 6.

Furthermore, the size of a TTL-formula ψ is a positive natural number $s(\psi)$ recursively defined as follows:

(1) $s(p(t_1,..., t_n)) = s(t_1) + ... + s(t_n) + 1$, for all predicate symbols p.
(2) $s(\neg\varphi) = s((\forall x) \varphi) = s((\exists x) \varphi) = s(\varphi) + 1$, for all TTL-formulae φ and variables x.
(3) $s(\varphi\&\chi) = s(\varphi|\chi) = s(\varphi\Rightarrow\chi) = s(\varphi) + s(\chi) + 1$, for all TTL-formulae φ, χ.

In this way, for example, the complexity of behavioural property BP1 amounts to 53, and the complexity of behavioural property BP2 is 32. As a result, the complexity of the complete behavioural specification for the stimulus-response case (which is determined by BP1 & BP2) is 85.

Using this formalisation of a complexity measure as the size function defined above, the complexity measures for environmental, internal cognitive, and behavioural dynamics for the considered cases of stimulus-response, delayed response, goal-directed and learning behaviours have been determined. Table 1 provides the results (see the Appendix for all properties).

Table 1. Temporal complexity of environmental, behavioural and cognitive dynamics

Case	Environmental dynamics	Behavioural dynamics	Cognitive dynamics
Stimulus-response	262	85	85
Delayed response	345	119	152
Goal-directed	387	234	352
Learning	661	476	562

The data given in Table 1 confirm the Complexity Monotonicity Thesis put forward in this paper, that the more complex the environmental dynamics, the more complex the types of behaviour an agent needs to deal with the environmental complexity, and the more complex the behaviour, the more complex the internal cognitive dynamics.

7 Discussion

In this paper, the temporal complexity of environmental, behavioural, and cognitive dynamics, and their mutual dependencies, were explored. As a refinement of Godfrey-Smith's Environmental Complexity Thesis [4], the Complexity Monotonicity Thesis was formulated: for more complex environments, more complex behaviours are needed, and more complex behaviours need more complex internal cognitive dynamics. A number of example scenarios were formalised in a temporal language, and the complexity of these formalisations was measured. Complexity of environment, behaviour and cognition was taken as temporal complexity of dynamics of these three aspects, and the formalisation of the measurement of this temporal complexity was based on the complexity of the syntactic expressions to characterise these dynamics in a predicate logic language, as known from, e.g., [7]. The outcome of this approach is that the results support the Complexity Monotonicity Thesis.

Obviously, the results as reported in this paper are no generic proof for the correctness of the Complexity Monotonicity Thesis. Instead, the paper should rather be seen as a case study in which the thesis was tested positively. However, the approach taken for this test was not completely arbitrary: the used complexity measure is one of the standard approaches to measure complexity of syntactical expressions [7]. Moreover, the formal specifications were constructed very carefully, to ensure that no shorter specifications exist that are equivalent. Although no formal proof is given that the used specifications are indeed the shortest possible ones, the construction of these specifications has been an iterative process in which multiple authors have participated. To represent the specifications, the language TTL was just used as a vehicle. Various similar temporal languages could have been used instead, but we predict that this would not significantly influence the results.

Nevertheless, there are a number of alternative possibilities for measuring complexity that might in fact influence the results. Among these is the option to use complexity measures from information theory based on the amount of entropy of a system, such as [1]. In future work, such alternatives will be considered as well. Another challenging direction for future work is the possibility to establish a uniform approach for specification of dynamic properties for environment, behaviour, and cognition. Such an approach may, for example, prescribe a limited number of predefined concepts that can be used within the dynamic properties.

Another issue that is worth some discussion is the fact that the Complexity Monotonicity Thesis can also be considered in isolation of Godfrey-Smith's Environmental Complexity Thesis. Although it was used as a source of inspiration to explore for the more refined Complexity Monotonicity Thesis, the Environmental Complexity Thesis as such was not investigated in this paper. Doing this, again from an agent-based modelling perspective, is another direction for future work. To this end, techniques from the area of Artificial Life may be exploited, e.g., to perform social simulations and observe whether more complex agents evolve in a way that supports the Environmental Complexity Thesis.

In [4], in particular in Chapters 7 and 8, mathematical models are discussed to support the Environmental Complexity Thesis, following, among others [9] and [12]. These models are made at an abstract level, abstracting from the temporal dimension of the behaviour and the underlying cognitive architectures and processes. Therefore, the more detailed temporal complexity as addressed in this paper is not covered. Based on the model considered, Godfrey-Smith [4] concludes that the flexibility to accommodate behaviour to environmental conditions, as offered by cognition, is favoured when the environment shows (i) unpredictability in distal conditions of importance to the agent, and (ii) predictability in the links between (observable) proximal and distal. This conclusion has been confirmed to a large extent by the formal analysis described in this paper. Comparable claims on the evolutionary development of learning capabilities in animals are made in work such as [13] and [10]. According to these authors, learning is an adaptation to environmental change. All these are conclusions at a global level, compared to the more detailed types of temporal complexity considered in our paper, where cognitive processes and behaviour extend over time, and their complexity can be measured in a more detailed manner as temporal complexity of their dynamics.

References

1. Berlinger, E.: An information theory based complexity measure. In: Proceedings of the Natural Computer Conference, pp. 773–779 (1980)
2. Bosse, T., Jonker, C.M., Meij, L., van der Sharpanskykh, A., Treur, J.: Specification and Verification of Dynamics in Cognitive Agent Models. In: IAT 2006. Proceedings of the Sixth International Conference on Intelligent Agent Technology, pp. 247–254. IEEE Computer Society Press, Los Alamitos (2006)
3. Darwin, C.: The Descent of Man. John Murray, London (1871)
4. Godfrey-Smith, P.: Complexity and the Function of Mind in Nature. Cambridge University Press, Cambridge (1996)
5. Hills, T.T.: Animal Foraging and the Evolution of Goal-Directed Cognition. Cognitive Science 30, 3–41 (2006)
6. Hunter, W.S.: The delayed reaction in animals. Behavioral Monographs 2, 1–85 (1912)
7. Huth, M., Ryan, M.: Logic in Computer Science: Modelling and reasoning about computer systems. Cambridge University Press, Cambridge (2000)
8. McMillan, K.L.: Symbolic Model Checking: An Approach to the State Explosion Problem. PhD thesis, School of Computer Science, Carnegie Mellon University, Pittsburgh, 1992. Published by Kluwer Academic Publishers (1993)
9. Moran, N.: The evolutionary maintenance of alternative phenotypes. American Naturalist 139, 971–989 (1992)
10. Plotkin, H.C., Odling-Smee, F.J.: Learning, Change and Evolution. Advances in the Study of Behaviour 10, 1–41 (1979)
11. Sharpanskykh, A., Treur, J.: Verifying Interlevel Relations within Multi-Agent Systems. In: ECAI 2006. Proceedings of the 17th European Conference on Artificial Intelligence, pp. 290–294. IOS Press, Amsterdam (2006)
12. Sober, E.: The adaptive advantage of learning versus a priori prejustice. In: From a Biological Point of View, Cambridge University Press, Cambridge (1994)
13. Stephens, D.: Change, regularity and value in evolution of animal learning. Behavioral Ecology 2, 77–89 (1991)
14. Tinklepaugh, O.L.: Multiple delayed reaction with chimpanzees and monkeys. Journal of Comparative Psychology 13, 207–243 (1932)
15. Vauclair, J.: Animal Cognition. Harvard Univerity Press, Cambridge (1996)
16. Wilson, O.: The Diversity of Life. Harvard University Press, Cambridge (1992)

Structured Argumentation in a Mediator for Online Dispute Resolution

Ioan Alfred Letia and Adrian Groza

Technical University of Cluj-Napoca
Department of Computer Science
Baritiu 28, RO-400391 Cluj-Napoca, Romania
{letia,adrian}@cs-gw.utcluj.ro

Abstract. Online dispute resolution is becoming the main method when dealing with a conflict in e-commerce. A family of defeasible reasoning patterns is used to provide a useful link between dispute resolution agents and legal doctrines. The proposed argumentation framework combines defeasible logic with temporal reasoning and argumentation with level of certainty. The evaluation of arguments depends on the stage of the dispute: commencement, discovery, pre-trial, arbitration, according to current practice in law. By applying the open world assumption to the rules, the argumentative semantics of defeasible logic is enriched with three types of negated rules which offer symmetrical means of argumentation for both disputants. A corollary of this extension consists in defining a specialized type of undercutting defeater. The theory is illustrated with the help of a concrete business-to-client case in a prototype implemented system.

1 Introduction

Online Dispute Resolution (ODR) promises to become the predominant approach to settle e-commerce disputes. To reach this statute it needed ten years of fast and sustained development [1]: starting in 1996 as a hobby, an experimental stage sustained by academics and non-profit organizations during 1997-1998, an entrepreneurial stage from 1999 (75% rate of success as business), and beginning with 2003 there have been much governmental effort and many projects to institutionalize the online dispute resolution process. It started initially in the USA, followed by Australia where automatic ODR systems are functioning under a legal framework (for distributing the marital property in divorce cases), and now Europe gives sensitive attention to ODR services.

From the business viewpoint the enthusiasm for ODR is caused by two main points. Firstly, the business entities manifest less concern over obtaining the best solution, but they are more interested in processing the cases faster and cheaper than can be done in a trial. Secondly, the ODR process is private, meaning that no inside information of the companies is revealed to third parties. From the academic perspective ODR involves more than simply integrating e-mail communications, chat rooms, or video streaming. The first book [2] published

M. Baldoni et al. (Eds.): DALT 2007, LNAI 4897, pp. 193–210, 2008.
© Springer-Verlag Berlin Heidelberg 2008

on this issue suggests that technology comes in as a fourth party in ODR, thereby integrating the earlier ideas of computer expert systems with the idea of easy access to justice. Practically, ODR is shaping the way we handle disputes in the technological age [3].

In order to face the increasing number of disputes in e-commerce, there is an acute need for flexible ODR support systems, both to enhance the expertise level of the mediator, and to structure argumentation. We approach the mediation to be carried out by software agents from the point of view of human negotiation where the capacity or ability to get things done covers the *power* of: competition, legitimacy, risk taking, commitment, expertise, the knowledge of "needs", investment, rewarding or punishing, identification, morality, precedent, persistence, persuasive capacity, attitude. Very important dimensions of such a real problem are also *time* and *information*. Quite aware of the difficulties that lie ahead of such a task, we embark in this research on the road of developing a reasonable flexible argumentation framework, according to the current practice in law, which can be effectively employed in online dispute resolution agents. In recent years several researchers acknowledged the value of argumentation theory for ODR [4]. Flexibility in configuring ODR systems is both an opportunity and a challenge. The opportunity is that any business can, quite quickly, have its own "court" specialized in disputes that might occur in its specific business domain. The challenge is that the technical instrumentation must simultaneously satisfy the business viewpoint asking for trust [5] and the legal viewpoint, which requires accordance with the current practice in law.

In the next section we formalize the argumentation framework by defining both sustaining and defeating rules for a claim. In section 3 we empower agents with defeasible reasoning patterns, followed by guidelines about how this method can be suitably applied to current practice in law in section 4. Section 5 illustrates how mediator agents can deal with different phases of the dispute resolution process. We end with related work and conclusions.

2   Argumentation Framework

The proposed framework exploits the argumentation semantics of defeasible logic, which is proved to be the most suitable choice for legal reasoning [6]. We enrich the defeasible logic of Governatori [7] with: i) interval-based temporal reasoning, ii) level of certainty, and iii) negated rules. By introducing interval-based reasoning we attempt to provide a more appropriate framework for practical scenarios, having the possibility to model contract deadlines. The levels of certainty for weighting arguments are meant to better handle incomplete information, vagueness, or fuzziness of the terms implied in the dispute, but also they could be very useful when taking decision of accepting or not an argument, depending on the dispute phases (see section 5). The negated rules aim to offer symmetrical means of argumentation between disputants.

Definition. *A theory in temporal defeasible logic (TDL) is a structure $\langle F, R \rangle$ formed by a finite set of facts $f(\beta)[a, b] \in F$ valid at time t, $a \leq t \leq b$, and a finite set of rules $r(\gamma) \in R$, with certainty factors $\beta, \gamma \in (0..1]$. A fact $f(\beta) \in F$ is strict if $\beta = 1$ and defeasible if $\beta < 1$.*

The rules are split in two disjoint sets: the set of support rules R_{sup} which can be used to infer conclusions and the set of defeaters R_{def} that can be used only to block the derivation of some conclusions.

Definition. *A rule $r(\gamma) \in R_{sup}$ is strict ($\rightarrow$) iff $\gamma = 1$, with the set of strict rules $R_s = \{r(\gamma) \in R_{sup} | \gamma = 1\}$. A rule $r(\gamma) \in R_{sup}$ is defeasible ($\Rightarrow$) iff $\gamma < 1$, with the set of defeasible rules $R_d = \{r(\gamma) \in R_{sup} | \gamma < 1\}$.*

Strict rules are rules in the classical sense, that is whenever the premises are indisputable, then so is the conclusion, while defeasible rules are rules that can be defeated by contrary evidence. Following Pollock's terminology [8], a defeasible conclusion q can be defeated either by inferring the opposite one $\sim q$ with a superior certainty factor (rebuttal defeater), or by attacking ($\rightsquigarrow q$) the link between the premises and the conclusion q (undercutting defeater[1]).

Facts within TDL are enhanced with validity intervals. For premise $a[x, y]$ and a conclusion $b[u, v]$ the following weak semantics is used: if a is valid in at least one moment within $[x, y]$, then b is valid in all moments from $[u, v]$. In this interpretation (imprecise premise, precise conclusion), the validity interval [a,b] of a rule depends on the activation intervals of its own premises: $r_i(\gamma)[a, b]: q_1(\beta_1)[a_1, b_1], ...q_k(\beta_k)[a_k, b_k] \Rightarrow q_0(\beta_0)[a_0, b_0]$, with $a = min(a_i)$ and $b = max(b_i), i \in [1..k]$. For the particular case when a defeasible rule has only one premise, its activation interval is synonym to the validity of that premise: $q_1[a_1, b_1] \Rightarrow q_0[a_0, b_0] \Leftrightarrow (q_1 \Rightarrow q_0[a_0, b_0])[a_1, b_1]$. This feature is used in nested rules[2].

Similar to facts, the rules acting as premises or conclusion within the body of a nested rule can appear negated. We use the following notations: $\nrightarrow$ for $\neg (a \rightarrow b)$, meaning that "a does not strictly determine b", $\nRightarrow$ for $\neg (a \Rightarrow b)$, meaning that "a does not defeasibly determine b", and $\not\rightsquigarrow$ for $\neg (a \rightsquigarrow b)$ meaning that "a does not defeat b". We note by R_{ns} the set of negated strict rules, by R_{nd} the set of negated defeasible rules, and by R_{ndef} the set of negated defeaters. The problem consists in giving a proper interpretation to a negated rule. Firstly, the negated rule represents a counterargument to the opposite rule, negated rules having the same role as an undercutting defeater, attacking the links between the premises and the conclusion. The difference consists in the fact that a defeater of the consequent

---

[1] Intuitively, an undercutting defeater argues that the conclusion is not sufficiently supported by its premises.

[2] In our approach, rules are allowed to appear as premises or conclusions within other rules. The general case of such nested rule is represented by: $r_i(\gamma_i): r_j[a_2, b_2] \Rightarrow r_k[a_3, b_3]$, where the existence of the rule r_j fires the conclusion r_k, which can be seen as a dynamic rule. Another technical approach [9] consists in using an objectivation operator to translate a meta-level expression to an object-level expression.

Claim: Harry is a British subject now.
Datum: Harry was born in Bermuda in 1937.
    Harry is become an American citizen[1966,1966].
    Very probably Harry speaks English.
Warrant: A man born in Bermuda will generally be a British subject.
    English speakers are usually British subject.
Backing: Civil Code 123 provides that persons born in Bermuda
    are generally British subjects.
Exception: An American Citizen cannot be a British subject.
Counter-example: Speaking English does not mean one is a British subject.

$Harry\_Born\_Bermuda(1.0)[1937, 1937]$
$Harry\_American\_Citizen(1.0)[1960, 1960]$
$Harry\_Speaks\_English(0.95)[1937, now]$
$r_1 : (0.9) : Born\_Bermuda[t, t] \Rightarrow British\_Subject[t, now]$
$r_2 : (0.5) : Speak\_English[1, 1] \Rightarrow [t, t]British\_Subject[t, t]$
$r_3 : (0.9)Harry\_American\_Citizen[1, 1] \rightsquigarrow British\_Subject[2, 2]).$
$r_4 : (0.9)Speak\_English[1, 1] \nrightarrow British\_Subject[t, t]).$
$r_5 : valid\_code\_123[0, t] \rightarrow (Born\_Bermuda[t, t] \Rightarrow British\_Subject[t, now]).$

Fig. 1. A special type of undercutting defeater: negated rules

q attacks all rules which sustain q, whilst the negated rule attacks a single rule
sustaining the respective conclusion[3]. The version of Toulmin's standard example
about British citizenship in figure 1 illustrates this difference. Here, the rule r_4
attacks only the rule r_2, which is defeated. Opposite, the undercutting defeater
r_3 attacks both r_1 and r_2 with a stronger certainty factor, blocking the claim
$+\partial British\_Subject : now$. We use Pollock's undercutting defeaters to model
exceptions and negated rules in representing counter-examples. Undercutting
defeaters or negated rules cannot be used to draw a conclusion, their only use is
to prevent some conclusions. Practically, introducing negated rules, we extend
the open world assumption to the rules. A relation between two terms a and
b can be positive $(a \rightarrow b)$, negative $(a \nrightarrow b)$, or unspecified. Pairs of relations

φ	$\sim \varphi$
q	$\neg q, X \rightarrow \neg q, X \Rightarrow \neg q$
$A \rightarrow q$	$\neg q, X \rightarrow \neg q, A \nrightarrow q$
$A \Rightarrow q$	$\neg q, X \rightarrow \neg q, X \Rightarrow \neg q, X \rightsquigarrow \neg q, A \nRightarrow q$
$A \rightsquigarrow q$	$A \not\rightsquigarrow q$
$A \nrightarrow q$	$A \rightarrow q$
$A \nRightarrow q$	$A \Rightarrow q$
$A \not\rightsquigarrow q$	$A \rightsquigarrow q$

Fig. 2. Attacking a sentence φ depends on its type

---

[3] If defeaters represent rules used to block the derivation of some conclusion q, the
negated rules are used to block the activation of a specific support argument for q.

provide symmetrical means of argumentation for both disputants. The type of counterargument depends on the type of the current sentence φ: fact, support rule, defeater (figure 2). Here, one can see that the support rules ($\rightarrow$, $\Rightarrow$) can be attacked in different ways. The negated rule $A \not\rightarrow q$ represents an argument in favor of q, because it attacks the undercutting defeater $A \rightsquigarrow q$. The second utility of the negated rules is the dynamic elimination of some arguments from the knowledge base. The existence of a negated rule allows the deactivation of a rule, when the certainty factor is strong enough.

3 Types of Agents for ODR

A family of defeasible reasoning patterns is discussed next, employed in dispute resolution agents for more flexibility of the decision. The strategy of an agent consists of three orthogonal components which modularly capture different concerns of the problem: basic component, tactical component, and attitude component.

3.1 Basic Component

Fuzzy Inference. Using the weakest link principle for deductive arguments [8], the conclusion q_0 is as good as the weakest premise, given by $min(\beta_1, ..., \beta_k)$. Additionally, the certainty factor is also influenced by the strength γ of the inferencing rule (figure 3). The figure presents the generalized modus ponens where given the premises $q_i(\beta_i)[t_i]$ valid at time t_i required by the rule r_i, the conclusion q_0 is inferred with a strength equal to the minimum between the strength of the premises β_i and the strength of the rule r_i.

$$rule\_r_i : \_q_0[a_0, b_0] \xleftarrow{\gamma} q_1[a_1, b_1] \wedge .... \wedge q_k[a_k, b_k]$$
$$facts : \_q_1(\beta_1)[t_1], a_1 \le t_1 \le b_1................., q_k(\beta_k)[t_k], a_k \le t_k \le b_k$$
$$\overline{\rule{0pt}{0pt}\hspace{6cm}}$$
$$q_0(min(\beta_1, ..., \beta_k, \gamma)[a_i], \forall a_i, a_0 \le a_i \le b_0$$

Fig. 3. Inferring the conclusion q_0 when no valid defeaters exist

Probabilistic inference. A probabilistic approach of computing the certainty factor of a conclusion would multiply the certainty factors of all premises. Practically, the certainty factor depends on the number of premises. In this probabilistic context, the temporal persistence issue can also be considered. Suppose the fact a having the certainty factor β_a is valid at time t. The following interpretation could arise: if a at t then there is a defeasible reason to infer a at $t + \Delta t$, the certainty factor for a being a monotonic decreasing function of argument Δt. A typical scenario might be: the probability that the new business partner will breach the contract is 0.2. This probability decreases as time passes and the contract meets its time of maturity. Similarly, an agent believes that his business partner is trust-able with a factor of 0.6. If nothing defeats this believe in time, the agent increases the trust in the partnership as the business runs. By default we consider that the certainty factor is constant in time and we provide mechanisms to adjust it for each scenario.

3.2   Tactical Component

The same conclusion q can be sustained by several arguments with different degrees of reliance. The tactical component defines how an agent handles the accrual of such valid arguments. Let n be the number of valid derivations of the consequent q and $cf[q_i]$ the certainty factor of the inference number i of q, $i \in [1..n]$. Similarly, m is the number of valid undercutting defeaters (both defeaters and negated rules) of the sentence q and we note by $cf[\sim q_j]$ the certainty factor of the j defeater of q, $j \in [1..m]$. If p is the number of valid rebuttal defeaters, we note with $cf[\neg q_k]$ the certainty factor of the k rebuttal defeater for q, $k \in [1..p]$.

Persuasion Agent. In some situations, independent reasons supporting the same action provide stronger arguments in favor of that conclusion. For instance, the testimony of two witnesses is required in judicial cases. This approach is appropriate for *practical reasoning*, when the decision is about what actions to perform [8] or evidential reasoning [10]. One issue related to this agent regards the difficulty to identify independent reasons. Thus, an argument presented in different forms contributes with all its avatars to the certainty factor. Similarly, an argument subsumed by another general argument also contributes to the certainty factor. Correlated to the same judicial example, if the two witnesses are kin or they conferred with each other, only one testimony is accepted in the trial. The accrual of dependent arguments is not necessarily useless. Changing the perspective, this case can be valuable in persuasion dialogs, where an agent, by repeatedly posting the same argument in different representations, will end in convincing his partner to accept that sentence.

A persuasion agent computes the certainty factor of the thesis q under dispute as follows. Firstly, it considers all the accepted arguments supporting the claim q at time t. This amount is decreasing by all his objections about deriving q, in our case all the undercutting defeaters. If the remaining certainty factor is still greater than all the existing support for the opposite conclusion $\neg q$, the thesis is successfully established. Formally, the model of persuasion based on the defeasible pattern of inference becomes:

$$
cf[q] = \begin{cases} min(1, \sum_{i=1}^{n} cf[q_i] - \sum_{j=1}^{m} cf[\sim q_j]), & \sum_{i=1}^{n} cf[q_i] - \sum_{j=1}^{m} cf[\sim q_j] > \sum_{k=1}^{p} cf[\neg q_k] \\ 0, & \text{otherwise} \end{cases}
$$

Epistemic Agent. In reasoning about what to believe or *epistemic reasoning* the accrual of arguments does not hold [8]. The sentence q is inferred if it has a greater support than any of the undercutter or rebuttal defeaters, but the certainty factor is not diminished:

$$
cf[q] = \begin{cases} max(cf[q_i]), & max(cf[q_i]) > max(cf[\neg q_k], cf[\sim q_j]) \\ 0, & \text{otherwise} \end{cases}
$$

The choice between a persuasion or an epistemic agent depends on the context. A hybrid agent would include modalities such as *action* or *knowledge* for capturing practical and, respectively, epistemic reasoning, with the certainty factor of the conclusion computed accordingly.

Rigorous Agent. A rigorous agent will treat differently each type of defeater. Thus, only the strongest undercutting defeater contributes to the decreasing of the certainty factor. If the remaining strength of the conclusion overwhelms the most powerful rebuttal defeater, the respective conclusion is derived.

$$cf[q] = \begin{cases} max(cf[q_i]) - max(cf[\sim q_j]), & max(cf[q_i]) - max(cf[\sim q_j]) \\ & > max(cf[\neg q_k]) \\ 0, & \text{otherwise} \end{cases}$$

Next we present the derivation formula of a consequent according to the reasoning strategy of the rigorous agent. A conclusion in TDL is a tagged literal which can have the following forms: i) $+\Delta q : t \Leftrightarrow q$ is definitely provable at time t in TDL, using only strict facts and rules (figure 4); ii) $-\Delta q : t \Leftrightarrow q$ is not definitely provable at time t in TDL; iii) $+\partial q : t \Leftrightarrow q$ is defeasibly provable at time t in TDL (figure5); iv) $-\partial q : t \Leftrightarrow q$ is not defeasibly provable at time t in TDL.

$+\Delta$:
    If $P(i+1) = +\Delta q : t$ then
        (1) $\exists q(\beta)[u, v] \in F$ and $\beta = 1$ and $u \leq t \leq v$ or
        (2) $\exists r \in R_s[q[u, v]]$ with $u \leq t \leq v$ such as
            (2.1)$\forall a[x_1, y_1] \in A(r)\exists t' : +\Delta a : t' \in P(1..i)$ and $x_1 \leq t' \leq y_1$
            (2.2) $\nexists ns \in R_{ns}[r]$

Fig. 4. Definite proof for the consequent q at time t for the rigorous agent

A conclusion q is strictly provable at time t (figure 4) if (1) q is a strict fact valid at time t or (2) there exists a strict rule with conclusion $q[u, v]$ and the instant of time t within $[u, v]$, which rule, (2.1) for all its antecedents $a[x_1, y_1]$, there is a time t' when they are strictly valid and (2.2) there is no strict negated rule ns, attacking rule r.

Defeasible derivations have an argumentation like structure [7]: firstly, we choose a supported rule having the conclusions q we want to prove, secondly we consider all the possible counterarguments against q, and finally we rebut all the above counterarguments showing that, either some of their premises do not hold, or the rule used for its derivation is weaker than the rule supporting the initial conclusion q. The sentence q is defeasibly provable at time t (figure 5) if (1) it is strictly provable at t, or (2) there is a valid support for q either (2.1) it is a defeasible fact valid at t, or (2.2) there exists a rule with all premises valid sustaining that conclusion q and it is not defeated by (2.3) a negated rule with a stronger certainty factor, or (2.4) by an undercutting defeater def where (2.4.1) time t is not within the validity interval of the defeater, or (2.4.2) the defeater

$+\partial$:

If $P(i+1) = +\partial q : t$ then

(1) $+\Delta q : t \in P(1..i)$ or

(2) q is supported

(2.1) $\exists q(\beta)[u,v] \in F$ and $\beta < 1$ and $t \in [u,v]$ or

(2.2) $\exists r(\gamma_r) \in R_{sup}[q[u,v]], \forall a[x_1,y_1] \in A(r) \exists t'$ such as $+\partial a : t' \in P(1..i)$ and $t' \in [x_1,y_1])$

and not defeated

(2.3) $\forall nd(\gamma_{nd}) \in R_{nd}[r] \cup R_{ns}[r]], \gamma_r > \gamma_{nd}$ and

(2.4) $\forall def(\gamma_{def}) \in R_{def}[q[u_1,v_1]]$or

(2.4.1) $t \notin [u_1,v_1]$ or

(2.4.2) $\exists a[x_1,y_1] \in A(def) \ \forall t' \in [x_1,y_1] - \partial a : t'$ or

(2.4.3) $\exists ndef(\gamma_{ndef}) \in R_{ndef}[def], \ \gamma_{ndef} > \gamma_{def}$ and

(2.5) $\forall d(\gamma_d) \in R_{sup}[\sim q[u_2,v_2]]$ with
$\forall a[x_2,y_2] \in A(d), \exists t' \in [x_2,y_2] + \partial a : t', t \in [u_2,v_2]$ either

(2.5.1) $\exists nnd(\gamma_{nnd}) \in R_{nd}[d] \cup R_{ns}[d], \gamma_{nnd} > \gamma d$, or

(2.5.2) $\gamma_r - \gamma_{def} > \gamma_d$

Fig. 5. Defeasible derivation of consequence q at time t for the rigorous agent

has an antecedent a which cannot be derived, or (2.4.3) there exists a negated defeater stronger than def, and (2.5) for all valid rebuttal defeaters d either (2.5.1) there is a negated rule which defeats d or (2.5.2) the support for conclusion q after it is attacked by the undercutter defeaters remains stronger than all the valid rebuttal defeaters. The strict order relation in (2.3), (2.4.3), and (2.5.2) provides a skeptical reasoning mechanism, meaning that none of $q : t$ and $\sim q : t$ is derived when they have equal support. Allowing the ambiguity propagation increases the number of inferred conclusions, useful in the argumentation process of ODR systems oriented towards solution rather than finding the degree of guilt.

3.3   Attitude Component

The attitude component defines the argumentative attitude of an agent towards other participants, making a distinction between the agent's private collection of arguments and its public uttered sentences. We adapt the claim-attitude and concede-attitude [11], defining the level of proof sufficient to convince the opponent that a given sentence is true, to our defeasible formalism.

The following standards of proofs from current legal practice are modeled: *scintilla of evidence, reasonable suspicion*[4], *preponderance of evidence*[5], *clear and convincing evidence*, and *beyond reasonable doubt*[6].

---

[4] Reasonable suspicion is a low standard of proof used to determine whether a brief investigative stop or a brief search by a police officer is warranted.

[5] Also known as the "balance of probabilities", this standard is met if the proposition is more likely to be true than not true.

[6] This means that the proposition must be proved to the extent that there is no "reasonable doubt" in the mind of a reasonable person, such as 90% certain in the US.

Definition. *Claim-attitude at time t*

- *A confident agent can claim any sentence $q : t$ for which there is a valid support rule $r \in R_{sup}$ (scintilla of evidence).*
- *A careful agent can claim any proposition $q : t$ if there is no valid rebuttal defeater sustaining the opposite sentence $\neg q : t$ (reasonable suspicion).*
- *A precaution agent can claim any proposition $q : t$ if there is no valid rebuttal or undercutting defeater for the opposite sentence $\neg q : t$ (preponderance of evidence).*
- *A thoughtful agent can claim any proposition $q : t$ for which it can construct a defeasible proof $+\partial q : t$ (clear and convincing evidence).*
- *A strict agent can claim any proposition $q : t$ for which it can construct a definite proof $+\Delta q : t$ according to its theory (beyond reasonable doubt).*

Definition. *Concede-attitude at time t*

- *A credulous agent can concede to any sentence $q : t$ for which it has a valid support rule $r \in R_{sup}$ (scintilla of evidence).*
- *A cautious agent can concede to any proposition $q : t$ if it is not able to provide a stronger rebuttal defeater for the opposite sentence $\neg q : t$ (reasonable suspicion).*
- *A vigilant agent can concede to any proposition $q : t$ if it is not able to provide a stronger rebuttal or undercutting valid defeater (preponderance of evidence).*
- *A skeptical agent can concede only to those propositions $q : t$ for which it can construct a defeasible proof $+\partial q : t$ (clear and convincing evidence).*
- *A wary agent can concede to any proposition $q : t$ for which it can construct a definite proof $+\Delta q : t$ according to its theory (beyond reasonable doubt).*

During the argumentation process, a confident agent might claim any proposition for which it is able to construct an argument (propositions which are not credible can also be uttered). When, for example, the knowledge base of the agent consists of the rules $r_1 : (0.5) : a[1,1] \Rightarrow q[2,2]$, and $r_2 : b[1,1] \rightarrow \neg q[2,2]$ where a and b are strict valid facts, then it is still presumable for the agent to claim q, even if it is aware of the existence of the stronger counterargument r_2 sustaining the opposite consequent. A careful agent does not communicate a sentence if it is conscious about the validity of a rebuttal defeater, no matter what certainty factor that argument has. Similarly, a precaution agent additionally considers the validity of an undercutter defeater in order to minimize the risk of a potential counterattack from the other disputants. A more critical attitude is the thoughtful one, where an agent will claim propositions for which it is able to construct an acceptable argument, an argument which is defeasibly provable from its knowledge base. A strict agent does not take any risk to be combated in its claims, therefore it conveys only sentences supported by strict inference according to its defeasible theory. The concede-attitudes are used similarly to the claim-attitudes.

4   Choosing the Proper Strategy

Various situations might be encountered. (i) The market may have substantial authority, and the same mediation strategy is imposed to all disputants. (ii) Consistent with party autonomy, the agents may settle on different mediation strategies at contracting time or just prior to the arbitration. This approach increases the flexibility and efficiency, because the agents are the ones who know what type of mediation strategy better protects their interests[7]. (iii) All the above mediator's strategies might be used during the resolution process[8].

In markets where the consumer protection is the main concern, the mediator may provide different interfaces to the disputants. For instance, the persuasion strategy might guarantee high level of protection to the client being irritated by several issues. The strategies may also be correlated to the current dispute: persuasion strategy is connected to cases involving fairness or good faith. Similarly, the persuasion strategy is adequate in the first stage of the dispute, the so called evidential phase, when the factual information is collected.

On the one hand, a probabilistic approach is a good candidate when the dispute process is in its early stages, when there is little information available, and the mediator tries to figure out if the initial claim is warranted[9]. It also may be considered when the information sources are not trust-able. On the other hand, when the process reaches its maturity stage, the irrelevant facts become clear. Therefore, within a fuzzy inference, the unimportant facts do not influence the decision. Legal rules are often open to several interpretations because some terms within legal texts are vague. It is the mediator who gives the appropriate interpretation to terms such as *reasonable* or *sufficient*. The agent strategy depends on the active legal doctrines within the market. If the required standard of proof is *preponderance of evidence*, the probabilistic approach fits better, but when *beyond a reasonable doubt* doctrine is active, the fuzzy reasoning is appropriate.

The attitude component is relevant in the context of revealing information. Sometimes, the arguments uttered, either fact or rule, represent private information. The agents must assign a utility cost to revealing information, as well as a utility to winning an argument. The strategy depends on the rules of dialog game where the agent participates. When the dialog protocol stipulates that a claim which has been defeated by a party cannot be uttered again, then a strict or thoughtful attitude must be considered. Opposite, a confident attitude is adequate when a party wants to find information, because his opponent defeats the claim by revealing his private arguments.

---

[7] Mediators and arbitrators are humans who might have biases and prejudices. Frequently, the disputants have the opportunity to select the arbitrator who is likely to be sensitive to their predicament.

[8] Most of the human mediators use a form of the co-mediation model. Having two mediators can be an effective way to deal with many different ODR challenges, fitting well to legal systems based on jury.

[9] The *probable cause* doctrine may be invoked which requires a fair probability that a breach took place. Courts vary when determining what constitutes a "fair probability," some say 30%, others 40%, others 51%.

The relevant question concerns the validity of the semantic model. This question requires empirical evaluations with realistic test cases[10] in order to choose the best suited defeasible pattern within a particular market. The common disputes can be translated into defeasible theories[11], and the agent's decision would be compared with the one given by the human mediator. The highest scored strategy is provided to the disputant who might better anticipate the verdict and the execution timing. The advantage here consists in the fact that judicial cases that are not conforming to a pattern useful in deriving rules, are not treated as noise and removed. Simply, they are considered exceptions and encapsulated as defeaters or strong defeasible rules.

5   Dispute Resolution Phases

The client orders a hardware object through a shop-on-line web site (scenario adapted from [13]). The seller has published general contractual conditions on the web site. One of the clauses c_1 stipulates that *"if the product sent is defective, the client has the right to get it repaired or replaced, depending on the seller's choice"*. After an order is made at t_0, the seller sends the item. When the client receives it at t_7, he notices both that it does not work and its design was not quite similar to the picture on the web site. The seller accepts that the hardware might be defective, but invokes the mentioned clause c_1. His default choice is to repair the item, but he also proposes to replace the product if the client accepts to pay the transport fee. The client replies that he will only pay half the fee. The client asks an ODR system for arbitration, submitting his argumentation. The seller asks the product to be replaced. The ODR system accepts to lead the arbitration and notifies the seller. The seller accepts and submits his own argumentation.

5.1   Commencement of Dispute

A dispute action is commenced by filling a complaint. If minimum of evidence is provided[12], the mediator takes into consideration the plaintiff's claim. Consequently, a judicial summon is addressed to the defendant. The probabilistic rigorous mediator with a credulous concede attitude is appropriate for this stage. Suppose the plaintiff believes with a certainty factor of 0.9 that the picture illustrating the item was irrelevant (fact f_2 in figure 6). Considering the rule r_5, such a mediator will prove the $+\partial replace : 7$ conclusion with a certainty factor of $0.9 * 0.95 = 0.855$. Because this value is greater than the threshold of 0.2, set for this phase of the dispute, the complaint is accepted and a resolution process starts.

---

[10] See http://www.as.uky.edu/polisci/ulmerproject/index.html for a collection of such legal dataset.
[11] ILP techniques are available for deriving defeasible theories from legal datasets [12].
[12] The claim is supported with 20% certainty factor.

5.2 Discovery

The discovery is the pre-trial phase in a lawsuit in which each disputant can request evidence from the other party. Under the *duty of disclose* doctrine, the disputants have the obligation to share their own supporting evidence without being requested to by the other party. Failure to do so can preclude that evidence from being used in trial[13]. Modern dispute resolution strategies try to set the dispute in its early stages. Thus, the discovery phase is meant to clarify what the lawsuit is about, and perhaps to make a party realize it should settle or drop the claim, all before wasting court resources[14]. Because this early phase is mainly about evidence, a probabilistic epistemic mediator is recommended. Also, confident or careful claim attitudes prevail in obtaining information. During this dialog, the following facts become known: the item might be defective (defeasible fact f_1 has a certainty factor of 0.9), and the seller option is to repair the item (f_3). He advocates this through the contractual clause c_1 accepted by the buyer when the contract has been signed and representing within the defeasible theory by the rules r_1, r_2, r_3, and r_4. The seller proposes to repair the product if the client accepts to pay the transport fee (the strict rule r_6). The client might agree to pay half the fee (the defeasible rule r_7) in order to derive the *seller_choice_replace* consequent. The seller response r_8, which is an undercuting defeater, explicitly defeats the derivation of the conclusion *seller_choice_replace* based on the premise *half_transport_fee*.

5.3 Pre-trial

The pre-trial represents the last gate-keeping function before trial, answering the question of whether the claim could even go to the arbitration phase. In this stage, the movant can affirmatively negate the claim, whilst the plaintiff may provide different arguments to support the claim. Therefore, a probabilistic persuasion strategy is appropriate in this stage. Because the negation of claims is modeled by rebuttal defeaters, the vigilant concede attitude functioning under the *reasonable suspicion* doctrine is recommended. The rebuttal defeater r_9 is conveyed by the defendant who argues that usually (70% of the cases) he does not replace items to non-premium customers. The probabilistic persuasion mediator will derive the *replace* conclusion as follows. The *replace* consequent is supported by the rule r_5 with a certainty factor of $0.95 * 0.9 = 0.855$ and by the rule r_2 with a certainty factor of $0.5 * 0.9 = 0.45$. Due to the persuasion component the aggregated support is 1.305. In the same time, the conclusion is undecuttingly attacked by the rule r_4 with a strength of $0.6 * 0.8 = 0.48$. After this amount is decreased from the initial support, the *replace* conclusion is sustained by $1.305 - 0.48 = 0.852$. Because this confidence factor is stronger than the rebuttal rules (in this case only the rule r_9 supports the opposite conclusion $\neg replace$ only with a strength of $0.7 * 1.0 = 0.7$), the replace consequent will be derived.

---

[13] This applies only to evidence that supports their own case, not anything that could harm their case.

[14] A procedural rule stipulates that parties have the right to query 25 questions to each other in order to reveal information.

5.4   Arbitration

This phase is the presentation of the evidence gathered during earlier stages (figure 6). In the next step, the mediator decides to which jurisdiction the case belongs and loads the corresponding legal doctrines encapsulated as defeasible theories. He uses both the hard law (enactments, i.e. rule r_{10}) and the soft law (usages, customs within the e-market, i.e rule r_{11}) to activate the rules or to adjust the certainty factor of the disputants' arguments. As nested rules are allowed in our framework the activation can be done dynamically (rule r_{11}). For this phase, a fuzzy rigorous mediator with a skeptical concede attitude is recommended in order to compute the expected outcome. Consider that *offer*, *acceptance*, and *consideration* accepted as strict facts, based on the rule r_{10}, the contract is validated with a certainty factor of 0.9^{15}. Thus, the dynamic rule is activated with a certainty factor of $min(0.9, 0.8) = 0.8$ (and $0.9 * 0.8 = 0.72$ in case of the probabilistic inference), resulting the rule $r'_5(0.8) : irrelevant\_picture \Rightarrow replace$ (respectively, $r''_5(0.72) : irrelevant\_picture \Rightarrow replace$ in the probabilistic case) which, based on the *lex posteriori* legal principle[16], takes the place of the rule r_5 in figure 6. This mechanism provides the mediator the ability to dynamically adjust priorities among rules[17].

Users can also explore hypothetical situations when mediators have different strategies: fuzzy, probabilistic, persuasion or epistemic. How the dispute outcome depends on each defeasible mediator type is shown in figure 7. In order to trace

$f_1 : defective\_item(0.9)[t_7, t_7].$

$f_2 : irrelevant\_picture(0.9)[t_7, t_7].$

$f_3 : seller\_choice\_repair(0.8)[t_0, t_7].$

$f_4 : \neg premium\_customer(1.0)[t_0, t_7].$

$r_1 : (0.5)defective\_item[t_0, t_7] \Rightarrow repair[t_0, t_7]$

$r_2 : (0.5)defective\_item[t_0, t_7] \Rightarrow replace[t_0, t_7]$

$r_3 : (0.6)seller\_choice\_replace[t_0, t_7] \rightsquigarrow repair[t_0, t_7]$

$r_4 : (0.6)seller\_choice\_repair[t_0, t_7] \rightsquigarrow replace[t_0, t_7]$

$r_5 : (0.95)irrelevant\_picture[t_0, t_7] \Rightarrow replace[t_0, t_7]$

$r_6 : transport\_fee[t_0, t_7] \rightarrow seller\_choice\_replace[t_0, t_7]$

$r_7 : (0.9)half\_transport\_fee[t_0, t_7] \Rightarrow seller\_choice\_replace[t_0, t_7]$

$r_8 : half\_transport\_fee[t_0, t_7] \nrightarrow seller\_choice\_replace[t_0, t_7]$

$r_9 : (0.7)\neg premium\_customer[t_0, t_7] \Rightarrow \neg replace[t_0, t_7]$

$r_{10} : (0.9)offer[t_0, t_0], acceptance[t_0, t_0], consideration[t_0, t_0] \Rightarrow contract\_valid[t_0, t_7]$

$r_{11} : (0.8)contract\_valid[t_0, t_0] \Rightarrow (irrelevant\_picture[t_0, t_7] \Rightarrow replace[t_0, t_7])$

Fig. 6. Sample of arguments collected during the run of a dispute

---

[15] In order to accommodate some exceptions like "the signer is under 18".

[16] Under the legis posterior doctrine, the most recent law or precedent case takes precedence when computing the outcome.

[17] Under most laws, the arbitrator can assign as much probatory force as he believes they deserve, as long as this assessment is not arbitrary [13]. In the long run of ODR it is necessary to create specialized jurisdiction for e-commerce cases, where the certainty factor would be fine tuned according to precedents and mediator experience.

$+\partial replace : t_7$	Persuasion	Epistemic	Rigorous
Probabilistic	$No_{0.45+0.64-0.6<0.7}$	$No_{max(0.45,0.64)<max(0.6,0.7)}$	$No_{max(0.45,0.64)-0.6<0.7}$
Fuzzy	$No/Yes_{0.5+0.8-0.6=0.7}$	$Yes_{max(0.5,0.8)>max(0.6,0,7)}$	$No_{max(0.5,0.8)-0.6<0.7}$

Fig. 7. Answer for query $+\partial replace : t_7$ depends on mediator type

the results depicted here, figure 8 recalls only the relevant rules for the derivation of the *replace* consequent. Here, the dynamic rule r'_5 is active in a fuzzy approach, whilst the dynamic rule r_5" is the consequence of a probabilistic inference.

In the probabilistic approach (first data raw in figure 7) the claim *replace* is sustained by the rules r_2 with $0.5 * 0.9 = 0.45$ and by the rule $r"_5$ with $0.72 * 0.9 = 0.64$. The same claim is undercutingly defeated by the rule r_4 with $0.6 * 0.8 = 0.48$, and rebutally defeated by the rule r_9 with $0.7 * 1.0 = 0.7$. In the case of the persuasion strategy, the total support of $0.45 + 0.64 = 1.09$ decreased by the undercutting defeaters with 0.6 is not enough to beat the strength of the opposite conclusion $\neg replace$, which is 0.7. In the case of the epistemic strategy, the maximum support for the *replace* consequent $max(0.45, 0.64) = 0.64$ also is not enough to overwhelms the most powerful defeater, given by $max(0.6, 0.7) = 0.7$. Similarly, in a rigorous approach, the most strength supporting argument $max(0.45, 0.64) = 0.64$, decreased by the strength 0.6 of the undercutting defeater, results in a less confidence in the *replace* consequent compared with the strength of 0.7 of the opposite conclusion.

In the fuzzy approach (second data raw in figure 7), the rule r'_5 supports the consequent with $min(0.8, 0.9) = 0.8$, whilst the rule r_2 with $min(0.5, 0.9)$. The undercutting defeater r_4 challenges the consequent with a confidence of $min(0.6, 0.8) = 0.6$, while the rule r_9 sustains the negated conclusion with a certainty factor of $min(0.7, 1.0) = 0.7$. In the case of the persuasion strategy, the aggregated support of $0.5 + 0.6 = 1.3$, decreased by the strength of the undercuting defeater 0.6 equals the confidence of the opposite conclusion 0.7. Here, in case the ambiguity propagation is enabled, the fuzzy persuasion agent proves the consequent, whilst under a skeptical reasoning it is not inferred. In the case of an epistemic mediator, the strongest supporting argument, given by $max(0.5, 0.8) = 0.8$ wins in front of the strongest defeater, given by

$$f_1 : defective\_item(0.9)[t_7, t_7].$$
$$f_2 : irrelevant\_picture(0.9)[t_7, t_7].$$
$$f_3 : seller\_choice\_repair(0.8)[t_0, t_7].$$
$$f_4 : \neg premium\_customer(1.0)[t_0, t_7].$$
$$r_2 : (0.5)defective\_item[t_0, t_7] \Rightarrow replace[t_0, t_7]$$
$$r_4 : (0.6)seller\_choice\_repair[t_0, t_7] \rightsquigarrow replace[t_0, t_7]$$
$$r'_5 : (0.8)irrelevant\_picture[t_0, t_7] \Rightarrow replace[t_0, t_7]$$
$$r_5" : (0.72)irrelevant\_picture[t_0, t_7] \Rightarrow replace[t_0, t_7]$$
$$r_9 : (0.7)\neg premium\_customer[t_0, t_7] \Rightarrow \neg replace[t_0, t_7]$$

Fig. 8. Supporting and attacking rules for the *replace* consequent

$max(0.6, 0.7) = 0.7$. If a rigorous approach is preferred, the strongest supporting argument $max(0.5, 0.8) = 0.8)$, decreased by the undercutting defeater with 0.6, no longer overwhelms the support 0.7 of the $\neg replace$ consequent. Users are also able to have dialogs with the system to explore what would happen if some of their claims were rejected or just partially accepted[18].

5.5 Post-trial

After the arbitration is done two paths might follow: the enforcement of judgment and appealing the results of the arbitration process. Appealing after the trial may be quite difficult. To facilitate trust in e-commerce, many governs have enacted a norm similar to the next one: *"Any item achieved in online transaction can be returned within 15 days, without reason."*. Under these circumstances, the seller concedes to replace the defective item within 3 days if the client requests this: $r_{20} : request[t_8, t_8] \rightarrow must\_replace\_item[t_8, t_{10}]$. If the client is satisfied this obligation is no longer active: $r_{21} : satisfied[t_8, t_{10}] \rightarrow \neg must\_change\_item[8, 10]$. The last role of the system is to monitor contract enactment. This is done simply by trying to prove $+\partial must\_change\_item : 10$. If the client asked for the replacement and within 3 days he did not get satisfaction, the obligation still stands.

6 Related Work

The need for computerized mechanisms for decision support comes from well known limits of human knowledge processing. One aim is to provide disputants information about the expected outcome of the resolution process[19]. The other goal is to enrich the mediator's ability to process knowledge and weight arguments. By enhancing the expertise level of the mediator we argue that such decision support system can be looked at as a fourth party as defined in [2].

In the DiaLaw system [15], if the respondent of an argument accepts all the premises of a valid argument, he must also accept the conclusion, in case the respective inductive rule was previously accepted. In our framework, in the light of new information, an undercutting defeater might be used to attack the link between the premises and the consequent. In our view, the existence of a finite set of pre-agreed rules is not feasible for practical applications[20]. Thus, both

---

[18] For the scenario in figure 8 if the certainty factor of *irrelevant_picture* fact is greater than 0.8 a persuasion mediator will also infer the *replace* conclusion.

[19] In the negotiation literature this is called BATNA: Know your best alternative to a negotiated agreement [14].

[20] By accepting a jurisdiction parties practically agree on a set of legal rules. Through a signed contract, parties agree not only on some contractual clauses, but also regarding several specific doctrines under which that contract is enacted (such as expectation damages, opportunity costs, reliance damages). Due to the open character of both legal rules and contractual clauses, there are situations when supplementary rules have to be considered.

facts and rules may be dynamically asserted and retracted within the defeasible framework.

In the Carneades argumentation framework [16] three kinds or premises are used: ordinary premises, presumptions, and exceptions, where presumptions are used to model uncertain knowledge. In our approach, the nondeterminacy inherent in the early stages is handled by probabilistic reasoning, whilst defeaters deal with exceptions and information obtained during the resolution process. The framework also deals with information about dialectical status of a sentence: undisputed, at issue, accepted, rejected. We treated this issue elsewhere [17], by defining defeasible commitment machines as a flexible mechanism to adapt the life-cycle of the conveyed facts.

An ODR system was modeled within a multi-agent context by identifying and representing the types of communication between the different actors: parties, mediator, arbitrator, experts, witnesses, ODR-administrator, system-administrator, visitors [13]. Our approach does not regard the architectural requirements of an ODR system, but rather the reasoning capabilities of the arbitrator.

Rule-based systems are suitable for modeling the logical structure of legislation and are practically successful when the gap between factual and legal language is small and the regulations are uncontroversial, but they fail to model legal argument. Defeasible logic, through its argumentative semantics, overcomes this drawback. It is also adequate in practical applications due to its low complexity [18]. As a simulation tool, the ODR system designer may obtain results regarding what types of strategies better suit the e-market or how information sharing can be used to settle the dispute.

The formalization of virtual organizations and contracts based on commitments [19] opens another path for ODR by enabling to capture the social structure. Changes of organizations impose some treatment for the dynamics of enacted contracts.

7   Conclusions

There is a strong motivation for the need of ODR systems to reflect different types of argumentation patterns, mainly those models where persuasion can be functionally embedded into negotiation protocols [4]. From the knowledge representation viewpoint the implemented system accommodates temporal defeasible reasoning, nested rules, and a dynamic notion of priority over the rules[21]. From the argumentative semantics viewpoint the system introduces negated rules to model counter-examples, whilst Pollock's style undercutting defeaters are used to represents exceptions.

We advocate two strong points of this approach: (i) the *flexibility* of the framework due to the different patterns of weighting arguments and to the property of defeasible logic to model exceptions; (ii) the *accordance to legal practice*, by establishing a connection between these patterns and disputes phases as they

---

[21] A prototype based on LISA (Lisp-based Intelligent Software Agents) is available at http://cs-gw.utcluj.ro/~adrian/odr.html.

appear in current practice in law. This view on the ODR issue does not insist on the temporal aspects included in the logic. They can be subject to further investigation regarding the application of the framework to contract enactment [19]. Our future work regards the enrichment of the logical framework with explanation capabilities of the outcome, needed to achieve trustworthiness and practical usability in a dispute resolution system.

Acknowledgments

We are grateful to the anonymous reviewers for useful comments. Part of this work was supported by the grant 27702-990 from the National Research Council of the Romanian Ministry for Education and Research.

References

1. Tyler, M.C., Bretherton, D.: Seventy-six and counting: An analysis of ODR sites. In: Workshop on Online Dispute Resolution at the International Conference on Artificial Intelligence and Law, Edinburgh, UK, pp. 13–28 (2003)
2. Katsh, E., Rifkin, J.: Online Dispute Resolution: Resolving Conflicts in Cyberspace. John Wiley, Chichester (2001)
3. Lodder, A., Thiessen, E.: The role of artificial intelligence in online dispute resolution. In: Workshop on Online Dispute Resolution at the International Conference on Artificial Intelligence and Law, Edinburgh, UK (2003)
4. Walton, D., Godden, D.: Persuasion dialogues in online dispute resolution. Artificial Intelligence and Law 13, 273–295 (2006)
5. Rule, C., Friedberg, L.: The appropriate role of dispute resolution in building trust online. Artificial Intelligence and Law 13, 193–205 (2006)
6. Hage, J.: Law and defeasibility. Artificial Intelligence and Law 11, 221–242 (2003)
7. Governatori, G.: Representing business contracts in RuleML. Journal of Cooperative Information Systems 14 (2005)
8. Pollock, J.L.: Defeasible reasoning with variable degrees of justification. Artificial Intelligence 133, 233–282 (2001)
9. Pollock, J.L.: How to reason defeasibly. Artificial Intelligence 57, 1–42 (1992)
10. Prakken, H.: A study of accrual of arguments, with applications to evidential reasoning. In: 10th International Conference on Artificial Intelligence and Law, New York, NY, USA, pp. 85–94 (2005)
11. Parsons, S., Wooldridge, M., Amgoud, L.: Properties and complexity of some formal inter-agent dialogues. Journal of Logic and Computation 13, 347–376 (2003)
12. Johnston, B., Governatori, G.: An algorithm for the induction of defeasible logic theories from databases. In: Australasian Database Conference, pp. 75–83 (2003)
13. Bonnet, V., Boudaoud, K., Gagnebin, M., Harms, J., Schultz, T.: Online dispute resolution systems as web services. ICFAI Journal of Alternative Dispute 3, 57–74 (2004)
14. Bellucci, E., Lodder, A.R., Zeleznikow, J.: Integrating artificial intelligence, argumentation and game theory to develop an online dispute resolution environment. In: 16th International Conference on Tools with Artificial Intelligence, pp. 749–754. IEEE Computer Society Press, Los Alamitos (2004)

15. Lodder, A.: DiaLaw: On Legal Justification and Dialogical Models of Argumentation. Kluwer, Dordrecht (1999)
16. Gordon, T., Walton, D.: The Carneades argumentation framework: Using presumptions and exceptions to model critical questions. In: 1st International Conference on Computational Models of Argument, pp. 208–219. IOS Press, Amsterdam (2006)
17. Letia, I.A., Groza, A.: Running contracts with defeasible commitment. In: Ali, M., Dapoigny, R. (eds.) IEA/AIE 2006. LNCS (LNAI), vol. 4031, pp. 91–100. Springer, Heidelberg (2006)
18. Maher, M.J.: Propositional defeasible logic has linear complexity. Theory and Practice of Logic Programming 1, 691–711 (2001)
19. Udupi, Y.B., Singh, M.P.: Contract enactment in virtual organizations: A commitment-based approach. In: 21st National Conference on Artificial Intelligence, pp. 722–727. AAAI, Stanford (2006)

Extending Propositional Logic with Concrete Domains for Multi-issue Bilateral Negotiation

Azzurra Ragone[1], Tommaso Di Noia[1], Eugenio Di Sciascio[1],
and Francesco M. Donini[2]

[1] SisInfLab, Politecnico di Bari, Bari, Italy
{a.ragone,t.dinoia,disciascio}@poliba.it
[2] Università della Tuscia , Viterbo, Italy
donini@unitus.it

Abstract. We present a novel approach to knowledge-based automated one-shot multi-issue bilateral negotiation handling, in a homogeneous setting, both numerical features and non-numerical ones. The framework makes possible to formally represent typical situations in real e-marketplaces such as *"if I spend more than 20000 € for a sedan then I want a navigator pack included"* where both numerical (price) and non-numerical (sedan, navigator pack) issues coexist. To this aim we introduce $\mathcal{P}(\mathcal{N})$, a propositional logic extended with concrete domains, which allows to: model relations among issues (both numerical and not numerical ones) via logical entailment, differently from well-known approaches that describe issues as uncorrelated; represent buyer's request, seller's supply and their respective preferences as formulas endowed with a formal semantics. By modeling preferences as formulas it is hence possible to assign a utility value also to a bundle of issues, which is obviously more realistic than the trivial sum of utilities assigned to single elements in the bundle itself. We illustrate the theoretical framework, the logical language, the one-shot negotiation protocol we adopt, and show we are able to compute Pareto-efficient outcomes, using a mediator to solve a multi-objective optimization problem.

1 Introduction

Bilateral negotiation between agents is a challenging problem, with applications in several scenarios, each one with its own peculiarities and issues. In this work we focus on automated negotiation in e-marketplaces [30]. In such domains we do not simply deal with undifferentiated products (commodities as oil, cement, etc.) or stocks, where only price, time and quantity have to be taken into account; also other features must be considered during the negotiation process. For instance, when a potential buyer browses an e-marketplace about automobiles, she looks for a car fulfilling her needs and/or wishes. So, not only the price is important, but also warranty or delivery time, as well as look, model, comfort and so on. In such domains it is difficult to model the request/offer descriptions, and even more difficult to find the best suitable agreement. Recently, there has been a growing interest towards multi-issue negotiation, also motivated by the idea that richer and expressive descriptions of demand and supply can boost e-marketplaces [29]. However, to the best of our knowledge, and also in recent literature, issues are

M. Baldoni et al. (Eds.): DALT 2007, LNAI 4897, pp. 211–226, 2008.

usually described as uncorrelated terms, without considering any underlying semantics. Notable exceptions are discussed in Section 8. In our approach we use knowledge representation in two ways: (1) exploiting a logical theory to represent relations among issues and (2) assigning utilities to formulas to represent agents having preferences over different bundles of issues. For what concerns the former, we introduce a logical theory that allows to represent, *e.g.*, through logical implication, the fact that a Ferrari is an Italian car (Ferrari $\Rightarrow$ ItalianMaker) or that an Italian car is not a German car (ItalianMaker $\Rightarrow$ ¬GermanMaker). Furthermore we can express agent preferences over a bundle of issues, *e.g.*, the buyer can state she would like to have a car with navigator pack, where the meaning of navigator pack is in the formula (NavigatorPack $\Leftrightarrow$ SatelliteAlarm $\wedge$ GPS_system). In this case, the utility assigned to a bundle is obviously not necessarily the sum of utilities assigned to single elements in the bundle itself. Moreover issues are often inter-dependent: the selection of one issue depends on the selection made for other issues: in our framework agents can express conditional preferences as *I would like a car with leather seats if its color is black* (ExternalColorBlack $\Rightarrow$ Leather_seats). We propose an extended propositional logic, $\mathcal{P}(\mathcal{N})$ enriched with concrete domains, which allows—as it is in the real world—to take into account preferences involving both numerical features and non-numerical ones, *e.g.*, the seller can state that if you want a car with a GPS system you have to wait at least one month: (GPS_system $\Rightarrow$ deliverytime ≥ 31) as well as preferences can involve only numerical ones: *e.g.*, the buyer can state that she can accept to pay more than 25000€ only if there is a warranty lasting more than two years (price $> 25000 \Rightarrow$ year_warranty > 2). Contributions of this paper include:

1. the framework for automated multi-issue bilateral negotiation,
2. the logical language to represent existing relations between issues and preferences as formulas, which is able to handle both numerical features and non-numerical ones as correlated issues w.r.t. a logical theory, and
3. the one-shot protocol we adopt, which allows to compute Pareto-efficient agreements, exploiting a mediator that solves a multi objective optimization problem.

The rest of the paper is structured as follows: next section discusses the scenario and the assumptions we make; then we illustrate the modeling of issues through our logical language and the negotiation mechanism. Section 4 presents the multi-issue bilateral negotiation problem, Section 5 describes the computation of utilities for numerical fetures. Section 6 shows how to compute Pareto-efficient agreements and Section 7 summarizes the bargaining process. Related work and discussion close the paper.

2 Negotiation Scenario

We start by introducing the negotiation mechanism and the assumptions characterizing our framework. According to Rosenschein and Zlotkin [25], we define the *Space of possible deals*, the *Negotiation Protocol* and the *Negotiation Strategy*. For what concerns the *Space of possible deals*, since we solve a multi-objective optimization problem, possible deals are all the solutions of the problem that satisfy the constraints, even if they do not maximize the objective function (the so called *feasible region* [11]). The *Negotiation Protocol* we adopt is *one-shot*, with the presence of a mediator. Differently from the classical *Single-shot* bargaining [23], where one player proposes a deal and the other player may only accept or refuse it [2], in our framework we hypothesize the presence of an electronic mediator, that may automatically explore the negotiation space and discover Pareto-efficient agreements to be proposed to both parties. Such parties may then accept or refuse agreements. We recall that two basically different approaches to automated negotiation exist: *centralized* and *distributed*. In the former, agents elicit their preferences and then a mediator, or some central entity, selects the most suitable deal based on them. In the latter, agents negotiate through various negotiation steps reaching the final deal by means of intermediate deals, without any external help [5]. Distributed approaches do not allow for the presence of a mediator [14, p.25] because agents cannot agree on any entity, so they do not want to disclose their preferences to a third party, that, missing any relevant information, could not help agents. In dynamic system a predefined conflict resolution cannot be allowed, so the presence of a mediator is discouraged. On the other hand the presence of a mediator can be extremely useful in designing negotiation mechanisms and in practical important commerce settings. According to MacKie-Mason and Wellman [17], negotiation mechanisms often involve the presence of a mediator[1], which collects information from bargainers and proposes an efficient negotiation outcome. In Section 8 some approaches adopting a centralized approach are described. Although the main target of an agent is reaching a satisfying agreement, this objective alone may not be enough to satisfy the agent, since this agreement should also be Pareto-efficient. It is fundamental to assess *how hard* is to find Pareto-efficient agreements and check whether a given agreement is also Pareto-efficient. The presence of a trusted third party can help parties to reach a Pareto-efficient agreement. As pointed out by Raiffa et al. [24, p.311], usually bargainers may not want to disclose their preferences or utilities to the other party, yet they can be more willing to reveal these information to a trusted – automated – mediator, helping negotiating parties to achieve efficient and equitable outcomes. The presence of a mediator and the one-shot protocol is an incentive for the two parties to reveal the true preferences, because they can trust in the mediator and they have a single possibility to reach the agreement with that counterpart. Therefore in our framework we propose a one-shot protocol with the intervention of a *mediator* with a proactive behavior: it suggests to each participant a *fair* Pareto-efficient agreement. For what concerns *strategy*, the players reveal their preferences to the mediator and then, once it has computed a solution, they can accept or refuse the agreement proposed to them; they refuse if they think possible to reach a better agreement looking for another partner, or another shot, or for a different set of bidding rules. Notice that here we do not consider the influence of the *outside options* in the negotiation strategy [18].

---

[1] The most well-known—and running—example of mediator is eBay, where a mediator receives and validates bids, shows the current highest bid and finally determines the auction winner [17]. Observe also that eBay retains private information of actors, such as selling reservation values.

3 Representation of Issues

We divide issues involved in a negotiation in two categories. Some issues may express properties that are true or false, like, *e.g.*, in an automotive domain, ItalianMaker, or AlarmSystem. We represent them as propositional atoms $A_1, A_2, \ldots$ from a finite set $\mathcal{A}$. Other issues involve numerical features like deliverytime, or price. We represent them as variables $f_1, f_2, \ldots$, each one taking values in its specific domain $D_{f_1}, D_{f_2}, \ldots$, such as $[0, 90]$ (days) for deliverytime, or $[1,000, 20,000]$ (euros), for price. The variables representing numerical features are always constrained by comparing them to some constant, like price $< 20,000$, or deliverytime ≥ 30, and such constraints can be combined into complex propositional requirements – also involving propositional issues – *e.g.*, ItalianMaker $\wedge$ (price $\leq 25,000$) $\wedge$ (deliverytime < 30) (representing a car made in Italy, costing no more than 25,000 euros, delivered in less than 30 days), or AlarmSystem$\Rightarrow$ (deliverytime > 30) (expressing the seller's requirement "if you want an alarm system mounted you'll have to wait more than one month"). We now give precise definitions for the above intuitions, borrowing from a previous formalization of so-called *concrete domains* [1] from Knowledge Representation languages.

Definition 1 (Concrete Domains, [1]). *A* concrete domain *D consists of a finite set $\Delta_c(D)$ of numerical values, and a set of predicates $C(D)$ expressing numerical constraints on D.*

For our numerical features, predicates will always be the binary operators $C(D) = \{\geq, \leq, >, <, =, \neq\}$, whose second argument is a constant in $\Delta_c(D)^2$. We note that in some scenarios other concrete domains could be possible, *e.g.*, colors as RGB vectors in an agricultural market, when looking for or selling fruits.

Once we have defined a concrete domain and constraints, we can formally extend propositional logic in order to handle numerical features. We call this language $\mathcal{P}(\mathcal{N})$.

Definition 2 (The language $\mathcal{P}(\mathcal{N})$). *Let $\mathcal{A}$ be a set of propositional atoms, and F a set of pairs $\langle f, D_f \rangle$ each made of a feature name and an associated concrete domain D_f, and let k be a value in D_f. Then the following formulas are in $\mathcal{P}(\mathcal{N})$:*

1. *every atom $A \in \mathcal{A}$ is a formula in $\mathcal{P}(\mathcal{N})$*
2. *if $\langle f, D_f \rangle \in F$, $k \in D_f$, and $\circ \in \{\geq, \leq, >, <, =, \neq\}$ then $(f \circ k)$ is a formula in $\mathcal{P}(\mathcal{N})$*
3. *if ψ and φ are formulas in $\mathcal{P}(\mathcal{N})$ then $\neg\psi$, $\psi \wedge \varphi$ are formulas in $\mathcal{P}(\mathcal{N})$. We also use $\psi \vee \varphi$ as an abbreviation for $\neg(\neg\psi \wedge \neg\varphi)$, $\psi \Rightarrow \varphi$ as an abbreviation for $\neg\psi \vee \varphi$, and $\psi \Leftrightarrow \varphi$ as an abbreviation for $(\psi \Rightarrow \varphi) \wedge (\varphi \Rightarrow \psi)$.*

In order to define a formal semantics of $\mathcal{P}(\mathcal{N})$ formulas, we consider interpretation functions $\mathcal{I}$ that map propositional atoms into {true, false}, feature names into values in their domain, and assign propositional values to numerical constraints and composite formulas according to the intended semantics.

---

[2] So, strictly speaking, $C(D)$ would be a set of unary predicates with an infix notation, *e.g.*, $x > 5$ is in fact a predicate $P_{>5}(x)$ which is true for all values of D_x greater than 5 and false otherwise; however, this distinction is not necessary in our formalization.

Definition 3 (Interpretation and models). *An interpretation $\mathcal{I}$ for $\mathcal{P}(\mathcal{N})$ is a function (denoted as a superscript $\cdot^{\mathcal{I}}$ on its argument) that maps each atom in $\mathcal{A}$ into a truth value $A^{\mathcal{I}} \in \{\text{true}, \text{false}\}$, each feature name f into a value $f^{\mathcal{I}} \in D_f$, and assigns truth values to formulas as follows:*

- *$(f \circ k)^{\mathcal{I}} = \text{true}$ iff $f^{\mathcal{I}} \circ k$ is true in D_f, $(f \circ k)^{\mathcal{I}} = \text{false}$ otherwise*
- *$(\neg \psi)^{\mathcal{I}} = \text{true}$ iff $\psi^{\mathcal{I}} = \text{false}$, $(\psi \wedge \varphi)^{\mathcal{I}} = \text{true}$ iff both $\psi^{\mathcal{I}} = \text{true}$ and $\varphi^{\mathcal{I}} = \text{true}$, etc., according to truth tables for propositional connectives.*

Given a formula φ in $\mathcal{P}(\mathcal{N})$, we denote with $\mathcal{I} \models \varphi$ the fact that $\mathcal{I}$ assigns true to φ. If $\mathcal{I} \models \varphi$ we say $\mathcal{I}$ is a model for φ, and $\mathcal{I}$ is a model for a set of formulas when it is a model for each formula.

Clearly, an interpretation $\mathcal{I}$ is completely defined by the values it assigns to propositional atoms and numerical features.

Example 1. Let $\mathcal{A} = \{\text{Sedan}, \text{GPL}\}$ be a set of propositional atoms, $D_{\text{price}} = \{0, \ldots, 60000\}$ and $D_{\text{year\_warranty}} = \{0, 1, \ldots, 5\}$ be two concrete domains for the features price, year_warranty, respectively. A model $\mathcal{I}$ for both formulas:

$$\left\{ \begin{array}{l} \text{Sedan} \wedge (\text{GPL} \Rightarrow (\text{year\_warranty} \geq 1)), \\ (\text{price} \leq 5{,}000) \end{array} \right\}$$

is $\text{Sedan}^{\mathcal{I}} = \text{true}$, $\text{GPL}^{\mathcal{I}} = \text{false}$, $\text{year\_warranty}^{\mathcal{I}} = 0$, $\text{price}^{\mathcal{I}} = 4{,}500$.

Given a set of formulas $\mathcal{T}$ in $\mathcal{P}(\mathcal{N})$ (representing an ontology), we denote *model* for $\mathcal{T}$ as $\mathcal{I} \models \mathcal{T}$. An ontology is *satisfiable* if it has a model. $\mathcal{T}$ logically implies a formula φ, denoted by $\mathcal{T} \models \varphi$ iff φ is true in all models of $\mathcal{T}$. We denote with $\mathcal{M}_{\mathcal{T}} = \{\mathcal{I}_1, \ldots, \mathcal{I}_n\}$, the set of all models for $\mathcal{T}$, and omit the subscript when no confusion arises.

We assume the following restrictions for the concrete domains of our e-marketplace-oriented scenarios:

1. domains are *discrete*, with a *uniform* discretization step ϵ_f. If the seller states he cannot deliver a car before one month, he is saying that the delivery time will be at least in one month and one day ($\text{deliverytime} \geq 32$), where $\epsilon_d = 1$ (in days).
2. domains are *finite*; we denote with $\max(D_f)$ and $\min(D_f)$ the maximum and minimum values of each domain D_f.
3. even for the same feature name, concrete domains are *marketplace dependent*. Let us consider price in two different marketplace scenarios: pizzas and cars. For the former one, the discretization step ϵ_p is the €-cent: the price is usually something like 4.50 or 6.00 €. On the other hand, specifying the price of a car we usually have 10,500 or 15,000 €; then the discretization step in this case can be fixed as 100 €.

The above Point 1 and the propositional composition of numerical constraints imply that the operators $\{\geq, \leq, >, <, =, \neq\}$ can be reduced only to $\geq, \leq$.

Definition 4 (successor/predecessor). *Given two contiguous elements k_i and k_{i+1} in a concrete domain D we denote by:*

- *$s : D \to D$ the successor function: $s(k_i) = k_{i+1} = k_i + \epsilon_f$*
- *$p : D \to D$ the predecessor function: $p(k_{i+1}) = k_i = k_{i+1} - \epsilon_f$*

Clearly, $\max(D_f)$ has no successor and $\min(D_f)$ has no predecessor. Based on the above introduced notions, we can reduce $C_m(D)$ to $\{\leq, \geq\}$ using the following transformations:

$$f = k \qquad\qquad\qquad \longrightarrow (f \leq k) \wedge (f \geq k) \tag{1}$$

$$f \neq k \qquad\qquad\qquad \longrightarrow (f < k) \vee (f > k) \tag{2}$$

$$f > k \longrightarrow f \geq (k + \epsilon_f) \longrightarrow f \geq s(k) \tag{3}$$

$$f < k \longrightarrow f \leq (k - \epsilon_f) \longrightarrow f \leq p(k) \tag{4}$$

4   Multi Issue Bilateral Negotiation in $\mathcal{P}(\mathcal{N})$

Following [21], we use logic formulas in $\mathcal{P}(\mathcal{N})$ to model the buyer's demand and the seller's supply. Relations among issues, both propositional and numerical, are represented by a set $\mathcal{T}$ – for Theory – of $\mathcal{P}(\mathcal{N})$ formulas.

In a typical bilateral negotiation scenario, the issues within both the buyer's request and the seller's offer can be split into *strict requirements* and *preferences*. Strict requirements represent what the buyer and the seller want to be necessarily satisfied in order to accept the final agreement – in our framework we call strict requirements *demand/supply*. Preferences denote issues they are willing to negotiate on – this is what we call *preferences*.

Example 1. *Suppose to have a buyer's request like "I would like a sedan with leather seats. Preferably I would like to pay less than 12,000 € furthermore I'm willing to pay up to 15,000 € if warranty is greater or equal than 3 years. (I don't want to pay more than 17,000 € and I don't want a car with a warranty less than 2 years)". In this example we identify:*

demand: I want a sedan with leather seats. I don't want to pay more than 17,000 €. I don't want a car with a warranty less than 2 years
preferences: Preferably I would like to pay less than 12,000 , furthermore I'm willing to pay up to 15,000 € if warranty is greater or equal than 3 years.

Definition 5 (Demand, Supply, Agreement). *Given an ontology $\mathcal{T}$ represented as a set of formulas in $\mathcal{P}(\mathcal{N})$ representing the knowledge on a marketplace domain*

- *a buyer's demand is a formula β (for Buyer) in $\mathcal{P}(\mathcal{N})$ such that $\mathcal{T} \cup \{\beta\}$ is satisfiable.*
- *a seller's supply is a formula σ (for Seller) in $\mathcal{P}(\mathcal{N})$ such that $\mathcal{T} \cup \{\sigma\}$ is satisfiable.*
- *$\mathcal{I}$ is a possible deal between β and σ iff $\mathcal{I} \models \mathcal{T} \cup \{\sigma, \beta\}$, that is, $\mathcal{I}$ is a model for $\mathcal{T}, \sigma,$ and β. We also call $\mathcal{I}$ an agreement.*

The seller and the buyer model in σ and β the minimal requirements they accept for the negotiation. On the other hand, if seller and buyer have set strict attributes that are in conflict with each other, that is $\mathcal{M}_{\mathcal{T} \cup \{\sigma, \beta\}} = \emptyset$, the negotiation ends immediately because, it is impossible to reach an agreement. If the participants are willing to avoid the *conflict deal* [25], and continue the negotiation, it will be necessary they revise their strict requirements.

In the negotiation process both the buyer and the seller express some preferences on attributes, or their combination. The utility function is usually defined based on these preferences. We start defining buyer's and seller's preferences and their associated utilities: u_β for the buyer, and u_σ for the seller.

Definition 6 (Preferences). *The buyer's negotiation preferences $B \doteq \{\beta_1, \ldots, \beta_k\}$ are a set of formulas in $\mathcal{P}(\mathcal{N})$, each of them representing the subject of a buyer's preference, and a utility function $u_\beta : B \rightarrow \Re^+$ assigning a utility to each formula, such that $\sum_i u_\beta(\beta_i) = 1$.*

Analogously, the seller's negotiation preferences $S \doteq \{\sigma_1, \ldots, \sigma_h\}$ are a set of formulas in $\mathcal{P}(\mathcal{N})$, each of them representing the subject of a seller's preference, and a utility function $u_\sigma : S \rightarrow \Re^+$ assigning a utility to each formula, such that $\sum_j u_\sigma(\sigma_j) = 1$.

Buyer's request in Example 1 is then formalized as:

$$\beta = \texttt{Sedan} \wedge \texttt{Leather\_seats} \wedge (\texttt{price} \leq 17,000) \wedge$$
$$(\texttt{year\_warranty} \geq 2)$$
$$\beta_1 = (\texttt{price} \leq 12,000)$$
$$\beta_2 = (\texttt{year\_warranty} \geq 3) \wedge (\texttt{price} \leq 15,000)$$

As usual, both agents' utilities are normalized to 1 to eliminate outliers, and make them comparable. Since we assumed that utilities are additive, the *preference utility* is just a sum of the utilities of preferences satisfied in the agreement.

Definition 7 (Preference Utilities). *Let B and S be respectively the buyer's and seller's preferences, and $\mathcal{M}_{T \cup \{\alpha, \beta\}}$ be their agreements set. The* preference utility *of an agreement $\mathcal{I} \in \mathcal{M}_{T \cup \{\alpha, \beta\}}$ for a buyer and a seller, respectively, are defined as:*

$$u_{\beta, \mathcal{P}(\mathcal{N})}(\mathcal{I}) \doteq \Sigma\{u_\beta(\beta_i) \mid \mathcal{I} \models \beta_i\}$$
$$u_{\sigma, \mathcal{P}(\mathcal{N})}(\mathcal{I}) \doteq \Sigma\{u_\sigma(\sigma_j) \mid \mathcal{I} \models \sigma_j\}$$

where $\Sigma\{\ldots\}$ stands for the sum of all elements in the set.

Notice that if one agent *e.g.*, the buyer, does not specify soft preferences, but only strict requirements, it is as $\beta_1 = \top$ and $u_{\beta, \mathcal{P}(\mathcal{N})}(\mathcal{I}) = 1$, which reflects the fact that an agent accepts whatever agreement not in conflict with its strict requirements. From the formulas related to Example 1, we note that while considering numerical features, it is still possible to express strict requirements and preferences on them. A strict requirement is surely the *reservation value* [24]. In Example 1 the buyer expresses two reservation values, one on price *"more than 17,000 €"* and the other on warranty *"less than 2 years"*.

Both buyer and seller have their own reservation values on each feature involved in the negotiation process. It is the maximum (or minimum) value in the range of possible feature values to reach an agreement, *e.g.*, the maximum price the buyer wants to pay for a car or the minimum warranty required, as well as, from the seller's perspective the minimum price he will accept to sell the car or the minimum delivery time. Usually, each participant knows its own reservation value and ignores the opponent's one. Referring to price and the two corresponding reservation values $r_{\beta,\text{price}}$ and $r_{\sigma,\text{price}}$ for the buyer and the seller respectively, if the buyer expresses $\text{price} \leq r_{\beta,\text{price}}$ and the seller $\text{price} \geq r_{\sigma,\text{price}}$, in case $r_{\sigma,\text{price}} \leq r_{\beta,\text{price}}$ we have $[r_{\sigma,\text{price}}, r_{\beta,\text{price}}]$ as a **Z**one **O**f **P**ossible **A**greement — $ZOPA(\text{price})$, otherwise no agreement is possible [24]. More formally, given an agreement $\mathcal{I}$ and a feature f, $f^{\mathcal{I}} \in ZOPA(f)$ must hold.

Keeping the price example, let us suppose that the maximum price the buyer is willing to pay is 15,000, while the seller minimum allowable price is 10,000, then we can set the two reservation values: $r_{\beta,\text{price}} = 15,000$ and $r_{\sigma,\text{price}} = 10,000$, so the *agreement price* will be in the interval $ZOPA(\text{price}) = [10000, 15000]$.

Obviously, the reservation value is considered as private information and will not be revealed to the other party, but will be taken into account by the mediator when the agreement will be computed. Since setting a reservation value on a numerical feature is equivalent to set a strict requirement, then, once the buyer and the seller express their strict requirements, reservation values constraints have to be added to them (see Example 1).

In order to formally define a Multi-issue Bilateral Negotiation problem in $\mathcal{P}(\mathcal{N})$, the only other elements we still need to introduce are the *disagreement thresholds*, also called disagreement payoffs, t_β, t_σ. They are the minimum utility that each agent requires to pursue a deal. Minimum utilities may incorporate an agent's attitude toward concluding the transaction, but also overhead costs involved in the transaction itself, *e.g.*, fixed taxes.

Definition 8 (MBN-$\mathcal{P}(\mathcal{N})$). *Given a $\mathcal{P}(\mathcal{N})$ set of axioms $\mathcal{T}$, a demand β and a set of buyer's preferences $\mathcal{B}$ with utility function $u_{\beta,\mathcal{P}(\mathcal{N})}$ and a disagreement threshold t_β, a supply σ and a set of seller's preferences $\mathcal{S}$ with utility function $u_{\sigma,\mathcal{P}(\mathcal{N})}$ and a disagreement threshold t_σ, a Multi-issue Bilateral Negotiation problem (MBN) is finding a model $\mathcal{I}$ (agreement) such that all the following conditions hold:*

$$\mathcal{I} \models \mathcal{T} \cup \{\sigma, \beta\} \tag{5}$$

$$u_{\beta,\mathcal{P}(\mathcal{N})}(\mathcal{I}) \geq t_\beta \tag{6}$$

$$u_{\sigma,\mathcal{P}(\mathcal{N})}(\mathcal{I}) \geq t_\sigma \tag{7}$$

Observe that not every agreement $\mathcal{I}$ is a solution of an MBN, if either $u_\sigma(\mathcal{I}) < t_\sigma$ or $u_\beta(\mathcal{I}) < t_\beta$. Such an agreement represents a deal which, although satisfying strict requirements, is not worth the transaction effort. Also notice that, since reservation values on numerical features are modeled in β and σ as strict requirements, for each feature f, the condition $f^{\mathcal{I}} \in ZOPA(f)$ always holds by condition (5).

5   Utilities for Numerical Features

Buyer's/seller's preferences are used to evaluate how good is a possible agreement and to select the best one. On the other hand, also preferences on numerical features have to be considered, in order to evaluate agreements and how good an agreement is w.r.t. another one. Let us explain the idea considering the demand and buyer's preferences in Example 1.

Example 2. Referring to β, β_1 and β_2 in Example 1 let us suppose to have the offer [3]:

$$\sigma = \text{Sedan} \wedge (\text{price} \geq 15{,}000) \wedge (\text{year\_warranty} \leq 5)$$

Three possible agreements between the buyer and the seller are, among others:

$$\mathcal{I}_1 : \{\text{Sedan}^{\mathcal{I}_1} = \text{true}, \text{Leather\_seats}^{\mathcal{I}_1} = \text{true},$$
$$\text{price}^{\mathcal{I}_1} = 17{,}000, \text{year\_warranty}^{\mathcal{I}_1} = 3\}$$
$$\mathcal{I}_2 : \{\text{Sedan}^{\mathcal{I}_2} = \text{true}, \text{Leather\_seats}^{\mathcal{I}_2} = \text{true},$$
$$\text{price}^{\mathcal{I}_2} = 16{,}000, \text{year\_warranty}^{\mathcal{I}_2} = 4\}$$
$$\mathcal{I}_3 : \{\text{Sedan}^{\mathcal{I}_3} = \text{true}, \text{Leather\_seats}^{\mathcal{I}_3} = \text{true},$$
$$\text{price}^{\mathcal{I}_3} = 15{,}000, \text{year\_warranty}^{\mathcal{I}_3} = 5\}$$

Looking at the values of numerical features, $\mathcal{I}_1$ is the best agreement from the seller's perspective whilst $\mathcal{I}_3$ is the best from the buyer's one. In fact, the buyer the less he pays, the happier he is and the contrary holds for the seller! The contrary is for the warranty: the buyer is happier if he gets a greater year warranty. On the other hand, $\mathcal{I}_2$ is a good compromise between buyer's and seller's requirements.

The above example highlights the need for utility functions taking into account the value of each numerical feature involved in the negotiation process. Of course, for each feature two utility functions are needed; one for the buyer — $u_{\beta,f}$, the other for the seller — $u_{\sigma,f}$. These functions have to satisfy at least the basic properties enumerated below. For the sake of conciseness, we write u_f when the same property holds both for $u_{\beta,f}$ and $u_{\sigma,f}$. :

1. Since u_f is a utility function, it is normalized to $[0\ldots,1]$. Given the pair $\langle f, D_f \rangle$, it must be defined over the domain D_f.
2. From Example 2 we note the buyer is happier as the price decreases whilst the seller is sadder. Hence, u_f has to be monotonic and whenever $u_{\beta,f}$ increases then $u_{\sigma,f}$ decreases and vice versa.
3. There is no utility for the buyer if the agreed value on price is greater or equal than its reservation value $r_{\beta,\text{price}} = 17{,}000$ and there is no utility for the seller if the price is less than or equal to $r_{\sigma,\text{price}} = 15{,}000$. Since concrete domains are finite, for the buyer the best possible price is $\min(D_{\text{price}})$ whilst for the seller is $\max(D_{\text{price}})$. The contrary holds if we refer to year warranty.

Definition 9 (Feature Utilities). *Let $\langle f, D_f \rangle$ be a pair made of a feature name f and a concrete domain D_f and r_f be a reservation value for f. A **feature utility function** $u_f : D_f \rightarrow [0\ldots,1]$ is a monotonic function such that*
– if u_f monotonically increases then (see Figure 1)

$$\begin{cases} u_f(v) = 0, v \in [\min(D_f), r_f] \\ u_f(\max(D_f)) = 1 \end{cases} \tag{8}$$

---

[3] For illustrative purpose, in this example we consider an offer where only strict requirements are explicitly stated. Of course, in the most general case also the seller can express his preferences.

– *if u_f monotonically decreases then*

$$\begin{cases} u_f(v) = 0, v \in [r_f, \max(D_f)] \\ u_f(\min(D_f)) = 1 \end{cases} \tag{9}$$

Given a buyer and a seller, if $u_{\beta,f}$ increases then $u_{\sigma,f}$ decreases and vice versa.

Clearly, the simplest utility functions are the two linear functions:

$$u_f(v) = \begin{cases} 1 - \frac{v - \min(D_f)}{r_f - \min(D_f)} \, , v \in [\min(D_f), r_f[\\ \\ 0 \, , v \in [r_f, \max(D_f)] \end{cases} \tag{10}$$

if it monotonically decreases and

$$u_f(v) = \begin{cases} 1 - \frac{v - \max(D_f)}{r_f - \max(D_f)} \, , v \in [r_f, \max(D_f)[\\ \\ 0 \, , v \in [\min(D_f), r_f] \end{cases} \tag{11}$$

if it monotonically increases (see Figure 1).

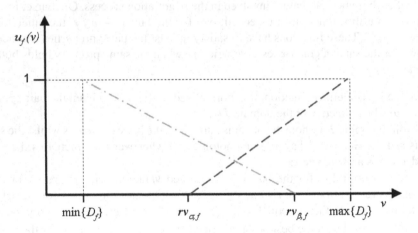

Fig. 1. Linear utility functions

6   Computing Pareto Agreements in $\mathcal{P}(\mathcal{N})$

Among all possible agreements that we can compute, given a theory $\mathcal{T}$ as constraint, we are interested in agreements that are Pareto-efficient and *fair* for both the participants, in order to make them equally, and as much as possible, satisfied. We now outline how an actual solution can be found solving a multi objective optimization problem.

First of all, let $\{B_1, \ldots, B_k, S_1, \ldots, S_h\}$ be $k + h$ new propositional atoms, and let $\mathcal{T}' = \mathcal{T} \cup \{B_i \Leftrightarrow \beta_i | i = 1, \ldots, k\} \cup \{S_j \Leftrightarrow \sigma_j | j = 1, \ldots, h\}$ – that is, every preference in $\mathcal{B} \cup \mathcal{S}$ is equivalent to a new atom in $\mathcal{T}'$.

6.1   Objective Functions

Here we define functions to be maximized to find a solution to a multi objective optimization problem. In order to formulate functions to be maximized involving preferences expressed as formulas in $\mathcal{P}(\mathcal{N})$, let $\{b_1,\dots,b_k\}$ the $(0,1)$-variables one-one with $\{B_1,\dots,B_k\}$ and similarly $\{s_1,\dots,s_h\}$ for $\{S_1,\dots,S_h\}$. The functions representing respectively buyer's and seller's utility over preferences can hence be defined as:

$$u_{\beta,\mathcal{P}(\mathcal{N})} = \sum_{i=1}^{k} b_i u_\beta(\beta_i) \tag{12}$$

$$u_{\sigma,\mathcal{P}(\mathcal{N})} = \sum_{j=1}^{h} s_j u_\sigma(\sigma_j) \tag{13}$$

As highlighted in Section 5, also utilities over numerical features have to be taken into account while finding the best solution for both the buyer and the seller. Hence, for each feature f_t involved in the negotiation process we have a *feature utility function* for the buyer u_{β,f_t} and one for the seller u_{σ,f_t}. For instance, if we consider `price` and the linear function in equations (10) and (11) we likely will have:

$$u_{\beta,\texttt{price}}(v) = \begin{cases} 1 - \dfrac{v-\max(D_{\texttt{price}})}{r_{\beta,\texttt{price}}-\max(D_{\texttt{price}})} \\ 0 \end{cases}$$

$$u_{\sigma,\texttt{price}}(v) = \begin{cases} 1 - \dfrac{v-\min(D_{\texttt{price}})}{r_{\sigma,\texttt{price}}-\min(D_{\texttt{price}})} \\ 0 \end{cases}$$

6.2   The Multi Objective Optimization Problem

Given the objective functions to be optimized – the *feature* utility functions and the *preference* utility functions – in order to compute a Pareto agreement we reduce to a multi objective optimization problem (MOP). The functions to be optimized are utility functions both for the buyer and the seller, as we want them equally satisfied.

In addition to the set of functions to maximize (or minimize), in a MOP there are a set of constrained numerical variables. In our setting, we have three different sets of constraints:

1. the (modified) ontology $\mathcal{T}'$ —see the beginning of Section 6
2. strict requirements β and σ, including reservation values over numerical features
3. conditions (6) and (7) of an MBN on disagreement thresholds t_β and t_σ — see the definition of MBN-$\mathcal{P}(\mathcal{N})$ at the end of Section 4

Notice that the ones involving disagreements thresholds are already linear constraints. In order to model as linear constraints also the ones described in points 1 and 2 of the above enumeration, proceed as follows.

Clause reduction. Obtain a set of clauses T'' s.t. each clause contains only one single numerical constraint and T'' is satisfiable iff $T' \cup \{\sigma, \beta\}$ does. In order to have such clauses, if after using standard transformations in clausal form [16] you find a clause with two numerical constraints $\chi : A \vee \dots (f_i \circ_i k_i) \vee (f_j \circ_j k_j)$ pick up a new propositional atom $\overline{A}$ and replace χ with the set of two clauses[4]

$$\left\{ \begin{array}{l} \chi_1 : \overline{A} \vee A \vee \dots \vee (f_i \circ_i k_i), \\ \chi_2 : \neg\overline{A} \vee A \vee \dots \vee (f_j \circ_j k_j) \end{array} \right\}$$

As a final step, for each clause, replace $\neg(f \le k)$ with $(f \ge s(k))$ and $\neg(f \ge k)$ with $(f \le p(k))$ (see (3) and 4).

Example 3. Suppose to have the clause

$$\chi : \texttt{ItalianMaker} \vee \neg\texttt{AirConditioning} \vee$$
$$(\texttt{year\_warranty} \ge 3) \vee \neg(\texttt{price} \ge 20,500)$$

First of all split the clause in the following two

$$\chi_1 : \overline{A} \vee \texttt{ItalianMaker} \vee \neg\texttt{AirConditioning} \vee$$
$$(\texttt{year\_warranty} \ge 3)$$
$$\chi_2 : \neg\overline{A} \vee \texttt{ItalianMaker} \vee \neg\texttt{AirConditioning} \vee$$
$$\neg(\texttt{price} \ge 20,500)$$

then change the second one in

$$\chi_2 : \neg\overline{A} \vee \texttt{ItalianMaker} \vee \neg\texttt{AirConditioning} \vee$$
$$(\texttt{price} \le 20,000)$$

Here we consider $\epsilon = 500$ for the concrete domain $D_{\texttt{price}}$.

Encoding clauses into linear inequalities. Use a modified version of well-known encoding of clauses into linear inequalities (*e.g.*, [19, p.314]) so that every solution of the inequalities identifies a model of T''. If we identify true with values in $[1 \dots \infty]$ and false with values in $[0 \dots 1[$ each clause can be rewritten in a corresponding inequality.

- map each propositional atom A occurring in a clause χ with a $(0,1)$-variable a. If A occurs negated in χ then substitute $\neg A$ with $(1-a)$, otherwise substitute A with a.
- replace $(f \le k)$ with $\frac{1}{\max(D_f)-k}(\max(D_f) - f)$ and $(f \ge k)$ with $\frac{1}{k}f$.

After this rewriting it is easy to see that, considering $\vee$ – logical *or* – as classical addition, in order to have a clause true the evaluation of the corresponding expression must be a value grater or equal to 1.

Example 4. If we consider $\max(D_{\texttt{price}}) = 60,000$, continuing Example 3 we have from χ_1 and χ_2 the following inequalities respectively:

$$\overline{a} + i + (1-a) + \frac{1}{3}\texttt{year\_warranty} \ge 1$$

$$(1-\overline{a}) + i + (1-a) + \frac{1}{60,000 - 20,000}(60,000 - \texttt{price}) \ge 1$$

---

[4] It is well know that such a transformation preserves logical entailment [27].

where $\bar{a}$, i, a are $(0,1)$-variables representing propositional terms $\overline{A}$, ItalianMaker and AirConditioning.

Looking at the example below, it should be clear the reason why only one numerical constraint is admitted in a clause.

Example 5. Let us transform the following clause without splitting in the two corresponding ones

$$\overline{\chi} : \texttt{ItalianMaker} \vee (\texttt{year\_warranty} \geq 3) \vee (\texttt{price} \leq 20\,000)$$

the corresponding inequality is then

$$i + \frac{1}{3}\texttt{year\_warranty} + \frac{1}{60\,000 - 20\,000}(60\,000 - \texttt{price}) \geq 1$$

The interpretation $\{\texttt{year\_warranty} = 2, \texttt{price} = 19\,500\}$ is not a model for $\overline{\chi}$ while the inequality is satisfied.

7 The Bargaining Process

Summing up, the negotiation process covers the following steps:

Preliminary Phase. The buyer defines strict β and preferences $\mathcal{B}$ with corresponding utilities $u_\beta(\beta_i)$, as well as the threshold t_β, and similarly the seller σ, $\mathcal{S}$, $u_\sigma(\sigma_j)$ and t_σ. Here we are not interested in how to compute $t_\beta, t_\sigma, u_\beta(\beta_i)$ and $u_\sigma(\sigma_j)$; we assume they are determined in advance by means of either direct assignment methods (Ordering, Simple Assessing or Ratio Comparison) or pairwise comparison methods (like AHP and Geometric Mean) [20]. Both agents inform the mediator about these specifications and the theory $\mathcal{T}$ they refer to. Notice that for each feature involved in the negotiation process, both in β and σ their respective reservation values are set either in the form $f \leq r_f$ or in the form $f \geq r_f$.

Negotiation-Core phase. For each $\beta_i \in \mathcal{B}$ the mediator picks up a new propositional atom B_i and adds the axiom $B_1 \Leftrightarrow \beta_i$ to $\mathcal{T}$, similarly for $\mathcal{S}$. Then, it transforms all the constraints modeled in β, σ and (just extended) $\mathcal{T}$ in the corresponding linear inequalities following the procedures illustrated in Section 6.2 and Section 6.2. Given the preference utility functions $u_{\beta,\mathcal{P}(\mathcal{N})} = \sum_{i=1}^{k} b_i u_\beta(\beta_i)$ and $u_{\sigma,\mathcal{P}(\mathcal{N})} = \sum_{j=1}^{h} s_j u_\sigma(\sigma_j)$, the mediator adds to this set of constraints the ones involving disagreement thresholds $u_{\beta,\mathcal{P}(\mathcal{N})} \geq t_\beta$ and $u_{\sigma,\mathcal{P}(\mathcal{N})} \geq t_\sigma$.

With respect to the above set of constraints, the mediator solves a MOP maximizing the *preference* utility functions $u_{\beta,\mathcal{P}(\mathcal{N})}$, $u_{\sigma,\mathcal{P}(\mathcal{N})}$ and for each feature f involved in the negotiation process also the *feature* utility functions $u_{\beta,f}$ and $u_{\sigma,f}$. The returned solution to the MOP is the agreement proposed to the buyer and the seller. Notice that a solution to a MOP is always Pareto optimal [11], furthermore the solution proposed by the mediator is also a *fair* solution, because among all the Pareto-optimal solutions we take the one maximizing the utilities of both the buyer and the seller (see Sec. 6.1). From this point on, it is a *take-it-or-leave-it* offer, as the participants can either accept or reject the proposed agreement [12]. Let us present a tiny example in order to better clarify the approach. Given the toy ontology in $\mathcal{P}(\mathcal{N})$,

$$\mathcal{T} = \left\{ \begin{array}{l} \texttt{ExternalColorBlack} \Rightarrow \neg\texttt{ExternalColorGray} \\ \texttt{SatelliteAlarm} \Rightarrow \texttt{AlarmSystem} \\ \texttt{NavigatorPack} \Leftrightarrow \texttt{SatelliteAlarm} \wedge \texttt{GPS\_system} \end{array} \right.$$

the buyer and the seller specify their strict requirements and preferences:

β = Sedan $\wedge$ (price $\leq 30{,}000$) $\wedge$ (km_warranty $\geq 120{,}000$) $\wedge$ (year_warranty ≥ 4)
β_1 = GPS_system $\wedge$ AlarmSystem
β_2 = ExternalColorBlack $\Rightarrow$ Leather_seats
β_3 = (km_warranty $\geq 140{,}000$)
$u_\beta(\beta_1)$ = 0.5
$u_\beta(\beta_2)$ = 0.2
$u_\beta(\beta_3)$ = 0.3
t_β = 0.2

σ = Sedan $\wedge$ (price $\geq 20{,}000$) $\wedge$ (km_warranty $\leq 160{,}000$) $\wedge$ (year_warranty ≤ 6)
σ_1 = GPS_system $\Rightarrow$ (price $\geq 28{,}000$)
σ_2 = (km_warranty $\leq 150{,}000$) $\vee$ (year_warranty ≤ 5)
σ_3 = ExternalColorGray
σ_4 = NavigatorPack
$u_\sigma(\sigma_1)$ = 0.2
$u_\sigma(\sigma_2)$ = 0.4
$u_\sigma(\sigma_3)$ = 0.2
$u_\sigma(\sigma_4)$ = 0.2
t_σ = 0.2

Then the final agreement is:

$$\mathcal{I} : \{ \texttt{Sedan}^{\mathcal{I}} = \text{true}, \texttt{ExternalColorGray}^{\mathcal{I}} = \text{true},$$
$$\texttt{SatelliteAlarm}^{\mathcal{I}} = \text{true}, \texttt{GPS\_system}^{\mathcal{I}} = \text{true},$$
$$\texttt{NavigatorPack}^{\mathcal{I}} = \text{true}, \texttt{AlarmSystem}^{\mathcal{I}} = \text{true},$$
$$\text{price}^{\mathcal{I}} = 28{,}000, k^{\mathcal{I}} = 160{,}000, \text{year\_warranty}^{\mathcal{I}} = 5 \}$$

Here, for the sake of conciseness, we omit propositional atoms interpreted as false.

8 Related Work and Discussion

Automated bilateral negotiation among agents has been widely investigated, both in artificial intelligence and in microeconomics research communities, so this section is necessarily far from complete. Several definitions have been proposed in the literature for bilateral negotiation. Rubinstein [26] defined the *Bargaining Problem* as the situation in which "two individuals have before them several possible contractual agreements. Both have interests in reaching agreement but their interests are not entirely identical. What 'will be' the agreed contract, assuming that both parties behave rationally?" In game theory, the bargaining problem has been modeled either as *cooperative* or *non-cooperative* games [10]. AI-oriented research has been more focused on automated negotiation among agents and on designing high-level protocols for agent interaction [15]. Agents can play different roles: act on behalf of buyer or seller, but also play the role of a mediator or facilitator. Approaches exploiting a mediator include among others

[8,13,9]. In [8] an extended alternating offers protocol was presented, with the presence of a mediator, which improves the utility of both agents. In [13] a mediated-negotiation approach was proposed for complex contracts, where inter dependency among issues is investigated. In [3] the use of propositional logic in multi-issue negotiation was investigated, while in [4] weighted propositional formulas in preference modeling were considered. However, in such papers, no semantic relation among issues is taken into account. In our approach we adopt a logical theory, *i.e.*, an ontology, which allows *e.g.*, to catch inconsistencies between demand and supply or find out a feasible agreement in a bundle, which is fundamental to model an e-marketplace. Self-interested agents negotiating over a set of resources to obtain an optimal allocation of such resources have been studied in [7,6,5]. Endriss et al. [7] propose an optimal resource allocation in two different negotiation scenarios: one, with money transfer, determines an allocation with maximal social welfare; the second is a money-free framework, which results in a Pareto outcome. In [5] agents negotiate over small bundles of resources, and a mechanism of resource allocation is investigated, which maximizes the social welfare by means of a sequence of deals involving at most k items each. Both papers [7,5] extend the framework proposed in [28], which focused on negotiation for (re)allocating tasks among agents. We borrow from [31] the definition of agreement as a model for a set of formulas from both agents. However, in [31] only multiple-rounds protocols are studied, and the approach leaves the burden to reach an agreement to the agents themselves, although they can follow a protocol. The approach does not take preferences into account, so that it is not possible to guarantee the reached agreement is Pareto-efficient. Our approach, instead, aims at giving an *automated* support to negotiating agents to reach, in one shot, Pareto agreements. The work presented here builds on [22], where a basic propositional logic framework endowed of a logical theory was proposed. In [21] the approach was extended and generalized and complexity issues were discussed. In this paper we further extended the framework, introducing the extended logic $\mathcal{P}(\mathcal{N})$, thus handling numerical features, and showed we are able to compute Pareto-efficient agreements, solving a multi objective optimization problem adopting a one-shot negotiation protocol.

References

1. Baader, F., Hanschke, P.: A schema for integrating concrete domains into concept languages. In: Proc. of IJCAI 1991, pp. 452–457 (1991)
2. Binmore, K.: Fun and Games. A Text on Game Theory. D.C. Heath and Company (1992)
3. Bouveret, S., Lemaitre, M., Fargier, H., Lang, J.: Allocation of indivisible goods: a general model and some complexity results. In: Proc. of AAMAS 2005, pp. 1309–1310 (2005)
4. Chevaleyre, Y., Endriss, U., Lang, J.: Expressive power of weighted propositional formulas for cardinal preference modeling. In: Proc. of KR 2006, pp. 145–152 (2006)
5. Chevaleyre, Y., Endriss, U., Lang, J., Maudet, N.: Negotiating over small bundles of resources. In: Proc. of AAMAS 2005, pp. 296–302 (2005)
6. Dunne, P.E., Wooldridge, M., Laurence, M.: The complexity of contract negotiation. Artif. Intell. 164(1-2), 23–46 (2005)
7. Endriss, U., Maudet, N., Sadri, F., Toni, F.: On optimal outcomes of negotiations over resources. In: Proc. of AAMAS 2003, pp. 177–184 (2003)

8. Fatima, S., Wooldridge, M., Jennings, N.R.: Optimal agendas for multi-issue negotiation. In: Proc. of AAMAS 2003, pp. 129–136 (2003)
9. Gatti, N., Amigoni, F.: A decentralized bargaining protocol on dependent continuous multi-issue for approximate pareto optimal outcomes. In: Proc. of AAMAS 2005, pp. 1213–1214 (2005)
10. Gerding, E.H., van Bragt, D.D.B., La Poutre, J.A.: Scientific approaches and techniques for negotiation: a game theoretic and artificial intelligence perspective. Technical report, SEN-R0005, CWI (2000)
11. Hillier, F., Lieberman, G.: Introduction to Operations Research. McGraw-Hill, New York (2005)
12. Jennings, N.R., Faratin, P., Lomuscio, A.R., Parsons, S., Wooldridge, M.J., Sierra, C.: Automated negotiation: prospects, methods and challenges. Int. J. of Group Decision and Negotiation 10(2), 199–215 (2001)
13. Klein, M., Faratin, P., Sayama, H., Bar-Yam, Y.: Negotiating complex contracts. In: Proc. of AAMAS 2002, pp. 753–757 (2002)
14. Kraus, S.: Strategic Negotiation in Multiagent Environments. MIT Press, Cambridge (2001)
15. Lomuscio, A.R., Wooldridge, M., Jennings, N.R.: A classification scheme for negotiation in electronic commerce. Int Journal of Group Decision and Negotiation 12(1), 31–56 (2003)
16. Loveland, D.W.: Automated theorem proving: A logical basis. North-Holland, Amsterdam (1978)
17. MacKie-Mason, J.K., Wellman, M.P.: Automated markets and trading agents. In: Handbook of Computational Economics, North-Holland, Amsterdam (2006)
18. Muthoo, A.: On the strategic role of outside options in bilateral bargaining. Operations Research 43(2), 292–297 (1995)
19. Papadimitriou, C.H., Steiglitz, K.: Combinatorial optimization: algorithms and complexity. Prentice-Hall, Inc, Englewood Cliffs (1982)
20. Pomerol, J.C., Barba-Romero, S.: Multicriterion Decision Making in Management. Kluwer Series in Operation Research. Kluwer Academic Publishers, Dordrecht (2000)
21. Ragone, A., Di Noia, T., Di Sciascio, E., Donini, F.M.: A logic-based framework to compute pareto agreements in one-shot bilateral negotiation. In: Proc. of ECAI 2006, pp. 230–234 (2006)
22. Ragone, A., Di Noia, T., Di Sciascio, E., Donini, F.M.: Propositional- logic approach to one-shot multi issue bilateral negotiation. ACM SIGecom Exchanges 5(5), 11–21 (2006)
23. Raiffa, H.: The Art and Science of Negotiation. Harvard University Press, Cambridge (1982)
24. Raiffa, H., Richardson, J., Metcalfe, D.: Negotiation Analysis - The Science and Art of Collaborative Decision Making. The Belknap Press of Harvard University Press, Cambridge (2002)
25. Rosenschein, J.S., Zlotkin, G.: Rules of Encounter. MIT Press, Cambridge (1994)
26. Rubinstein, A.: Perfect equilibrium in a bargaining model. Econometrica 50, 97–109 (1982)
27. Russell, S., Norvig, P.: Artificial Intelligence: A Modern Approach. Pearson Education-Prentice Hall, London (2003)
28. Sandholm, T.: Contract types for satisficing task allocation: I theoretical results. In: Proceedings of the AAAI Spring Symposium (1998)
29. Trastour, D., Bartolini, C., Priest, C.: Semantic Web Support for the Business-to-Business E-Commerce Lifecycle. In: Proc. WWW 2002, pp. 89–98 (2002)
30. Wellman, M.P.: Online marketplaces. In: Practical Handbook of Internet Computing, CRC Press, Boca Raton (2004)
31. Wooldridge, M., Parsons, S.: Languages for negotiation. In: Proc of ECAI 2004, pp. 393–400 (2000)

Component-Based Standardisation of Agent Communication

Frank Guerin and Wamberto Vasconcelos

Dept. of Computing Science, Univ. of Aberdeen, Aberdeen AB24 3UE, UK
{fguerin,wvasconc}@csd.abdn.ac.uk

Abstract. We address the problem of standardising the semantics of agent communication. The diversity of existing approaches suggests that no single agent communication language can satisfactorily cater for all scenarios. However, standardising the way in which different languages are specified is a viable alternative. We describe a standard meta-language in which the rules of an arbitrary institution can be specified. In this way different agent communication languages can be given a common grounding. From this starting point, we describe a component based approach to standardisation, whereby a standard can develop by adding component sets of rules; for example to handle various classes of dialogs and normative relations. This approach is illustrated by example. Eventually we envisage different agent institutions publishing a specification of their rules by simply specifying the subset of standard components in use in that institution. Agents implementing the meta-language can then interoperate between institutions by downloading appropriate components.

1 Introduction

We are interested in facilitating interoperability for agents interacting with different institutions on the Internet. For example, consider a personal agent of a professor who is invited to participate in a conference (say to give a keynote address and chair a session). The personal agent may connect with the conference site and enter a collaborative dialogue with the agents of the various other speakers, and the conference organiser, in order to arrange the schedule of events. Subsequently the agent will connect to various online travel sites to procure airline tickets and accommodation, most likely by means of some auction mechanism. Finally the agent may discover that an airline ticket it has bought does not conform to what was advertised, thus it may seek compensation, lodging an appeal with some arbitration site, and bringing evidence to support the claim. Each of these interactions occurs in a different institution; the requirements for the agent communication language (ACL) in each institution are quite different. Yet, would it be possible to provide a standard language which encompasses all requirements?

Past attempts to standardise agent communication [8,15,7][1] have managed to standardise certain syntactic or pragmatic aspects, but fared poorly when it

---

[1] Note that the FIPA'97 specification is cited here because the communication language semantics has not changed since then.

M. Baldoni et al. (Eds.): DALT 2007, LNAI 4897, pp. 227–244, 2008.

comes to the issue of the semantics of the communication language. In practice, implementers who claim to be using a particular standard ACL tend to ignore those aspects of the standard that pose difficulties for their implementation (often the formal semantics are ignored); additionally they often create ad hoc extensions when none of the constructs of the standard quite fits their needs. Effectively they invent their own custom dialect, which will not be understood by any other system [22]. Given the diverse needs of different domains, it is probably not feasible to come up with a single standard ACL which will cater for the needs all possible agent systems. Furthermore, a standard ACL would be rigid, precluding the possibility of agents negotiating the semantics of their own custom ACL on the fly, for a particular purpose. The ACL would seem to be the wrong level to standardise at; instead, it would seem appropriate to have a standard way of specifying semantics, to allow developers (or agents themselves) to create their own languages in a standard and structured way. Our proposal is to create a standard meta-language which would allow different interaction languages to be defined for different domains.

The core language, on which developers will build, must be sufficiently expressive to allow any reasonable language to be specified. For this purpose we identify a class of agent communication languages which are universal in the sense that they could be used to simulate any other agent communication language which is computable. We specify one such language and demonstrate its generality by showing how it allows the specification of institutions in which agents can change the rules of the institution itself. With this core in place, we envisage a standard evolving gradually by adding "components". Note that we are using a non-standard meaning of "component", i.e. we are not talking in the software engineering sense where it encapsulates functions and communicates with other components. However it does share some properties of a software component in that it should be reusable and composable with other components. By "component" we mean a set of rules to govern a certain aspect of an interaction. For example, a component may provide rules for normative relations, defining abstractions such as permissions and obligations, and how these change as messages are sent. Further components could then use these abstractions to specify high-level protocols. High level protocols themselves can be specified as components, and so composed with other protocols for flexible interactions. In this way we can give developers the flexibility to define their own components, and publish the specifications, so that others can develop further components, and agents, to work with that language. It is hoped that this could bring together the efforts of the community as similar efforts have done in software engineering by specifying standards for programming languages. A further advantage of the component based approach is that all agents in a society do not necessarily need to support the same components. Some agents may be less sophisticated than others and may support simple reactive protocol components, while other more sophisticated agents may be able to use components which allow them to express their intentions and desires, with a well defined meaning. When agents wish to communicate they would firstly discover which components they support in common, and then they can determine the level at which they can interact. This ability to implement lightweight versions of an agent communication language is one of the desiderata for agent communication languages outlined by Mayfield et al. [19].

In this paper we will illustrate the proposed approach with some examples. We must stress that we are not advocating that the components described in this paper be adopted as a standard; we merely provide simple examples to demonstrate the feasibility of the component-based approach. This paper will focus exclusively on the semantic issues as these have proved to be the most problematic for the standardisation of agent communication. We therefore ignore all pragmatic issues, e.g. how to find the name of an agent who provides some service, authentication, registration, capability definition and facilitation [16]. We assume an agent platform which can take care of all these issues. Pragmatic issues are of course important, but they would require a full treatment in their own right. Furthermore, the types of ACL which we will consider will be restricted to those that have a social semantics; the primary reason for this is the impossibility of verifying languages with mental semantics in an open system, where agents' internals cannot be easily inspected [22].

This paper is organised as follows. Section 2 looks at the most general framework within which all practical ACLs could be specified. Section 3 defines an agent communication language which allows unlimited extensions, and so forms the base component which we later build on. Section 4 adds a component for normative relations. Section 5 discusses how protocols can be added in general, and adds an auction protocol. Section 6 describes a temporal logic component we have added. Section 7 discusses related work and Section 8 concludes with a look to the future.

2 Definition of an Agent Communication Language

In this section we want to define what an ACL is in the most general terms, and to have a formal framework which captures the space of possible ACLs. Following Singh's seminal work on social commitments [22,23], there does seem to be a consensus in the community that the semantics of communication for open systems should be based on social phenomena rather than agents' private mental states [25,9,4,5]. We follow this social approach and we consider that all "reasonable" languages for use in an open system must be of the social type. We do not restrict ourselves to commitments: we allow arbitrary social facts[2].

We define an ACL by specifying an institution. The existence of a communication language presumes the existence of an institution, which defines the

---

[2] This means that we are not precluded from representing mental states that have been publicly expressed by an agent [12]. This can be handled by treating the agent's publicly expressed mental attitudes as part of the state of affairs in the institution. The difference between this and earlier mentalistic semantics [8,15,7] is that we do not require that agents actually hold the mental states which they have publicly expressed.

meaning of language. Institutions are man-made social structures created to regulate the activities of a group of people engaged in some enterprise. They may be created deliberately, as is the case for formal organisations, or they may be created by conventions evolving over time, as is the case for human culture. Institutions regulate the activities of their members by inventing *institutional facts*, a term due to Searle [21]. Some institutional facts take the form of *rules* while others merely describe a *state of affairs* in the institution. *Rules* describe how institutional facts can be created or modified. An example of an institutional fact of the *state of affairs* type is having the title "doctor"; examples of institutional facts which are rules are the rules in a University which describe how the title can be awarded and by whom. The *rule* type of facts can be used to provide a relationship between the real physical world and the institution; rules can have preconditions which depend on the physical world and/or on other institutional facts. For example, the submission of a thesis physically bound in a specified format is a necessary precondition to the awarding of the title "doctor"; the passing of an examination (a purely institutional fact) is another precondition.

Rules relating to the physical world describe how events or states of the world (typically the actions of members) bring about changes in the institutional facts. The classic example of this is where an utterance by a member of an institution can bring about an institutional fact, for example the naming of a ship: "I hereby name this ship the Queen Elizabeth." [3]. It is not possible for institutional facts to bring about changes in the physical world because the institution itself, being a collection of intangible institutional facts, cannot directly effect any physical change in the world.[3] Institutions may describe their rules in a form which specifies physical effects in the world, but such rules are not strictly true because the physical effects are not guaranteed to happen; the only way in which the institution can influence the actions of its members is through the threat of further institutional facts being created. For example a legal institution may prescribe a term of imprisonment as the consequence of an institutional fact, but it cannot directly bring about the imprisonment of a member; instead it can state that a policeman should use physical force to bring the member to prison, and the policeman can be threatened with the loss of his job if he does not. The rule prescribing imprisonment can be reformulated as a rule which states that if the policeman does not imprison the member by physical force or otherwise, then the policeman loses his job. Thus all the rules relating to the physical world take the form of descriptions of how events or states of the world bring about changes in the institutional facts.

---

[3] Institutions may indirectly affect the physical world if agents of the institution take physical actions in response to institutional facts. We consider a bank balance to be an institutional fact; it happens that banks have implemented physical agents which act on this institutional fact and dispense money. Nevertheless, the bank balance itself is not a physical fact. Likewise, if certain institutional facts are valued or feared by agents, then they will act in response to them (hence the institutional facts affect the physical world only through the agents).

A further point to note is that the institutional facts being modified by a rule could be rules themselves. Many institutions do modify their rules over time; a legal institution may allow arguments about the rules by which argumentation should take place. This is accommodated by the framework described above, because a rule can modify an institutional fact, and that institutional fact could be another rule.

If we assume that any relevant change in the world's state can be translated into an event, then we can say (without loss of generality) that the institutional facts change only in response to events in the world (we do not allow rules to refer to states of the world). In a typical agent system we rely on the agent platform to handle the generation of events. Typical events include messages being transmitted, timer events and possibly other non communicative actions of agents or events such as agent death. Let E be the set of possible events and let $\mathcal{F}$ be the set of possible institutional facts. Let $update$ be a function which updates the institutional facts in response to an event; $update : E \times 2^{\mathcal{F}} \to 2^{\mathcal{F}}$. Now in an institution $\mathcal{I}$, it is the institutional rules R which indirectly define this update function. The institution interprets the rules in order to define the update function, let the interpreter function be I, where I maps R to some update function. An institution $\mathcal{I}$ can then be fully specified by specifying the interpreter I and the facts $F \subset \mathcal{F}$. F is itself composed of the *rule* type of facts R and the *state of affairs* type of facts A, so $F = \langle R, A \rangle$. Therefore institution $\mathcal{I}$ can be represented by a tuple $\langle I, F \rangle$. The F component fully describes the facts and rules which currently hold in the institution.

This gives us the most general view of agent communication languages; by specifying the tuple $\langle I, F \rangle$ we can specify any ACL. It describes how institutional facts F change in response to events as the multi-agent system runs. Given an institution described by $\langle I, F_0 \rangle$ at some instant, and a subsequent sequence of events $e_1, e_2, e_3 \ldots$, we can calculate the description of the institutional facts after each event, obtaining a sequence of facts descriptions: $F_0, F_1, F_2, \ldots$, where each F_i is related to F_{i-1} as follows: $F_i = update_{i-1}(e_i, F_{i-1})$ where $update_{i-1} = I(R_{i-1})$ (and $F_i = \langle R_i, A_i \rangle$ for all i). Interpreter I remains fixed throughout runs.

2.1   A Universal Agent Communication Machine

The rule interpreter I specified above is the immutable part of an institution. The choice of I can place limits on what is possible with that institution, or give it universal expressive power. Just as a universal Turing machine can simulate the behaviour of any Turing machine, we can have an analogous universal agent communication machine.

Definition 1. *A universal agent communication machine is a machine which can simulate the behaviour of any computable agent communication language.*

By "simulate" here we mean that (given an appropriate set of input rules) it could generate the same sequence of institutional facts in response to the same sequence of events. In fact a universal Turing machine is a universal agent communication machine. The input R to the machine produces the function $update$.

Any update function that is computable can be produced in this way. Any Turing complete programming language can be used to implement a universal agent communication machine.

3   Specifying Extensible Languages

Given a universal agent communication machine it is possible to specify an ACL which has *universal expressive power*, in the following sense.

Definition 2. *An agent communication language is said to have universal expressive power if the agents using it can transform its rules so that it simulates the behaviour of any computable agent communication language.*

Given a language defined by an institutional specification $\mathcal{I} = \langle I, \langle R, A \rangle \rangle$ (as described above), if I is a universal agent communication machine, then the language will have universal expressive power if the rules R allow messages sent (i.e. events) to program the machine in a Turing complete way.[4] Languages with universal power are of particular interest because they allow unlimited extension. It is our thesis that a minimal language with universal expressive power is an appropriate basis for standardising agent communication; i.e. the specification of the programming language and core code can be agreed upon and published. Such a choice of standard does not restrict agents to the rules given because it can provide a mechanism through which agents can change the rules at runtime; this can allow agents to introduce new protocols at runtime, for example. Such protocols could come from trusted libraries, or could be generated by the agents on the fly for the scenario at hand. If necessary, agents could also have a phase of negotiation before deciding on accepting some new rules.

We define one such language in Fig. 1. We make use of Prolog as the logic programming paradigm is particularly appropriate for agent communication; there is also evidence that Prolog already enjoys considerable popularity in the agent communication semantics community [1,20,14]. The `interpretEvent/3` predicate takes as input the current set of facts `F` and an event `Event`, and generates the new set of facts `NewF`. In line *3* the event is converted from its predicate form to a list form, so that line *4* can append the old and new facts variables to it. In line *5* the event is converted back from list form to its predicate form. The next step will be to match the head of the event with the appropriate rule in `Rules` (this corresponds to R in the formal model); however, we do not want to change the rule itself by unifying its variables, this is why we make a clean copy of it in line *6* before doing the matching in line *7*, via the `member/2` predicate. Now that the body of the rule (`Tail`) has been retrieved, we can invoke it in line *8* via `callPred/2`. Lines *9* to *17* define the recursive `callPred/2` predicate. Line *10* handles the case where the rule body to be executed invokes another rule within `Rules`, in which case `callPred/2` is called to handle it. Line

---

[4] This expressiveness implies undecidability, hence it may be impossible to prove properties for a system of agents using the language. However, if desired one can specify a restricted and decidable language on top of this, by restricting the agents' ability to modify rules, as described in the sequel.

```
 1 interpretEvent(F,Event,NewF):-
 2   F=[Rules,Asserts],
 3   Event=..EventAsList,
 4   append(EventAsList,[F,NewF],NewEventAsList),
 5   Pred=..NewEventAsList,
 6   copy_term(Rules,Rules2),
 7   member([_|[Pred|Tail]],Rules2),
 8   callPred(Tail,Rules).

 9 callPred([],_).
10 callPred([HeadPred|Tail],Rules):-
11   copy_term(Rules,Rules2),
12   member([_|[HeadPred|NestTail]],Rules2),
13   callPred(NestTail,Rules),
14   callPred(Tail,Rules).
15 callPred([HeadPred|Tail],Rules):-
16   call(HeadPred),
17   callPred(Tail,Rules).
```

Fig. 1. Extensible Communication Language in Prolog

15 handles the case where the rule body to be executed invokes a built in Prolog predicate, in which case it is called directly via `call/1`. It is important that `interpretEvent/3` forces the event to use a rule from `Rules` (i.e. it checks that the rule is a member of `Rules` before passing control to `callPred/2` so that agents are unable to directly invoke Prolog predicates with their messages; their messages are interpreted first. Without this precaution our interpreter would not truly have universal expressive power, as it would always accept Prolog predicates, which could be used to reprogram it; hence it would be impossible to define a language which restricted the possible things which events could change.

Rules stored in R are written in the form of lists, with an index number at the head of each rule. A Prolog clause of the form "`pred1(A,B):-pred2(A)`, `pred3(B)`" becomes "`[1,pred1(A,B),pred2(A),pred3(B)]`". This corresponds to the Horn clause $pred2(A) \land pred3(B) \rightarrow pred1(A, B)$. Some sample rules are:

```
[ [ 1, addRule(Rule,[R1,A1],[NewR1,A1]),
       append(R1,[Rule],NewR1)                ],
  [ 2, deleteRule(Index,[R2,A2],[NewR2,A2]),
       delete(R2,[Index|_],NewR2)             ]
]
```

Let the above program be called *prog* and the interpreter $I = \langle prog, Prolog \rangle$. Let the assertions A be initially empty and rules R be the two rules above.

Theorem 1. *The ACL specified by institution $\langle I, \langle R, A \rangle \rangle$ has universal expressive power.*

The truth of this follows from that fact that Prolog is Turing-complete, and `addRule` can be used to add arbitrary predicates, and can therefore give subsequent events access to the underlying Prolog language (or restrict their access). Despite the ease with which this can be done, to our knowledge this is the first

example of such an ACL. We propose that an ACL such as this would form
the core component of a standard. This is only the first step of standardisation
however. Standards will also need to define libraries and tools which will make
the base machine more usable.

Let us briefly illustrate how we can begin to use the above ACL. The following
is an example of an event:

```
addrule([3,assert(Fact,[R,A],[R,[Fact|A]])])
```

After interpreting this event, the rules R will be updated so that subsequent
assert events cause the addition of an element to the assertions A. For example, a subsequent event assert(alive(agent1)) would add alive(agent1)
to A. Note that this is invoking our rule 3 and not Prolog's built-in assert/1
predicate. At this point we will avoid giving an extended example of the kind
of interaction we can capture. Instead we want to show the component based
approach to standardisation, so we will eventually illustrate only a very simple
auction protocol, but we will build it upon some useful components.

We now add some basic "housekeeping" rules. We will have a *timer* predicate
in A, which records the current time, e.g. *timer(524)*. We will assume that our
agent platform generates timer events at regular intervals. Whenever a timer
event happens we want to update the clock and execute a set of housekeeping
rules. These rules perform housekeeping checks, for example to see if an agent
has failed to meet a deadline. The following rule (in R) handles the timer event:

```
[ 3, timer(Time,[R,A],[NewR,NewA]),
    replace(A,timer(Time),UpdatedA),
    housekeeping([R,UpdatedA],[NewR,NewA])
]
```

Here we have assumed the existence of a *replace* predicate which replaces a
named predicate in A with a new version. The initial *housekeeping* predicate
simply preserves the institutional facts F; subsequent components will modify
the predicate, adding their own rules.

It is desirable to add another layer for the interpretation of agent communications. We create a *speechAct* rule for this purpose. Agents communicate by
sending messages (events) of the form *speechAct(sender, receiver, performative,
content)*. We must rely on the platform's message handling layer to discard any
messages where the *sender* parameter is falsified; there is no way to do this
once the event is processed by the interpreter. We also rely on the platform to
distribute the message to the intended recipients. The message event is then
handled by our *speechAct* rule. With this in place we protect the lower level
operations from direct access by the agents. We do not want agents to be able to
directly invoke the timer event or the rule changing events; however, if desired,
we can still create speech acts which allow the modification of certain rules in R
by suitably empowered agents. Now the *speechAct* predicate becomes particularly useful to gather together all those operations which need to be done during
the processing of any message (e.g. check roles, permissions and empowerments).
This is described in Section 4.

It is worth noting that agents can only process the events they have observed; hence, when the update rule is implemented in agents, they only build a view of the institutional facts from their individual perspectives. If each agent applies the rules on limited information in this way, it is entirely possible that the institutional facts from the perspective of two different agents may have contradictory assertions. This is not a problem, so long as the developer bears this in mind when designing components (protocols for example). Specifications of norms should not create "unfair" rules, for example creating an obligation for an agent to do something, and leaving the agent unaware of the existence of the obligation. In most practical systems which we envisage, there will be no need for any agent to maintain this global view and indeed in a large system it might not be feasible to maintain it; it will be sufficient for each agent to maintain an individual perspective, which coincides with the perspective of other agents for any interactions they share.

Obviously we need to be particularly careful if we allow agents to change the rules R, lest conversational participants have contradictory beliefs about the meanings of the messages they are exchanging. At least two solutions can be envisaged: either all members of the institution need to be informed of any change, or a subgroup can decide to set up a virtual organisation (having new communicative actions and corresponding rules which apply only within that virtual organisation, the old ones still applying outside). The later solution is probably the more practical of the two.

4 Normative Relations Component

Various different notions are employed by institutions to describe their rules; Sergot distinguishes between notions of power, permission and practical possibility [13]. Power is the ability of a member to bring about changes in the institutional facts; i.e. for each event which changes F we can describe which members of the institution can effect those changes. For convenience it is common to define roles and define the power of a role. This is because the occupants of roles often change, while the powers associated with the role do not.

Permission can be used to describe those actions which ought or ought not to be taken. Permission is distinct from power because a member may be empowered to do something even though he is not permitted; in this case: if he does it then it counts, i.e. it creates the institutional fact. For example, an examiner could award a student a pass on submission which falls short of the required standards as set out by the institution. In this case the examiner's action is not permitted but still counts as a pass under the rules of the institution; the examiner may be subject to some sanction if the abuse is discovered, but this may not necessarily revoke the fact that the student has passed.

The notion of permission leads to its dual: obligation; obligation is equivalent to "not permitted not to". Obligation can be captured by a rule which specifies a sanction if an action is not done. Because we will be testing agents' compliance over finite models, we must always specify a time-limit for obligations. It is no good for an agent to promise something and deliver "eventually", if there is no upper bound on the time taken.

Practical possibility is another distinct notion which some institutions may need to represent explicitly. For example, suppose there is a rule defining the sanction to be placed on a member in the case of failing to fulfil an obligation, there may be a need to exempt the case where the member was physically incapable of fulfilling the obligation at the time. Thus there could be institutional facts to represent the physical capabilities of each agent; i.e. a rule will define the events in the physical world which *count as* the agent being recognised by the institution as being capable or incapacitated. We do not implement practical possibility however.

4.1   Implementing Norms

The normative relations we implement are defined by predicates stored in the assertions A. Relations can apply to agents directly or via *roles*; an agent occupies one or more roles (also stored in the assertions A). There are four types of normative predicate: *power, permitted, obliged* and *sanction*. Sanctions are defined for actions which agents should not do. Permitted or obliged actions are treated as exemptions to these sanctions, i.e. the sanction applies unless the agent was permitted or obliged. Power and permission have arity 3: the first parameter is the agent name (or role name), the second is the performative of the speech act he is empowered/permitted to do, and the third is a condition. For example

```
power(bidder,bid,[Content=[C],C>47])
```

means that any agent in the role of bidder is empowered to send a *bid* speech act provided it complies with the following conditions: the content of the act must be a list containing a single number whose value is greater than 47. If the condition is the empty list then it is always true. Sanctions and obligations add a further (fourth) parameter, which is the "sanction code". Following [20] we will associate a 3-figure "sanction code" with each norm violation (similar to the error codes used in the Internet protocol HTTP), in our case higher numbers are used for more egregious violations. The sanction codes gathered by each agent as it commits offences are merely recorded in a list. The use of codes is just a convenient way to record sanctions without yet dealing with them; we would require a separate component to impose some form of punishment. Finally the obligation adds a fifth parameter which is the deadline by which the specified speech act must be sent.

The algorithm shown in Fig. 2 is added to the *speechAct* rule to handle the normative relations, it effectively defines an operational semantics for the normative relations. With this implementation we make obligation imply permission and power. It is in this algorithm that roles are consulted to retrieve the names of the agents occupying the roles; e.g. when checking if an agent who has just sent a message is obliged (and hence permitted), the algorithm will consult the facts to see what roles the sending agent occupies. We also need to add the following to the *housekeeping* rule (recall that the housekeeping rule is invoked on every timer event):

– For each obligation check if it has timed out. If so, apply the sanction to the agent (or all agents occupying the obliged role) and remove the obligation from A.

Note that we are assuming that the existence of a *speechAct* rule is an agreed standard across component developers, so that any new components can add checks and guards to this rule.

algorithm HANDLE-NORMS

1. Input: a speech act with *Sender, Receiver, Performative, Content*
2. Check if there is an obligation which requires that *Sender* (or one of the roles he occupies) send this speech act. If so remove the obligation from A and jump to 5.
3. Check if there is a sanction for *Sender* (or one of the roles he occupies) sending this speech act: If not, go to the next step; If so,
   o check if there is a permission for *Sender* (or one of the roles he occupies) to send this speech act: If so, go to the next step; If not, apply the specified sanction.
4. Check if *Sender* (or one of the roles he occupies) is empowered to send this speech act: If not, discard the act and exit this algorithm.
5. Process the act as normal.

Fig. 2. Algorithm to Handle Normative Relations

5   Protocol Components

Protocols are additional components of the ACL, they are each encoded via their own rules in R. Each protocol has a unique name and may be represented by a number of clauses in R. Protocols essentially determine what actions are to be taken next, given the current state and an event that happens. They do this by consulting the current state and modifying the normative relations according to the event that has just happened. Agents initiate protocols by using the special speech act *initProtocol*; the *speechAct* predicate passes control to the protocol on initiation. A protocol initiates a "sub-conversation" within the institution. All the assertions describing the protocol's state of execution are gathered together as an indexed list within A. In order to ensure the index is unique, the initiator will compose an index by concatenating his name with a positive integer which increases with each new protocol he initiates. Subsequently all speech acts indexed with the protocol's identifier will be processed by the protocol's rules (instead of the standard rules which process speech acts that are not part of any protocol). Normative relations defined within the protocol's "space" in A only apply to messages that are part of that protocol. Timer events are processed by all protocols running at any time. Agents are free to enter multiple parallel protocols, each being a separate sub-conversation. Sending a *exitProtocol* message terminates the protocol and removes its assertions from A.

5.1   Example Protocol: Auction

The Vickrey auction protocol below is expected to be invoked by a speech act with content [*Index,Protocol,Item,OffersOver,ClosingTime*]. These then become variables accessible to the initiator clause of the protocol rule, along with the initiator of the protocol and the list of receivers. Each clause has access to the variables *Sndr* and *Rcvr* from the event that invoked the clause (we cannot use the names *Sender* and *Receiver* as these are used by content checking conditions). The Prolog-style pseudocode below describes a series of clauses, one to handle each speech act that can happen during the execution of the protocol. To keep the presentation concise we have avoided presenting the example in real Prolog code.

```
initiator:
 add role(Sndr,auctioneer)
     // sender of initiating message takes on role of auctioneer
 for each Rcvr add role(Rcvr,bidder)
     // each receiver of initiating message takes on role of bidder
 add power(bidder,bid,[Content>OffersOver])
 add permitted(bidder,bid,[Receiver=R,
              role(R,auctioneer),Content>OffersOver])
     // bidders are empowered and permitted to bid
     // provided the content satisfies the specified constraints
 add sanction(bidder,bid,[],100)
     // any other bid incurs a sanction
 retrieve global.timer(Time)
 add timeout(closingTime+Time)
     // timeout is simply a newly defined predicate in the social facts
 add item(Item)
 add high1(0)
 add high2(0)

if bid([auctioneer,NewBid])
 retrieve high1(High1)
 retrieve high2(High2)
     // the current highest and second highest bids
 if NewBid>High1 then replace winner(_) with winner(Sndr)
                      replace high1(_) with high1(NewBid)
 else if NewBid>High2 then replace high2(_) with high2(NewBid)

if timer(Time)
 retrieve timeout(T)
 if Time>T then
   retrieve high1(High1)
   retrieve high2(High2)
   NewTime = Time+50
   if High1=High2 then
       // if nobody has bid then exit
     obliged(auctioneer,exitProtocol,[Receiver=bidder],101,250)
   else
       // else declare the winner
```

```
remove power(bidder,bid,_)
add power(auctioneer,inform,[])
retrieve winner(Winner)
add obliged(auctioneer,inform,
            [Receiver=Winner,Content=[won,High2]],103,NewTime)
add obliged(auctioneer,exitProtocol,
            [Receiver=[bidder]],101,NewTime)

if inform([won,Price]) then
retrieve global.timer(Time)
retrieve winner(Winner)
retrieve item(Item)
NewTime = Time + 150
    // this is the time by which payment must be made
add global.obliged(auctioneer,inform,
  [Receiver=bank,Content=[transfer,Item,Winner]],102,NewTime)
add global.obliged(Winner,inform,[Receiver=bank,
  Content=[credit,Price,auctioneer]],102,NewTime)
```

Note that the final clause creates obligations which are to persist after the protocol's termination (this is the meaning of add global...). When this is done the agent's name is put in the obligation instead of the role name. This is because the role will cease to exist on termination of the protocol (i.e. the fact asserting it is within the indexed list of facts for that protocol, and hence will be deleted when the protocol terminates), whereas we want the agent to still be obliged to pay even after the auction is finished.

5.2   Auction Animation

The initiating speech act is

```
speechAct(alice, [bob,claire], initProtocol,
           [alice1,auction,IPRowner,47,200])
```

Here *initProtocol* is the performative and *auction* is the protocol to be initiated. This starts a new conversation state, having its assertions as an indexed list within *A*. The index is *alice1*. Subsequent messages which are part of this protocol execution must be tagged with this index at the head of their content list. After this the following assertions hold within the indexed list

```
role(alice,auctioneer)
role(bob,bidder)
role(claire,bidder)
power(bidder,bid,[Content=[C],C>47])
power(auctioneer,exitProtocol,[Receiver=[bob,claire]])
permitted(bidder,bid,[Receiver=R,role(R,auctioneer),Content=[C],>47])
sanction(bidder,bid,[],100)
```

The next speech act is a bid by *bob*:

```
speechAct(bob, alice, bid, [alice1,53])
```

The only effect of this is to add a predicate recording this as the highest bid. Bidders still retain the power and permission to revise their bids. Next we have *claire* bidding 51, which adds a predicate recording the second highest bid. Then the timeout event happens. This results in the power to bid being revoked. Agents are still permitted to bid, but it has no effect. We now have the following norms for the auctioneer:

```
power(auctioneer,inform,[])
obliged(auctioneer,inform,[Receiver=bob,Content=[won,51]],103,250)
obliged(auctioneer,exitProtocol,[Receiver=[bob,claire]],101,250)
```

Note that the auctioneer is empowered to inform anything to the bidders; whatever he says, it counts. However, he is obliged to announce the winner and losers as expected in a Vickrey auction. The auctioneer's next messages are

```
speechAct(alice, bob, inform, [alice1,won,52])
speechAct(alice, [bob, claire], exitProtocol,[alice1])
```

This terminates the protocol and generates two obligations which exist in the "root" of A, i.e. not in the sublist indexed by *alice1*.

```
obliged(alice,inform,[Receiver=bank,
        Content=[transfer,IPRowner,bob]],102,400)
obliged(bob,inform,[Receiver=bank,Content=[credit,52,alice]],102,400)
```

Note that *alice* has overcharged *bob*. Without any third party monitoring, there is no way for him to know. However, we could imagine a subsequent dialog where *claire* reveals her bid to him and he lodges a complaint with an arbitration authority. If the evidence is deemed to be sufficient, the protocol specification can be consulted again to determine the appropriate sanction, i.e. that sanction 103 should be enforced on *alice*.

6   Temporal Logic Component

Our *obliged* predicate only allows us to specify that an action must be done before some future time. We have also added a temporal logic component which allows us to express more complex conditions. For example we can specify that an agent is obliged to ensure that a certain condition holds true, where the condition is expressed in a simple temporal logic (a subset of LTL), but ultimately refers to the truth values of predicates in A. We are interested in making these kinds of normative specifications for the behaviour of agents, and then testing their compliance with the specification by observing their behaviour at runtime (by observing finite runs of the system). This is the same type of testing as described by Venkatraman and Singh [24]; i.e. given an observed run of the system we can determine if the agents have complied so far, but not if they will comply in other circumstances. We have found that the standard temporal logic operator ◇ (at some time in the future) is not very useful for our specifications. The linear temporal formula ◇p promises that p will eventually true, but there is no way to falsify it in a finite model; i.e. if we require that an agent perform some action eventually, it is not possible to be non compliant in a finite model. Hence this formula becomes meaningless when referring to agent behaviour in a finite observed sequence. A typical type of formula we need to specify is that some condition must hold continuously before a deadline. This can be done with the $\mathcal{U}$ (until) operator. The formula $p\mathcal{U}q$ means that p must hold continuously until q becomes true, and q should eventually become true (this second part is of course redundant in our finite sequences). We include Boolean connectives $\neg, \wedge$ and $\vee$ in the language. The $\square$ operator (now and at all future times) is not included in our language because, in a finite sequence, $\square p$ is the same as $p\mathcal{U}false$. Despite the fact that our temporal logic only has one temporal operator, it is still quite expressive, as nestings of $\mathcal{U}$ can be used, as well as the Boolean connectives.

Using this simple language we have constructed a model checking component which keeps track of the temporal formulae which an agent is obliged to keep true; i.e. the checker "carries forward" the pending formulae and checks each new state as timer events are processed. This allows the formulae to be used in normative specifications, and sanctions to be triggered automatically when the formulae are falsified. We use the method of particle tableau from [18] to check the formulae. This allows an efficient incremental construction of the relevant portion of the tableaux.

7   Related Work

There are few recent works which address standardising agent communication semantics. It appears that the effort has been abandoned since the attempts of FIPA and KQML [8,15,7] in the 90's. However, in terms of technical ideas, there are some recent proposals which are moving in directions similar to what we propose.

In [10] it is demonstrated that a system of production rules can be used to implement many agent institutions that had originally been specified with very diverse formalisms. This is similar to our proposal as it is given a common computational grounding to proposals which were previously hard to compare. It also shows that if we are considering computational implementations of agent communication, then one simple language will be sufficient to implement whatever diverse notions we choose to employ to govern the agents.

In [20] the possibility of agents modifying the rules of the institution is mentioned; it is stated that this would require "interpretable code or some form of dynamic compilation". In [2] the event calculus formalism has been implemented to animate a specification of a rule governed agent society, but it is also stated that features of the underlying programming language could be made accessible to complement the event calculus formalism; this comes closer to the flavour of our proposal. In [11] normative relations are implemented in the Jess production rule system. The authors mention the possibility of "societal change", where societies may "evolve over time by altering, eliminating or incorporating rules". This societal change facility is not actually implemented in [11], but the authors do specify norms in a computationally grounded language based on observable phenomena.

In [6] there is a proposed development methodology which is similar to the "component based" aspect of our approach; generic protocols are specified, and then *transformers* can be applied to them to capture variations of the protocol for specific contexts. The work of [26] advocates the need for tools to assist developers in protocol design, while also showing how protocols can be built on the social commitments approach to agent communication semantics; this type of tool support and structured development is exactly what we expect will be needed to take our standardisation approach forward.

8   Conclusions and Future Work

There are two requirements which should be fulfilled as a precondition to making a standard for agent communication which has a reasonable prospect of actually being adopted. One is the expressive power to allow developers to do what they want, and the second is the ease of use (for which tools are required). The first aspect is easy, as we have shown, the second will take more effort. Even with the few components we described, we can see already that programming moves to a higher level as we add more components. We expect that standardisation will need to proceed by means of evolving libraries and tools which make the agent developers job easier. In this process the role of a standards body would be to accredit components and publish them, and to standardise the form of their documentation.

One avenue for future work is to explore the possibility of creating a component which defines a more intuitive semantics for common speech acts. The auction example above is a very mechanistic protocol, in that there is little room for flexibility and innovation among the agents. The social facts we created were solely concerned with describing sufficient information for the execution of the auction. Thus the semantics of these messages was purely procedural. In more flexible protocols we could create social facts which capture more of a natural human style of communication. For example, a "request for information" message sent by an agent could create a social fact which describes that the sender has expressed a desire to know something. Other participants in the society could then be creative in how they respond, because they can recognise the need of the speaker, rather than being constrained to only reply according to some rigid protocol, as would be the case for procedural semantics.

Another direction we are currently experimenting with is our temporal logic component which model checks temporal logic formulae. We plan to extend the expressiveness of its language. Argumentation is yet more interesting as it typically requires the use of nonmonotonic logics: an agent may undercut another agent's argument, and so force a conclusion to be retracted. Here we would code the rules defining acceptability of an argument. The ability of a meta-interpreter to specify a depth limit on proofs is particularly useful for this purpose; in order to have a common consensus on what arguments are accepted we need to specify the limits on the resource bounded reasoning [17]. Argumentation also introduces the possibility of negotiating changes to the rules of the institution itself. There will also no doubt be considerable interest in developing components for various logics such as the C+ action language (which is gaining popularity [2,6]) and various modal logics.

Eventually it is hoped that different electronic institutions could publish the components which comprise their communication language in a machine readable format, so that a roaming agent could come and join the institution without needing to be programmed to use that particular language in advance. This is an ambitious goal, as the agent would need not to just know the rules, but also its strategy for participation. However, if we restrict our attention to certain types of dialog, and their variants (e.g. auctions) then it does seem feasible.

References

1. Agerri, R., Alonso, E.: Semantics and Pragmatics for Agent Communication. In: Bento, C., Cardoso, A., Dias, G. (eds.) EPIA 2005. LNCS (LNAI), vol. 3808, Springer, Heidelberg (2005)
2. Artikis, A., Sergot, M., Pitt, J.V.: Specifying Norm-Governed Computational Societies. Technical Report 06-5, Dept. of Computing, Imperial College, London, UK (2005)
3. Austin, J.L.: How To Do Things With Words. Oxford University Press, Oxford (1962)
4. Bentahar, J., Moulin, B., Meyer, J.-J.C., Chaib-Draa, B.: A Computational Model for Conversation Policies for Agent Communication. In: Leite, J.A., Torroni, P. (eds.) Computational Logic in Multi-Agent Systems. LNCS (LNAI), vol. 3487, Springer, Heidelberg (2005)
5. Chaib-Draa, B., Labrie, M.-A., Bergeron, M., Pasquier, P.: An Agent Communication Language Based on Dialogue Games and Sustained by Social Commitments. Autonomous Agents and Multi-Agent Systems 13(1), 61–95 (2006)
6. Chopra, A.K., Singh, M.P.: Contextualizing Commitment Protocols. In: AAMAS. Procs. 5th. Int'l Conf. on Autonomous Agents and Multi-Agent Systems, ACM Press, New York (2006)
7. Cohen, P.R., Levesque, H.J.: Communicative Actions for Artificial Agents. In: Int'l Conf. on MASs, pp. 65–72. MIT Press, Cambridge (1995)
8. FIPA. [FIPA OC00003] FIPA 97 Part 2 Version 2.0: Agent Communication Language Specification. In: Website of the Foundation for Intelligent Physical Agents (1997), http://www.fipa.org/specs/fipa2000.tar.gz
9. Fornara, N., Vigano, F., Colombetti, M.: Agent communication and artificial institutions. Autonomous Agents and Multi-Agent Systems (2006), doi:10.1007/s10458-006-0017-8
10. Garcia-Camino, A., Rodriguez-Aguilar, J., Sierra, C., Vasconcelos, W.: A Rule-based Approach to Norm-Oriented Programming of Electronic Institutions. SIGEcomm Exchanges 5(5) (2006)
11. Garcia-Camino, A., Rodriguez-Aguilar, J.-A., Noriega, P.: Implementing Norms in Electronic Institutions. In: AAMAS. Procs. 4th Int'l Conf. on Autonomous Agents & Multiagent Systems, ACM Press, New York (2005)
12. Guerin, F., Pitt, J.V.: A semantic framework for specifying agent communication languages. In: ICMAS 2000. Fourth International Conference on Multi-Agent Systems, pp. 395–396. IEEE Computer Society, Los Alamitos (2000)
13. Jones, A.J.I., Sergot, M.J.: A formal characterisation of institutionalised power. Journal of the IGPL 4(3), 429–445 (1996)

14. Labrou, Y.: Semantics for an agent communication language. PhD thesis, Baltimore, MD: University of Maryland Graduate School (1996)
15. Labrou, Y., Finin, T.: A semantics approach for kqml – a general purpose communication language for software agents. In: CIKM 1994. Third International Conference on Information and Knowledge Management, pp. 447–455 (1994)
16. Labrou, Y., Finin, T., Peng, Y.: The current landscape of agent communication languages (1999)
17. Loui, R.P.: Process and policy: Resource-bounded nondemonstrative reasoning. Computational Intelligence 14(1), 1 (1998)
18. Manna, Z., Pnueli, A.: Temporal Verification of Reactive Systems (Safety), vol. 2. Springer, New York (1995)
19. Mayfield, J., Labrou, Y., Finin, T.: Desiderata for agent communication languages. In: AAAI 1995 Spring Symposium. Proceedings of the AAAI Symposium on Information Gathering from Heterogeneous, Distributed Environments, pp. 347–360. Stanford University, Stanford (1995)
20. Pitt, J., Kamara, L., Sergot, M., Artikis, A.: Formalization of a voting protocol for virtual organizations. In: AAMAS 2005. Proceedings of the Fourth International Joint Conference on Autonomous Agents and Multi-Agent Systems, Utrecht, ACM Press, New York (2005)
21. Searle, J.R.: What is a speech act? In: Martinich, A.P. (ed.) Philosophy of Language, 3rd edn., Oxford University Press, Oxford (1965)
22. Singh, M.: Agent communication languages: Rethinking the principles. IEEE Computer 31(12), 40–47 (1998)
23. Singh, M.: A social semantics for agent communication languages. In: IJCAI Workshop on Agent Communication Languages, Springer, Berlin (2000)
24. Venkatraman, M., Singh, M.P.: Verifying compliance with commitment protocols: Enabling open web-based multiagent systems. Autonomous Agents and Multi-Agent Systems 2(3), 217–236 (1999)
25. Verdicchio, M., Colombetti, M.: A logical model of social commitment for agent communication. In: Proceedings of the second international joint conference on Autonomous agents and multiagent systems table of contents, Melbourne, Australia, pp. 528–535 (2003)
26. Yolum, P.: Towards design tools for protocol development. In: AAMAS 2005. Proceedings of the fourth international joint conference on Autonomous agents and multiagent systems, pp. 99–105. ACM Press, New York (2005)

Author Index

Lecture Notes in Artificial Intelligence (LNAI)

Vol. 4682: D.-S. Huang, L. Heutte, M. Loog (Eds.), Advanced Intelligent Computing Theories and Applications. XXVII, 1373 pages. 2007.

Vol. 4676: M. Klusch, K.V. Hindriks, M.P. Papazoglou, L. Sterling (Eds.), Cooperative Information Agents XI. XI, 361 pages. 2007.

Vol. 4667: J. Hertzberg, M. Beetz, R. Englert (Eds.), KI 2007: Advances in Artificial Intelligence. IX, 516 pages. 2007.

Vol. 4660: S. Džeroski, L. Todorovski (Eds.), Computational Discovery of Scientific Knowledge. X, 327 pages. 2007.

Vol. 4659: V. Mařík, V. Vyatkin, A.W. Colombo (Eds.), Holonic and Multi-Agent Systems for Manufacturing. VIII, 456 pages. 2007.

Vol. 4651: F. Azevedo, P. Barahona, F. Fages, F. Rossi (Eds.), Recent Advances in Constraints. VIII, 185 pages. 2007.

Vol. 4648: F. Almeida e Costa, L.M. Rocha, E. Costa, I. Harvey, A. Coutinho (Eds.), Advances in Artificial Life. XVIII, 1215 pages. 2007.

Vol. 4635: B. Kokinov, D.C. Richardson, T.R. Roth-Berghofer, L. Vieu (Eds.), Modeling and Using Context. XIV, 574 pages. 2007.

Vol. 4632: R. Alhajj, H. Gao, X. Li, J. Li, O.R. Zaïane (Eds.), Advanced Data Mining and Applications. XV, 634 pages. 2007.

Vol. 4629: V. Matoušek, P. Mautner (Eds.), Text, Speech and Dialogue. XVII, 663 pages. 2007.

Vol. 4626: R.O. Weber, M.M. Richter (Eds.), Case-Based Reasoning Research and Development. XIII, 534 pages. 2007.

Vol. 4617: V. Torra, Y. Narukawa, Y. Yoshida (Eds.), Modeling Decisions for Artificial Intelligence. XII, 502 pages. 2007.

Vol. 4612: I. Miguel, W. Ruml (Eds.), Abstraction, Reformulation, and Approximation. XI, 418 pages. 2007.

Vol. 4604: U. Priss, S. Polovina, R. Hill (Eds.), Conceptual Structures: Knowledge Architectures for Smart Applications. XII, 514 pages. 2007.

Vol. 4603: F. Pfenning (Ed.), Automated Deduction – CADE-21. XII, 522 pages. 2007.

Vol. 4597: P. Perner (Ed.), Advances in Data Mining. XI, 353 pages. 2007.

Vol. 4594: R. Bellazzi, A. Abu-Hanna, J. Hunter (Eds.), Artificial Intelligence in Medicine. XVI, 509 pages. 2007.

Vol. 4585: M. Kryszkiewicz, J.F. Peters, H. Rybinski, A. Skowron (Eds.), Rough Sets and Intelligent Systems Paradigms. XIX, 836 pages. 2007.

Vol. 4578: F. Masulli, S. Mitra, G. Pasi (Eds.), Applications of Fuzzy Sets Theory. XVIII, 693 pages. 2007.

Vol. 4573: M. Kauers, M. Kerber, R. Miner, W. Windsteiger (Eds.), Towards Mechanized Mathematical Assistants. XIII, 407 pages. 2007.

Vol. 4571: P. Perner (Ed.), Machine Learning and Data Mining in Pattern Recognition. XIV, 913 pages. 2007.

Vol. 4570: H.G. Okuno, M. Ali (Eds.), New Trends in Applied Artificial Intelligence. XXI, 1194 pages. 2007.

Vol. 4565: D.D. Schmorrow, L.M. Reeves (Eds.), Foundations of Augmented Cognition. XIX, 450 pages. 2007.

Vol. 4562: D. Harris (Ed.), Engineering Psychology and Cognitive Ergonomics. XXIII, 879 pages. 2007.

Vol. 4548: N. Olivetti (Ed.), Automated Reasoning with Analytic Tableaux and Related Methods. X, 245 pages. 2007.

Vol. 4539: N.H. Bshouty, C. Gentile (Eds.), Learning Theory. XII, 634 pages. 2007.

Vol. 4529: P. Melin, O. Castillo, L.T. Aguilar, J. Kacprzyk, W. Pedrycz (Eds.), Foundations of Fuzzy Logic and Soft Computing. XIX, 830 pages. 2007.

Vol. 4520: M.V. Butz, O. Sigaud, G. Pezzulo, G. Baldassarre (Eds.), Anticipatory Behavior in Adaptive Learning Systems. X, 379 pages. 2007.

Vol. 4511: C. Conati, K. McCoy, G. Paliouras (Eds.), User Modeling 2007. XVI, 487 pages. 2007.

Vol. 4509: Z. Kobti, D. Wu (Eds.), Advances in Artificial Intelligence. XII, 552 pages. 2007.

Vol. 4496: N.T. Nguyen, A. Grzech, R.J. Howlett, L.C. Jain (Eds.), Agent and Multi-Agent Systems: Technologies and Applications. XXI, 1046 pages. 2007.

Vol. 4483: C. Baral, G. Brewka, J. Schlipf (Eds.), Logic Programming and Nonmonotonic Reasoning. IX, 327 pages. 2007.

Vol. 4482: A. An, J. Stefanowski, S. Ramanna, C.J. Butz, W. Pedrycz, G. Wang (Eds.), Rough Sets, Fuzzy Sets, Data Mining and Granular Computing. XIV, 585 pages. 2007.

Vol. 4481: J. Yao, P. Lingras, W.-Z. Wu, M.S. Szczuka, N.J. Cercone, D. Ślęzak (Eds.), Rough Sets and Knowledge Technology. XIV, 576 pages. 2007.

Vol. 4476: V. Gorodetsky, C. Zhang, V.A. Skormin, L. Cao (Eds.), Autonomous Intelligent Systems: Multi-Agents and Data Mining. XIII, 323 pages. 2007.

Vol. 4460: S. Aguzzoli, A. Ciabattoni, B. Gerla, C. Manara, V. Marra (Eds.), Algebraic and Proof-theoretic Aspects of Non-classical Logics. VIII, 309 pages. 2007.

Vol. 4457: G.M.P. O'Hare, A. Ricci, M.J. O'Grady, O. Dikenelli (Eds.), Engineering Societies in the Agents World VII. XI, 401 pages. 2007.

Vol. 4456: Y. Wang, Y.-m. Cheung, H. Liu (Eds.), Computational Intelligence and Security. XXIII, 1118 pages. 2007.

Vol. 4455: S. Muggleton, R. Otero, A. Tamaddoni-Nezhad (Eds.), Inductive Logic Programming. XII, 456 pages. 2007.

Vol. 4452: M. Fasli, O. Shehory (Eds.), Agent-Mediated Electronic Commerce. VIII, 249 pages. 2007.

Vol. 4451: T.S. Huang, A. Nijholt, M. Pantic, A. Pentland (Eds.), Artifical Intelligence for Human Computing. XVI, 359 pages. 2007.

Vol. 4442: L. Antunes, K. Takadama (Eds.), Multi-Agent-Based Simulation VII. X, 189 pages. 2007.

Vol. 4441: C. Müller (Ed.), Speaker Classification II. X, 309 pages. 2007.